The Hope of Glory

The Hope of Glory
A Theology of Redemption

Ian A. McFarland

© 2024 Ian A. McFarland

First edition
Published by Westminster John Knox Press
Louisville, Kentucky

24 25 26 27 28 29 30 31 32 33—10 9 8 7 6 5 4 3 2 1

All rights reserved. No part of this book may be reproduced or transmitted in any form or by any means, electronic or mechanical, including photocopying, recording, or by any information storage or retrieval system, without permission in writing from the publisher. For information, address Westminster John Knox Press, 100 Witherspoon Street, Louisville, Kentucky 40202-1396. Or contact us online at www.wjkbooks.com.

Unless otherwise indicated, Scripture quotations are taken from the New Revised Standard Version Updated Edition. Copyright © 2021 National Council of Churches of Christ in the United States of America. Used by permission. All rights reserved worldwide. Scripture quotations marked NIV are from the Holy Bible, New International Version. Copyright © 1973, 1978, 1984, 2011 by Biblica, Inc.® Used by permission of Zondervan. All rights reserved worldwide. Scripture quotations marked NRSV are from the New Revised Standard Version of the Bible, copyright © 1989 by the Division of Christian Education of the National Council of the Churches of Christ in the U.S.A., and used by permission. All emphasis is the author's.

Excerpt, with revisions, from Ian A. McFarland, "Sin and the Limits of Theology: A Reflection in Conversation with Julian of Norwich and Martin Luther," *International Journal of Systematic Theology* 22, no. 2 (April 2020), is reprinted by permission.

Some material in chapter 5 originally appeared in Ian A. McFarland, "Eschatology," in the *New Cambridge Companion to Christian Doctrine* (Cambridge: Cambridge University Press, 2023).

Book design by Drew Stevens
Cover design by Mark Abrams

Library of Congress Cataloging-in-Publication Data

Names: McFarland, Ian A. (Ian Alexander), 1963-, author.
Title: The hope of glory : a theology of redemption / Ian A. McFarland.
Description: First edition. | Louisville : Westminster John Knox Press,
    [2024] | Includes bibliographical references and index. | Summary:
    "Christians hope for life in glory, but according to Scripture, such
    life is not to be conceived as leaving this world behind. On the
    contrary, Christians hope for the renewal of this world: it is the same
    creation that God made "in the beginning" that God glorifies and redeems
    at the end"-- Provided by publisher.
Identifiers: LCCN 2024023486 (print) | LCCN 2024023487 (ebook) | ISBN
    9780664267001 (paperback) | ISBN 9781646983933 (ebook)
Subjects: LCSH: Eschatology. | Redemption--Biblical teaching. |
    Hope--Religious aspects--Christianity. | Glory--Religious
    aspects--Christianity.
Classification: LCC BT821.33 .M444 2024 (print) | LCC BT821.33 (ebook) |
    DDC 234/.3--dc23/eng/20240609
LC record available at https://lccn.loc.gov/2024023486
LC ebook record available at https://lccn.loc.gov/2024023487

Most Westminster John Knox Press books are available at special quantity discounts when purchased in bulk by corporations, organizations, and special-interest groups. For more information, please email SpecialSales@wjkbooks.com.

When we on that final journey go
That Christ is for us preparing,
We'll gather in song, our hearts aglow,
All joy of the heavens sharing,
And there will join God's endless praise,
With angels and saints adoring.

—N. F. S. Grundtvig

Contents

Preface	ix
Introduction: The Problem of Hope	1
The Tension between Hope and Glory	2
Resolving the Tension: The Resurrection	6
Resurrection's Form: Persons and Natures	9
Resurrection's Content: Living by God's Word	13

PART 1: HOPE

1. False Hope	**19**
Escapism: Rescue from the World	20
Titanism: Control of the World	26
False Hope as Rejection of the Past	32
2. Hope Refused	**39**
Naturalism: Hope as Incredible	40
Protest: Hope as Monstrous	50
Hope Refused as Rejection of the Future	56
3. "Jesus Our Hope"	**61**
From Creation to Redemption	63
The Form of Hope	66
Enacting Hope	76

INTERLUDE

4. The Mystery of Evil and the Limits of Eschatology	**89**
The Case of Julian	93
The Case of Luther	99
Evaluation	104

PART 2: GLORY

5. Jesus, the Lord of Glory	**113**
Advent	116
Judgment	120
Heaven and Hell	125

viii   *Contents*

6. **The Transformation of the Self**   **135**
   Death   137
   Resurrection   142
   Life Everlasting   149

7. **The Transformation of the World**   **159**
   Signs and Portents   161
   A New Heaven and a New Earth   166
   Sabbath   171

   Conclusion: A Theology of Glory   **179**
   The Challenge of the Cross   180
   The Hope of Glory   186

   Bibliography   **189**

   Scripture Index   **199**

   Name and Subject Index   **206**

Preface

This book is a study in what since the nineteenth century Christian theologians have typically called eschatology, though I think its theme is probably more clearly communicated using the term that I have used in the subtitle: redemption, by which I mean God's comprehensive and definitive vindication of creation from the power of evil.[1] Because I argue that the hope of redemption is centered on the person of Jesus of Nazareth, whose resurrection from the dead defines our future as well as his, this book is also a sequel to my earlier *The Word Made Flesh: A Theology of Incarnation*.[2] And insofar as that book was itself something of a sequel to *From Nothing: A Theology of Creation*, the present volume can be seen as the conclusion to a three-part project.[3]

And yet though the topics of creation, incarnation, and redemption covered in these books correspond to the three main episodes in the Christian account of God's dealings with the world (the divine "economy," or in more modern parlance, "salvation history"), the focus of each is too narrow, and the material covered in them thus far too selective, for the ensemble to constitute anything like a "systematic theology." The three books are better understood as a sequence of case studies, each of which explores a particular problem within a much larger doctrinal complex. In the first my concern was to explain the meaning of the Christian claim that God creates from nothing; in the second to defend the classical confession of Jesus as one person in two natures; and in this book to make sense of Paul's characterization of "the mystery of Christ among you" as "the hope of glory" (Col. 1:27).[4]

In pursuing this aim, I will make every effort to keep the use of jargon (theological and otherwise) to a minimum, though I will continue my practice of

---

1. Although the term "eschatology" was coined in the seventeenth century, it did not come into general use among theologians until rather later. Earlier theological convention in the West (dating to the fifteenth century) was to treat these topics under the rubric *De novissimis*. See Sigurd Hjelde, *Das Eschaton und die Eschata: Eine Studie über Sprachgebrauch und Sprachverwirrung in protestantischer Theologie von der Orthodoxie bis zur Gegenwart* (Munich: Christian Kaiser, 1987), 37; and Paul J. Griffiths, *Decreation: The Last Things of All Creation* (Waco, TX: Baylor University Press, 2014), 8–9. The identification of eschatology with redemption derives from Karl Barth, who intended the final volume—planned but unwritten—of his *Church Dogmatics* to bear the title, *The Doctrine of Redemption*.

2. Ian A. McFarland, *The Word Made Flesh: A Theology of the Incarnation* (Louisville, KY: Westminster John Knox, 2019).

3. Ian A. McFarland, *From Nothing: A Theology of Creation* (Louisville, KY: Westminster John Knox, 2014).

4. My translation. The NRSV's and NRSVue's "Christ in you" obscures the fact that the Greek text uses the second-person plural pronoun *hymin*; I have translated the preposition *en* as "among" in order to bring out the point that Paul is not speaking of Christ living inside individual Christians, but rather in the midst of the gathered community of faith (cf. Matt. 18:20; Luke 17:21).

ix

selectively drawing on traditional Christian doctrinal formulations where I judge that the risks of obfuscation that come with the use of technical vocabulary are offset by gains in conceptual clarity. My driving interest is to address what I see as the inherent tension between "hope" on the one hand and "glory" on the other that can appear to make talk of a "hope of glory" a contradiction. The tension I perceive is this: as much as it may be the case that (as Paul taught) "hope that is seen is not hope" (Rom. 8:24; cf. 2 Cor. 5:7), hope must nevertheless have some connection with the present in order to qualify as hope, rather than simply wishful thinking. And yet for Christians glory has no such connection, since it refers to the displacement of the corruption and mortality intrinsic to life now by the incorruption and immortality of the resurrection—a displacement that neither does nor can have any ground in our present existence just because it comes upon us as an utterly gracious gift rather than either a natural development or a merited reward (1 Cor. 15:50–53).[5]

Nor is this attempt to reconcile the themes of hope and glory simply a conceptual or semantic puzzle. It is rather deeply bound up with the reality of human life in this world. For the Christian proclamation of glory as the object of hope is rooted in the recognition that the human experience of mortality is not neutral or indifferent but shot through with injustice, brutality, pain, and want. To hope for glory is to hold that these soul-crushing realities are not the last word for our existence, so that when faced with them "we do not lose heart" but trust instead that they are "producing for us an eternal weight of glory beyond all measure" (2 Cor. 4:16–17).

In the latter half of the twentieth century, in the aftermath of two world wars, the Holocaust, and the unleashing of atomic weaponry, theologians in Europe and North America sought to expand reflection on Christian hope to include the form of human life within history as well as the promise of eternal glory beyond it.[6] Christian hope, it was argued, is not rightly deferred either to an otherworldly existence on the far side of death or a supernaturally transformed creation at the end of time, but looks for the transformation of the conditions of life here and now. These theologies of hope generated considerable excitement in academic circles, and yet early on James Cone raised the complaint that they were "influenced too much by German and American philosophical discourse on hope and too little by the actual bearers of hope in our social existence."[7]

---

5. Frederic Jameson has argued that this tension is also endemic to secular utopian thinking, which struggles between visions of utopia that are simply projections of the cultural situation of the writer (and her public) on the one hand, and a recognition that the transition to a truly novel social situation is by reason of its very novelty indescribable. See Frederic Jameson, *Archaeologies of the Future: The Desire Called Utopia and Other Science Fictions* (London: Verso, 2005), Part One; cf. 289, where he argues that science fiction as a genre serves "to bring home . . . our constitutional inability to imagine Utopia itself: and this, not owing to any individual failure of imagination but as the result of the systemic, cultural and ideological closure of which we are all in one way or another prisoners."

6. The seminal work in this genre was Jürgen Moltmann, *Theologie der Hoffnung. Untersuchungen zur Begründung und zu den Konsequenzen einer christlichen Eschatologie* (Munich: Christian Kaiser Verlag, 1964); ET: *Theology of Hope: On the Ground and the Implications of a Christian Eschatology*, trans. James W. Leitch (London: SCM, 1967). See pp. 3–6 below for a more detailed discussion of this text.

7. Cone continues that if would-be theologians of hope "continue their talk about hope primarily in relation to Pierre Teilhard de Chardin, Alfred North Whitehead, Moltmann, and Pannenberg, while ignoring the hope disclosed in the songs and tales of black slaves, then we can only conclude that white theology's hope is a reason for despair on the part of the oppressed and thus alien to the gospel of Jesus." James H. Cone, *God of the Oppressed* (New York: Seabury, 1975), 127.

Preface xi

Cone's point was simple: however putatively this-worldly its focus, theological talk about hope will provide only false consolation unless it takes its bearings from those who bear the brunt of worldly affliction. For theologians located in North America, he insisted, this means that "there can be no talk of hope in the Christian sense unless it is talk about the freedom of black, red, and brown people."[8]

Cone's warning has lost none of its pungency since it was first written half a century ago, especially as I reflect on it from the perspective of my own privileged background. Even if Paul's experience of hunger, thirst, flogging, beating, stoning, imprisonment, and shipwreck (2 Cor. 11:23–27), culminating (according to tradition) in his martyrdom under Nero, lend existential weight to his words when he insists that earthly afflictions are only "slight" and "momentary" in comparison with the glory to come, how can such assurances be echoed with any credibility by me—a well-established white, male scholar who has never known want or debilitating disease but whose life, to the contrary, has been blessed in immeasurable ways, not least in the companionship of a wise and understanding spouse, together with whom I have shared the inestimable privilege of seeing our two daughters grow to healthy and confident adulthood? Even my sins, many (not to mention shameful and embarrassing) though they are, have not aroused public scandal or led to widespread alienation of family or friends. On what basis then can I possibly speak about hope to those whose paths have been beset by experiences of deprivation, humiliation, and pain that I cannot imagine?

The plain truth is that I can't, at least not in a way that will provide any advance guarantee that my speaking will avoid either presumption or absurdity. And yet avoiding the topic is not an option, because it is not permitted for the Christian theologian (whatever that theologian's personal circumstances) to remain silent on the question of hope, given that Scripture enjoins the faithful always to be "ready to make your defense to anyone who demands from you an accounting for the hope that is in you" (1 Pet. 3:15).

But if I can't avoid the suspicion that any account of hope I might provide will be compromised by the all-too-limited prospects of my own experience, I can try to mitigate this risk by attending to the voices of those who have suffered in ways that I have not. Given the many very different forms that suffering can take, this effort cannot take the form of explicit engagement with all the particular experiences of suffering that will be known to the readers of this book. It can mean no more than to try to ensure that articulation of the Christian conviction that it is right to hope even in the face of the most extreme forms of suffering, and thus that such suffering is not the final word to be spoken over any human life, does not entail—ever—forgetfulness of suffering. Indeed, it seems to me that this principle is the essential truth in Luther's theology of the cross: that the revelation of God in the crucified Jesus means that no talk about God can be credible that ignores or bypasses the fact of earthly suffering. In this context, the work of Black and womanist theologians, especially James Cone and Delores Williams, has been particularly important for my own theological formation. Although I address their thinking explicitly only in the final

8. Cone, *God of the Oppressed*, 128.

chapter—because it is there that the tensions associated with my articulation of the content of Christian hope come to a head—their common insistence that the measure of good theology is its capacity to bring good news to the poor and marginalized has informed my thinking throughout, calling me always to remember experiences different than my own in the face of the temptation—ever-present for an author whose whiteness is inseparable from a presumption of mastery—to provide too tidy an account of the Christian hope.

Whatever success I may have in achieving this goal, I owe to the wisdom of many people—teachers and colleagues like Cone and Williams, of course, but also students, family, friends, pastors, and others—who have influenced me for the good in ways of which I am all too often unaware. One set of debts I can readily acknowledge, however, is to the people at Westminster John Knox Press, especially Bob Ratcliff, who commissioned the text; Bridgett Green, who reviewed the entire manuscript, which is much the better for her editorial suggestions; Dan Braden, Julie Tonini, and all the other production staff whose efforts, both known and unknown to me, have brought this book to print. I am also grateful to Dean Doug Sweeney and the faculty of the Beeson Divinity School of Samford University, whose gracious invitation to give the Reformation Heritage Lectures in 2023 gave me the opportunity to present much of the material in chapters 5 and 6 before an engaged and probing audience. But my deepest thanks go to my colleagues at Emory University's Candler School of Theology, who have provided a home for dogmatic reflection like no other I have experienced in over a quarter century in theological education: one where I find myself pressed to attend to the demands of voices all too frequently ignored by an institutional ethos that at every point connects formation for church leadership with attention to context. While I have been aware of Candler's unique character as an institution of theological education since I was first hired in 2005, it is only since my return after five (in their own right wonderful) years in Cambridge that I have come to appreciate fully the indispensability of this community of learning for whatever integrity my own work—on this topic in particular—may possess. I am profoundly grateful for it.

Candler School of Theology
May 2023
The Feast of St. Philip and St. James

Introduction

The Problem of Hope

For what do Christians hope? That is the fundamental question of Christian eschatology, or the doctrine of "the last things" (*ta eschata* in Greek), and at one level, the Christian tradition offers pretty clear answers. Christians hope for the return of the Lord Jesus, the coming of God's kingdom, and the life of the world to come. In short, the Christian hope is a "hope of sharing the glory of God" (Rom. 5:2). But what do these phrases mean concretely? Over the last century or so, in response to the worry that traditional interpretations of Christian hope failed to take seriously God's concern for human life in this world, two different ways of approaching this question emerged within Western academic theology, each with its own characteristic problems. The first, exemplified by the social gospel movement and by political and liberation theologies, risks historical reduction, in which Christian hope is focused on the possibilities for the transformation of the conditions of human existence in this world. The second, reflected in mid-twentieth-century kerygmatic theologies as well as more recent forms of postliberalism, tends toward ahistorical abstraction, in which hope is largely decoupled from future expectation and is instead reinterpreted in terms of a transformed quality of life in the present, whether in the form of the existential freedom secured by the individual's decision for faith or the pursuit of virtue in the community of the church.[1]

Although each of these alternatives has very able exponents who seek to avoid the one-sided simplifications I have just described, neither has much to say about glory. Indeed, it is striking that in the debates between these two approaches over the past century (in which the progressive optimism of the social gospel gave way to the professed realism of dialectical theologies, only for the latter to be charged with their own form of socioeconomic naiveté by liberationists, who, in their turn, were accused by postliberals of reducing the gospel to a secular political program, and so on), the eschatological topics associated with glory—the Parousia, resurrection, and eternal life—have tended to drift to the margins and thus effectively surrendered to proponents of those otherworldly interpretations of Christian hope that were the stimulus for the formulation of these modern alternatives in the first place. Yet the fact that these otherworldly perspectives, far from having been displaced, dominate popular expressions of Christian faith across the globe (not least among the Pentecostal

---

1. These two perspectives correspond roughly with what Markus Mühling characterizes as eschatologies "from ahead" and "from above," respectively. See Markus Mühling, *T&T Clark Handbook of Christian Eschatology*, trans. Jennifer Adams-Maßmann and David Andrew Gilland (London: Bloomsbury T&T Clark, 2015 [2007]), 14–22.

2   *The Hope of Glory*

churches that represent the fastest-growing branch of contemporary Christianity) show that such surrender is a mistake. For the end of Christian hope, to which the traditional creedal and biblical symbols relating to "the last things" point, is ineluctably a "hope of *glory*" (Col. 1:27; cf. Rom. 5:2; Titus 2:13) and thus rightly and necessarily "otherworldly," in that glory—which properly and finally belongs to God alone—exceeds every possibility and potential of life in this world. Consequently, for all the objections that must (and in the following pages will) be raised against the eschatological vision on display in the Left Behind series and similar books,[2] insofar as such texts testify to a refusal to give up the hope of glory, they challenge those of us who swim in the waters of mainline academic theology to answer the question "What then are *we* to say about these things?" (Rom. 8:31).

The Tension between Hope and Glory

But it is one thing to register the need for such an answer and quite another to provide one that is credible. For the impulses giving rise to the eschatologies that I have rather cavalierly accused of "historical reduction" and "ahistorical abstraction" remain compelling. Thanks to the insights of the natural sciences, we have a level of knowledge about the structure, history, and destiny of the physical universe that renders literalistic interpretations of topics like a new heaven and earth, in which death, suffering, and pain will be no more, difficult to accept, since they seem flatly inconsistent with our best understanding of how the world is put together. For as much as Christians are called to join Paul in affirming that "hope that is seen is not hope" (Rom. 8:24), nevertheless a hope that is completely divorced from what can be "seen"—that is, from some relation to present experience—seems better described as wishful thinking or even delusion. I can hope for a cure for cancer, the end of poverty, even a female pope. But it seems a misuse of the word to speak of a hope that I will acquire the powers of Superman, that the sun will turn blue, or that two plus two will someday equal five.[3]

In short, to the degree that the life in glory for which Christians hope lacks grounding in present experience, it is inconsistent with the basic character of hope, which is fundamentally a matter of anticipation, in which that for which we hope, while not reducible to extrapolation of worldly processes, is sufficiently rooted in what we know of the world and our place in it to motivate activity consistent with its future realization (see especially 2 Cor. 3:12; cf. 1 Cor. 9:10; 1 Tim. 4:10; Heb. 6:11).[4] If the object of my hope is completely

2. Left Behind includes sixteen books (named for the first in the series: *Left Behind: A Novel of the Earth's Last Days*), all written by Tim LaHaye and Jerry B. Jenkins, and published between 1995 and 2007. Reflecting one version of the kind of otherworldly eschatological vision discussed in detail in the first section of chapter 1 below, the series has commanded a wide readership among conservative Protestants in particular and has given rise to a separate series intended for a teenage audience (Left Behind: The Kids), as well as to film adaptations and video games.

3. "It is just crazy, clearly, to be hopeful . . . about an outcome one believes has literally no chance of occurring or that one believes is certain to occur." Adrienne Martin, *How We Hope: A Moral Psychology* (Princeton: Princeton University Press, 2013), 51.

4. Vincent Lloyd summarizes the founding insights of Black theology along just these lines as a rejection of the "reduction of hope to either a plan for the future or a desire for an improbable but fantasized

Introduction 3

discontinuous with what I experience now, then its fulfillment bears no intrinsic relationship whatsoever to anything I do or neglect to do now. To be sure, the glory for which one hopes may be conceived as a reward for certain sorts of behavior in this life, but to the extent that glory is understood to supervene on rather than to emerge from worldly possibilities, this connection will invariably appear arbitrary: a collection of admissions criteria to be fulfilled in the present that could be expanded, contracted, or even radically transformed, without any implications for the character of the life to come.

These considerations suggest that the "hope of glory" is almost oxymoronic, since the this-worldly demands of hope are simply incompatible with the otherworldly character of glory. Indeed, the difficulty of thinking hope and glory together provides a plausible explanation for the tendency in much twentieth-century eschatology to opt for either a hope without glory (by way of a this-worldly focus on strategies for ameliorating the human condition) or glory that is decoupled from hope (in which there is a transformed vision of the world but little expectation that its essential character can be changed within the confines of history). These alternatives take concrete form in probably the two most influential treatments of hope and glory written since the Second World War: Jürgen Moltmann's *Theology of Hope* (1964) and Hans Urs von Balthasar's multivolume *The Glory of the Lord* (1961–1969), respectively, in both of which one topic is treated in almost complete disregard of the other.[5]

The subject of glory is all but absent from *Theology of Hope*: the word itself appears only a handful of times and is nowhere the subject of sustained analysis or reflection. Nor is this omission surprising when it is recognized that Moltmann's explicit aim in this book was to develop an eschatology that is "forward looking and forward moving, and therefore also revolutionizing and transforming the present" over against otherworldly alternatives.[6] He sees this need as all the more urgent given that neither the much-celebrated rediscovery of the eschatological character of Jesus' teaching by Johannes Weiss and Albert Schweitzer at the turn of the twentieth century nor the stress on eschatology in the dialectical theology of subsequent decades led to a renewed emphasis on the theological significance of earthly history as the context for the realization of God's kingdom. Instead, eschatology was interpreted merely as a sign of the strangeness of Jesus' proclamation, in which the promise of the kingdom was decoupled from life in the world and deployed instead as a transcendental

---

future," on the grounds that neither of these perspectives "captures hope as a disposition or virtue . . . a way of responding to dire circumstances, without despair. Such a virtue necessarily finds expression in concrete, worldly terms: desires for *this* and *that*, obtainable through *these* channels." Vincent Lloyd, *Religion of the Field Negro: On Black Secularism and Black Theology* (New York: Fordham University Press, 2018), 134. For resolutely secular defenses of the same point, see Ernst Bloch, *The Principle of Hope*, 3 vols. (Oxford: Oxford University Press, 1986 [1954–1959]), and Martin, *How We Hope*.

5. This is not to say that either author is unaware of the need for a balance between the two dimensions of eschatology, only that neither succeeds in striking it. Balthasar, for example, has written, "Man must give himself completely in two directions: *the horizontal 'forward' and the vertical 'upward.'* And this should be accomplished in such a way that each direction does not hinder the other but, on the contrary, furthers it." Hans Urs von Balthasar, *A Short Primer for Unsettled Laymen*, trans. Michael Waldstein (San Francisco: Ignatius, 1985), 33.

6. Jürgen Moltmann, *Theology of Hope: On the Ground and Implications of a Christian Eschatology*, trans. James W. Leitch (London: SCM, 1967 [1965]), 16. From the side of biblical scholarship, N. T. Wright has also defended the resolutely this-worldly character of biblical eschatology in his book *New Heavens, New Earth: The Biblical Picture of the Christian Hope* (London: Grove, 1999).

4   *The Hope of Glory*

principle for the critique of all worldly politics.[7] While this approach performed the service of discrediting those forms of Christianity that simply identified God's will with any worldly political order, it also painted human history as essentially hopeless. Over against this position, Moltmann insisted that Christian hope entails attention to history as the arena where human beings are called by God to realize new possibilities for life in this world.[8]

On the other hand, Balthasar's account of glory, with its emphasis on theology's grounding in the discernment of form—specifically the form of "the indivisible God-man," Jesus Christ—results in an emphasis on the vision of the risen Lord's glory now rather than on any expectation of future transformation of the conditions of life in this world.[9] To be sure, Balthasar is clear that the revelation of God's glory in Christ is completed only eschatologically, when the form that is Christ will have taken every creature up into itself; but his focus is on the present, defending Christ's status as the form of God's glory by showing how he can and should be understood as the unifying center of all human experience, gathering together the disparate threads of nature and history into a single, focused frame.[10] Because this attention to form leads to the prioritization of sight as central to the perception and analysis of theological truth,[11] faith and love are the theological virtues that take center stage, with hope rarely coming into focus as an object of extended reflection.[12]

---

7. Moltmann, *Theology of Hope*, 37–40.

8. "A missionary exposition of the biblical witness to man's history and mission will therefore agree with the existentialist interpretation in enquiring about the new possibilities which entered the world through Israel and Christianity. It, too, will have to present these past existential possibilities as possibilities of the present understanding of existence. But it will interpret these existential possibilities as new possibilities for man's future. It will not interpret the phenomena of history on the ground of the possibilities of human existence, but on the contrary, it will interpret the new possibilities of human existence on the basis of the 'phenomenon' of God's promise and mission and of the 'phenomenon' of the resurrection and future of Christ. It will be able to open up to man today new possibilities, prospects and goals through its exposition of that event which paves the way for the eschatological future." Moltmann, *Theology of Hope*, 287–88.

9. Hans Urs von Balthasar, *Seeing the Form*, vol. 1 of *The Glory of the Lord: A Theological Aesthetics*, trans. Erasmo Leiva-Merikakis (Edinburgh: T&T Clark, 1982 [1961]), 437.

10. This focus on the present is partly a function of Balthasar's concern to defend the possibility of the *theologia gloriae* against Protestant critiques: "For Protestantism beauty remains eschatological; but if the *eschaton* which is Christ has appeared in the midst of history, and if the rays of his resurrection already begin to brighten that history, then we should be permitted to speak of Christian beauty even here below." (Balthasar, *Seeing the Form*, 659; cf. the critique of Luther on 57–58).

11. "Jesus is the Word, the Image, the Expression and Exegesis of God.... He is what he expresses—namely God.... How greatly therefore the power of sight is demanded and presupposed at the point of origin." Balthasar, *Seeing the Form*, 29. This emphasis on sight is partly intended to counter the Protestant emphasis on faith and hearing (following Rom. 10:17) as precluding the possibility of present vision (see ibid., 333; cf. 120, 200–201). And although he also states that "we do not need to argue over whether precedence goes to hearing or seeing," he effectively subverts that claim by adding that "hearing must be assigned particularly to imitative faith, while . . . seeing is more properly assigned to archetypal faith. . . . Furthermore, within the archetypal experience we can assign hearing . . . predominantly to the Old Testament, and seeing . . . predominantly to the New" (ibid., 309–10).

12. The English translation of *Herrlichkeit* runs to seven volumes and over 3,500 pages (the German original is in three, with the third in two parts). In the programmatic first volume, *Seeing the Form*, there are only a few, widely scattered references to hope, and even where it is mentioned the theological accent falls on present experience more than anticipation of the future. Thus, even where hope does come into discussion (at the end of each of the last two volumes of the English translation), it is largely by way of warning: in the first case indicting the messianic hope of postexilic Israel as one of several abortive "attempts to force the glory of God into the open" (Hans Urs von Balthasar, *Theology: The Old Covenant*, vol. 6 of *The Glory of the Lord: A Theological Aesthetics*, trans. Brian McNeil and Erasmo Leiva-Merikakis (Edinburgh: T&T Clark, 1991 [1967]), 303); and in the second in connection with the rejection of all "political theology" (Hans Urs von Balthasar, *Theology: The New Covenant*, vol. 7 of *The*

Introduction 5

Importantly, the one-sidedness of both Moltmann's theology of hope and Balthasar's theology of glory can be understood as motivated by sound theological concerns. For although neither thinker comments directly on his decision to treat one topic in comparative disregard of the other, both clearly wish to stress God's love for this creation in all its quotidian concreteness in opposition to theologies with a more subjective or otherworldly focus.[13] Both their respective strategies may thus be understood as acknowledging that while hope and glory are both integral to Christian faith, each has an inherent tendency to turn theological attention away from life in this world, albeit in different ways. In the case of hope, the risk of displacement is temporal (or "horizontal"): from the present to the future; while for glory it is rather spatial (or "vertical"): from the ambiguities of earth "below" to the heavenly realm "above" where God is ever visible.[14] By choosing hope or glory as the focus of attention, each theologian runs the risk of a displacement of eschatological discourse along either the "horizontal" or "vertical" axis but is thereby enabled to give full attention to the dimension they choose. Thus, by exploring hope without much reference to glory, Moltmann maintains a horizon for Christian faith and practice that, while resolutely forward looking, remains firmly bound to the possibilities and promise of this-worldly historical existence. Likewise, although Balthasar's focus on glory pulls attention "upward" to the exalted Christ, his intent is to provide a comprehensive vision of the world as experienced here and now.[15]

Nevertheless, the trade-offs involved in the work of both theologians raises the question of whether the attempt to provide an integrated account of the "hope of glory" will not invariably give rise to an eschatology that fails to take seriously God's commitment to the flourishing of the present world, owing to the expectation of its (more or less imminent) replacement by a new creation that is utterly discontinuous with that which we now inhabit. In other words, linking hope (which points away from the present to the future) to glory (which points away from earthly possibility to heavenly reality) threatens a double displacement that risks evacuating the present of any genuine significance for

---

Glory of the Lord: A Theological Aesthetics, trans. Brian McNeil [Edinburgh: T&T Clark, 1989, {1969}], 502). Of course, *Herrlichkeit* is not Balthasar's last word on eschatology; but even in *The Last Act*, the final volume of his five-volume *Theo-Drama*, his emphasis is from the beginning on the realized dimension of Christian eschatology: *"the New Testament no longer envisages the idea of a self-unfolding of horizontal theo-dramas; there is only a vertical theo-drama in which every moment of time . . . is directly related to the exalted Lord."* Hans Urs von Balthasar, *The Last Act*, vol. 5 of *Theo-Drama: Theological Dramatic Theory*, trans. Graham Harrison (San Francisco: Ignatius, 1998 [1983]), 48.

13. In this context—and in keeping with the fact that both projects date from the 1960s and the heyday of kerygmatic theology—both Balthasar and Moltmann frequently define their own positions over against that of Bultmann and his school, which they associate with a deprecation of interest in the objective conditions of human life in time and space (viz., history) in favor of an emphasis on faith as a purely subjective decision (viz., "historicity" as a condition of personal responsibility). See, e.g., Balthasar, *Seeing the Form*, 124: "The 'glory' of Christian transfiguration is in no way less resplendent than the transfiguring glory of worldly beauty, but the fact is that the glory of Christ unites splendour and radiance with solid reality."

14. Here and in what follows, unless otherwise stated "heaven" is reserved for the created but invisible realm, beyond space and time, where God's glory is eternally visible, while "earth" and "earthly" refer to the whole visible realm of time and space (and not simply to planet Earth). This usage is intended to reflect that of the Nicene Creed, in which the phrase "heaven and earth" functions as a summary description of everything that God created, both "seen and unseen."

15. See also his interpretation of the transfiguration as a demonstration "that the Son of Man's form in his humiliation is a function of his glorified form . . . and not primarily an anticipation of the eschatological manner of existence after the Resurrection" (Balthasar, *Seeing the Form*, 670).

6 *The Hope of Glory*

life with God in a way that is impossible to square with Jesus' dedication to the healing and renewal of creation.[16] For if the glory for which Christians hope is utterly beyond the experience of life in this world, then this world seems to be reduced to little more than a purgatorial prelude to another that sits uneasily with the divine declaration that heaven and earth and all that is in them are "very good" (Gen. 1:31).[17]

To reject these alternatives as inadequate to Christian confession means accepting the challenge of finding a way to think hope and glory together. Here, as in all matters of Christian teaching, theology finds its proper point of orientation in the life of Jesus—all the more so because Paul equates "the hope of glory" with "Christ among you" (Col. 1:27). And because it is only possible to speak of Christ—who was crucified, dead, and buried—among us insofar as he has been raised from the dead, it follows that the resurrection will prove crucial for assessing the significance of Jesus for Christian hope. Certainly Paul, in proclaiming Jesus to be "the first fruits of those who have died" (1 Cor. 15:20), seems to hold that Jesus' resurrection provides the template for the destiny of all those whose life he came to share. Finding a way to think hope and glory together thus entails clarifying what it means to say that God raised Jesus from the dead, since death seemingly marks the end of all hope, and yet for Jesus it became the occasion for him to be "crowned with glory and honor" (Heb. 2:9).

Resolving the Tension: The Resurrection

In the quest to understand what resurrection entails, it must first of all be distinguished from resuscitation. The latter refers to the restoration of a dead person to earthly life, examples of which are recorded not only in both the Old and New Testaments (e.g., 2 Kings 4:32–37; John 11:1-44) but also in many other

---

16. "When immortality is thought of simply as grace . . . then it takes flight into the realm of the miraculous and loses its claim on the serious attention of thinking people." Joseph Ratzinger, *Eschatology: Death and Eternal Life*, 2nd ed., trans. Michael Waldstein (Washington, DC: Catholic University of America Press, 1988 [1977]), 154.

17. In this context, it is necessary to say something about Giorgio Agamben's view that divine glory is merely a cover for what is ultimately empty, rather like the fire and smoke distracting from the nonentity behind the curtain in the film *The Wizard of Oz*. Agamben argues that to posit glory as an intrinsic property of God implies that God is inherently "inoperative." This essential divine inactivity implies that there is nothing to say about God, in the face of which "glory" is introduced as that which "must cover with its splendor the unaccountable figure of divine inoperativity." Giorgio Agamben, *The Kingdom and the Glory: For a Theological Genealogy of Economy and Government*, trans. Lorenzo Chiesa (Stanford: Stanford University Press, 2011 [2007]), 163; cf. 224, where he goes on to ask, "Why must God be continually praised, even if the theologians . . . never tire of assuring us that he has no need of it? Does the distinction between internal [intrinsic] and external [ascribed] glory . . . really constitute a sufficient explanation? Does it not rather betray the attempt . . . to hide something that it would be too embarrassing to leave unexplained?" Leaving aside the considerable difficulties with Agamben's historical account of the relation between "theology" and "economy" in patristic Trinitarian theology, the fundamental problem with his analysis is his inability to conceive of creation as gift, insisting rather that if God is conceived as existing apart from the world, it must follow that God is "foreign" to it, and that the world must therefore be understood as "extraneous" (140)—the product of an arbitrary act of will that, being groundless, is essentially empty—and therefore in need of being covered over or concealed by the ascription of glory. That a God who is love might freely (yet, precisely because God is love, non-arbitrarily) choose to share that love externally by bringing creatures into being evidently fails to occur to him.

Introduction 7

religious traditions and, for that matter, in the annals of modern medicine. Those who are merely resuscitated, however, will eventually die again and for good: in being "raised," they have been granted only a temporary reprieve. By contrast, "Christ, being raised from the dead, will never die again; death no longer has dominion over him" (Rom. 6:9; cf. Luke 20:36).

This difference between resurrection and resuscitation means that Jesus' rising from the dead cannot be understood as just one more (albeit extraordinary) event in his life story, alongside his birth, baptism, trial, and the like.[18] Such an interpretation would vitiate the Christian confession that Jesus (as the one in whom, according to Col. 2:9, "the whole fullness of deity dwells bodily") is the definitive revelation of God's will for creation. For if Jesus were to continue to live—that is, to experience and respond to events—on the far side of Easter in the same way that he did during the period from his birth through his death, then we could no longer be confident that the divine will for our salvation revealed in Jesus' earthly lifespan was final or definitive. If in his risen state Jesus continued to develop as a character via interactions with various features of his environment (even if on a higher, heavenly plane), what guarantee would we have that one of these postmortem events would not disclose that God's favor was in fact less expansive than suggested by Jesus' life on earth? In order for this possibility to be excluded—as it must be if the gospel that "Christ Jesus came into the world to save sinners" is indeed to be regarded as "sure and worthy of full acceptance" (1 Tim. 1:15)—resurrection must not be confused with a return to or resumption of earthly life, but must rather be understood as the divine vindication of that life in its entirety, from Jesus' birth to his death. To confess Jesus as risen therefore means to acknowledge that his death marks the absolute and definitive boundary to his life story, so that the mode of Jesus' life after Easter is quite different from that which he experienced between Christmas and Good Friday: from his birth to his death Jesus lived out his identity as the Son in time; in the resurrection, he lives eternally just as the person whose life is bounded by his birth from Mary at one end and his crucifixion under Pilate at the other. It follows that if Jesus is the one from whom we take our eschatological bearings, then the content of Christian hope is not to be conceived as an otherworldly sequel to the life we live here and now, but rather as the eternal affirmation of our lives as they have been lived on earth.

Hope is thus anchored in our life now because it is just this life's vindication, even though the fact that hope pertains to the *whole* of this life also means that it cannot be realized in this world but only on the far side of death, as that which marks the end of this life. So far, so good—but only so far. For it does not take much reflection to realize that serious questions arise when this christological template of postmortem vindication is applied to human beings in general. It is, after all, one thing to speak of the eternal affirmation of Jesus' earthly life, since he is without sin (Heb. 4:15). But what sense can be made of the claim that God would affirm the life of any human being *other* than Jesus, "since all have

---

18. The Sadducees' query to Jesus about the postmortem status of the woman who married seven brothers in succession suggests that they understood the idea of resurrection in just this sense (Matt. 22:23–28 and pars.). See pp. 114–15 below for further discussion of this point.

8 *The Hope of Glory*

sinned and fall short of the glory of God" (Rom. 3:23; cf. 1 John 1:18)?[19] Is it really good news to hear that lives marked by selfishness, vanity, faithlessness, or greed—let alone those whose record includes torture, rape, or murder—will be received into eternal glory?

Of course, this problem was known to Israel long before the coming of Jesus, as shown by the psalmist's question, "If you, O LORD, should mark iniquities, Lord, who could stand?" (Ps. 130:3). When human life is considered in itself, with reference to what an individual has done or failed to do, there can be no possibility of vindication: because everyone has sinned, no one can stand. Nor is this judgment arbitrary, as though this universal condemnation derived from God having set absurd or impossible criteria for human beings to meet. Quite the contrary, the essential mystery of sin is that there is no accounting for it on these or any other terms, because for a creature to sin is to turn from God and thereby—since God is the sole ground of every creature's being—to cut itself off from the very power that secures its existence. In bringing us into being, God wills that we should stand; but in committing sin (where "sin" refers to any action or inaction by which we turn from God's will for us) we reject the only power by which we *can* stand.

Yet however great the mystery of sin may be, Scripture teaches that the mystery of love, whereby God refuses to allow that creatures' fate should be defined by their failures, is greater still. "If you, O LORD, should mark iniquities, Lord, who could stand?" But, the psalmist continues, "there is forgiveness with you, so that you may be revered" (Ps. 130:3–4). Forgiveness is God's declaration that what the sinful creature has done or failed to do is not decisive for its relationship with God. Importantly, in making this declaration, God does not undo what has been done: the fact of sin remains part of the creature's history; but in forgiving the sin God declares that the creature's being is not reducible to its history, so that the lives of sinners may be affirmed without thereby affirming their sin. In other words, through the forgiveness of sin, our lives are redeemed.

Here, too, the resurrection remains central, for according to Scripture it is only on the basis of the news that Jesus has risen from the dead that "repentance and forgiveness of sins is to be proclaimed in his name to all nations" (Luke 24:47; cf. Acts 5:31; 10:43; 13:38; 26:18; Col. 1:14). This is not because Jesus' death somehow makes forgiveness possible by satisfying some divine requirement that mercy be purchased at the price of some compensatory quantity of punishment. Leaving aside the fact that even in human practice to forgive is precisely to *forgo* the demand for punishment, the Gospels are full of stories of Jesus forgiving people's sin without the evangelists offering any account of Jesus satisfying any moral, legal, or cultic requirements as a condition of his doing so.

The link between incarnation and the gospel of forgiveness therefore needs to be conceived in different terms. As already noted, in sin we turn away from God, undermining the very conditions of our existence (since God is the only condition of our existence) in a way that invariably leads to our destruction. In taking flesh, God checks this process by uniting God's own life, which cannot

---

19. Catholics will, of course, hold Mary of Nazareth to be one further exception to this truth, but this does not affect the basic point being made.

Introduction 9

be destroyed, to ours. The result is that our life, too, is now reconstituted in such a way as to be unable to be held by death. Nor is this just a future hope. The gospel is not that Jesus has gone on to a life in glory that the rest of us will share some day, but that because Jesus has been glorified our lives have *already* been transformed:

> [W]e are convinced that one has died for all; therefore all have died. And he died for all, so that those who live might live no longer for themselves, but for the one who for their sake died and was raised. From now on, therefore, we regard no one from a human point of view; even though we once knew Christ from a human point of view, we no longer know him in that way. So if anyone is in Christ, there is a new creation: everything old has passed away; look, everything has become new! (2 Cor. 5:14–17, alt.)

In light of Jesus' resurrection, no one is any longer to be regarded "from a human point of view"—that is, according to the potentials and possibilities of their earthly lives.[20] For because it is true of the risen Jesus that "the life he lives, he lives to God" (Rom. 6:10; cf. 2 Cor. 13:4), so no human life is to be considered apart from God. We, too, are to be regarded as sharing Jesus' risen life, because (as Paul goes on to inform the Corinthians), in him "God was reconciling the world to himself, not counting their trespasses against them, and entrusting the message of reconciliation"—that is, the gospel of forgiveness of sins—"to us" (2 Cor. 5:19). The life that is consummated in resurrection is already active in us now by virtue of the baptism through which we, experiencing our dying to sin in anticipation of our dying in the body, likewise begin to experience renewed life with God prior to the general resurrection: "So you also must consider yourselves dead to sin and alive to God in Christ Jesus" (Rom. 6:11).[21]

Resurrection's Form: Persons and Natures

But how does the resurrection make it possible for mere words—even if they are God's words of forgiveness—to change the human situation so radically? It is, after all, one thing to recognize the capacity of a well-placed word to sustain the weary in a time of weakness (Isa. 50:4) but quite another to argue that a word has the capacity to secure our lives in the face of death. To answer this question, it is necessary to take a slight detour through the technicalities of Christian teaching about Jesus' person in order to recognize the connection between Jesus' rising from the dead and the confession that he is at once fully divine and fully human. In the classic form adopted at the Council of Chalcedon in 451, this teaching turns on the conceptual distinction between *person*

---

20. This Greek of 2 Cor. 5:16 translated in the NRSVue as "from a human point of view" is *kata sarka*—literally "according to the flesh," to which the implicit alternative is *kata pneuma*, or "according to the Spirit." The point is to contrast what God is doing with that which appears either real or possible on the basis of creaturely considerations (cf. Matt. 19:26 and pars.).

21. "Thinking of who we are after baptism is analogous to thinking about who we will be after the resurrection: still ourselves, particularly and recognizably so, though metamorphosed. . . . The self at baptism isn't just analogous to the resurrected self—the self at baptism approximates the self upon resurrection." Lauren Winner, *The Dangers of Christian Practice: On Wayward Gifts, Characteristic Damage, and Sin* (New Haven, CT: Yale University Press, 2018), 112.

10 The Hope of Glory

(or hypostasis) and *nature*, according to which Jesus is confessed to be just *one* person but with *two* (viz., divine and human) natures, as follows:

> the same Lord Jesus Christ, the only begotten Son, must be acknowledged in two natures, without confusion or change, without division or separation. The distinction between the natures was never abolished by their union but rather the character proper to each of the two natures was preserved as they came together in one person and hypostasis. He is not split or divided into two persons, but he is one and the same only begotten Son, God the Word, the Lord Jesus Christ.[22]

The claim that the divine and human natures were united in Jesus "without confusion or change" means, on the one hand, that God did not cease to be God in taking flesh and, on the other, that the flesh that God took was perfectly ordinary, so that with respect to his humanity Jesus, like every other human being, was dependent on a vast network of creaturely structures and processes, both physical and social, to sustain his earthly life. This ordinariness was recognized by Jesus' contemporaries and, indeed, was what made his claims to authority so puzzling to them (see, e.g., Mark 6:3; John 1:46; 8:57): with respect to his human nature, he was indeed like us "in every respect" (Heb. 2:17).[23]

This insistence that the union of divinity and humanity in Jesus did not violate the integrity of either nature means that the incarnation does not entail any change in the fundamental relationship between God as Creator and the world as created: even in the person of Jesus, the natures of Creator and creature remain distinct, so that considered as a human being, Jesus is no more divine than you or I. The crucial difference between Jesus and other human beings has to do with that other crucial category in the Chalcedonian definition: his person, or "hypostasis," meaning his identity, or *who* he is. All human beings are "hypostases" in this Chalcedonian sense of the term (that is, every individual human being is some*one* in addition to being some*thing*), but only in the case of Jesus, Christians claim, is the someone in question God; that is, only in his case can a human being be said to have (or, more accurately, to be) a *divine* hypostasis, so that Jesus is rightly identified as none other than the eternal Word, the Second Person of the Trinity.[24] This means that while it is no more true of Jesus than of me or you that when he eats a piece of bread, for example, God is the immediate ground of that action (since as Creator God is the necessary and

---

22. *Compendium of Creeds, Definitions, and Declarations on Matters of Faith and Morals*, 43rd ed., ed. Heinrich Denzinger, Peter Hünermann, et al. (San Francisco: Ignatius Press, 2012) [hereafter DH], §301–02; translation slightly altered.

23. Although Jesus also performed miracles, the fact that he himself attributed this capacity to God's Spirit (Matt. 12:28; cf. John 3:34) implies that the "mechanics" (if you will) of his teaching and miracles were no different than that of the prophets who preceded him or his disciples who would come after (see John 14:12)—and thus implies no qualification of the judgment that his humanity was perfectly ordinary. Similarly, Jesus' virginal conception does not in any fundamental sense qualify the ordinariness of the humanity thereby conceived (nor is it in any sense an ontologically necessary corollary of his being the Word incarnate, which, as discussed below, is a function of his hypostasis rather than his human nature).

24. When I characterize my explication of the term "hypostasis" as Chalcedonian, I do not mean to suggest that the word was understood in this sense when it was used in the definition of 451. Instead, my interpretation reflects the more precise meaning the word came to have as the result of further clarification by theologians who sought to defend the Chalcedonian definition over the subsequent 250 years (most especially in the first half of the sixth century).

Introduction   11

sufficient condition of every creaturely happening), in the case of Jesus alone can it be said that God is also the actor. To say that Jesus is the Word made flesh is thus to say that when Jesus eats, talks, or breathes, the one eating, talking, and breathing is God: whatever Jesus does, God does—and that is not true of any other human being.

Now, this feature of Jesus' existence carries with it certain further implications. All other human beings come into being as (human) hypostases together with their (human) natures, such that we become someone just in coming to be something (viz., a human being). In other words, it is just because I have been born a human being that I also subsist as a human hypostasis. The structure of the earthly life of human beings is thus one in which the nature sustains the hypostasis, meaning that human beings subsist as persons by virtue of their being human, that is, because "humanity" names a kind of nature that in being individuated is also "personalized."[25] By contrast, Jesus' identity as the eternal Word means that the relation between hypostasis and human nature is different in his case. Because his hypostasis is divine, his hypostatic status as someone is not contingent upon his having a human nature as yours or mine is. Rather, because the Word subsists eternally as a hypostasis of the divine nature, and thus independently of incarnation, Jesus' hypostasis may be said to "preexist" his humanity in a way that is not true of any other human being.[26] Consequently, while the Word who has taken flesh lives his incarnate life in Roman Palestine by means of the same processes of respiration, digestion, and so forth characteristic of the nature he shares with all other human beings, the Word is not dependent on that nature and its processes in the same way as the hypostases of other human beings are. Rather, because Jesus is God, the Second Person of the Trinity, he is the one human being for whom it is the case that his hypostasis subsists (viz., in the divine nature) prior to his humanity.[27]

It is this feature of Jesus' ontology that distinguishes him from a "mere human being" (what the Greek fathers called a *psilos anthrōpos*), in spite of the ordinariness of his humanity. And it is also this feature which ensures that death—the cessation of those biological functions that sustain a living creature in active relation with its external environment—affects Jesus differently

---

25. Importantly, this is not to say that the nature *causes* the hypostasis, for that would imply that the hypostasis were a part or attribute of the nature (that is, some *thing*—one property of the nature alongside others) rather than the identity of the one who instantiates the nature. One might say that my nature "causes" me to have brown hair, two arms, the capacity to reason, even to exhibit particular personality traits; but it does not cause me to be Ian. In other words, I am the hypostasis I am as the one who has this particular body, with this personality, will, intellect, and so forth; but because (as Christians will want to confess) my identity as this particular hypostasis persists in spite of the most radical changes to any of these features, it cannot be derived from any of them. Thus, although my hypostasis has no existence apart from my nature (since it is a hypostasis at all only as it is a hypostasis of that nature), it cannot be derived from any individual feature or set of features of that nature.

26. I put "preexist" in quotation marks because although it is impossible to talk about the incarnation except in terms that connote temporal sequence (e.g., "took flesh," "became incarnate," etc.), the fact that the Word's taking flesh is not an evolution in the life of the Word (which, as eternal, does not subsist in temporal sequence), but simply the projection of an eternal reality into time, makes the use of temporal modifiers misleading.

27. That is the force of the Scholastic doctrine of "anhypostasia," according to which Jesus' human nature has no existence (i.e., is "anhypostatic") except as hypostatized by the divine Word. See pp. 139–42 below for a discussion of how it is possible to speak of human hypostases being upheld by God—though not properly subsisting—apart from actively hypostatizing a human nature.

12   *The Hope of Glory*

than other human beings. For every other human being, death's destruction of human nature (traditionally described as the separation of soul and body) claims the hypostasis as well, which cannot subsist apart from the nature that sustains it.[28] To be sure, for Jesus, too, the death of his human nature also entails the death of his hypostasis: that is just what it means to confess (in line with the vindication of the theopaschite formula at the Second Council of Constantinople) that one of the Trinity died on the cross;[29] but precisely because Jesus, as the Word of God, *is* one of the Trinity, his hypostasis is also inseparable from the immortal divine nature, with the result that the process of death works itself out differently in his case. Unlike the rest of us, after Jesus dies in his humanity, he is also and necessarily raised again from the dead in that same humanity, "because it was impossible for him" as the eternal Word who eternally hypostatizes the divine nature "to be held in [death's] power" (Acts 2:24). Because the inherent immortality of the divine nature means that the hypostasis of the Word cannot be held by death, the human nature to which that hypostasis has bound itself in taking flesh cannot be held by death either. That is just what it means for Jesus to be raised from the dead: to live anew before God as the Word *incarnate*—that is, with a human nature and therefore as a human being.

As already noted, this mode of life is different from a mere return to earthly life, although the Bible does not give much information about the characteristics of resurrected existence. According to Paul, it entails the acquisition of a "spiritual" body in place of our current "psychic" (i.e., soul-animated) one (1 Cor. 15:44), but this information is of limited value, since Paul does not give any detail about what a "spiritual body" is. The resurrection narratives in the Gospels give a mixed picture: on the one hand, a spiritual body seemingly has some sort of substantial reality (since John 21:4, 9–13, for example, depicts Jesus cooking and serving breakfast); on the other, it also has the very un-substantial properties of being able to pass through closed doors (John 20:19, 26) and to vanish from sight (Luke 24:30–31). While there seems little point in trying to work out the biophysics of all this, the upshot is clearly that a spiritual body lives in a manner that is qualitatively different from human bodies on the hither side of death.

This difference can be described in Chalcedonian language in terms of a shift in the relation between nature and hypostasis. Again, so long as Jesus lived an earthly life, his hypostasis, like that of every human being, was sustained through the operation of his human nature, and thus by the mediation of the same sorts of physical interactions on which all living organisms depend. Since such interactions are subject to disruptions (for example, by the withholding of food or the infliction of injury) that render creatures vulnerable to death, the claim that after Easter "death no longer has dominion over" Jesus means that his resurrected human nature is no longer threatened by such disruptions; it is free from them because it now subsists not by its own power, but rather by the

---

28. If death is understood as the separation of the soul from the body, the hypostasis continues to subsist in the soul (since it is precisely the soul of somebody or other); but in a state of separation from the body, neither the soul nor the hypostasis can be said to be fully alive prior to its being reunited to the body in the resurrection. See the discussion in chapter 6 below.

29. "If anyone does not confess that he who was crucified in the flesh, our Lord Jesus Christ, is true God, Lord of glory and one of the Holy Trinity, let him be anathema." DH §432.

Introduction 13

power of the divine hypostasis, which cannot be held by death and with which Jesus' human nature has been united. In short, whereas during his earthly life as a human being the incarnate Word's human nature sustained his hypostasis, in the resurrection it is the hypostasis that sustains his human nature. Thus, while the risen Jesus remains human, with a "spiritual body" that maintains enough of the characteristics of his earthly body (most especially, his wounds) to be recognized precisely as the body of Jesus, that body now subsists independently of the network of physical causes that sustained it prior to Good Friday.

This independence is manifest during the forty days after Easter in the risen Jesus' ability to vanish and appear spontaneously, but it is established definitively in his ascension to the right hand of God (Mark 16:19; Eph. 1:20; 1 Pet. 3:22), for the point of the ascension is precisely to affirm that Jesus continues to subsist humanly (that is, as a psychosomatic whole rather than as an angel or other form of disembodied spirit), but that he does so "in heaven"—that is, outside of the network of interdependence that marks creatures' existence in time and space. As risen and ascended, Jesus occupies a "place" in the presence of God that is outside of created space: the place of glory. Of course, as the eternal Word Jesus is always in the Father's presence in his divine nature (for he is God together with the Father and the Holy Spirit); but by virtue of having taken flesh, died, risen, and ascended, he now lives before the Father according to his human nature as well. Again, he does not do this by any power of his human nature, but rather by virtue of his hypostatic identity as the Word. That is why Jesus is no longer to be regarded "from a human point of view," that is, as defined by the constraints of his earthly existence in first-century Palestine.

Resurrection's Content: Living by God's Word

This rather long christological detour provides a framework allowing us to address the question of how the hope of glory can rest on God's word of forgiveness. Again, the hope of glory is, according to Paul, none other than Christ among us (Col. 1:27). In the period between Christ's ascension and return, Christ is among us in the message of forgiveness that comes to us through word and sacrament, and through this message the human nature of the sinner, too, comes to be sustained through her hypostasis rather than the other way round. After all, forgiveness—that which affirms the lives of sinners apart from their sin—is spoken to the hypostasis, since it is the person (i.e., Mary or Peter or Ian) not the nature that is forgiven. Unlike Jesus, our hypostases are not divine; but because our hypostases have been claimed by the Word in the face of the judgment that would otherwise rightly fall on us, it becomes true for us as well that our natures are sustained by our hypostases—which is simply to say that we live by the power of God's word of forgiveness rather than by any power of our own.[30] Prior to the resurrection this promise of life before God is not fully

---

30. One might draw a parallel here with Thomas Aquinas's way of contrasting how humans know in this life and in glory: in glory they know things immediately ("from above," we might say) through direct vision of the eternal ideas in the divine mind, whereas in history they know things only via abstraction from sensory perception of particular objects ("from below"). See Thomas Aquinas, *Summa Theologiae* 1.78–84, 60 vols., Blackfriars ed. (London: Eyre & Spottiswood, 1964–1981).

14 *The Hope of Glory*

realized. We do not live in glory yet: we remain on earth, where Christ is hidden from our sight until his return; but the life of glory is nevertheless anticipated now as we receive the gospel of forgiveness, which declares that nothing can separate us from the love of God shown forth in Christ Jesus (Rom. 8:39).

The Bible teaches that human beings live not "by bread alone, but by every word that comes from the mouth of God" (Matt. 4:4 and par.; cf. Deut. 8:3). To receive the gospel of the forgiveness of sins is to experience, incompletely but genuinely, what it means to live by God's word alone. For to hear this word is to know that one's identity is not defined by one's past actions, but solely and definitively by God's word of grace. That is why none of us is to be regarded "from a human point of view": not because we have ceased to be human, but because our humanity is no longer defined by the possibilities and limits of existence in space and time, but rather by the power of God's word. As creatures we were, of course, already products of this Word, through whom we and all things were made (John 1:3); but in Jesus Christ that Word is now spoken to us personally, calling us to rest on its power alone rather than on any of the various created realities on which we might otherwise be tempted to rely.[31] To confess that we live "not by bread alone, but by every word that comes from the mouth of God" is thus simply to acknowledge that in the last analysis our lives are not secured by our natural powers, but by God who, in addressing us as persons, upholds our natures as well.[32]

It is on these grounds that it becomes possible to think hope and glory together without contradiction, because the glory for which Christians hope, while not in any sense reducible to what can be seen now, or to what can be grasped by extrapolation from present experience, nevertheless has an anchor in that experience. For the object of this hope is just the risen life of Jesus: a life that is both fully human and, having overcome death, is secure in its humanity against every conceivable threat. And while we are not yet risen, we experience something of that eschatological vindication now when and as we receive Jesus' word of forgiveness, which gives us the assurance of a life sustained by grace from above rather than by our efforts from below. For when it is known that a person's life is finally secured by the word of pardon and adoption that comes to them from God in Christ rather than by what they have done or failed to do, then it becomes impossible to regard anyone "from a human point of view."

Fine words—and fine words butter no parsnips. How in practice do we honor the demand to regard no one "from a human point of view" while still remaining attentive to the concrete realities of human sin and suffering here and

---

31. Cf. Maximus the Confessor, *Quaestiones ad Thalassium* 61 (*PG* 90: 640B-C): "the righteous man will not be in a 'place' [*thesin*] describable in terms of 'where' at all, having by grace received God himself as his 'place' instead of any spatial 'where' [*hyper to pou*]. . . . For God does not admit of 'where'; he is unqualifiedly beyond all 'where.' In him will be the sure foundation of all who are saved." Cited in Maximus the Confessor, *On the Cosmic Mystery of Jesus Christ: Selected Writings from St. Maximus the Confessor*, trans. Paul M. Blowers and Robert Wilken (Crestwood, NY: St. Vladimir's Seminary Press, 2003), 142; translation altered.

32. Cf. Kathryn Tanner, *Jesus, Humanity and the Trinity* (Edinburgh: T&T Clark, 2000), 110: "In short, there is an approximation to the hypostatic union that the world enjoys through grace, most particularly after the world's death, when it transpires that, like Christ, the only life or existence we have is in and through God. . . . When the fire of our own lives grows cold, we come to burn with God's own flame."

Introduction 15

now? What prevents the assurance of God's favor from turning into complacency before the ongoing injustices that blight the existence of the vast majority of the world's human population—as well as threatening the extinction of vast numbers of nonhuman organisms? And—perhaps most seriously of all—how does a focus on forgiveness as the heart of the gospel avoid a construal of the Christian message that speaks far better news to those who have perpetrated injustice than to those who have suffered its effects, thereby betraying Jesus' identification of the gospel with good news to the poor in particular (Matt. 11:5 and par.; Luke 4:18)?

The balance of this book will attempt to address these questions by exploring more fully how the reality of life lived now in the light of the gospel is to be related to the hope of eschatological glory to come. The argument falls into two parts, focused on the topics of hope and glory, respectively. Part 1 begins with an examination of false hope (chapter 1), which takes the contrasting forms of otherworldly fantasy on the one hand, and Promethean efforts to control the future on the other, both of which so focus attention on what is to come that they fail to recognize the degree to which the experience of present pain casts doubt on the credibility of any promise of future flourishing. I then turn to the refusal of hope (chapter 2) found among those whose appreciation for the depth of pain in this life leads them to dismiss the promise of a redeeming God as neither credible nor desirable, before going on to show how the person and work of Jesus provide a basis for a hope in which confidence in God's saving power keeps faith with those who suffer now (chapter 3). After an interlude in which I explore the inherent limitations of eschatological speech (chapter 4), part 2 examines the glory that is the final object of Christian hope from three different perspectives: first, the confession of Jesus' return and the Last Judgment (chapter 5); second, the transformation of the individual that centers on the doctrine of bodily resurrection (chapter 6); and third, the transformation of the cosmos implied by the biblical promise of a new heaven and a new earth (chapter 7). The book then concludes with a reflection on the possibility of a theology of glory that sits within rather than against a theology of the cross.

Throughout the course of this argument, I aim to show that because the accounts of hope and glory at the heart of the Christian doctrine of redemption are firmly rooted in the present realities of created existence, a dogmatic account of the redeemed life should never lead to the turning of theological attention away from the travails of this world and its creatures. In the book's first part I do this by linking *hope*, with its risk of "horizontal" displacement of attention from the present to the future, with the experience of *suffering* in the here and now. Tethering talk of future hope to present suffering serves to guard against glibness. This sort of safeguard, it is important to stress, does not make it possible to talk about hope in the presence of burning children (to talk about *anything* in the presence of burning children is to have misdiagnosed what the situation demands). Its aim is rather the more modest one of ensuring that talk of forgiveness does not have the effect of licensing forgetfulness. Along similar lines, I seek in part 2 to keep the promise of eschatological *glory*, with its risk of "vertical" displacement of attention upward from earth to heaven, bound to *corporeality*, or embodiment, as a defining and irrevocable feature of human being. Associating glory with the fate of bodies serves to check the temptation

16   *The Hope of Glory*

to interpret redemption as an escape from the world: because to have a body—whether earthly or spiritual—is to be in relation to other bodies, to proclaim the resurrection of the body is to affirm that the life of one is inseparable from the life of all and thus from the fate of the whole creation.[33]

Finally (and with the details to be developed further in what follows), it must be stressed that to confess that the glory for which Christians hope is beyond every possibility of life in this world does not mean that there is anything illegitimate about seeking to realize in this world whatever possibilities for righteousness are available to us here and now. Quite the contrary, the biblical command to "seek the welfare of the city where I have sent you into exile" on the grounds that "in its welfare you will find your welfare" (Jer. 29:7) applies to us now just as much as it did when spoken to the Israelites in Babylon. And yet the specification that the city whose welfare we are to seek is identified as a place of exile serves as a permanent reminder that "here we have no lasting city, but we are looking for the city that is to come" (Heb. 13:14). Again, this conviction must not be taken as an excuse for dismissing the significance of life in the present, but rather as encouragement not to lose heart when (as inevitably happens) our efforts toward improving the welfare of our earthly habitation fall short. It should, in short, be taken as a reminder that the shape of the church's hope is not finally determined by our discernment of what may prove possible in the present. For however much the discernment of such possibilities is crucial to Christians' day-to-day efforts to be faithful witnesses to the kingdom, from a human point of view the hope of glory is not a "possibility" at all. But this is precisely why we are instructed not to regard anything from a human point of view: not because we have license to ignore the realities of the present in the smug or desperate expectation that it will all be wiped away and miraculously replaced by some faultless facsimile, but rather out of the conviction (which, because it is founded in Jesus, is neither smug nor desperate) that because the kingdom has already dawned in the life, death, and resurrection of Christ, we may discern even now, in our lives and the lives of those around us, the lineaments of glory and proclaim in wonder, "Look, everything has become new!"

---

33. Linking glory with corporeality reflects the etymology of the Hebrew *kābōd*, which refers to weight or heaviness, in contrast to the Greek *doxa*, which is more suggestive of external appearance. (Cf. Paul's reference to the promise of "an eternal *weight* of glory" in 2 Cor. 4:17.)

PART 1

Hope

1. False Hope

The apostle Paul puts hope at the heart of Christian life, writing that we were saved for hope—specifically the hope for "the redemption of our bodies" (Rom. 8:23–24). In this hope we are to "rejoice" (Rom. 12:12), because it does not "disappoint" (Rom. 5:5, NRSV) and, indeed, makes us "act with great boldness" (2 Cor. 3:12, NRSV). But to speak of hope is invariably to walk a fine line, because hope can easily be misplaced: "The senseless have vain and false hopes, and dreams give wings to fools" (Sir. 34:1). To hope for something is not simply to wish for it to happen; genuine hope must, rather, be grounded in a realistic assessment of what may be expected. If Christians hope for the fulfillment of God's promises in the future, such hope can only be justified if rooted in the conviction that God has proved faithful in the past (see, e.g., Acts 2:25–26). It is because genuine hope is not simply fanciful that Christians are admonished always to "be ready to make your defense to anyone who demands from you an accounting for the hope that is in you" (1 Pet. 3:15).

At the same time, neither should hope be confused with extrapolation from present circumstances: "hope that is seen is not hope, for who hopes for what one already sees?" (Rom. 8:24; cf. 2 Cor. 5:7). If something is certain to happen, or is a calculable outcome of a particular course of behavior, it cannot properly characterized as an object of hope in the theological sense.[1] For while it is possible to give an account of one's hope (as well as, for that matter, the other "theological virtues" of faith and love) by explaining its content and warrants, that is quite different from providing a detailed description of how it will come to be actualized—let alone proving that it will be.

It is the aim of this chapter to show that the Christian hope for redemption becomes false when it veers in either of these two directions: toward wishful thinking on the one hand, or toward futuristic calculation on the other. The former fails to take seriously God's commitment to the creation that God has brought into being by hoping for future divine action that is utterly

---

1. Even in Scripture, "hope" can be used loosely to refer to matters of worldly calculation (Luke 6:34; Acts 16:10) as well as to wishful thinking (e.g., Job 3:9; Acts 24:26); but such colloquial usage must be distinguished from the term's theological sense. In this context, it is important to stress that although Christian hope's invisibility means it can never be reduced to calculation, that fact does not render it (as opposed to worldly hope) uncertain (cf. the reference to "sure and certain hope" in the rite for the burial of the dead in the *Book of Common Prayer*). I therefore part company with William Lynch's characterization of hope as "a sense of the possible" (William F. Lynch, *Images of Hope: Imagination as Healer of the Hopeless* [Notre Dame, IN: University of Notre Dame Press, 1965], 32): realistic assessment of the possible is certainly an important skill, but it is not the meaning of hope, which is grounded in God, whose capacities are not defined by what is humanly possible (Luke 18:27).

disconnected from—and thus simply overwhelms—the being and actions of creatures. The latter, by contrast, renders the content of the hoped-for future immanent to the created order, and thus ultimately a product of human work rather than divine grace. At first glance these two varieties of false hope seem to err in opposite ways, but closer examination suggests that although both can plausibly be seen as responses to the experience of suffering, their orientations to the future, for all their differences in appearance, are characterized by shared forgetfulness of (and thus ultimately disregard for) the past that renders them unable finally to take suffering seriously.

Escapism: Rescue from the World

As noted in the introduction, the content of Christian hope is "the manifestation of the glory of our great God and Savior, Jesus Christ" (Titus 2:13), who, having been raised from the dead to sit at the right hand of the Father, will (in the words of the Nicene Creed) "come again . . . to judge the living and the dead," and whose "kingdom will have no end." Yet as much as the promise of life with the risen Lord constitutes the stable center of Christian eschatology, there remains significant disagreement among Christians over whether or not that promise is fulfilled within history (i.e., on this earth, in the same framework of space and time in which we live at present) or only beyond it, in the new heaven and new earth that will follow the passing away of the current spatio-temporal order (Rev. 21:1; cf. Isa. 65:17; 66:22; 2 Pet. 3:13).[2] This disagreement turns on respective parties' understanding of the meaning of the millennium, the thousand-year reign of Christ and the saints mentioned at the end of the book of Revelation:

> Then I saw thrones, and those seated on them were given authority to judge. I also saw the souls of those who had been beheaded for their testimony to Jesus and for the word of God. They had not worshiped the beast or its image and had not received its brand on their foreheads or their hands. They came to life and reigned with Christ a thousand years. (The rest of the dead did not come to life until the thousand years were ended.) This is the first resurrection. Blessed and holy are those who share in the first resurrection. Over these the second death has no power, but they will be priests of God and of Christ, and they will reign with him a thousand years. (Rev. 20:4–6)

For most of the church's history, the dominant interpretation of this passage, given classic articulation by Augustine of Hippo in the fifth century, has been that the millennium refers to the period of time between Jesus' first and second comings, and thus to the present age of the church.[3] An alternative reading,

2. There is broad agreement among Christians that life with the risen Lord is realized in a provisional sense (i.e., apart from the experience of bodily resurrection that will come only with the eschaton) for the faithful who die prior to Christ's return. For further discussion and assessment of this belief, see chapter 6 below.

3. "Thus, the devil is bound throughout the whole period embraced by the Book of Revelation, that is, from the first coming of Christ until the end of the world, which will be Christ's second coming. . . .

1. False Hope

however, sees this passage as describing a temporal sequence in which Christ's second coming inaugurates (instead of concluding) the millennium, which is understood as referring to a future historical epoch during which believers will be raised from the dead to reign with Christ on earth for an extended period, only after which will come the general resurrection and the Last Judgment.

While this latter perspective, known since the time of Augustine as "millenarian" and, more recently (and precisely), as "premillennial" (because it anticipates Christ returning *before* the millennium) had significant—though by no means universal—support in the early church,[4] it was eclipsed as a mainstream theological position after the fourth century.[5] It has, however, seen a marked resurgence since the mid-nineteenth century, beginning in the United Kingdom through the work of John Nelson Darby and the Plymouth Brethren and then spreading widely among self-described evangelical Protestants in America and beyond, especially in the wake of the publication of the Scofield Reference Bible in 1909. At the same time, there are significant disagreements among contemporary premillennialists, with some placing themselves explicitly in the line of early Christian millenarianism, which they argue differs in important ways from the version popularized by Scofield (and, more recently, the Left Behind books).[6]

Although premillennialists draw on eschatological passages from both the Old and New Testaments in attempting to provide a chronology of the end times, Revelation plays a central role by virtue of its containing the only explicit biblical reference to the millennium. Against this background, contemporary premillennialists share the belief that Revelation's final chapters describe a

---

But while the devil is bound for a thousand years, the saints reign with Christ, also for a thousand years, which are without a doubt to be understood . . . as the period beginning with Christ's first coming." Augustine, *The City of God against the Pagans*, 20.8–9, ed. and trans. R. W. Dyson (Cambridge: Cambridge University Press, 1998), 983, 987; cf. 20.6 (975–78), where Augustine (citing John 5:25–26; 2 Cor. 5:14–15) explains that in this scheme the "first resurrection" refers to the resurrection of the soul in baptism (see Rom. 6:11).

4. Examples include Irenaeus of Lyon (*Against Heresies* 5:32–34), Tertullian (*Against Marcion* 3.24), Victorinus of Pettau (*On the Creation of the World*), and Lactantius (*Divine Institutes*, 7.24, 26), all of whom are listed by Jerome as following the millenarian views of the second-century bishop Papias of Hierapolis in Jerome, *De Viris Illustribus* 18, https://www.newadvent.org/fathers/2708.htm. See also Justin Martyr, *Dialogue with Trypho* 80–81. At the same time, Eugenio Corsini has argued on the basis of an extensive survey of Christian texts before 200 that millenarian interpretations were not predominant. See Eugenio Corsini, *Apocalisse di Gesù Cristo secondo Giovanni* (Turin: Società Editrice Internazionale, 2002); cf. Francis J. Moloney, SDB, *The Apocalypse of John: A Commentary* (Grand Rapids: Baker Academic, 2020), 20–25.

5. This eclipse, which took the form of a shift to a symbolic understanding of the millennium, is often seen as a result of the conversion of Constantine and the consequent yoking of the church's fortunes to those of the Roman Empire—not least because of the overt hostility to millennialism shown by Constantine's "court theologian," Eusebius of Caesarea. But Origen (who died from tortures endured under the Decian persecution) defended a non-literal interpretation of the millennium long before Constantine (see his *De Principiis* 2.11.2); and the fact that a symbolic interpretation was also defended by Tyconius among the persecuted Donatists as well as by Christians who lived outside of or under persecution by the Christian Empire (viz., the Church of the East and the Oriental Orthodox Churches) suggests that the change in perspective cannot be explained simply as a consequence of Christian establishment.

6. The position of Darby and Scofield is typically referred to as "dispensational premillennialism," owing to its framing of eschatological teaching within a broader division of salvation history into (usually) seven divine "dispensations," each of which corresponds to a distinct way in which God relates to human beings. For a detailed comparison between this approach and that of Christians who identify with the "historical premillennialism" of the early church, see Sung Wook Chung and David Mathewson, *Models of Premillennialism* (Eugene, OR: Cascade, 2018).

future historical sequence defined by three events: first, Christ's return (Rev. 19:11–21); second, the millennial reign of Christ with the saints on earth (Rev. 20:1–6); third, the Last Judgment (Rev. 20:7–15). There is equally broad agreement that these three events will be preceded by a fourth that is not explicitly mentioned in Revelation's later chapters: "the great tribulation"—a period of worldwide catastrophe that will include war, famine, and various natural disasters.[7] Disagreement emerges when it comes to relate these occurrences to a further anticipated end-time event that is not mentioned in Revelation at all: the "rapture" of faithful Christians, living and dead, who "will be caught up [*rapiemur* in the Latin Vulgate] in the clouds . . . to meet the Lord in the air" (1 Thess. 4:17). Those who follow in the wake of Darby hold that the rapture will take place *before* the tribulation (the "pre-trib" position). By contrast, premillennialists who place themselves in the line of early Christian teaching identify the rapture with Christ's second coming and thus locate it *after* the tribulation (the "post-trib" view).[8]

When delving into the minutiae of such debates (which include still further variants, including, as one might guess, "mid-trib" positions), it is tempting to dismiss the whole of contemporary premillennial speculation out of hand. After all, the seemingly interminable character of the debates over the timing of the rapture arguably reflect a fundamental hermeneutical problem with the whole approach: that it is based on a very selective aggregation of disparate biblical passages, read with little if any attention to genre or context, and then forced into a continuous narrative that is not independently attested anywhere in the Bible. The results therefore cannot help but seem arbitrary and the disagreements between various positions correspondingly irresolvable.[9] To read Revelation as providing a clear future chronology, let alone one that can be intercalated with the visions of Ezekiel and Daniel, the end-time predictions ascribed to Jesus in the Gospels, and Paul's remarks to the Thessalonians, reflects a failure to appreciate its character as an apocalyptic text, the language of which is symbolic rather than literal, and whose author is far more concerned with present circumstances than future prognostication. After all, the whole sequence of visions in Revelation 4–22 follows on from (and thus invariably

---

7. The phrase is found in Rev. 7:14 (KJV, NIV) in reference to a vision of uncounted multitudes standing before the throne of the Lamb "who have come out of the great tribulation"; Matt. 24:21 also speaks of a period of eschatological suffering (also rendered as "great tribulation" in the KJV, translating the same Greek word—*thlipsis*—found in Revelation 7). Modern premillennialists typically identify the tribulation with the catastrophes of the last of the seventy "weeks" described in Dan. 9:24–27.

8. While contemporary "post-trib" premillennialists often identify their position with the millennialism of the church's early centuries (see, e.g., *A Case for Historic Premillennialism: An Alternative to "Left Behind" Eschatology*, ed. Craig Blomberg and Sung Wook Chung [Grand Rapids: Baker Academic, 2009]), the categories of the tribulation and the rapture do not play the role in ancient accounts that they do in contemporary debates. Thus, insofar as Irenaeus and Tertullian (for example) do not speak of a rapture before Christ's Parousia, they may be said to have a post-tribulationist position; but because they do not identify either "tribulation" or "rapture" as discrete theologoumena, their positions do not map easily onto current debates.

9. To give an example, pre-tribulationist appeal to passages like 1 Thess. 1:10 ("Jesus . . . rescues us from the coming wrath") and 5:9 ("God has destined us not for wrath but for obtaining salvation") as supporting their position, while post-tribulationists will use texts like Rev. 13:10 ("If you are to be taken captive, into captivity you go; if you kill with the sword, with the sword you must be killed. Here is a call for the endurance and faith of the saints") to defend their point of view; but none of these passages speaks of "tribulation" (*thlipsis*)—surely a significant point if one holds to the technical understanding of this term defended by both sides in the debate.

1. False Hope

points back to) the concrete situation of the seven first-century churches, all located in the Roman province of Asia, addressed in chapters 1–3. The author views this situation as dire, but he also believes it will be subject to a great reversal in which Rome will be overthrown and Christians vindicated. That the book is meant as a summons to steadfastness and hope in a time of trial is clear; but to read its various apocalyptic symbols (including the millennium) as providing a literal description of future events simply fails to reckon with the kind of text it is.[10] And given our ignorance of the circumstances out of and for which it was written, it seems doubtful that even the symbolic import of the writer's visions is fully recoverable to any present-day reader.[11]

And yet however problematic the interpretive strategies underlying such eschatologies may be, the premillennial hope of an earthly kingdom reflects legitimate theological concerns. In this respect, one of the earliest defenses of the millenarian position remains one of the most compelling:

> it behoves the righteous first to receive the promise of the inheritance which God promised to the fathers, and to reign in it, when they rise again to behold God in this creation, and that the judgment should take place afterwards. For it is just that in the very creation in which they toiled or were afflicted, being proved in every way by suffering, they should receive the reward of their suffering; and that in the creation in which they were slain because of their love to God, in that they should be revived again; and that in the creation in which they endured servitude, in that they should reign.[12]

Importantly, the issue is not simply one of fairness—that because saints, like all earthly creatures, were made for life in this world, they should enjoy life in this world. It is rather rooted in the internal logic of responsible human action. As the young Karl Barth argued, because a person who acts with a definite moral objective must regard that objective "as a goal of *history*"—and thus as intending the transformation of the conditions of historical existence—the logic of the

---

10. B. B. Warfield (who had as high a view of biblical inerrancy as any in the tradition) made this point a century ago: "in the simple fact that we are brought face to face here with a series of visions significant of events—we are to bear continually in mind that the whole fabric of the book is compact of symbols. The descriptions are descriptions not of the real occurrences themselves, but of symbols of the real occurrences; and are to be read strictly as such. Even more than in the case of parables, we are to avoid pressing details in our interpretation of symbols: most of the details are details of the symbol, designed purely to bring the symbol sharply and strongly before the mind's eye, and are not to be transferred by any method of interpretation whatever directly to the thing symbolized." Benjamin Breckenridge Warfield, "The Millennium and the Apocalypse," in *Biblical Doctrines* (Oxford: Oxford University Press, 1929), 643–44.

11. Here I concur with the judgment of David Bentley Hart, *That All Shall Be Saved: Heaven, Hell, and Universal Salvation* (New Haven, CT: Yale University Press, 2019), 106–7: "The whole book is to my mind an intricate and impenetrable puzzle, one whose key vanished long ago along with the particular local community of Christians who produced it. The tradition of apocalyptic literature on which it draws, moreover, is one of such farraginous allegory . . . that we delude ourselves if we imagine that—across a distance of two millennia, and without any knowledge of the secretive community from which the text arose, and without any inkling of the cryptadia concealed beneath its countless figural layers—we could hope to grasp even a shadow of a fragment of its intended message." And yet recognizing this fact does not render the book useless for the church, so long as it is read with its symbolic frame in mind: "The ascertainment of the meaning of the Apocalypse is a task . . . not directly of verbal criticism but of sympathetic imagination: the teaching of the book lies not immediately in its words, but in the wide vistas its visions open to the fancy." Warfield, "The Millennium and the Apocalypse," 644.

12. Irenaeus of Lyon, *Against Heresies* 5.22, in *The Apostolic Fathers with Justin Martyr and Irenaeus*, 561.

24   *The Hope of Glory*

millennium cannot be avoided, whatever one's views about the proper interpretation of Revelation 20: "Ethics can no more exist without millenarianism . . .
than without the idea of moral personality. The man who claims he is happily
free from this *judaica opinio* has either not yet learned or has forgotten what
the ethical problem really is."[13] As noted earlier, where the outcome of faithful action now is expected entirely and exclusively in an otherworldly sphere,
the relationship between present action and future state (whether of reward or
punishment) cannot be judged other than completely arbitrary. God may stipu-
late a present course of action for the believer, but it will have no connection to
that person's future destiny than the brute fact of this divine *fiat*.[14]

Yet while such considerations disclose the *particula veri* in millenarian thinking, premillennial eschatologies (whatever their take on the relative chrono-
logical position of the rapture) are beset by serious problems that also relate
to the question of the continuity between present experience and future hope.
To put the matter bluntly, if the appeal of premillennialism lies in its refusal
to decouple the content of future hope from life in time and space, its Achilles
heel is its failure to think through that connection consistently. One sign of this
problem is the way in which the premillennialist focus on Jesus' second coming eclipses attention to the first. To be sure, all Christian eschatology contrasts
Jesus' first advent in humility with his second in glory, but precisely because
premillennialists insist that the second coming inaugurates a historical kingdom (and thus as a further development in Jesus' earthly career), the effect of
the second coming is to subvert the first: the humility, mercy, and solidarity
with the vulnerable that marked Jesus' ministry in Palestine (see Luke 22:27)
ends up telling us nothing fundamental about the character of Jesus' lordship,
which will on his return be marked by the same naked exercise of brute force
of any earthly potentate.[15] The effect is to reduce Jesus to something of a cipher:
a required object of faith whose past life and ministry have no particular significance for the content of future hope.[16] Granted, within this scheme faith in
Jesus includes assent to an array of beliefs about his earthly life (e.g., virgin
birth, miracle working, atoning death, and so on), but there is no intrinsic connection between the various features of his life in Palestine and the character of
his millennial rule.[17] Jesus is significant not because he tells us anything about

---

13. Karl Barth, *The Word of God and the Word of Man*, trans. Douglas Horton (n.p.: The Pilgrim Press,
1928), 158. Cf. Catherine Keller's critique of the Augustinian rejection of millenarian hopes common
to Orthodox, Catholic, and most historic Protestant churches: "it is not apocalypse per se which has
been undermined . . . but rather the apocalypse of collective, utopian aspirations for greater justice
in history." Catherine Keller, *Apocalypse Now and Then: A Feminist Guide to the End of the World* (Minneapolis: Fortress, 2005 [1996]), 102.
14. See p. 3 above.
15. This is not to say that premillennialists simply ignore Jesus' earthly ministry, but they tend to
view his characteristic humility as a corollary of the perfect obedience that was required for him to
accomplish the work of atoning for human sin, and thus as a function of the economy that reveals
nothing about the essential character of divine sovereignty.
16. It is consistent with this perspective that the popular premillennial writer Hal Lindsey defends
his emphasis on the second coming on the grounds that there are far more Old Testament prophecies
that speak of Christ's return in glory than of his earthly existence. See Hal Lindsey, with C. C. Carlson,
The Late Great Planet Earth (Grand Rapids: Zondervan, 1970), 41; see also 171.
17. As James Cone puts it, in this perspective Jesus "becomes a magical name which gives people
a distorted hope in another life. Through identification with a name, unbearable suffering becomes
bearable. . . . In reality, this is not the perspective of biblical faith but, rather, an expression of a hopeless

1. False Hope

God, but only because his is "the name . . . given among mortals by which we must be saved" (Acts 4:12).[18]

Within a premillennial framework, there is, correspondingly, little sense that Jesus inaugurated the kingdom in his first coming: the kingdom is not somehow both already and not yet, but strictly that which is to come, a future reality that will be actualized only with Jesus' return. In this way, the christological issues raised by premillennial eschatologies reflect a broader difficulty with the relationship they posit between present reality and future hope. For whichever relative sequencing of Christ's return and the rapture that the premillennialist defends, the fact that both events are unilateral divine actions breaking in on history from above renders the connection between present and hoped-for future experience more apparent than real. Although the millennial hope is that the saints will reign with Christ on this earth, because this reign is the result of sudden, overpowering divine intervention in history, realized independently of anything human beings do or fail to do, the vital connection between present action and future expectation that Barth rightly identified as the compelling claim of millenarian doctrine is lacking. The resulting vision, according to which the course of future history will proceed according to a certain sequence that bears no relation to human action is profoundly hopeless, even nihilistic, for there can be no hope for the future where one's actions in the world bear no relation to the future's shape.[19] The present is a matter of interest solely to the degree that it shows forth, through the fulfillment of various prophetic signs, its own irrelevance in light of Jesus' imminent return.

It might be objected at this point that such charges go too far, since it is certainly true that for premillennialists there is one crucial respect—namely, the decision to believe in Jesus Christ—that the action or inaction of people directly affects their own participation in Christ's millennial rule. Moreover, it is also clear that adherence to the premillennial framework is consistent with public action in the form of evangelistic activity that seeks to persuade as many people as possible to believe in Christ and so ensure their own salvation.[20] But

---

faith which cannot come to terms with the reality of this world." James H. Cone, *Black Theology and Black Power* (New York: Seabury, 1969), 122–23.

18. This is not to deny that Jesus is the one in whose name we are saved, but only to insist that this claim is only good news when that name is connected with the particular commitments shown forth in Jesus' ministry. Otherwise, it is simply a mark of arbitrariness on the part of a God who decided on the name of Jesus, but might just as well have chosen Moses or the Buddha—or Hitler. See Lindsey, *Late Great Planet Earth*, 186: "If you truly desire to receive Jesus Christ into your life, then you have enough faith to enter God's family and change your eternal destiny." A more dismal understanding of the gospel is hard to imagine (and how the specification of this very clear condition of divine acceptance is compatible with the affirmation—on the very next page!—of "God's unconditional acceptance of us" is never explained).

19. The claim that the premillennial perspective (in its "pre-trib" form) represents "the most thrilling, optimistic view of what the future could hold for any individual" (as claimed in Lindsey, *The Late Great Planet Earth*, 5) is remarkable, given the concomitant belief that the vast majority of human beings will be subject to enormous suffering on earth, followed by eternal damnation. The idea that the prospect of my future "rapture" would bring me joy in spite of my certain knowledge of the subsequent misery that would be experienced by countless millions reflects once again the gap between this vision of Christ the king and that of the shepherd who lays down his life for the sheep (John 10:15).

20. "[F]ar from being pessimistic and dropping out of life, we should be rejoicing in the knowledge that Christ may return at any moment. This should spur us on to share the good news of salvation in Christ with as many as possible." Lindsey, *Late Great Planet Earth*, 187.

a little reflection shows that neither consideration is truly indicative of hope, since in both cases what is at stake is not commitment to the world and its future, but rather escape from it. The central conviction animating this eschatological perspective is that the various processes and concomitant possibilities that God instituted in creation are destined only for destruction. Even the birth of Jesus did nothing substantively to renew creation; the purpose of his ministry was solely to provide a means of escape from creation's futility. To this extent, premillennialism, ironically, arguably suffers from the same problem as the Augustinian eschatology it opposes: for insofar as the shape of the world's future is finally disconnected from this-worldly activity, its character remains as otherworldly as if it were located in the highest heaven, however much its proponents may insist that it will be actualized on earth.[21]

Titanism: Control of the World

Seemingly at the other extreme from an eschatological vision in which human actions are irrelevant for the shape of the world's future is one in which the shape of the future is intimately bound up with human activity here and now. And this position, too, has its theological advocates. Indeed, if premillennialism saw a resurgence in the nineteenth century, nevertheless the dominant trend among Protestants in particular during that period was far more "postmillennial" in character. As the name suggests, this perspective refers to the belief that Christ's return comes *after*, rather than before, the millennium, which is (in traditional Augustinian fashion) identified with the present age of the church. In contrast to the classical Augustinian position, however, the term "postmillennialism" refers to those who view the time of the church as one of steady and, indeed, triumphant growth.[22] Associated with a broad range of theological positions, from the liberalism of the social gospel to the conservative "Princeton theology" of Charles Hodge and B. B. Warfield, postmillennialism does not conceive the kingdom bursting on the world suddenly, as in the various forms of premillennialism, but rather following as a natural development from the spread of the gospel, so that Christ's return and the fulfillment of the kingdom build on human action rather than simply overruling it.[23] Consequently, when postmillennial thinkers look for signs of Christ's advent, they are less inclined

21. Thus, while the image of escape applies most straightforwardly to dispensationalists who look to a pre-tribulation rapture that simply removes the saints from the sphere of worldly history altogether, it is also applicable to post-tribulationists who affirm the suffering of the saints in the period before the kingdom's advent.

22. While both the classical Augustinian and these later eschatological accounts are "postmillennial" in the technical sense of the term, the term "amillennial" has come to be applied to the former as a means of distinguishing the two. Since the designation is both inaccurate (since its proponents do not deny that there is a millennium) and rarely used by those whose position it is supposed to describe, I will not make use of it and will instead refer to the majority teaching of the Greek and Latin churches over the last fifteen hundred years simply as the Augustinian position.

23. "Perhaps these nineteen centuries of Christian influence have been a long preliminary stage of growth, and now the flower and fruit are almost here. If at this juncture we can rally sufficient religious faith and moral strength . . . the generations yet unborn will mark this as that great day of the Lord for which the ages waited." Walter Rauschenbusch's *Christianity and the Social Crisis* (New York: Macmillan, 1907), 422. Cf. Warfield: "there is a 'golden age' before the Church—at least an age relatively golden gradually ripening to higher and higher glories as the Church more and more fully conquers the world and all the evil of the world; and ultimately an age absolutely golden when the

1. False Hope

to turn to Revelation than to Jesus' promise that the "good news of the kingdom will be proclaimed throughout the world, as a testimony to all the nations, and then the end will come" (Matt. 24:14; cf. Mark 13:10; Rom. 11:25).[24]

The conviction that the kingdom is not a purely future reality but has already been inaugurated is an obvious strength of the postmillennial position, given the Gospels' teaching that the kingdom has drawn so near with Jesus' earthly ministry (Matt. 4:17; Mark 1:15) that it can rightly be said to be present now (Luke 17:20; cf. Matt. 11:12). Moreover, the postmillennial emphasis on the ongoing growth of the kingdom through the worldwide missionary preaching for which Jesus commissioned his disciples (Matt. 28:19–20; Mark 16:15; cf. Luke 24:45–48) points to God's commitment to the processes and possibilities of the created order as integral to actualizing God's ultimate purposes for creation.[25] In sharp contrast to modern premillennial perspectives, Jesus' earthly ministry is not simply a rescue operation designed to save a few from a doomed creation, but rather inaugurates creation's renewal, in which Christians are called to participate through the use of their creaturely capacities. In these respects, classical postmillennialism has some claim to witness to a genuinely Christian hope.

And yet though in postmillennial perspective the ultimate fulfillment of God's purposes remains God's business, the logic of the position can lead to a triumphalism in which hope is transformed into presumption. The fact that the missionary impulse that was the most widespread and notable manifestation of postmillennial thought in the modern period frequently functioned as an arm of Western colonial and imperial ambitions, with little evidence of a willingness (or even ability) to distinguish between submission to the gospel and submission to the cultural and political hegemony of the great North Atlantic powers, shows just how serious this risk is. Indeed, even in those forms of postmillennialism like the North American social gospel, in which attention to urban poverty gave rise to a trenchant critique of the excesses of industrial capitalism, there was not only a near total disregard of the systemic racism that brutalized Native Americans and people of African descent but also in some cases an outright embrace of an explicitly racist, jingoistic nationalism.[26]

---

perfected Church is filled with the glory of the Lord in the new earth and under the new heavens." Warfield, "The Millennium and the Apocalypse," 663.

24. See, e.g., Charles Hodge, *Systematic Theology*, IV.iii.4.2 (Grand Rapids: William B. Eerdmans, 1940 [1872]). In the whole of the discussion of the Parousia and its attendant signs in Hodge's text (viz., IV.iii), Revelation is quoted directly only once (Rev. 2:16 in IV.iii.3). The popularity of this mindset is indicated by the stated aim of the Student Volunteer Movement for Foreign Missions (founded 1888) "to evangelize the world in this generation" (also encapsulated in the book *The Evangelization of the World in This Generation*, by John R. Mott, one of the movement's leading lights).

25. "That the conversion of the Gentile world is the work assigned the Church under the present dispensation, and that it is not to fold its hands and await the second coming of Christ to accomplish that work for it, seems evident from what has already been said, (1.) This is the work which Christ commanded his Church to undertake. (2.) He furnished it with all the means necessary for its accomplishment. . . . (3.) The Apostles and the Church of that age so understood the work assigned and addressed themselves to it with a devotion and a success, which, had they been continued, the work, humanly speaking, had long since been accomplished. (4.) There is no intimation in the New Testament that the work of converting the world is to be effected by any other means than those now in use. (5.) It is to dishonour the Gospel, and the power of the Holy Spirit, to suppose that they are inadequate to the accomplishment of this work." Hodge, *Systematic Theology*, IV.iii.4.7.

26. This confluence of progressivism and nativism is most striking in the figure of Josiah Strong (1847–1916): "Strong's confidence in applied science and guided evolution was boundless. His

28

The Hope of Glory

Perhaps the most telling sign of the theological fragility of postmillennialism, however, was its virtual collapse during the second quarter of the twentieth century, as the impact of two world wars and the Great Depression rendered the idea of steady progress of the kingdom incredible.[27] The "mainline" churches that were the bastion of postmillennial sentiment continued to fund foreign missionaries (albeit in greatly reduced numbers) and to address issues of social justice through denominational boards of church and society, but the dreams of the "Christian century" that gripped the Protestant imagination especially at the turn of the twentieth century had all but evaporated by the turn of the twenty-first.[28]

Of course, Christianity has no monopoly on the expectation of an ideal future, in which the limitations and injustices of the present order are overcome. There are any number of secular variants on the theme in the modern West, even if many of these are themselves profoundly shaped by the Christian eschatological vision.[29] Moreover, although the most prominent examples are resolutely atheistic, they nevertheless combine human activity with attention to suprahuman forces (albeit conceived in terms of scientific laws rather than supernatural agency) in a way that echoes Christian wrestling with the relative weight of divine and human agency in bringing about the millennial transformation. Most influential politically has been Marxism, which anticipates a future egalitarian social order on "scientific" (viz., materialist) rather than idealistic (or "utopian") grounds by arguing that the material processes governing the evolution of the conditions of production will naturally terminate in a classless (and therefore stateless) society that will, in turn, allow for the unlimited development of human productive capacity.[30] Although by the end of the

---

nationalism and his defense of imperialism have become almost infamous. Taken as a whole, however, his views were those which constituted the core program of the social gospel movement. In fact, without Strong's contribution, the very term 'movement' would hardly be warranted." Sydney E. Ahlstrom, *A Religious History of the American People* (New Haven, CT: Yale University Press, 1972), 799.

27. Among "evangelical" Protestants in the United States, the collapse of postmillennialism can be dated earlier. As Robert Jones has noted, the despondency among white Americans in the South that followed the Confederacy's defeat in the US Civil War precipitated not merely the decline of what had been the postmillennial consensus of antebellum southern Protestantism, but a sharp turn to premillennial thought—as exemplified by the fact that the Scofield who published the stridently premillennial *Scofield Reference Bible* was himself a Confederate veteran. See Robert P. Jones, *White Too Long: The Legacy of White Supremacy in American Christianity* (New York: Simon & Schuster, 2020), 93–94.

28. In the US context the early years of the postwar civil rights movement can be seen as the last gasp of postmillennial optimism, finding classic expression in Martin Luther King Jr.'s "I Have a Dream" speech, with its egalitarian vision of America's future. Here, too, however, hopes for fulfillment of the dream (not least on the part of King himself) faded rapidly over the course of the 1960s. For a specifically theological assessment, see James H. Cone, *Martin & Malcolm & America: A Dream or a Nightmare?* (Maryknoll, NY: Orbis, 1991).

29. For representative assessments of the impact of Christian eschatology on secular futurology, see, e.g., Norman Cohn, *The Pursuit of the Millennium: Revolutionary Messianism in Medieval and Reformation Europe and Its Bearing on Modern Totalitarian Movements*, 2nd ed. (New York: Harper & Row, 1961); Karl Löwith, *Meaning in History: The Theological Implications of the Philosophy of History* (Chicago: University of Chicago Press, 1957); Edward Hyams, *The Millennium Postponed: Socialism from Thomas More to Mao Tse-tung* (London: Secker & Warburg, 1974); John Gray, *Straw Dogs: Thoughts on Humans and Other Animals*, new ed. (London: Granta, 2003). See also Celia Deane-Drummond, "The Technologization of Life," in *Technofutures, Nature and the Sacred: Transdisciplinary Perspectives*, ed. Celia Deane-Drummond, Sigurd Bergman, and Bronislaw Szerszynski (Farnham, UK: Ashgate, 2015), 153: "the transcendence that surfaces for the most part in more rampant transhuman projects . . . amounts to a secularized eschatology, seeking to fill the void once occupied by Christian theology."

30. "Active social forces work exactly like natural forces: blindly, forcibly, destructively, so long as we do not understand, and reckon with, them. But when once we understand them . . . it depends only

1. False Hope 29

twentieth-century Marxism as a political movement had suffered an erosion of credibility as catastrophic as Christian postmillennialism, its claims for the historical malleability of human nature and corresponding attention to praxis as the basis for theoretical reflection on the human have nevertheless proven profoundly influential for many both inside and outside the church.[31]

If Marxism looks to dynamics of economic production and consumption as the force driving history forward toward its denouement, the most significant alternative secular vision of the future looks to technological advance as the engine that will bring humanity into a promised land that includes not simply material prosperity, but personal immortality. Particularly as encapsulated in the intellectual movement known as transhumanism, this perspective predicts that an imminent, exponential increase in information processing power will generate a combination of advances in genetic engineering, nanotechnology, and robotics that will transform the very conditions of human (and, indeed, cosmic) existence in unimaginable ways.[32] Theologians have generally been wary of the more extravagant transhumanist visions of the future, not least because of a tendency among some of the movement's leading proponents to subscribe to a strong anthropological dualism, in which individual identity is understood exclusively in terms of mental processes (analogous to computer software) having no necessary connection with the body, which is regarded as little more than a disposable material substrate (viz., just one possible hardware platform). At the same time (and in recognition of the fact that human beings have always been tool-using animals), a desire to take seriously the positive potential of technology for human flourishing has meant that theological reception of transhumanism has not been uniformly negative.[33]

It is beyond the scope of the present study to assess the concrete claims of movements like Marxism and transhumanism, whether with respect to the plausibility of their prognostications about humanity's future or their analyses

---

on ourselves to subject them more and more to our own will, and by means of them to reach our own ends." Friedrich Engels, "Socialism: Utopian and Scientific," in *The Marx-Engels Reader*, 2nd ed., ed. Robert C. Tucker (New York: W. W. Norton, 1978), 713. Of course, Marxist socialism has also been criticized as utopian in the broader sense of failing to acknowledge human limitations, so that "questions about the practical-political value of Utopian thinking and the identification of socialism and Utopia, very much continue to be unresolved topics today." Frederic Jameson, *Archaeologies of the Future: The Desire Called Utopia and Other Science Fictions* (London: Verso, 2005), xi–xii.

31. The influence of Marxism on Latin American liberation theology in particular is well known; for perhaps the most systematic theological deployment of Marxist categories, see Juan Luis Segundo, *A Theology for Artisans of a New Humanity*, 5 vols., trans. John Drury (Maryknoll, NY: Orbis, 1973–80).

32. For especially forceful articulations of the transhumanist vision, see Hans Moravec, *Robot: Mere Machine to Transcend Mind* (Oxford: Oxford University Press, 1999); and Ray Kurzweil, *The Singularity Is Near: When Humans Transcend Biology* (London: Duckworth, 2016). For a somewhat idiosyncratic variant, in which a non-Christian argues that the kinds of exponential improvements in information processing predicted by transhumanists, combined with the insights of contemporary physics and cosmology, imply the truth of at least some Christian eschatological claims, see Frank J. Tipler, *The Physics of Immortality: Modern Cosmology, God, and the Resurrection of the Dead* (New York: Doubleday, 1994).

33. See, e.g., Philip Hefner, *Technology and Human Becoming* (Minneapolis: Fortress, 2003), especially chapter 6. For a sampling of theological assessments of transhumanism, see *Transhumanism and Transcendence: Christian Hope in an Age of Technological Enhancement*, ed. Ronald Cole-Turner (Washington, DC: Georgetown University Press, 2011). The positive view of technology in shaping humanity's future found in the writings of Pierre Teilhard de Chardin is suggestive of the possibilities of strong Christian confluence with transhumanism, though Teilhard had died before the word "transhumanist" was coined. See, e.g., the essays collected in Pierre Teilhard de Chardin, *The Future of Man*, trans. Norman Denny (New York: HarperCollins, 1964 [1959]).

30   *The Hope of Glory*

of the ways in which social and physical forces define the parameters of cultural evolution. Even allowing that such utopian visions may be rooted in genuine insights into the laws governing human evolution, however, the enormous complexity of large-scale social and physical systems guarantees that the introduction of even the most carefully considered social policies (for the Marxist) and technologies (for the transhumanist) will give rise to consequences as unexpected as they are unwelcome.[34] And the significance of such considerations is only amplified when one looks to the dismal (if not downright terrifying) results of large-scale efforts to implement secular visions of utopia in the recent past:

> When the twentieth century has tried to carry out the utopian plans of the past, it has failed miserably; it has created all-powerful States which control the means of production and distribution, but which have not abolished starvation; States encouraging scientific discoveries and developing production, but failing to give to every citizen a decent standard of life; States which claimed to institute perfect equality, but which have given birth instead to new privileged classes and new inequalities perhaps more appalling than the old; States which have made people into Taylorised robots, subordinated by the machines they serve, brutalised by propaganda; States which have created conditions where all individual thought is regarded as criminal, where literature, music and art cease to be the expression of the individual and instead eulogise the regime where servitude to the old religion is replaced by that to the State and its new gods.[35]

From a theological perspective such catastrophes are arguably just what one would expect from human efforts to inaugurate the millennium, since the Christian doctrine of original sin (most especially in its Western, Augustinian form) is clearly inconsistent with the idea that human beings are sufficiently transparent to themselves to be able to act at any point—let alone consistently—in ways sufficiently free from self-interest and malice to create an earthly paradise. It is precisely the fantasy of full control of the conditions of life in this world (in the form of limitless food, physical invulnerability, and universal rule) with which Jesus is tempted in the wilderness—and which he unequivocally rejects.[36]

---

34. On the problem of unexpected consequences, see Paul J. Griffiths, *Decreation: The Last Things of All Creatures* (Waco, TX: Baylor University Press, 2014), 348–50.

35. Marie Louise Berneri, *Journey through Utopia* (New York: Schocken Books, 1950), 309. Cf. Keller, *Apocalypse Now and Then*, 165: "The hope for a manmade heaven and earth picks up precisely where Columbus left off. . . . The heroic masculinity of the scientist shrouds itself in the eschatological order of the coming 'Supermen,' an entire race of revelatory 'discoverers.' But if for the conquistadores 'she'—the 'other' as place, the Place of the Other—was the exotic world of the natives and their lands, for the Scientist she is Nature herself. . . . The new virile rationalism thus reinscribes apocalypse in the material bodies and the intertextual tropes of slaves, women, children, and nature." Cf. Albert Camus, *The Rebel: An Essay on Man in Revolt*, trans. Anthony Bower (New York: Vintage, 1991 [1956]), 208: "Utopia replaces God by the future. Then it proceeds to identify the future with ethics; the only values are those which serve this particular future. For that reason Utopias have almost always been coercive and authoritarian."

36. "The temptations of Jesus . . . express the expectation to perfection: bread from desert soil, signs and wonders, assured political power over the entire world. The Messiah of temptations in the wilderness—the Messiah of human expectation—is defined by his promises of consumer satisfaction and power over others." Joseph Ratzinger, *Eschatology: Death and Eternal Life*, 2nd ed., trans. Michael Waldstein (Washington, DC: Catholic University of America Press, 1988 [1977]), 61.

1. False Hope   31

And yet it would be churlish for Christians to dismiss even the most resolutely secular of such utopian visions out of hand. In the face of the staggering
levels of deprivation and violence that afflict vast numbers of human beings
(with the burden falling disproportionately on people of color, and on women
of all backgrounds), the church has no stake in a quietism that diminishes the
prospects for improvement in the this-worldly conditions of human existence.
Moreover, given the Christian conviction that God's own work in creating and
redeeming the world takes the form of sustained and inexhaustible giving that
has as its goal the realization of a peaceable kingdom in which all creatures
are able to flourish, there is good theological reason to resist succumbing to
a vision of this world, even in its postlapsarian state, as nothing more than a
charnel house of competition, scarcity, and violence.[37] Thus, while a Christian
theologian cannot help but view secular utopian programs as characterized by
presumption, the fact that such programs seek to sustain hope renders them
far closer to Christian understanding of the world's future than any outlook—
including putatively Christian ones—more or less resigned to the gross injustices of the status quo.[38]

Meaningful theological criticism of secular utopian visions will therefore
center neither on their decidedly this-worldly orientation nor on their hopeful-
ness (however naively the latter may be articulated in particular cases), but
rather on their failure finally to be able to sustain genuine hope. The problem
here is the converse of that identified in dispensationalist forms of premillennialism: where the latter finally undermine hope for creation by cutting it off
from creation's own processes and potentialities, titanic visions collapse the
two together so as to reduce eschatology to futurology—the mere extrapolation of contemporary processes.[39] But, again, the impossibility of predicting
the future states of complex, dynamic systems, whether social or physical, renders all such projections finally incapable of sustaining hope.[40] For precisely
because hope can never be reduced to what can be predicted on the basis of
present observation (cf. Rom. 8:24), when such prediction is the only ground
presented for hope, then hope must fail, because honest assessment of the creaturely processes that are the basis for such predictions disallows any firm conclusions about their future evolution. Only as hope is anchored in a promise
for the future made by God who, as Creator, is sovereign over (and thus not
constrained by) the limitations of created processes can hope be sustained in

---

37. See, e.g., Kathryn Tanner, *Economy of Grace* (Minneapolis: Fortress, 2005); and Kathryn Tanner,
Christianity and the New Spirit of Capitalism (New Haven, CT: Yale University Press, 2019). A similar
argument, albeit from a very different perspective, is made by the proponents of Radical Orthodoxy;
see, e.g., John Milbank, *Beyond Secular Order: The Representation of Being and the Representation of the
People* (Malden, MA: Wiley Blackwell, 2014); and John Milbank and Adrian Pabst, *The Politics of Virtue:
Post-liberalism and the Human Future* (London: Rowman and Littlefield, 2016).

38. While among Christians the tendency to resignation before the limitations of postlapsarian existence is perhaps most famously associated with the "Christian realism" of Reinhold Niebuhr, an even
more striking recent example is Paul Griffiths's characterization of the present world as "the devastation" (Griffiths, *Decreation*, 4).

39. For the distinction between eschatology and futurology, see Carl E. Braaten, *The Future of God*
(New York: Harper & Row, 1969), 29.

40. Chaos theory gives mathematical form to these limitations, noting that in nonlinear systems far
from thermodynamic equilibrium, the sensitivity of individual components to variations in initial
conditions is such that the accurate prediction of future states becomes impossible, even assuming
a thoroughly deterministic relation between cause and effect among all the system's components.

32   *The Hope of Glory*

the face of the uncertainties and resistances that beset all attempts to actualize this-worldly changes in the conditions of human existence.[41]

False Hope as Rejection of the Past

Thus far I have characterized escapism and titanism as mirror-images of each other, with the former undermining hope by evacuating creaturely activity of any significance for the future and the latter granting it too much significance. Arguably, however, this difference between the two perspectives masks an underlying commonality, which is that both are united by a rejection of the past. In other words, the various forms of what I have termed "escapism" and "titanism" all view the character of life in this world from its origins up to the present day as fundamentally defective, a vast slaughter-bench, which, whatever its role in setting history on its course toward fulfillment (and on this point escapism and titanism offer sharply contrasting views), is to be left behind in the transition to a new order in which the deficiencies of the past will be overcome.[42] This shared perspective, moreover, reveals a further feature of false hope: a forgetfulness of suffering, which is understood precisely as a manifestation of the defective character of the present order, and which therefore has no significance other than as something to be overcome (or at least minimized) in moving to the glorious future. It is in this way that the hope proffered by both the escapist and titanist visions proves not simply conceptually incoherent (as argued in the previous two sections of this chapter) but false, because the rejection of the past and the forgetfulness of suffering that goes with it are both profoundly inconsistent with the biblical understanding of hope.

This may seem a questionable claim on at least two fronts. On the first, with respect to the shape of Christian teaching, does not Scripture itself encourage rejection of the past, and a corresponding forgetfulness of suffering? For example, does not Paul identify the "one thing" he does as "forgetting what lies behind and straining forward to what lies ahead" (Phil. 3:13)? Even more

---

41. "When we say . . . that hope is a virtue only when it is a theological virtue, we mean that hope is a steadfast turning toward the true fulfillment of man's nature, that is, toward good, only when it has its source in the reality of grace." Josef Pieper, *On Hope*, 7th ed., trans. Mary Francis McCarthy, SND, in *Faith, Hope, Love* (San Francisco: Ignatius, 1997 [1986]), 100. The fundamental disconnect that Pieper posits between natural and supernatural hope can be seen in the most expansive secular reflection on hope, that of the dedicated (if idiosyncratic) Marxist Ernst Bloch, for whom the advent of socialism is not a mechanical process, but is rather something that must be worked toward by those who reckon consistently with the fact of resistance and the possibility of defeat—which is precisely what gives hope a crucial role in the struggle to achieve the socialist future. For Bloch hope goes beyond the daydreams of wishful thinking, but it remains rooted in them: "revolutionary interest, with knowledge of how bad the world is, with acknowledgment of how good it could be if it were otherwise, needs the waking dream of world-improvement, keeps hold of it in a wholly unheuristic, wholly realistic way in both its theory and practice," so that through "a combination of courage and knowledge, the future does not come over man as fate, but man overcomes the future and enters it with what is his." Ernst Bloch, *The Principle of Hope*, 3 vols., trans. Neville Plaice, Stephen Plaice and Paul Knight (Oxford: Basil Blackwell, 1986 [1959]), 95, 198; cf. 146: "the *historical content* of hope . . . is *human culture referred to its concrete-utopian horizon*."

42. "But in contemplating history as the slaughter-bench at which the happiness of peoples, the wisdom of states, and the virtue of individuals have been sacrificed, a question necessarily arises: To what principle, to what final purpose, have these monstrous sacrifices been offered?" G. W. F. Hegel, *Reason in History: A General Introduction to the Philosophy of History*, trans. Robert S. Hartman (New York: The Library of Liberal Arts, 1953 [1840]), 27.

1. False Hope

explicitly, does he not write, "I consider that the sufferings of this present time are not worth comparing with the glory about to be revealed to us" (Rom. 8:18)? And is all this not made even worse by the apparent instrumentalizing of human misery implicit in his claim that "we also boast in our sufferings, knowing that suffering produces endurance, and endurance produces character, and character produces hope" (Rom. 5:3–4, NRSV; cf. Col. 1:24)?

Attention to the full context of these passages, however, blunts the force of such objections. For the object of Paul's forgetting in his letter to the Philippians is not his sufferings, but—quite the contrary—his accomplishments: specifically, all those matters of his past life that might otherwise be construed as establishing a claim to "a righteousness of my own that comes from the law" as opposed to "one that comes through faith in Christ" (Phil. 3:9). Thus, although there is a rejection of the past here, it has nothing to do with contempt for the value of the created order as such, but purely with his own estimation of where that value lies. What he leaves behind are not those things that are normally viewed as unpleasant or contemptible in the world—on the contrary, he argues elsewhere that these are precisely those things God has chosen to be instruments of God's redeeming work (1 Cor. 1:26–29; cf. 4:10–13)—but just those things on which human beings are tempted to rely as providing some basis for happiness and security independently of God's grace.

As for the passages from Romans, although Paul does speak of suffering in both of them, his point in so doing is not to suggest that suffering either will or should be forgotten. Far from dismissing suffering as nothing more than the ultimately senseless product of history's slaughter-bench that one can only seek (however unsuccessfully) to forget, Paul's claim is that precisely *because* of the character of Christian hope, sufferings are not to be forgotten, but may be received as a positive aspect of one's identity—a matter of boasting (Rom. 5:2–3). Suffering is, mysteriously, part of the economy whereby God brings the world to glory and, as such, is not to be understood merely as the product of the inexorable grinding on of impersonal natural forces, but rather as falling within the providence of God and thus (again, mysteriously) as open to redemption.[43] For this reason, there can be for Christians no forgetting of suffering. Indeed, because the risen Christ retains the scars of his passion (Luke 24:36–40; John 20:26–27), thereby showing that his sufferings, far from being forgotten, remain intrinsic to his identity into eternity, it is the custom in Christian iconography for the martyrs to be depicted with the marks of their ordeals as similarly constitutive of their eternal identities.[44] It is certainly integral to the Christian hope

---

43. Importantly, the claim that the scope of God's sovereignty is such that suffering is *open to redemption* must be distinguished from the very different claim that suffering *is itself redemptive*, which has been subject to searching critique by feminist and womanist theologians in particular. See pp. 180–81 below for direct engagement with the question of redemptive suffering.

44. See Augustine, *The City of God against the Pagans*, ed. R. W. Dyson (Cambridge: Cambridge University Press, 1998), 22.19: "I do not know why this is so, but the love we bear for the blessed martyrs makes us desire to see in the kingdom of heaven the marks of the wounds which they received for Christ's name; and it may be that we shall indeed see them. For this will not be a deformity, but a badge of honour, and the beauty of their virtue—a beauty which is in the body, but not of the body—will shine forth in it." Note here the contrast with Hegel's dictum that "The wounds of the Spirit heal, and leave no scars behind." G. W. F. Hegel, *Phenomenology of Spirit*, trans. A. V. Miller (Oxford: Oxford University Press, 1977 [1807]), 407.

34 *The Hope of Glory*

that in the kingdom there will be an end to the experience of death, mourning, crying and pain (Rev. 21:4), but not an end to the memory of them.[45]

But (to turn to the second front) even if Christianity can be cleared of the charge of rejecting the past and its suffering, cannot the same defense be made on behalf of escapism and titanism? Is not Marxism driven by a pressing awareness of the injustice suffered by workers who are systematically denied the rewards of their labor? Similarly, is not a vivid awareness of the agonies suffered by human beings in their present state a central concern behind the transhumanist vision of a future in which people are no longer subject to the limitations of biological existence? And is not a central image underlying premillennial yearning for the future that of the souls of the martyrs under the heavenly altar, who "cried out with a loud voice, 'Sovereign Lord, holy and true, how long will it be before you judge and avenge our blood on the inhabitants of the earth?'" (Rev. 6:10)? In all these cases a vibrant awareness of suffering's toll on human life seems to stand very much in the foreground in a way that seems flatly inconsistent with the charge that these perspectives are grounded in a forgetfulness of suffering.

In addressing this line of objections, it is important to stress that the charge of forgetfulness of suffering is not intended as either a psychological evaluation or a moral judgment. In other words, my claim is not that premillennialists, Marxists, transhumanists, or anyone else is indifferent to human suffering.[46] On the contrary (and in line with the thrust of the rhetorical questions in the previous paragraph), the desire to respond to the agony of human suffering is a (if not the) central motivation for all the movements I have identified as promoting false hope. Likewise, the charge that such movements reject the past does not mean that they regard the past as having no role in giving shape to the future. Marxists view the promise of the proletarian revolution as inconceivable apart from the changes in the mode of production brought about by capitalism, and transhumanists similarly recognize the dependence of future technological breakthroughs on past developments. Even premillennialists, for all their positing of a fundamental causal break between the present and future orders, understand the past dispensations of the divine economy as establishing the necessary conditions for human participation in Christ's earthly rule.

The charge of rejection of the past and forgetfulness of suffering in such movements therefore cannot be based on their respective accounts of the past (including its legacy of suffering) as such, but rather on the relation they posit between the past and the hoped-for future. For in escapist and titanist accounts

---

45. One further New Testament passage should be noted here: "When a woman is in labor, she has pain because her hour has come. But when her child is born, *she no longer remembers the anguish because of the joy* of having brought a human being into the world. So you have pain now, but I will see you again, and your hearts will rejoice, and no one will take your joy from you" (John 16:21–22). I take it that Jesus' point is not that the woman literally forgets the pain of labor, but rather (and in line with Paul's remarks in Rom. 8) that she does not regard the pain as comparable to the joy that follows the birth.

46. While such indifference is undeniable in the case of, e.g., premillennial celebrations of the fact that believers will be saved from "the most ghastly pestilence, bloodshed, and starvation the world has ever known" (Lindsey, *Late Great Planet Earth*, 138), this sort of "obsession with the avoidance of suffering" is also the focus of criticism within premillennial circles (see Craig L. Blomberg's foreword to Sung Wook Chung and David Matthewson, *Models of Premillennialism* [Eugene, OR: Cascade, 2018], viii). Similar points could be made regarding less palatable examples of Marxist and transhumanist discourse.

1. False Hope 35

alike this relation is one in which the future is simply the continuation of the past: however sharp the break between the present and future orders, time carries on as it always has, albeit under new and improved conditions. Thus, to the extent that these futures entail either the mitigation or outright elimination of suffering, the fact of suffering moves inexorably ever further into the past, so that over time it becomes either an increasingly distant memory (to the risen saints sharing in Christ's earthly reign) or simply unknown (to subsequent generations of the classless society or of the new transhumanist reality). The reality of the past, with its legacy of suffering, is certainly not denied, and its role in laying the groundwork for the new order may be freely acknowledged; but with the ongoing flow of time, it becomes less and less relevant. As it slips ever farther into the distance, the past can only be left behind as an ever-diminishing portion of the human story, whether considered collectively or individually. The problem with this vision is certainly not the prospect of a diminishment in the burden of human suffering (which can only be judged by Christians as a good thing), but rather that it leads to an account of hope in which the past and its legacy of suffering ultimately have no place in the story of creation.

Again, this feature of escapist and titanist movements has nothing to do with the personal qualities of their proponents. It is therefore not to be ascribed to lack of empathy or a failure of moral sensitivity; it is, rather, a function of the structure of the perspectives themselves, in which there is ultimately no redemption of suffering, only the assurance that it will fade with time into the increasingly distant past. The past and its weight of suffering can therefore only be rejected by way of a resolute turning toward the promised future through some combination of active labor and eager expectation. Until that future arrives, however, there is nothing to be done with suffering but to look past it and, finally, try to forget it.[47]

It would, of course, be foolish to deny that many forms of Christianity other than that represented by dispensationalist premillennialism have succumbed to such varieties of false hope. Although the language of white robes, golden streets, and "pie in the sky when you die" may be features of a uniquely North American form of Protestant revivalism that looks to the rapture and Armageddon as the only "solutions" to the problem of suffering, the displacement of attention from the exigencies of the here and now that these tropes signify has deep roots in Christian teaching and preaching across the ecumenical spectrum. Yet however tempting such rhetoric may have proven, it is deeply inconsistent with the Christian hope for life with God, precisely when the latter is considered in its otherworldly dimension. For the promise of glory—of life in and with the risen Lord—is not one that entails the temporal continuation of life through an ongoing series of events and experiences that simply extend the story of a person's earthly life on a higher plane. On the contrary, as with Jesus, so with all human beings, the sequence of events that define any particular individual's identity ends with death. When a human person dies, her life is over. Nothing that follows this event adds anything to it, for the simple reason that, strictly speaking, nothing follows it: to die is to come to the end of the whole panoply

---

47. For an example of this parallel between (Christian) escapism and (scientific) titanism, see Ellen F. Davis, *Scripture, Culture, and Agriculture: An Agrarian Reading of the Bible* (Cambridge: Cambridge University Press, 2009), 80–81.

36   *The Hope of Glory*

of temporal interactions—physiological, psychological, social, and so on—that establish one's character. Death is the end of life. As such, it defines the human creature's finitude in time in the same way that her bodily dimensions do in space. Whatever glory and the promise of heaven may mean, it is not that our stories go ever on and on, for with death they have come to an end.

But this means that insofar as suffering marks human life right up to the moment of death (indeed, climactically so in the case of Jesus and the martyrs), there can be no forgetting of suffering. Its dreadful weight cannot be avoided or mitigated through any imagining that it will become an ever more distant memory, an ever-shrinking percentage of an ever-expanding biographical storyline. No, the sufferings that have marked every human lifespan will retain all the starkness, the prominence, the weight they had at the moment of death.[48] That is part of what it means to portray the martyrs in glory with their wounds visible.

And yet it is no part of Christian hope that human beings in glory will continue to suffer through eternity. The promise is just the opposite: that for those who dwell with the Lord, suffering will end—and yet that they will live precisely as those who have suffered. In short, the Christian hope is that the finite, earthly span that defines every human life from birth to death will, with all its experiences of suffering and pain (as well as of triumph and joy), be glorified—sustained before God as good, and so experienced by the person whose life it is as good. Just how this will or can be we cannot say. But, however realized, this conviction that in glory the past will not be left behind and therefore is not to be rejected means that it can form no part of an authentically Christian response to suffering to minimize its significance by looking to the pleasures of an imagined future as a counterweight to present pain. Although it remains a part of Christian belief that "the sufferings of this present time are not worth comparing with the glory about to be revealed" (Rom. 8:18), this conviction must be understood as providing a basis for the endurance of suffering in the confidence of God's power to redeem it, not as suggesting that it should be disregarded as ultimately irrelevant to the meaning of life before God. For a faith that looks to the cross as central to the revelation of God's identity cannot view the suffering of any of those called to be God's children as merely incidental to the stories of their lives. True hope is precisely hope for the suffering, that their suffering will not simply register as an eternal debit which will, at best, be cancelled out or counterbalanced by a corresponding credit recorded elsewhere, but that it can be redeemed in such a way that the life scarred by it may be glorified, in spite of the fact that we cannot see glory in it now.

The challenge is to speak of this future glorification of human lives, including their suffering, without succumbing to the temptation (to which Christians down through the centuries have proved all too susceptible) of glorifying suffering in the present. For if false hope is to be rejected for its tendency

---

48. The fact that suffering is evidently very unevenly distributed, that in some lives the experience of suffering appears as uninterrupted as it is varied, while others seem touched by it only minimally, is a matter for which there can be no satisfactory accounting this side of glory. But the problem of the inequality of suffering is irrelevant to the point that, however much or little it may afflict any individual, the structure of human life as understood within the doctrine of Christian hope means that forgetting can play no part in a theological account of its redemption. See the further discussion on pp. 151–53 below.

1. *False Hope*

toward forgetfulness of suffering, a no less serious error involves so coming to terms with the reality of suffering as to collapse the distinction between present and future, with the result that the hoped-for glorification of the suffering life is made into a prescription for glorifying suffering itself here and now. Suffering then becomes something to be accepted or even welcomed in a way that is utterly incompatible with the fact that a defining feature of Jesus' ministry, as well as that of the apostles after him, was the mitigation of human suffering.[49] When this point is disregarded, the rejection of the past characteristic of false hope is all too easily supplanted by a rejection of the future by those who, finding the idea of an order to come that is different than the present incredible, eschew hope altogether. This second form of deviation from the Christian doctrine of hope is the subject of the next chapter.

49. See, e.g., Matt. 8:2–3, 5–10, 14–15; 9:2–7, 20–22, 23–25, 27–30; 15:22–28; 20:29–34 and pars.; John 5:2–9; 9:1–7; Acts 3:1–8; 9:32–41; 14:8–10; 28:8; cf. Matt. 9:35; Luke 7:22.

2. Hope Refused

"Hope does not disappoint," insists Paul (Rom. 5:5, NRSV)—or does it? As argued in the previous chapter, both escapism and titanism can be seen as forms of presumption, in that each succumbs to the temptation of viewing hope as a matter of calculation, whether by way of apocalyptic prediction or social and technical manipulation. In the face of the inevitable disappointments that follow from these forms of false hope, the refusal of hope can seem eminently rational. And while such refusal can take the form of despair, it need not. Despair, theologically understood, is a specifically Christian sin: the refusal to believe the promises of the God who took flesh in Jesus.[1] Where encounter with this God is not in view, one can (and, again in a strictly theological sense, will) certainly be without hope (see Eph. 2:12; cf. 1 Thess. 4:13), but that state need not be characterized by the feelings of dejection and gloom associated with despair; it can just as easily take the form of a sober acceptance of what are taken to be the hard and unalterable truths of earthly existence.

Whatever form refusal of hope takes, it is generally easier to regard with sympathy than is presumption. The false hope of presumption can appear facile and arrogant. By contrast, refusal of hope is bound up with an insistence on the enduring seriousness of earthly suffering for human existence and thus reckons with the ongoing burden of the past in a way that is not characteristic of escapism or titanism. At the same time, from a Christian perspective the refusal of hope is a far more serious error than false hope; for while the latter mistakes hope's proper object, the former denies that there is any suitable object on which hope might fasten in the first place.[2] To refuse hope is thus to deny that the future holds any promise that suffering might be redeemed. Suffering can only be endured, whether with resignation or defiance.

---

1. In this context, it is important to distinguish between the sin of despair and medical conditions like clinical depression, even if the two may not be disentangled easily in individual experience. Josef Pieper views despair (understood in this specifically theological sense) as the complement to presumption: whereas the latter is "a perverse anticipation of the fulfillment of hope," the former is, contrariwise, "a perverse anticipation of the nonfulfillment of hope." See Josef Pieper, *On Hope*, 7th ed., trans. Mary Francis McCarthy, SND, in *Faith, Hope, Love* (San Francisco: Ignatius, 1997 [1977]), 113.

2. "[P]resumption is less opposed to hope than is despair. For despair is the true antitype of hope, whereas presumption is but its *falsa similitudo*." Pieper, *On Hope*, 124.

40   *The Hope of Glory*

Naturalism: Hope as Incredible

As intimated at the end of the previous chapter, there is a specifically Christian form of resignation in the face of suffering that is especially insidious. At first glance this form of resignation may seem worlds removed from the refusal of hope, because it includes no rejection of God's promises and, indeed, ostensibly follows Paul in citing hope as a reason to boast in suffering. Nevertheless, it mistakes the character of Christian hope by conflating the promise of suffering's eschatological redemption with the very different claim that it is redeemed already; that is, suffering becomes an occasion for boasting not in the sense of a mystery that may be endured now in anticipation of the promise of future glory, but rather as directly willed by God, and thus as something that can already be welcomed as good here and now.

The refusal of hope here is subtle, since the experience of suffering is not divorced from trust in God, as though it were interpreted simply as meaningless misery without any possibility of redemption. The problem is rather that the relationship between suffering and belief in God is so construed that hope becomes practically indistinguishable from resignation: in the desire to vindicate God's sovereignty, the distinction between future hope and present experience is collapsed, such that all suffering is interpreted as somehow good in itself (as reflecting "God's will") instead of something whose worldly causes Christians may be called to resist.[3] To object to this stance is certainly not to deny that there are some forms of suffering—especially public persecution for righteousness's sake (Matt. 5:10; cf. 1 Pet. 4:16)—that Christians are called to accept as part of their witness to the lordship of Jesus (who when abused "did not return abuse; when he suffered, he did not threaten," 1 Pet. 2:23); but this in no way entails an expectation that such a stance should also be the rule when the name of Jesus is not in play.[4] The idea that there exists any general obligation on the part of Christians to accept suffering—whether caused by disease, violence, or injustice, on the grounds that it is willed by God—is belied by the consistency with which Scripture characterizes these forms of suffering as contrary to God's will—and thus to be resisted (e.g., Isa. 58:1–11; Jer. 22:13–17; Amos 5:10–15; Luke 13:11–16; cf. John 10:10).

Apart from this particularly Christian form, however, the stance of resignation tends to reflect an understanding of suffering as simply inevitable rather than as desirable: a product of the blind and purposeless interaction of impersonal forces rather than the will of a personal God. This form of resignation may be described broadly as "naturalism," in that it is grounded in the conviction that suffering is simply ingredient to the nature of things rather than being oriented

---

3. The refusal to view suffering as a direct manifestation of God's will, and thus as by definition good, does not entail the contrary claim that all creaturely suffering is to be viewed as evil. Precisely because divine transcendence renders the relationship between God's will and those worldly events that can be assigned a created cause opaque, axiological judgments about suffering would seem to be misplaced, at least where its created cause cannot be assigned to a conscious moral agent (viz., so-called natural evil). See pp. 46–50 below; cf. Ian A. McFarland, "The Problem with Evil," *Theology Today* 74, no. 4 (January 2018): 321–39.

4. The commands regarding nonresistance to evil in the Sermon on the Mount (Matt. 5:39–42) do not seem to me to be inconsistent with this claim, since Jesus is there specifically addressing his disciples (Matt. 5:1–2), whose witness demands that their behavior stand out from that of the public at large (Matt. 5:46–47).

2. Hope Refused

toward any higher purpose or goal. Proponents of resignation may well continue to describe suffering as an evil, but evil is here understood in purely subjective terms: that is, because suffering is intrinsic to human life—a brute fact of existence rather than an appropriate matter of axiological evaluation as something that should or should not be—the term "evil" does not refer so much to suffering's external causes as to the feelings of affliction to which those causes give rise in the one who suffers. The most appropriate response to suffering is, correspondingly, to develop habits of mind and body that mitigate these feelings. Thus, in the ancient Mediterranean world the cultivation of *ataraxia*, or equanimity, was championed in different ways by the Pyrrhonist, Epicurean, and Stoic schools of philosophy as crucial to human happiness in the face of the inevitable fact of suffering.[5] Beyond the confines of Western thought similar values are found in Buddhism, which teaches that suffering is intrinsic to sentient existence but also that its effects in this life may be mitigated (and, with this life's ending, eliminated) through the practices of the Noble Eightfold Path.[6] In these cases, because hope's focus on the future invariably distracts the mind from the realities of the present that are the proper object of its attention, it ultimately serves only to augment rather than diminish suffering and so should be rejected.[7]

Within the contemporary context, the intellectual movement of postmodernism (especially in the form known as deconstruction) has argued for a form of hope's refusal tied to the rejection of grand accounts ("metanarratives") of historical progress.[8] Unlike both ancient Mediterranean philosophical schools and Buddhism, this form of refusal reflects explicit opposition to Christian and post-Christian (e.g., Marxist) perspectives, in that it includes the denial that history has any inherent direction or goal, or indeed that it exhibits any sort of definitive narratable pattern at all. Also in contrast to late antique and Buddhist emphases, the focus of postmodern concern shifts from individual happiness to the social sphere, because the central problem with metanarratives is that they generate social practices of exclusion and oppression. For history can only be narrated if the seemingly chaotic and unpredictable world of appearance is anchored in a transcendent, unifying reality that makes it possible to organize temporal experience in terms of an emplotted sequence of events running from a beginning through a middle to a definite

---

5. In Pyrrhonism and Epicureanism, *ataraxia* is itself the content of happiness and thus the goal of life; in Stoicism it is rather a secondary effect of the life of virtue that is the immediate goal of human existence.

6. The parallels between Greco-Roman philosophy and Buddhism on these matters do not seem to be entirely accidental: Pyrrho of Elis, the founder of Pyrrhonism, traveled with Alexander the Great to India, where he seems to have been influenced by Buddhist teaching. See Christopher I. Beckwith, *Greek Buddha: Pyrrho's Encounter with Early Buddhism in Central Asia* (Princeton, NJ: Princeton University Press, 2015).

7. "I find in the writings of our Hecato that the limiting of desires helps also to cure fears: 'Cease to hope,' he says, 'and you will cease to fear.' . . . I am not surprised that [hope and fear] proceed in this way; each alike belongs to a mind that is in suspense, a mind that is fretted by looking forward to the future. But the chief cause of both these ills is that we do not adapt ourselves to the present, but send our thoughts a long way ahead." Seneca, "Letter V: On the Philosopher's Mean," in *Seneca Ad Lucilium Epistolae Morales*, trans. Richard M. Gummere, 3 vols. (London: William Heinemann, 1917), 24–25.

8. "Simplifying to the extreme, I define postmodern as incredulity toward metanarratives." Jean-François Lyotard, *The Postmodern Condition: A Report on Knowledge*, trans. Geoff Bennington and Brian Massumi (Minneapolis: University of Minnesota Press, 1984), xxiv.

42   *The Hope of Glory*

end—a future when all uncertainties will be resolved. Because this work of emplotment requires a selection of events whose inclusion in the narrative is ultimately determined by the needs of the plot, the logic by which history is written is not only inherently circular, but also requires the active suppression of everything that falls outside the narrative construct.[9] Postmodernists contend that all such efforts at mastery inevitably fail, because the reality of death shows that no narrative can control or contain time, thereby rendering hope for the anticipated goal of history ultimately unsustainable. Since belief in a historical *telos* leads people to disregard this fundamental inconsistency and to trust that all apparent disorder in their experience of the world is contained by (and thus in service to) a higher and supremely good order, hope is a manifestation of false consciousness—a mystification that entices people to accept rather than to resist present injustice.[10]

In the face of the temptation to ignore all those elements of experience that cannot be assimilated to any hopeful narrative, postmodern thought calls for a willingness to acknowledge the impossibility of containing reality within any sort of comprehensive system, and thus for the rejection of every demand to sacrifice one's own life (not to mention the lives of others) to the implacable demands of historical "necessity." Instead, the indeterminate and open-ended character of reality calls for what Mark C. Taylor has described as "erring": a "purposeless process" of wandering that has "no certain destination, goal, aim, purpose, or end."[11] The one who "errs" lives resolutely in the present, accepting the inevitability of uncertainty and loss, thereby liberating both the self (who no longer needs to obsess over a hoped-for future whose fulfillment is continually deferred) and the other (who no longer needs to be controlled as a condition of maintaining order). The project of history, with its implicit commitment to a conceptual framework marked by exclusion and totalization, gives way to the uncontainable and transgressive diversity of carnival—"an impious, polytheistic pluralism of competing goods and multiple goods"[12]—which in its openness to and acceptance of the particular evokes a clear-eyed denial of the "denial of death" to which narratives of hope are held to be bound.[13]

---

9. "Suspended between a past that has been lost and a future not yet possessed, history is the domain of discontent and restlessness, of striving and strife. . . . Paradoxically, the making of history is the suppression of time," because "the historical subject's apparent self-affirmation . . . is mediated by the negation of other subjects and objects." Mark C. Taylor, *Erring: A Postmodern A/theology* (Chicago: University of Chicago Press, 1984), 68–69. One might see an antecedent to this line of critique in Theodore Adorno's dictum "The whole is the untrue." Theodor W. Adorno, *Minima Moralia*, §29, trans. E. F. N. Jephcott (London: Verso, 1978), 50.

10. As John Caputo puts it, "victims . . . are usually victims of somebody's Good." John D. Caputo, *Against Ethics: Contributions to a Poetics of Obligation with Constant Reference to Deconstruction* (Bloomington: Indiana University Press, 1993), 34.

11. Taylor, *Erring*, 157. Cf. Jacques Derrida, "Différance," in *Margins of Philosophy*, trans. Alan Bass (Chicago: University of Chicago Press, 1982), 7: "In the delineation of *différance* [the recognition that meaning can never be fixed, because specifying the meaning of any given word entails reference to other words ad infinitum] everything is strategic and adventurous. Strategic because no transcendent truth present outside the field of writing can govern theologically the totality of the field. Adventurous because this strategy is not a simple strategy in the sense that strategy orients tactics according to a final goal . . . [but] a strategy without finality, what might be called blind tactics, or empirical wandering."

12. Caputo, *Against Ethics*, 33.

13. Taylor, *Erring*, 72; cf. 167.

2. Hope Refused

This postmodern refusal of hope does not entail either the embrace of despair or a stance of indifference in the face of the suffering of others.[14] Indeed (and as already noted), in contrast to the schools of classical philosophy, the aim of postmodern critique is not the cultivation of *ataraxia*, but the unmasking of that which has been occluded by the dominant ideology, with the aim of revealing possibilities for making things better. There can be no definitive justification for any given action, for that would entail commitment to some metanarrative. Actions born of "erring" must always be understood as provisional, subject to revision, and prone to ideological deformation; nevertheless, "if everything is subject to doubt, this means that every judgment is doubtful, not that judgment is precluded."[15] There even remains a motivational role for the kinds of ideals (e.g., perfect justice) characteristic of Christian hope.[16] But hope in the Christian sense of that which is sure and certain—and therefore "does not disappoint"— is refused as an ideological distortion. Hope is unworthy of belief, because to make it an object of belief is to turn one's attention away from the concrete realities of this world to a putative transcendent ground, and thereby to subvert (through the occlusion and suppression of those aspects of reality that do not fit its narrative categories) the very promise of human flourishing that hope's defenders claim to pursue.

Notwithstanding the considerable influence of postmodern thought in academic contexts, in contemporary Western culture a specifically scientific naturalism (especially as popularized in movements like secular humanism) is perhaps the most recognizable example of hope's being refused on the grounds of its being incredible.[17] Like ancient Epicureanism, naturalist metaphysics is

---

14. Likewise, in rejecting totalizing accounts of history, Frederic Jameson does not advocate nihilism, but rather argues for an understanding of history that "is *not* a text, not a narrative, master or otherwise, but that as an absent cause, it is inaccessible to us except in textual form." Fredric Jameson, *The Political Unconscious* (Ithaca, NY: Cornell University Press, 1981), 35.

15. David Newheiser, *Hope in a Secular Age: Deconstruction, Negative Theology, and the Future of Faith* (Cambridge: Cambridge University Press, 2019), 30. In this context, John Caputo rejects what he takes to be the totalizing pretensions of *ethics*, writing, "I have lost my faith in the Good, which must needs be One and Overarching, which must inspire Piety and command universal Consent (all in upper-case), which leaves a trail of bowed heads wherever it passes." But he affirms the pressing reality of *obligation* as "a matter of being claimed, in which something has a hold on us, something that is older than us, that has us before we have it." Caputo, *Against Ethics*, 31.

16. For example, Derrida writes: "We do not give up the dream of the pure gift in the same way that we do not give up the idea of pure hospitality. Even if we know that it is impossible and that it can be perverse. . . . Despite this perversion, despite this impossibility, we go on dreaming or thinking of pure hospitality, of pure gift. . . . We continue to desire, to dream, *through* the impossible." Jacques Derrida and Jean-Luc Marion, "On the Gift: A Discussion between Jacques Derrida and Jean-Luc Marion," in *God, the Gift, and Postmodernism*, ed. John D. Caputo and Michael Scanlon (Bloomington: Indiana University Press, 1999), 72. Similarly, Frederic Jameson views his own critical work as motivated by "a properly Utopian or collective impulse," that looks to a time when cultural products are no longer subject to the charge of being "basely functional or instrumental" tools of ideology. Frederic Jameson, *The Political Unconscious* (Ithaca, NY: Cornell University Press, 1981), 293.

17. Less centered on the natural sciences and more clearly impacted by questions of theodicy are those forms of black humanism for which "relatively sustained and oppressive world conditions bring into question the presence of any Being"—and thus of any hope—"beyond the human realm," and whose proponents seek instead "to combat oppression through radical human commitment to life and corresponding activity." Anthony B. Pinn, *Why Lord? Suffering and Evil in Black Theology* (New York: Continuum, 1999), 141. By contrast, the movement known as Afropessimism (or black nihilism) is more influenced by postmodern discourse and rejects even this-worldly possibilities of hope. See, e.g., Calvin L. Warren, *Ontological Terror: Blackness, Nihilism, and Emancipation* (Durham, NC: Duke University Press, 2018), 172: "Continuing to keep hope that freedom will occur, that one day the world will apologize for its antiblack brutality and accept us with open arms, is a devastating fantasy. It

44   *The Hope of Glory*

resolutely materialist: all that is real exists within the phenomenal realm of time and space and is therefore to be understood as the product of interactions between bits of matter. Science provides a means of explaining these interactions, such that any given state of affairs (i.e., a particular configuration of material objects) can be accounted for by reference to the predictable (because quantifiable) operation of physical laws on its component material parts. Since only that which is subject to such analysis is taken as real, science is the only legitimate measure of truth claims about the world.[18] This perspective is "naturalist" in that it allows for no causal explanations for observed states of affairs other than those based on processes that are "natural" in the sense of being an inherent part of the world's phenomenal structure, everywhere and always observable as operating in a manner capable of description in terms of mathematical relationships.[19] Appeal to the intervention of "supernatural" forces whose operation is not regularly observable, measurable, and predictable is excluded.[20]

Materialism is also a defining feature of the false hope promoted by Marxism and transhumanism.[21] What distinguishes the naturalists I am discussing here is a self-consciously sober realism regarding what human beings can claim to know and expect to accomplish. The Nobel Prize–winning physicist Steven Weinberg provides a particularly moving example of the implication of this realism for the naturalist understanding of humanity's place in the universe. First, he notes that scientific investigation provides no basis for the idea that human beings have any particular significance within or for the cosmos:

---

might give one motivation to fight on, but it is a drive that will only produce exhaustion and protest fatigue."

18. This stance does not deny the role of emotions and other aspects of human experience for a full human life, but only that appeal to such experiences can serve as justification for claims to knowledge of how things are. See, e.g., the text of the "Humanist Manifesto II," whose signatories affirm, "we are not advocating the use of scientific intelligence independent of or in opposition to emotion, for we believe in the cultivation of feeling and love. As science pushes back the boundary of the known, humankind's sense of wonder is continually renewed, and art, poetry, and music find their places, along with religion and ethics." American Humanist Association, "Humanist Manifesto II," https://americanhumanist.org/what-is-humanism/manifesto2/.

19. Of course, the degree to which any particular state of affairs may in practice be reduced to mathematical explanation varies with the complexity of the system under observation: the relative populations of species on the African savannah from year to year cannot be mathematically modeled with the same precision as the movement of balls on a billiard table. But such modeling remains the goal. Even if chaos theory posits a limit to the ability to calculate the future states of complex systems based on present data, this does not reflect any doubt that such systems evolve in a mathematically predictable fashion, but acknowledges only that there is a limit to our ability to measure the relevant quantities with the precision necessary to allow for accurate prediction. Even in the realm of quantum mechanics, where some level of ontological indeterminacy is a matter of near consensus among scientists, particular processes (e.g., the collapse of the wave function) operate according to a strictly deterministic mathematics.

20. For example, the signatories to "A Secular Humanist Declaration," issued in 1980 by the Council for Democratic and Secular Humanism (now the Council for Secular Humanism), declared themselves "opposed to all varieties of belief that seek supernatural sanction for their values" on the grounds that they "consider the universe to be a dynamic scene of natural forces that are most effectively understood by scientific inquiry." See https://secularhumanism.org/a-secular-humanist-declaration/.

21. It is important to add, however, that the two forms of materialism are not identical: transhumanist materialism is physicalist (affirming the priority of matter and the causal closure of physical systems *tout court*), while Marxist materialism is historical (asserting the priority of means of production rather than matter considered apart from socio-historical contexts).

2. Hope Refused

In studying the universe scientifically, you don't find a point. Now, what kind of point would you have wanted to find? I would love to believe that human beings are part of a drama which is built around us. . . . But, if you believe it, you're not going to find evidence to support it in the discoveries of science. You don't find hints of that in scientific knowledge. . . . Human beings are different from cactuses and roses but . . . when you begin to ask questions about why you can think, and why cactuses are the way they are, and spiders are the way they are, you get down eventually to a level of molecular biology and then organic chemistry and ultimately down to elementary particle physics, and at that level you don't find human beings playing an especially important role.

And yet this assessment does not lead Weinberg to conclude that human beings therefore have no basis for purposeful action in the world:

I don't mean that they [viz., human beings] don't [play an important role in the universe]. . . . I think in fact they do, but it's one that they . . . create as they go along. . . . Here we are in this great expanding universe, which doesn't pay much attention to us, and we're creating a little island of life in which there's beauty and scientific research and loving each other, and we do it all ourselves. We make it up as we go along. In a way I find that more beautiful and more noble than if we were just playing a part that had been laid out for us in advance.[22]

There is much to admire in this commitment to live out a particular vision of human existence in the absence of external supports, and thus in the recognition that there can finally be no justification for such a vision beyond the sheer determination of those who find themselves compelled by it. A similar stance is movingly depicted by Albert Camus in *The Plague* in the character of Dr. Rieux, who devotes himself to the care of the sick without any belief in a higher purpose or rationale for his actions, and even in the recognition that his efforts at healing may have little practical effect. It is the vision of William James, too, for whom our actions bring value to a world that is otherwise pure fact.[23]

To object that such a perspective provides no grounds for choosing one vision of human life over another—that of beauty and love rather than violence and cruelty, for example—rather misses the point, since it is precisely the conviction of thinkers like Camus and Weinberg that no such grounds exist.[24] Wishing that they did will not change that fact, and the attempt to posit grounds of this sort in the absence of scientific evidence for them will only (as the historical record makes abundantly clear) lead to the use of violence in order to enforce common commitment to them. Far better, from a naturalist perspective, to acknowledge that no such vision can claim the sort of transcendent warrant that might be

22. "Steven Weinberg on the Relationship between Scientific Inquiry and Everyday Living," interview with Bill Moyers, *A World of Ideas*, PBS, September 23, 1988; transcript at https://billmoyers.com/content/steven-weinberg-scientific-inquiry/.
23. See William James, "The Will to Believe," in *The Will to Believe and Other Essays in Popular Philosophy* (Cambridge, MA: Harvard University Press, 1979 [1897]).
24. There is a common ground here with the deconstructionism of Caputo: "That [a] child deserves to live a normal healthy life is not a law written in the stars. . . . But the upshot of this nonfoundationalist line of reasoning is not that anything goes, but only that the things we favor and endorse . . . only go so far. The claim of the child is finite and fragile. It is not absolutely commanding. . . . What law there is to come to the relief of the child is inscribed only on the face of the child." Caputo, *Against Ethics*, 38.

46   *The Hope of Glory*

thought to justify such violence.[25] Nor is the price of spurious claims to higher meaning simply the threat of external compulsion; it also includes psychological harm. For if the human venture is played out according to a preexisting script, so that life is indeed "playing a part that has been laid out for us in advance," then it follows that suffering, too, is part of the meaning, and thus something not simply to be endured but accepted as good. Here, too, far better to "live in an absurd, indifferent cosmos . . . than see every last human event encased in a pitiless framework of meaning which deprives people of even the consolation that suffering, though inevitable, is not entirely merited or earned."[26]

Insofar as a credible account of hope must keep faith with those who suffer, such considerations are fully merited: a hope that demands a confession of meaning where no meaning may be found is rightly rejected. If naturalism is to be criticized, it therefore cannot be on the grounds that it chooses confession of suffering's meaninglessness in preference to the idea that it should be understood as just deserts, part of a pedagogical program of "soul-making," the redemptive bearing of others' burdens, or some other purpose. The problem is not that a particular instance of suffering *might* be interpreted as having some sort of benefit (e.g., there seems nothing objectionable in viewing the suffering of unrequited adolescent love as a normal part of human maturation, or the suffering of a hangover as an object lesson on the dangers of drinking too much alcohol), but rather the presupposition that all suffering *must* be so interpreted if human life is to be confessed as having the kind of purpose that would justify hope. As seen in the kind of resignation before suffering described at the beginning of this section, Christians have certainly been tempted to think God's status as Creator implies that because the history as a whole has a meaning and purpose, so must every event within it. But that inference is illicit.

Admittedly, the reasons why it is illicit are not immediately evident. In cosmogonies like that of Plato's *Timaeus*, in which God makes the world from preexisting material, the presence of evil and suffering can be explained by the fact that the properties of the material from which the world is made place inherent limits on God's ability to realize God's intentions for it (so that for Plato the world can be no more than a moving—and therefore defective—image of the changeless perfection of eternity).[27] By contrast, Christians teach that God creates from nothing (*ex nihilo* in Latin), meaning that God is the sole antecedent condition of the world's existence. There is therefore no external, nondivine factor (nothing!) that constrains God's ability to actualize God's will for creation. And since Christians also confess that God is intrinsically and indefectibly

---

25. Of course, naturalism does not necessarily entail the conclusion that there is no basis for human action beyond the sheer exercise of freedom championed in different ways by Weinberg and Camus. Hedonists from Epicurus to John Stuart Mill have sought to provide a "naturalist" approach to ethics based on the objective and (in principle) quantifiable principle of maximization of pleasure, arguing that this strategy leads (in sharp contrast to popular caricatures) to a restrained, sober, and tolerant way of life.

26. Richard Rubenstein, *After Auschwitz: History, Theology, and Contemporary Judaism*, 2nd ed. (Baltimore, MD: Johns Hopkins University Press, 1992 [1966]), 18. Rubenstein is here describing what he takes to be Camus's position.

27. "Now the nature of the ideal being was everlasting, but to bestow this attribute in its fulness upon a creature was impossible. Wherefore [the Creator] resolved to have a moving image of eternity." Plato, *Timaeus* 37D, in *Gorgias and Timaeus*, trans. Benjamin Jowett (Mineola, NY: Dover, 2003 [1892]).

2. Hope Refused

good, it follows that because whatever God makes has its origins in God and God alone, everything that God makes is also good—indeed, "very good" (Gen. 1:31). The conclusion would therefore seem unavoidable that since suffering is indubitably a feature of the created order that God has brought into being, it, too, must be a product of God's will, and so also to be acknowledged as good.

Yet further consideration of the logic of creation from nothing shows that this conclusion does not follow. To see why this is the case, it is necessary to begin by emphasizing that creation from nothing has no true parallel in worldly experience, where all "creative" activity is conditioned by the Creator's own location within a wider network of observable causes and effects: like Plato's Creator, creatures who seek to make something new can only exploit as best they can the possibilities already latent in their environment, whether by making nests of twigs or symphonies of musical notes. As the sole condition of the world's existence, however, God's creative activity does not take place within any such wider context; rather, God is the "cause" of the world and its processes in an absolutely comprehensive sense, giving rise not simply to particular effects within time and space, but to the whole structure of space-time, including the systems of cause and effect that govern its evolution.

The nearest analogy to such comprehensive causation is that of a writer who is responsible for every aspect of the "world" of her novel.[28] For just as a novelist gives rise to the whole range of causal interactions that define the world of the story without herself being part of that world, so God, precisely as Creator (or, in the language of Scholastic theology, "primary cause") of all that is stands completely outside the sequence of created (or "secondary") causes that, as part of God's creative intention for the world, govern interactions between the entities in it. The practice of science is based on the study of the way these secondary causes connect entities within the world, such that any given state of affairs (understood as a more or less complex "effect") can always be explained as having been brought about by a previous state (its "cause"). Because God, as the source of this causal network in its entirety, is not part of it, God is (as scientific naturalists are entirely right to assert) not a possible object of scientific knowledge.[29] Rather, following the words of the prophet, the Creator is "a God who hides himself" (Isa. 45:15).

---

28. Even here the parallel is only rough, since the writer makes use of a preexisting stock of words and ideas that constitute an array of possibilities from which she constructs an actual novelistic or dramatic world. To take seriously the confession of God as the sole antecedent condition of worldly reality, and thus as the world's cause in an absolutely comprehensive sense, is to recognize that God's creative activity is not the actualization of any preexisting possibilities, but includes giving rise to the very conditions in which there are such things as possibilities that may be actualized.

29. While this line of reasoning is generally associated with Immanuel Kant, it also has specifically Christian antecedents: "God is one, without beginning, incomprehensible, possessing in his totality the full power of being, completely excluding the notion of time and quality in that he is inaccessible to all *and not discernible by any being on the basis of any natural appearance* [*ek physikēs emphaseōs*]" (Maximus the Confessor, *Chapters on Knowledge* 1.1 (PG 90:1084A), in Maximus the Confessor, *Selected Writings*, trans. G. C. Berthold (New York: Paulist Press, 1985), 129; translation altered). Even the sorts of inference from earthly phenomena to God's existence found in Thomas's five "ways" is consistent with this position. The upshot of these arguments is to locate the word "God" semantically within human language, as reflected in the fact that each of the five "ways" proceeds by noting how when human thought reaches its limits with respect to questions of causation, it necessarily posits some ultimate—which is "what everyone names 'God'" (Thomas Aquinas, *Summa Theologiae* [hereafter *ST*] 1.2.3, 60 vols., Blackfriars ed. [London: Eyre & Spottiswood, 1964–1981]; translation altered). Thus, while Thomas certainly wants to affirm that the idea of "God" is unavoidable, he also immediately

48   *The Hope of Glory*

Crucially, however, this hiddenness is not a matter of arbitrary divine decision, but intrinsic to God's status as Creator. Since scientific knowledge of an entity depends on observation of its location within the nexus of worldly cause and effect (i.e., it is known by reference to its relation to other things; e.g., as giving rise to a particular movement, sound, or scattering of light), God could not be other than hidden in the world without being part of that nexus—and thus without ceasing to be Creator in the Christian sense of the term. And this, in turn, has implications for the theological interpretation of suffering. For while the comprehensive character of God's (primary) causal activity means that nothing in creation is outside the scope of God's will, the fact that God has created a world with its own range of internal, secondary causes (from the regular operation of physical laws to the free actions of created agents to the random behavior of particles at the quantum level) precludes any direct correlation between created effects and God's will wherever secondary causes are operative. Only in those very few sorts of events (specifically, theophanies, miracles, sacraments, and the words and deeds of Jesus) where Christians claim that God is the causal agent in an unqualified sense (i.e., without reference to any intervening created cause) can a worldly event be regarded as the direct expression of the divine will, and thus effects of what in Scholastic theology is called God's *efficient* willing. In all other cases (i.e., wherever an event can be explained in terms of the secondary causal processes internal to the created order and thus without the need for any immediate reference to God), worldly events are properly described as the product of God's *permissive* will.[30] As such, while Christians will want to affirm that such events are not beyond the scope of God's willing, they will also deny that they can be characterized as God's actions in the direct or immediate sense connoted by the category of God's efficient willing.

This appeal to the category of divine "permission" is not meant to suggest that God at any point assumes the status of a passive bystander to worldly

---

cautions (in the preface to questions 3–11) that in confronting this idea we do not come to know anything about God beyond this unavoidability: "we cannot know what God is, but only what he is not; we must therefore consider the ways in which God does not exist, rather than the ways in which he does." Aquinas, *ST*, vol. 2, 19.

Similar observations may also be made with respect to Paul's teaching in Romans 1:19–20, according to which it is not *God* who is "understood and perceived through the things he has made," but rather "what can be known *about* God," namely, "his eternal power and divine nature," which, as Paul explicitly notes, are "invisible." In other words, because what can be known about God from creation is that the divine nature is invisible (and therefore *not* a possible object of knowledge), the error of the Gentiles is precisely that they deny this truth by identifying the divine with what can be perceived: "images resembling a mortal human being or birds or four-footed animals or reptiles" (Rom. 1:23). In this context, it is worth noting that Paul does not speak of God's power and nature as having been "revealed" (*apokalyptesthai*) in the world, as he does in the immediately preceding verses of God's righteousness and wrath (Rom. 1:17–18), and later of God's glory (Rom. 8:18); instead, he speaks of God having "shown" (*phaneroun*) them in such a way that they may be "perceived as objects of thought" (*nooumena kathoratai*). In short, our experience of the world certainly confronts us with profound mystery, but not with God.

30. Assuming that the Copenhagen interpretation of quantum mechanics is correct, events at the quantum level—e.g., the emission of an alpha particle by a specific U-235 atom as part of its cycle of decay—are ontologically random and thus cannot be assigned a cause in the normal sense; nevertheless, insofar as the rate of decay over a population of U-235 atoms is predictable and produces a regular sequence of isotopes, defined as its *natural* decay chain, it qualifies as part of the created causal order, and thus as a product of divine action only mediately (viz., by way of created causal structures) in the same way as events at the macroscopic level.

2. Hope Refused 49

events, as though God permitted an event to transpire in the same way that one might speak of an indulgent parent permitting a child to play with matches. That would be inconsistent with the doctrine of creation from nothing, since God's status as the sole antecedent condition of all created reality means that no creature can either be or act at any point independently of God's will. The category of permissive will serves instead to highlight this point by stressing that the lack of any creaturely parallel to God's creative activity rules out the possibility of explaining just *how* God causes the created order either to come into being or to continue in existence.[31] "Permission" is therefore intended less as a description of a mode of divine activity than as a term designed to highlight the fact that no such description is possible, because God's activity is hidden behind a network of mediating, secondary causes that at once constitutes and limits our understanding of how things come to be. In this way, talk of divine permission safeguards two fundamental theological convictions: first, that no created cause ever operates independently of God's will; and, second, that the way in which God's will relates to created causes eludes our grasp—most obviously in the free (and most especially sinful) actions of created agents, but no less so in the predictable operation of physical laws.[32]

If it is not possible to affirm that any worldly occurrence (with the very specific exceptions noted above) is a manifestation of God's will in a direct or unqualified sense, then there is no basis for viewing creaturely suffering as inherently meaningful, even granted that Christian belief that God created the world entails the conviction that God has a purpose for it. Because the God who creates from nothing is—for that very reason!—hidden, there can be no direct identification between the state of the world at any point in time between creation and consummation on the one hand, and God's will on the other. All theological counsels of patience in suffering reflect a failure to reckon with this point whenever they are based in the idea that the Christian commitment to God's all-encompassing sovereignty implies that all suffering must have a purpose, and thus be in some sense good. So understood, suffering does not need to be redeemed (and therefore cannot be addressed by a message of hope), because it cannot finally be judged evil.

Over against this position, the confession of God's hiddenness makes it possible to block the inference that the meaningfulness of history as a whole implies the meaningfulness of each of its constituent events. For Christians God certainly has a purpose for the world, but the way in which God ultimately achieves that purpose is not open to our inspection in a way that would justify affirming the purposefulness of every particular state of affairs that arises within creation on the way to that promised end. In other words, the purposefulness of the end does not entail the purposefulness of all suffering along the way. Contrariwise (and in opposition to the refusal of hope characteristic

31. In light of this difficulty, Katherine Sonderegger argues that the very category of "cause" should be avoided in reference to God's creative work (Katherine Sonderegger, *The Doctrine of God*, vol. 1 of *Systematic Theology* [Minneapolis: Fortress Press, 2015], 176–85). My own view is that while it is true (in this case as in all other matters of doctrine) that no words of human language, bound as they are to our experience of finite realities in time and space, are adequate to divinity, "cause," used with appropriate qualification, is no worse than any alternative.

32. For further discussion, see Ian A. McFarland, "Present in Love: Rethinking Barth on the Divine Perfections," *Modern Theology* 33, no. 2 (April 2017): 243–58.

50   The Hope of Glory

of naturalism), the fact that no meaning can be found in present experiences of suffering does not entail a lack of meaning in the whole course of history of which that suffering is a part. Against both these alternatives, Christians emphasize that the content of hope is not reducible to the extrapolation of present processes and thus cannot be assessed merely by attention to current states of affairs. Once again, the principle holds: "hope that is seen is not hope" (Rom. 8:24). But (*pace* the naturalist) the impossibility of seeing hope's object does not render it incredible, so long as one allows that hope presupposes that other factors also need to be taken into account that cannot be known on the basis of scientific inquiry.

Protest: Hope as Monstrous

Yet on what basis are such factors to be admitted, if they cannot be known in this way? And even if they are admitted, are they really adequate to the task? The first question will be addressed in the next chapter. But even if a satisfactory answer can be given to it, there seems ample reason to doubt that such factors—especially appeal to the power of an omnipotent God—will be sufficient to sustain hope. The previous section made the logical point that the utterly unique and comprehensive way in which a God creates (viz., from nothing) means that the claim that God intends a particular outcome for creation as a whole does not entail that God intends every event within creation (i.e., the meaningfulness of the whole does not entail the meaningfulness of each of its parts). For while the doctrine of creation from nothing entails that nothing in creation is outside the scope of God's willing, the fact that God has created a world with its own systems of (secondary) causes means that where an event can be explained by the operation of these causes, there can be no immediate ascription of divine intention to any worldly event; again, such intention can legitimately be claimed only in those limited cases where reference must be made to God's agency as the efficient cause of a worldly event.[33]

Yet while the unique character of God's relation to the world as primary cause may eliminate certain epistemological grounds for refusing hope (since in the vast majority of cases there is a logical gap between divine intention and worldly occurrence that blocks any inference about the former on the basis of observation of the latter), it does not address moral objections. After all, because the category of God's permissive will is intended to secure the theological point that nothing that happens in the world is outside of the scope of God's willing, it follows that even if in most cases it is not licit to infer from the fact of a particular event happening that God intended that event to happen, it remains both possible and necessary to say that God had the power to prevent it. Here the anthropomorphic implications of permission language are unavoidable, since the logic of creation from nothing means that even if God is not rightly

---

33. The specification of God's agency as a matter of *efficient* causation here is necessary in order to acknowledge that created causes may also be operative in such events. In the sacrament of baptism, for example, human agents are involved instrumentally in manipulating the water and speaking the words that communicate the divine promise; but it is God alone who effects the forgiveness of the baptized person's sin and that person's adoption as a child of God and member of the body of Christ.

2. Hope Refused

described as intending an occurrence of malignant cancer or the committing of a murder, God must nevertheless be said to allow such events to transpire. And in such cases the bracketing of divine intention can only seem rather cold comfort to the victims.

One solution to this problem, which finds its most consistent articulation in process theology, is to reject the doctrine of creation from nothing and, with it, the idea that God actually has the power to prevent any worldly occurrence. Process theologians propose instead a doctrine of creation from chaos in which God is a causal factor in and behind every worldly occurrence but not the sole cause of any of them, let alone of the world as a whole. Instead of being completely dependent on God for their being and action, all nondivine entities, even down to the level of subatomic particles, possess some degree of intrinsic and inalienable freedom that even God cannot override. Consequently, while God, being infinitely good, always seeks to bring about the best possible state of affairs in the world at every moment, God cannot be identified as the efficient cause of anything at all. Instead, God acts by way of persuasion, seeking at every moment to lure every other entity in the universe to exercise its freedom so as to maximize the ability of all entities to grow and flourish. If (as invariably happens) some entities fail to follow the lead of the divine lure, God is unable to prevent them from doing so—though God is always active in providing new lures to empower entities to produce the greatest possible good out of any given state of affairs.[34]

Although process thought in this way provides a fully consistent solution to the "problem of evil," the denial of divine omnipotence upon which this solution depends creates problems for a Christian doctrine of hope. For where the actions of creatures are finally outside the scope of God's will, as process theologians insist, then God cannot ensure (and thus cannot promise) that creation will in fact arrive at the state of glory God intends for it.[35] Process theologians can and do affirm with Paul that nothing can separate us from the love of God (Rom. 8:38), but they have difficulty affirming that the purposes of divine love will necessarily win out in the end.[36]

In any event, where God's omnipotence is viewed as nonnegotiable, as in the traditional teachings of Judaism as well as Christianity, the process solution is not an option.[37] Furthermore, the conviction common to the adherents of

---

34. For the classic introduction to process theology, see John B. Cobb Jr. and David Ray Griffin, *Process Theology: A Basic Introduction* (Philadelphia: Westminster, 1976).

35. Approaches like "open theism" and theological forms of free-will theodicy seek to avoid this difficulty by arguing that God voluntarily surrenders the exercise of divine omnipotence in order to generate a space for creaturely freedom; but such strategies simply reintroduce the problems associated with talk of God permitting evil. They are also metaphysically muddled, since it is unclear how a God who creates from nothing can detach creaturely action from divine causation in such a way as to give rise to the sort of creaturely freedom that open theists propose without violating the basic conditions of creaturely existence *ex nihilo* (viz., that every creature's existence at every moment and in every respect is dependent on God's actively sustaining it in being).

36. This is certainly not to say that process theologians have not tried to address this problem. See, for example, Marjorie Hewitt Suchocki, *The End of Evil: Process Eschatology in Historical Context* (Albany: State University of New York Press, 1988).

37. For the common commitment to creation from nothing across the three "Abrahamic" faiths of Judaism, Christianity, and Islam, see *Creation and the God of Abraham*, ed. David B. Burrell, Carlo Cogliati, Janet M. Soskice, and William R. Stoeger (Cambridge: Cambridge University Press, 2010); cf. Rubenstein, *After Auschwitz*, 157: "From the perspective of biblical and rabbinic Judaism, neither the justice nor the power of God can ever be denied."

52   *The Hope of Glory*

these faiths that God has broken out of the divine hiddenness by revealing the divine self in history in order to call human beings (specifically, the Jews and, through them, all nations) to life with God raises particular difficulties for any attempt to address the problem of suffering by appealing to the epistemological gap between divine intention and worldly occurrence. For in addition to the fact that belief in divine omnipotence inevitably makes it impossible to absolve God of ultimate responsibility for suffering, where God is confessed to have explicitly revealed God's intentions to creatures (viz., by electing the people of Israel to be an instrument of universal blessing), it seems problematic to view what happens to them as explicable without reference to those intentions.[38] Consistent with this judgment, there is a strong tendency among the biblical writers to view the suffering experienced by God's people (whether considered as Israel or the church) as intended by God, whether as justly deserved punishment for sin (e.g., Amos 3:2; Jer. 32:21–23; Heb. 12:5–6) or as somehow furthering the economy of redemption (e.g., Isa. 53:4–6; Phil. 1:29; Col. 1:24). Indeed, it is just this way of thinking—that suffering is in some way intended by God for the good, even if it is not immediately experienced as good by those who endure it—that underlies Paul's talk of boasting in suffering.

But can all suffering experienced by those who understand themselves to have been called by God plausibly be interpreted in these terms? More specifically, can suffering assume such fearful proportions that it can no longer be understood in that way? Perhaps no event in history has raised these questions so forcefully as the destruction of virtually the whole of European Jewry in the Holocaust. While some have sought to interpret this suffering in traditional terms (that is, as righteously ordained punishment for Jewish sin, or as redemptive suffering in service of Judaism's mission to the world),[39] many others have rejected absolutely any suggestion that the wholesale slaughter of the Holocaust might be understood as consistent with God's faithfulness to God's promises to Israel. In some cases, this conclusion leads to a denial neither of God's existence (along the lines of naturalism), nor (following process theology) of God's power. Instead, it gives rise to an indictment of God's goodness within the context of a refusal to give up on continuing relationship with God: a cry of protest that calls God to account for the suffering of God's people.

Far from seeking to qualify divine omnipotence, the stance of protest takes God's power for granted, since otherwise it would make no sense to confront God over human suffering. The dilemma has been stated forcefully by Richard Rubenstein, who argues, first, that within the context of Jewish belief, "it is impossible to affirm the existence of the biblical God of covenant and election without also affirming some sort of personal divine involvement at Auschwitz," and that, consequently "we can either affirm the innocence of Israel or the justice of God, but not both."[40] In light of the magnitude of Jewish suffering in the Holocaust, and the fact that so many of its victims were children,

---

38. "Given the classical theological positions of both Judaism and Christianity, the fundamental question posed by the Holocaust is not whether the existence of a just, omnipotent God can be reconciled with radical evil. That is a philosophical question. The religious question is the following: *Did God use Adolf Hitler and the Nazis as his agents to inflict terrible suffering and death upon six million Jews, including more than one million children?*" Rubenstein, *After Auschwitz*, 162.

39. For some examples, see Rubenstein, *After Auschwitz*, 159–68.

40. Rubenstein, *After Auschwitz*, 168, 171.

2. Hope Refused

Rubenstein has no doubt of the imperative of affirming Israel's innocence over divine justice.[41] And yet this does not entail for him a surrender of commitment to an ongoing relationship with God. Rubenstein put his predicament as follows: "We are enjoined to love God 'with all thy heart, with all thy soul, with all thy might,' but I cannot. I am aware of his holiness. I am struck with wonder and terror before His Nothingness, but I cannot love Him. I am affrighted before Him."[42] An even more sharply formulated response comes from David Blumenthal. Likening God's behavior toward Israel to that of an abusive parent, Blumenthal proposes that Jews should at once "try to accept God as God is" and also openly "accuse God of acting unjustly."[43]

Although taking particularly stark form in post-Holocaust theologies, this willingness to challenge God has deep roots within the Jewish tradition that long antedate the twentieth century.[44] Within Scripture itself instances of protest include not only the Gentile Job but also (and more specifically within the context of God's covenant with Israel) Abraham's argument with God over the fate of Sodom (Gen. 18:17–33) and Jeremiah's accusations of divine deception (Jer. 20:7–8, 14–18).[45] Stories that depict human defiance of God can also be found in rabbinic literature.[46] All are marked by a refusal to concede an epistemological gap between divine intention and human experience; and their point in refusing to acknowledge any such gap is seemingly not to bring consolation to the sufferer (e.g., by arguing that the suffering has some discernible meaning or purpose), but rather to provide a framework for ongoing engagement with God in which it is God rather than the faithful for whom the experience of human suffering might stand as a summons to repentance.[47] As such, while the

41. Importantly, not all Jews whose response to the Holocaust includes protest conceive the relation between human and divine innocence so starkly. Elie Wiesel, for example, argues that it is the task of the Jewish theologian "to opt for the Creator *and* his creation, refusing to pit one against the other." Elie Wiesel, *A Jew Today*, trans. Marion Wiesel (New York: Random House, 1978), 7; cf. 136, where he tells the story of a persecuted Jew who cries out to God, "In spite of me and in spite of You, I shall shout the Kaddish, which is a song of faith, for You and against You."

42. Rubenstein, *After Auschwitz*, 264.

43. David R. Blumenthal, *Facing the Abusing God: A Theology of Protest* (Louisville, KY: Westminster/John Knox, 1993), 267. The passage continues: "We cannot forgive God and concentrate on God's goodness. Rather, we will try to accept God—the bad along with the good—*and* we will speak our lament." Earlier on the same page he makes clear what he means by this combination of accusing and refusing to forgive God, as follows: "We will say, 'The fault was not ours. You are the Abuser. The fault was yours. You repent. You return to us.'"

44. "What is Jewish history if not an endless quarrel with God?" Wiesel, *A Jew Today*, 193.

45. Wiesel appeals explicitly to the Abraham story: "to be a Jew means . . . to serve God by espousing man's cause, to plead for man while recognizing his need of God. . . . Only the Jew opts for Abraham—who questions—*and* for God—who is questioned." Wiesel, *A Jew Today*, 7.

46. Perhaps the most famous example is the Talmudic story of the oven of *akhnai*, which recounts how even divine support (in the form of a heavenly voice) for a legal opinion of R. Eliezer was dismissed by R. Joshua on the grounds that no heed should be paid to heavenly voices, since God had already given the correct procedure for resolving disputes in the Torah. The story continues that when, years later, another rabbi asked the prophet Elijah how God had reacted to this event, Elijah replied, "The Holy One, Blessed be He, smiled and said: 'My children have triumphed over me'" (The William David Talmud, *Bava Metzia* 59b: https://www.sefaria.org/Bava_Metzia.59b.1?lang=bi&with=all&lang2=bi). As one writer has put it, "the *ad hominem* is at the core of Judaic argument, and manifests as *argumentum ad Deus* [sic] (an argument asking God to be consistent with God's stated values)." David A. Frank, "Arguing with God, Talmudic Discourse, and the Jewish Countermodel: Implications for the Study of Argumentation," *Argument and Advocacy* 41 (Fall 2004): 75.

47. As Rubenstein puts it, in the post-Holocaust context, religious practice is to be understood as "the way we share our predicament; it is never the way we overcome our condition." Rubenstein, *After Auschwitz*, 264.

54   *The Hope of Glory*

stance of protest does not presuppose any outcome in which all will be made well (and in this sense entails a refusal of any doctrine of eschatological hope in which all wrongs are made right), it also signals a rejection both of resignation and of despair.

While this attitude of protest is far less typical of traditional Christian faith and practice, biblical support for such a stance is not limited to the Old Testament. Most obviously, Jesus' cry of dereliction from the cross—"My God, my God, why have you forsaken me?" (Matt. 27:46 and par.)—places words of protest at the heart of the economy of redemption. To these might be added Paul's appeal to God to remove the mysterious "torment" from Satan with which he had been afflicted (2 Cor. 12:7–9) and the martyrs' cry of "How long?" from beneath the heavenly altar (Rev. 6:10), as well as Jesus' admonition to follow the example of the importunate widow and persist in prayer even in the face of apparent divine indifference (Luke 18:1–7). In later tradition, one might cite the mystics' "dark night of the soul" as pointing to an experience of desolation that is nevertheless understood as part of the believer's relationship with God rather than evidence against their being any such relationship.[48] In any event, in the wake of the Holocaust some Christian thinkers have sought to see these possibilities as providing a basis for a more explicit attitude of protest "in recognition that such defiance is crucial in struggles against despair."[49]

Advocates of protest have no interest in denying the presence of God as an unseen but present factor in the human story. On the contrary, it is precisely the conviction that God's presence is both real and inescapable—and, indeed, that it is rooted in the experience of God's explicit declaration of divine favor in the election of Israel and the church—that occasions the protest. It follows that for those who adopt this stance the claims of hope are not so much incredible (that is, unworthy of credence owing to a lack of evidence that there exists a power capable of fulfilling them) as outrageous, because they require the belief that events like the Holocaust can be interpreted as somehow consistent with God's plans for Israel, and thus with God's broader intention for the fulfillment of creation.[50] Over against the forgetfulness of the past characteristic of false hope, here the weight of the past is such that its painful legacy can never be overcome by any possible future act or achievement on God's part.[51]

---

48. Insofar as the "dark night" has since the time of St. John of the Cross (from whom the phrase comes) been understood as a stage on the road to mystical union with God, it might seem to fall short of the model of protest-without-resolution found in at least some strands of Jewish tradition. Yet (and without seeking to deny the genuine differences between the two faiths) the fact that for some the "dark night" can endure for decades (and, indeed, in the case of St. Teresa of Calcutta, apparently right up to the moment of her death) indicates that its experience cannot simply be reduced to a temporary setback and in this way seems at least analogous to Wiesel's paradox of hoping in God by hoping against God (see note 55 below).

49. John K. Roth, "A Theodicy of Protest," in *Encountering Evil: Live Options in Theodicy*, new ed., ed. Stephen T. Davis (Louisville, KY: Westminster John Knox, 2001), 4.

50. It is worth stressing here that traditional Jewish and Christian theodicies do not seek to show that God is free of all responsibility for evil, but only that God's responsibility for evil does not render God morally culpable. Thus, the so-called free-will defense admits that evil occurs because God honors the free decisions of creatures, but argues that this represents a greater good than were God not to create free beings. Even process theology views God as having some responsibility for evils like the Holocaust, since had God refrained from providing initial aims to entities in the primordial state of chaos, subsequent states of affairs of sufficient complexity to allow for genocide could not have arisen; here, too, the gambit is that the potential for good outweighs the risk of evil.

51. "The irretrievable waste of the past robs God of a convincing alibi. Only if God fraudulently obliterates the truth by wiping out the memory of victims can a disruptive, protesting and unreconcilable

2. Hope Refused

While one might suppose that the better counsel would simply be to leave talk of God aside, that possibility is simply not a live option for those who have heard and believed God's promises: in such circumstances going on in the world, *etsi Deus non daretur* (as if God did not exist) is no more plausible than (to invoke Blumenthal's analogy) for the grown child of abusive parents to pretend that they had not been abused. Moreover, to the extent that God's promises point precisely to the sort of vision of human flourishing that God's failure to prevent horrendous suffering belies, the religious practices sustained by those promises—including acts of protest against God's failure to honor those promises—can themselves function as a mark of ongoing human commitment to their actualization.[52] Here again, protest serves as an alternative to despair even as it refuses any facile assurance that all will come out right in the end.

It would be difficult to underestimate the moral seriousness of this position, for which the refusal to surrender the memory of history's victims is decisive. At the same time, this moral intensity is coupled with a conceptual instability that is difficult to ignore, and which follows precisely from the fundamental presupposition of protest: that God's goodness is not perfect, such that God can rightly be called to account for history's ills. For calling God to account only makes sense if God can be affected by those calls, such that the "rebellious care" for the integrity of creation that incites the creature's protests might somehow come to "grip God's heart."[53] The problem here isn't primarily that a God who is both eternal and less than perfectly good would be incapable of changing for the good, since Jewish and Christian convictions regarding divine freedom would seem to provide a plausible counter to any equation of the eternal with the necessary. It is rather that to the extent that a positive change in divine behavior—that God will be so gripped by human protest as to intervene to secure the triumph of righteousness—is judged possible, the denial of God's inherent goodness on which the position of protest is founded is compromised. For on what basis could such an appeal succeed unless God were already fundamentally good, and therefore touched (rather than repelled, angered, or left indifferent) by the creature's anguished pleas?[54]

In short, to the extent that protest actually seeks a divine hearing, its logic pushes toward hope.[55] Even if such hope remains in key respects sober, since it is never severed from the conviction that creaturely suffering creates an

---

'Why?' be stilled forever." Roth, "A Theodicy of Protest," 12.

52. "[T]he same realities [of suffering] that make one dissent against the promises [of God] can also be the facts that impel us to struggle toward them—unless, of course, we are willing to let the sufferings rage with impunity or resign ourselves to death as the end-in-itself." Roth, "A Theodicy of Protest," 15.

53. Roth, "A Theodicy of Protest," 16.

54. The objections that a God who was both eternal (as advocates of protest allow) and less than perfectly good would be incapable of change is made by Stephen T. Davis and David Ray Griffin (*Encountering Evil*, 22 and 26, respectively). The question of the possibility of God undergoing a change of heart is further complicated by the fact that Scripture speaks at various points of God repenting or changing God's mind (e.g., Gen. 6:6–7; Joel 2:13–14; Amos 7:1–6; Jonah 3:10), while in other places categorically denying that God either could or should do such a thing (Num. 23:19; 1 Sam. 15:29). Precisely because of their implications for divine reliability, within the Christian tradition the latter statements have generally been read literally and the former interpreted figuratively as referring to human perception rather than to divine reality.

55. Wiesel points in just this direction when he writes, "To have hope in God is to have hope against God." Elie Wiesel, *The Oath*, trans. Marion Wiesel (New York: Random House, 1973), 78; see also his *A Jew Today*, 196: "When all hope is gone, Jews invent new hopes. Even in the midst of despair we attempt to justify hope." Cf. Roth, "A Theodicy of Protest," 18: "A God encountered in Jewish

56   *The Hope of Glory*

existential deficit that can never fully be repaid, a stance of protest that looks for good to come would seem naturally to drift toward more or less patient expectation that is willing to wait on God. Alternatively, if God's moral ambiguity is understood as constitutional and irreducible, then protest drifts in the opposite direction: toward resignation before a forbidding brutality in the face of which appeal is ultimately pointless.[56] Either way, the stance of protest cannot be maintained. One can meaningfully make protest to God only where there is an expectation that God will ultimately prove good enough to hear and respond—but on that supposition protest can only be understood as a temporary expedient rather than a permanent stance. Alternatively, if and where belief in God's essential goodness has been abandoned, then protest loses its rationale and must give way to resignation, since there is ultimately no point in protesting to a God to whom protest makes no difference.

Hope Refused as Rejection of the Future

At first glance, the two forms of hope's refusal outlined in this chapter could not be more different, given that naturalism is premised on a denial of divine sovereignty over worldly events, while for protest the existence of a sovereign God is a fundamental presupposition.[57] As with the different forms of false hope, however, so in the case of hope's refusal this surface contrast masks underlying common ground. In this case, however, what is shared by those who refuse hope is not a denial of the significance of the past; on the contrary, for naturalism and protest alike, attention to the past is decisive for taking up an appropriate response to the hard facts of earthly existence, whether that response takes the form of resignation or complaint. Indeed, the characteristic shared by those who refuse hope is just the opposite of that which defines false hope: far from there being a risk that the past will be forgotten, its legacy assumes such proportions as to lead to a rejection of the future as holding any promise for the fundamental transformation in the conditions of human existence.

This claim might seem to be belied by those forms of protest in which appeal to God includes an expectation that God may respond to such appeals. As already noted, however, such a stance is fundamentally unstable; for if God's goodness is judged less than absolute (as the very act of protest would seem to

---

and Christian experience makes possible an option that keeps hope from dying, without making the dreary facts unreal."

56. This is effectively the concluding position offered by Rubenstein (*After Auschwitz*, 306): "The creative process is a totality. It is impossible to affirm the loving and the creative aspects of God's activity without also affirming that creation and destruction are part of an indivisible process. . . . Those who affirm the inseparability of the creative and the destructive in the divine activity thereby affirm their understanding of the necessity to pay in full measure with their own return to the Holy Nothingness for the gift of life."

57. The specification of divine *sovereignty* is important; for traditions like Epicureanism and Buddhism do not deny the existence of divinities (viz., supernatural beings) as such, but only that they determine the fundamental conditions of human existence. Alternatively, the conceptual importance of a sovereign deity for protest can be seen even in the work of a nonbeliever like Camus, who writes that insofar as "rebellion is a claim . . . against the suffering of life and death and a protest against the human condition," the rebel "is not definitely an atheist . . . but he is inevitably a blasphemer." Albert Camus, *The Rebel: An Essay on Man in Revolt*, trans. Anthony Bower (New York: Vintage, 1991 [1956]), 24.

2. Hope Refused

imply), then an expectation that God will respond to creaturely appeals, while not logically excluded, would appear to be sufficiently uncertain to raise significant doubt whether such expectation is anything more than wishful thinking. Alternatively, if God's goodness is taken as sufficiently secure to render such expectation credible, then the logic of protest is undermined, for in that case a fundamental, underlying trust that God is (and will eventually be seen to be) faithful to God's promises renders the attitude of protest, with its implicit claim that God has acted unjustly and therefore needs to repent, problematic.[58] While lament over the experience of pain and loss would certainly be justified under such circumstances, the cultivation of patient endurance would seem more appropriate than protest.

In short, protest would seem to make sense only in the expectation that it will produce some result (that is, on the assumption that it will give rise to a situation where protest becomes unnecessary, because appropriate redress will have been made). Were one to take the position that protest is an appropriate response even where no such expectation is in play—say, as a means of affirming human dignity in the face of the cold indifference of worldly occurrence—then indeed the attitudes characteristic of naturalism and protest become difficult to distinguish, as seen when a post-Holocaust theologian like Rubenstein offers what is effectively a counsel of resignation before suffering on the grounds that God's governance of the world is one in which "creation and destruction are part of an indivisible process" in which each of us must "pay in full measure with their own return to the Holy Nothingness for the gift of life."[59]

Nor does this blurring of the features between naturalism and protest pass only in one direction. Even as Rubenstein, a practicing Jew, can seem to echo a naturalist's counsel of resignation, so the atheist Camus can adopt an attitude of protest based on the principle that "to live is not to resign oneself."[60] The fact that the actions of resignation and protest can in these cases be decoupled from belief in the presence and power of God points again to underlying common ground between naturalism and protest: specifically, that the rejection of the future common to both is bound up with an assessment of the human condition as fundamentally tragic.[61] For the register of hope (whether true or false) is that of comedy, in Dante's sense of the term: a narrative that has a

---

58. The story of Job illustrates the inherent instability of this perspective of protest, insofar as Job holds at once to his own innocence, to God's responsibility, *and* to the conviction that God will vindicate him (see especially Job 13:15: "Though he slay me, yet will I trust in him" [KJV]). While the issue of divine responsibility for the evil Job suffers is clear in the narrative, the question of whether the book justifies ascription of guilt to God is another matter. Certainly there is no suggestion in the text that God either did or should repent.

59. Rubenstein, *After Auschwitz*, 306; see note 56 above.

60. Albert Camus, *The Myth of Sisyphus*, trans. Justin O'Brien (New York: Vintage, 1961), 113. The refusal of hope characteristic of Camus's position is clear from the full passage from which this quotation is taken: "From Pandora's box, where all the ills of humanity swarmed, the Greeks drew out hope after all the others as the most dreadful of all. I know of no more stirring symbol; for contrary to the general belief, hope equals resignation. And to live is not to resign oneself." Cf. Camus, *The Rebel*, 287: "What, then, should be the attitude of the rebel? He cannot . . . choose eternal life without resigning himself, in one sense, to evil."

61. Rubenstein explicitly appeals to the tragic to distinguish his position from that of modern secular society, which, he avers, "has yet to know what even the most archaic religions comprehended: that all human projects are destined to falter and fail. For technical society, failure is an incident to be overcome by further effort facilitated by the replacement of older units of manpower by newer units" (*After Auschwitz*, 27). Clearly, the secular vision he has in mind here is not that of Camus (whose work

58   *The Hope of Glory*

happy ending, however fraught with complications the process by which that ending is achieved.[62] By contrast, tragedy offers no such pleasing resolution, but is instead rooted in the conviction that all human aspirations are finally shipwrecked against the unremitting and implacable structures of the world within which human beings seek to realize them. According to the tragic vision, the human venture is ultimately one of frustration. This does not mean that it is without beauty or nobility; on the contrary, what renders the human situation tragic (rather than merely trivial or farcical) is the fact that human beings remain free and responsible agents, capable of acting with courage to promote life and beauty, even as they find themselves incapable of defeating the forces of physical entropy and human fallibility that inexorably bring all such efforts to naught. The tragic vision of life is without hope, but, whether taking the form of resignation or protest, it is not necessarily a counsel of despair.

This last point is important, because it can be tempting to see the refusal of hope, whether it veers toward more or less calm acceptance of the world's unconcern or a permanent attitude of protest against it, as fundamentally sterile because incapable of providing any motivation for action to change the world. After all, what point can there be in trying to change things, if the world is fundamentally incapable of change? And yet examination of the lives of those who have made a principled commitment to various forms of hope's refusal gives no evidence of any less dedication to the common good than is found among Christians—especially given that Christian hope (as pointed out at the beginning of this chapter) has itself in many cases proven susceptible of giving into a logic of resignation.[63]

If the refusal of hope is itself to be refused, then, it therefore cannot be on pragmatic grounds. For in the final analysis hope is not a principle to be invoked and evaluated as a motivational tool.[64] Indeed, it is hard to see how an appeal to hope made on pragmatic grounds can be anything other than false: a means of turning attention away from the agonies of past and present to an imagined compensatory future. And here those who refuse hope—and who thereby reject the idea that the future holds anything essentially different from the past—may claim to have at least the advantage of an honest and sober attention to the circumstances under which people live and die.

Even as there is much to admire about such a tragic sensibility, so, too, there is finally no way to disprove it—most certainly not by appeal to any imagined virtues ascribed to hope as such, or considered in the abstract. Hope as such is no more a virtue than is faith as such. Rather, even as faith may be counted

---

he cites approvingly at various points in *After Auschwitz*) but something more like the utopian visions of Marxism and transhumanism.

62. See Dante's letter to Can Grande: "comedy is a certain kind of poetic narration differing from all others. It differs . . . from tragedy in its content, in that tragedy begins admirably and tranquilly, whereas its end or exit is foul and terrible . . . whereas comedy introduces some harsh complication, but brings its matter to a prosperous end." Dante Alighieri, *A Translation of the Latin Works of Dante Alighieri* (Westport, CT: Greenwood Press, 1969 [1904]), 349–50.

63. See p. 40 above; cf. Camus's observation in note 60 above.

64. That hope be understood in this way is foundational to the philosophy of Ernst Bloch, as the title of his magnum opus, *The Principle of Hope*, suggests. It is also characteristic of Bloch's most consistent theological champion, Jürgen Moltmann, for whom (in the words of Werner Jeanrond) "hope is not so much a virtue than a call for eschatologically motivated action in the arena of the world." Werner G. Jeanrond, *Reasons to Hope* (London: T&T Clark, 2020), 50.

2. Hope Refused

virtuous only if and as it is placed in one who is worthy of it, so, too, is the case with hope: there is no virtue in believing a lie, however sincerely; nor is there any merit in hope for an illusion. Like faith, hope is finally rooted in *narrative*: that is, it arises from an account of the world that includes a particular vision of how the human story, having come to its present state through a particular series of events, is expected to move forward. One hopes not because it is a good thing to do in principle, but because one finds oneself caught up in a story of the world in which hope is simply the appropriate response to the way things are. One hopes because one is convinced that the way in which the story has transpired thus far gives reason for confidence in a future state that is better than the present.

And this means that where hope is true, there can thus be no forgetting of the past; hope for the future can only be articulated in terms of an account of the past. Nor can such an account be simply the identification of laws or principles that can be extended into the future in a more or less predictable or controllable way, for such an account is not a story but simply the relentless churning of impersonal processes. A story, by contrast, involves reference to an agent or agents whose actions will (at least if they are to be worthy of faith and so able to give rise to genuine hope) be counted reliable but never predictable. A story that gives rise to hope will thus be marked by paradox. For on the one hand, it will be grounded in the sober realization that the past is the sole source of our knowledge of the world; but on the other, it will allow that what *has* happened does not define the limits of what *will* happen, but leaves space for the possibility (and, indeed, the assurance) of the emergence of something genuinely new and good.

Of course, a story, however engaging and well told, is not a proof. Prior to hope's fulfillment, there is no demonstrating that the stance of Weinberg, Rubenstein, Camus, or anyone else who rejects the hope Christians affirm is wrong. One might object that the tragic vision that grounds such rejection finally has no true story, because—however many moments of beauty and dignity may emerge along the way—there is no expectation that the world is going anywhere, that there will be any resolution to the course of history, which, when all is said and done, really is just one damned thing after another; but the lack of a story in this sense does not show that the tragic account is false. And whether the Christian (or any other) alternative is true will finally only be known when history reaches its end.

It follows that the job of the believer is not to prove the validity of the hope the church proclaims, for, once again, "hope that it is seen is not hope." It is simply to be ready to give an account of it (1 Pet. 3:15), explaining what it means to have hope and how hope is equally distinct from wishing for the impossible on the one hand and resignation before the inevitable on the other. Such an account will center on Jesus, because his coming is the immediate object of Christian hope; but for this very reason it will need to reckon with the fact that the Jesus whom Christians hope will come in the future is the same one who has already come in the past—and thus that he is the one whose past holds the future open.

3. "Jesus Our Hope"

Analysis of hope's refusal has brought out an important feature of Christian understanding of the ways in which God relates to the world: the distinction between God's essential hiddenness *in* creation on the one hand and God's explicit self-disclosure *to* creatures on the other. The *particula veri* in the refusal of hope characteristic of both naturalist and protest perspectives lies in the fact that in a world created from nothing God's presence and activity are not visible.[1] Instead, God is hidden—a profound invisibility that is neither arbitrary (in the manner of a child hiding behind a bush) or penetrable by creaturely ingenuity (as is the case with the invisibility of magnetic fields or hydrogen). The invisibility of any created reality is at best partial and contingent: it remains firmly within the realm of worldly cause and effect and so is always in principle perceptible (even if not through the medium of sight) as the cause of some other spatio-temporal effect.[2] According to the doctrine of creation from nothing, however, God is not one causal factor among others giving rise to individual effects in the world; rather, God, as the single comprehensive ("primary") cause of the whole order of worldly (or "secondary") causes and effects, stands outside of that order in a way that precludes the possibility of tracing a line of creaturely effects to causes that terminates in God.[3]

1. "As the scriptural struggle is waged against idolatry in every form, so the struggle in the modern age, particularly in the West, is waged against the visibility of God. This is the theological significance of atheism in the contemporary world. . . . [A]theism *testifies* to the truth of the One God, his invisible Deity and Power, because God will not be left without His witnesses—even here, even in indifference and defiance." Katherine Sonderegger, *The Doctrine of God*, vol. 1 of *Systematic Theology* (Minneapolis: Fortress Press, 2015), 52–53.

2. If some version of the multiverse hypothesis should prove to be correct, then creatures in such universes would be insuperably invisible to one another; but, of course, this inherent invisibility is precisely what makes the concept of the multiverse a purely theoretical construct, which in scientific terms it must remain so long as distinct universes are understood to be causally isolated from one another. If, as in some accounts, gravitons can cross between universes, the existence of the multiverse could be established—but just in that case it would turn out that different universes are not causally isolated, and so not insuperably invisible to one another.

3. There is, of course, a venerable tradition (manifest especially in various forms of the "cosmological argument") that God's existence can be deduced from the world's, on the grounds that the latter is in its totality an effect demanding explanation in terms of a comprehensive cause. My own view (following David Hume and Bertrand Russell) is that the contingency of the world as a whole (i.e., its status as the effect of a cause) is not self-evident in the way that such arguments presuppose. While all realities and events in the world are evidently contingent, the world as a whole (precisely as the context for our experience of contingency) can be viewed as simply a brute fact, such that the query "Why is there something rather than nothing?" is properly understood as a plea to view the world as the effect of a (transcendent) cause rather than providing any warrant for believing it is to be such.

At best, arguments that attempt to reason from the experience of phenomenal reality back to a Creator God (the most significant of which are summarized by Thomas Aquinas in his *Summa Theologiae* [hereafter *ST*] 1.2, 60 vols., Blackfriars ed. [London: Eyre & Spottiswood, 1964–81]; see p. 47,

62   *The Hope of Glory*

Given this comprehensive character of God's creative work, it follows that however diverse creatures may be from one another, they are all utterly and equally other than God. Yet God's unique status as primary cause standing (so to speak) "over" the created realm of secondary causes does not mean that God is distant from the sphere of worldly occurrence. On the contrary, as primary cause God is more directly and intimately related to every worldly effect than is any created, or secondary, cause. Because it is created, a secondary cause produces worldly effects externally, through a transfer of energy (via physical impact, the communication of information, the raising of the ambient temperature, etc.) to another creature that exists to some extent independently of it. By contrast, God as primary cause brings about the totality of every created effect, including the operation of whatever secondary causes are in play, the being of the creature(s) they affect, and the whole system of mass-energy by which they are connected: every aspect of the causal interaction is in every respect directly upheld by God at every moment, such that if God were to withdraw in even the least respect, the whole complex would simply cease to exist. Again, it is precisely this comprehensive nature of God's creative activity—the fact that God is not one component in the worldly system of cause and effect but the One who sustains it all at every moment—that renders God inherently invisible.

This invisibility signals a fundamental asymmetry in the relationship between creature and Creator, which may be stated as follows: while creatures are always immediately present to (and thus known by) God, the form of divine relating to the world is such that God is not likewise intrinsically present to (and thus knowable by) creatures.[4] In relating to us as our Creator (that is, the One who both gives rise to and sustains our existence), God is the immediate, necessary, and sufficient cause of everything we are and do (cf. John 1:3). But while God's creative activity is absolutely unmediated and direct when

---

n. 29 above) identify what are sometimes called "limit experiences": points where we take note of the totality of our experience and then ask what lies beyond or behind it. "God" (as Thomas noted) is the word people use to fill in this blank, but precisely when used in this way (viz., as identifying the limits of our experiential knowledge), the word points not to something that is or can be known through process of inference from created effects, but rather to the *absence* of any scientifically knowable entity occupying that conceptual space. Because Christians argue that God has otherwise (viz., through revelation) made God's self known as the one who brought the whole of the world into being, it is natural enough that they should appropriate the term "God" to name the one they have come to know in this way. But (following the reasoning of Paul in his Areopagus speech in Acts 17), this is not a matter of becoming better acquainted with an already (if imperfectly) known being, but rather the proclamation of a God who was previously unknown. Thus, whatever claims about "God" people may make based on their experience of the phenomenal realm, such claims—even if aspects of them accord with Christian accounts of God's being and nature—can refer only to God of the *philosophes et savants*, and not to the God of Abraham, Isaac, and Jacob. As Scripture teaches, it is by faith, not reason, that "we understand that the worlds were prepared by the word of God, so that what is seen was made from things that are not visible" (Heb. 11:3).

4. Another way of describing this asymmetry is to say that while all creatures are other than God, the converse does not hold: God is *not* other than creatures. To see why this is the case, consider that if God could be described as "other" with respect to creatures, then God could be identified by the same processes of comparison and contrast (viz., here rather than there, now rather than then, or, most fundamentally, this rather than that) by which creatures are distinguished from one another. But precisely as Creator God simply cannot be put on the same ontological scale with creatures in this way. God is, rather, *totaliter aliter*—not "Wholly Other" but "wholly otherwise"—and therefore (in the words of Nicholas of Cusa) properly designated as "the Not Other." See Nicholas of Cusa, *On God as Not-Other: A Translation and an Appraisal of "De Li Non Aliud,"* 3rd ed., trans. Jasper Hopkins (Minneapolis: Arthur J. Banning Press, 1987 [1461]).

3. "Jesus Our Hope" 63

considered from God's side, from our side it is mediated and indirect: since it is not itself a possible object of our perception, all we can (and do) perceive naturally are the various sorts of secondary causes through which God effects God's creative intentions in the world. It is just this inherent asymmetry in the Creator-creature relation that would seem to render the hope of life in communion with God impossible; for we cannot live with God without being able to perceive and thereby know God, and for that to happen it would seem either that God would have to become a creature (and thus cease to be God), or that creatures would have to become divine (and thus cease to be other than God).

From Creation to Redemption

These considerations would indeed constitute an insuperable obstacle to the realization of the Christian hope—*if* creation were the only mode of God's relating to the world. But that is not the case. The difference between God's ways of relating to the world before and after Christ can be used to make sense of the Christian conviction that the gospel message establishes a this-worldly anticipation of and ground for the eschatological hope of life in communion with God. Central to this account is the claim that alongside the grace of creation by which God hiddenly makes and sustains the world, there is also the grace of redemption through which God reveals the divine self to creatures in order to enter into communion with them.[5] This latter grace takes definitive form within history in the incarnation, when God, by taking flesh and assuming a creaturely life, becomes an other present to—and thus able to be perceived and known by—creatures.

This act of self-disclosure does not involve any alteration in the divine nature, which remains as transcendent and (therefore) imperceptible as ever. Indeed, it is precisely the fact of divine transcendence that makes it possible for God to choose to identify the life of a particular creature—specifically, that of Jesus of Nazareth—as God's own. In so doing God does not need to change anything about the character of God's relation with the rest of creation, whether considered as a whole or in part. God neither is nor can be more intimately involved in sustaining Jesus' life than that of any other human being (or, for that matter, of any insect or toadstool), since the dependence of every creature's existence on the Creator is always already maximal. The difference between God's presence in Jesus and in any other creature is therefore not quantitative (as though there were or could be "more" of God in him than elsewhere), but qualitative: for God to take flesh in Jesus is for God to claim this creature's

---

5. David Kelsey distinguishes four modes of divine relating: creation (in the narrow sense of origination), providential care (understood as an entailment of creation that is nevertheless logically distinct from it), reconciliation, and eschatological consummation (David H. Kelsey, *Human Anguish and God's Power* [Cambridge: Cambridge University Press, 2020], 12–13; cf. 180–89, 200–203). My reduction of these four to two does not indicate any disagreement with Kelsey's analysis of the logical distinctions between God's different modes of relating to the world; it simply reflects my judgment that his fourfold categorization rests on a more basic, twofold distinction between God relating to creatures hiddenly on the one hand ("creation," combining the categories of creation and providential care) and God relating to creatures through self-disclosive communication on the other ("redemption," including the categories of reconciliation and eschatological consummation).

64   *The Hope of Glory*

life as God's own life, such that Jesus' thoughts and actions may be identified without qualification as God's thoughts and actions.[6] In short, the claim that the Word became flesh in Jesus means that God was born of Mary, grew up in Nazareth, ate with sinners, and died on a cross.

In the technical language of Chalcedonian Christology, to say that Jesus is God incarnate is to say that although his human nature—the various features of his body and soul that constitute *what* he is as a creature who lived in first-century Palestine—is created, his hypostasis—*who* he is—is divine. By becoming present in time and space in this way through assuming a human nature, God the Word is able to be heard, seen, touched, and thereby known by creatures (1 John 1:1), even though the divine nature remains invisible, intangible, and ineffable. And where creatures are able to know God as an other in this way, it becomes possible for them to live not only *under* God (by the grace of creation) but also *with* God (by the grace of redemption) and thereby to become "participants of the divine nature" (2 Pet. 1:4).

Of course, God's self-disclosure to human beings did not begin with Jesus. Scripture affirms that long before the first Christmas God also spoke "in many and various ways by the prophets" (Heb. 1:1). This belief is reflected in the New Testament writers' efforts to validate Jesus' ministry by showing that he fulfills the words of those prophets (Matt. 1:22; 2:15, 17, 23; 3:15 and *passim*; John 12:38; 13:18; 15:25; 19:24, 28, 36; cf. Matt. 5:17; Mark 14:49; Luke 4:21; 24:25–27, 44–47; John 5:46; Rom. 3:21; 1 Pet. 1:10; Rev. 10:7), and therefore is rightly confessed as sent by the same God who spoke through them (John 8:42; Gal. 4:4–5; cf. Luke 1:30–32; Acts 3:13; 13:22–23). From this perspective the life of Jesus is the climax of a history of divine address that goes back to the call of Abraham (Gen. 12:1–3).[7] Yet although it is the same God who speaks to human beings throughout, the distinction between God speaking "by the prophets" on the one hand and "by a Son" (Heb. 1:2) on the other reflects the belief that the Son, Jesus, unlike the prophets, *is* God: "the reflection of God's glory and the exact imprint of God's very being" (Heb. 1:3; cf. John 1:1; Col. 1:15–17). In the prophets God spoke *through* creatures without being identifiable *as* a creature in the way that

---

6. If, as suggested in the previous chapter, an analogy can be drawn between the comprehensive character of God's causality in creation and an author's giving rise to the whole of the "world" of her novel, a similar parallel may be drawn between the incarnation and an author's decision to identify a character in the novel as herself. Just as so doing does not render the author any less the source and sustainer of (and thus transcendent over) the whole novelistic world, neither does God's taking flesh in Jesus disrupt or cancel God's ongoing activity as Creator who holds the world as a whole and all its parts (including Jesus) in being. See Ian A. McFarland, *The Word Made Flesh: A Theology of the Incarnation* (Louisville, KY: Westminster John Knox Press, 2019), 81–84.

7. To the objection that the divine speaking to humankind should be dated all the way back to Adam and Eve, I concede that the doctrine of original sin does indeed imply a primordial divine communication that human beings disobeyed; but because we have no way of conceiving such a prelapsarian state, this original act of divine revelation (like the fall into sin that follows it) is better conceived as a presupposition for the confession of humanity's universal need for salvation than as a datable historical event. In other words, given the beliefs (which I take to be constitutive of Christian faith) that (1) humanity was created good and (2) that all people are nevertheless congenitally sinful (which itself follows from the conviction that because Jesus is rightly confessed as the Savior of all people without exception, all people without exception are intrinsically and not simply contingently in need of salvation), the confession of a primordial fall by virtue of which all persons have turned from God is unavoidable; but the associated presupposition of a primordial divine address should be taken as something like a necessary postulate of theological reason, not as a historical instance of the grace of redemption. See the discussion in Ian A. McFarland, *In Adam's Fall: A Meditation on the Christian Doctrine of Original Sin* (Malden, MA: Wiley-Blackwell, 2010), 159–61.

3. *"Jesus Our Hope"* 65

God is in Jesus. This difference is crucial, for so long as a distinction may be drawn between the identity of God and that of the human being who speaks in God's name, then even though what is spoken comes from God, it cannot be held to represent God's will in a full or final sense. For messengers can only speak what they are told, and they cannot guarantee that what they are told encompasses all that God has to say. Such a guarantee can only be had when the messenger, as one in whom "all the fullness of God was pleased to dwell" (Col. 1:19; cf. 2:9), can be identified as God.

As important as the distinction between God speaking through the prophets and God speaking as Jesus is, however, both are nevertheless manifestations of God's redemptive mode of relating to creatures, because across both the Old and New Testaments it is the self-same God who calls people to life with God. Indeed, insofar as Jesus is understood to be the fulfillment of all God's promises (2 Cor. 1:20), beginning with the declaration to Abraham that "in you all the families of the earth shall be blessed" (Gen. 12:3; cf. Gal. 3:16), it is possible to construe the whole history of revelation stretching between those two figures as a single, complex speech-act, through which God communicates God's Word and thereby discloses God's very self to human beings.[8] Through this address, extending from the election of Israel to the life of Israel's Messiah, God relates to human beings in a new way that supervenes on God's creative relating, treating them (as Luther put it) as "the kind of creatures with whom God would want to speak eternally and in an immortal manner."[9]

As argued in the introduction, this new mode of relating brings about a fundamental transformation in human existence that is encapsulated in the biblical teaching that human beings do not live "by bread alone, but by every word that comes from the mouth of God" (Matt. 4:4 and par.; cf. Deut. 8:3). As constituted by God's activity in creation, humans do indeed live by "bread," understood as shorthand for the whole ensemble of secondary causes that sustain our earthly existence, from the physical laws that hold our bodies together to the air we breathe to the interpersonal relationships without which we would perish in infancy. And, of course, even after God begins to speak to us, our earthly lives continue to depend on the goodness of the created order. For this reason, even as quoted by Jesus the words of Deuteronomy remain a promise rather than a statement of fact, since it is only in glory that our lives will in their entirety be sustained exclusively by God's Word apart from any created intermediaries.[10]

---

8. On this view the non-incarnate speech of God in the Old Testament is integral to God's incarnate speech in the New, such that (in line with the observations regarding the internal witness of Scripture in the previous paragraph), Jesus would not be known as God's Word apart from the prior witness of the prophets, whose words he fulfills. For though it is in Jesus alone that "all the fullness of God was pleased to dwell," such a confession is inseparable from the promise of his coming, since the God whose fullness Jesus reveals is precisely the God of Israel.

9. Martin Luther, *Lectures on Genesis: Chapters 26–30*, vol. 5 of *Luther's Works*, American ed., ed. Jaroslav Pelikan, Hilton C. Osvald, and Helmut T. Lehmann (St. Louis, MO: Concordia, 1970), 76. The preceding sentence reads: "Where and with whomever God speaks, whether in anger or in grace [viz., law or gospel], that person is surely immortal."

10. "For while our present life is active amongst a variety of multiform conditions, and the things we have relations with are numerous, for instance, time, air, locality, food and drink, clothing, sunlight, lamplight, and other necessities of life, none of which, many though they be, are God—that blessed state which we hope for is in need of none of these things, but the Divine Being will become all, and instead of all, to us, distributing Himself proportionately to every need of that existence. It is plain, too, from Holy Scripture that God becomes to those who deserve it, locality, and home, and clothing,

66   *The Hope of Glory*

Still, even now when we hear God's call and respond in faith, our lives, like Abraham's, are set on a new footing, because they are no longer defined solely by our past, whether in the form of the sins we have committed or the patterns of dependence to which those sins have bound us, but by the life to which God calls us: a life with God that lies ahead, and which, as a matter of grace, has no presupposition other than God's will that those who had lived *under* God as (faithless) servants by the grace of creation should by the grace of redemption come to live *with* God as (faithful) friends (John 15:15).

At the level of the individual, to experience God's work of redemption is to receive a *vocation*: to be called by God (Rom. 8:28; 1 Cor. 1:9; 7:17) to a particular form of life, which Paul describes as membership in the body of Christ.[11] Such callings take many forms, for "just as in one body we have many members, and not all the members have the same function" (Rom. 12:4), "so it is with Christ" (1 Cor. 12:12). And while all callings reflect the fact that human beings were made rational agents, capable of independent movement, speech, and the capacity to manipulate various features of their environment (so that the vocations of the redeemed are fully consistent with their human nature as created by God), the fact that vocation comes upon the individual from without, as a divine summons to give these general characteristics the specific form of (for example) butcher, baker, or candlestick-maker, means that a person's vocation cannot be predicted by simple extrapolation from these natural human attributes, which are distinctive precisely in that they render human nature open to an indefinite number of ways of fulfillment.[12] Because it is by God's grace rather than our own merit that we are both called to and live out redeemed lives (cf. 1 Cor. 15:10), the shape of an individual's vocation is sufficiently unpredictable to allow the righteous Pharisee Paul to be the apostle to the Gentiles, or the Gentile Ruth to become the spouse of the Jew Boaz. Precisely because it is a divine summons, vocation supervenes on an individual's capacities rather than simply deriving from them.[13]

The Form of Hope

Redeemed life is thus the result of a shift in the mode of God's relating to human beings, in which the hiddenness of God in creation is overcome through direct divine address that summons us to a life with God that begins now and reaches

---

and food, and drink, and light, and riches, and dominion, and everything thinkable and nameable that goes to make our life happy." Gregory of Nyssa, *On the Soul and the Resurrection*, in *Gregory of Nyssa: Dogmatic Treatises, Etc.*, vol. 5, *Nicene and Post-Nicene Fathers*, 2nd series, ed. Philip Schaff and Henry Wace (Boston: Hendrickson, 1995 [1893]), 452.

11. See also Hebrews 3:14, which speaks of Christians being *metochoi* of Christ, which may be translated "partners" (NRSVue) or "partakers" (KJV), and, like Paul's language of the body, entails the idea of sharing in Christ's life (see the JB, NIV, and RSV translations).

12. See Kathryn Tanner, *Christ the Key* (Cambridge: Cambridge University Press, 2010), 44–52.

13. Importantly, this does not mean that persons' vocations necessarily entail a radical break with the circumstances of their origin or upbringing. There is nothing to prevent the same God who called the fisherman Peter to be an apostle from equally graciously calling succeeding generations of Bachs to be musicians, or many members of the King family to the ministry. The point is simply that as much as a vocation may be expected to exploit a person's own characteristics and circumstances, in the final analysis its shape is determined from without through God's summons ("grace") rather than by simple extrapolation from a person's intrinsic merits or abilities ("works").

completion in glory; moreover, this shift entails a reorientation of human ontology in which God sustains the creature directly ("by every word that comes from the mouth of God") rather than indirectly ("by bread"). So described, however, this account of God's redemptive work remains too formal and schematic to serve as the basis for Christian hope. For while it may be assumed that the promise of life with God whose own inexhaustible goodness is the source of every good (Jas. 1:17) is eminently desirable, that by itself does not establish it as a legitimate object of hope. It could be (and often enough has been) dismissed as false hope, whether on the grounds that it leads to an escapist account of heaven above that is utterly disconnected from the basic conditions of created existence here below, or to a titanism that imagines it can bend those conditions to its own ends.

A faithful account of Christian hope must be able to answer such charges. Admittedly, because "hope that is seen is not hope," there can be no question of proving the truth of Christian claims: hope will always have the character of a wager, albeit one undertaken because the account of human life with which it is connected is judged irresistibly compelling rather than as the result of a formal calculation of the odds of success.[14] As already noted, that judgment will rest partly on being able to identify some elements of the hoped-for future in one's present experience (e.g., the forgiveness of sin as a foretaste of a future in which God's word is the sole—and thus unfailing—support for one's life), all the while recognizing a level of discontinuity between the two that precludes reducing the future to a simple extrapolation from the present. In other words, as much as the "unseen" character of hope entails an epistemic gap between what is and what is to come, the two cannot be separated, since they both pertain to the same person. Because the life for which I hope remains *my* life (that is, the glorification of someone who has already been created rather than a "new creation" in the strict sense), it must stand in continuity with the life I live now. Simply identifying elements common to life now and life in glory is insufficient; in order to sustain hope, those common elements must also form part of an overarching vision of human life within which what is hoped for appears plausible as well as desirable.

For Christians this vision is defined by Christ, since to receive a vocation is to find a place in his body, and thus to become part of his story. The ground of Christian hope is therefore the story of Jesus. As already noted, however, this story does not begin only with Jesus' birth. Because Jesus is confessed as the *Christ*—that is, the Messiah of *Israel*—his story cannot be separated from the redemptive history that begins with God's election of Abraham to be the ancestor of a people through whom all nations (Gen. 12:3) and, indeed, the whole of the created order (Isa. 11:6–9; 65:25) will find blessing. That Israel's story is intended to foster hope is clear from the characteristics of the life God intends for this people: it is to be characterized by justice, in which special provision is made for the vulnerable (Exod. 22:21–27; cf. Deut. 10:18; Isa. 1:17; Jer. 22:3); by peace, in which violence and oppression are cut off (Lev. 26:6; cf. Isa. 32:17; Ezek. 34:25; Zech. 8:12); and

---

14. Such judgment constitutes an exercise of what John Henry Newman called the "illative sense." See John Henry Cardinal Newman, *An Essay in Aid of a Grammar of Assent* (Notre Dame, IN: University of Notre Dame Press, 1979 [1870]), especially ch. 9.

68   *The Hope of Glory*

by equity, in which "those who gathered much had nothing over, and those who gathered little had no shortage" (Exod. 16:18; cf. Ps. 147:14). Indeed (and in keeping with the cosmic scope of God's eschatological promise), these principles of justice, peace, and equity extend even to the nonhuman creation: animals, too, are to enjoy the benefits of Sabbath rest (Exod. 20:10; Deut. 5:14; cf. 25:4), and the land is to be granted relief from use on a regular basis (Lev. 25:2–5).

So God intended. But the fact that this promise of a just, peaceful, and equitable society failed to be realized in Israel, which experienced instead conquest and occupation by a series of progressively more brutal foreign powers (see Dan. 7:2–7), cannot help but raise the question of whether Israel's hope proved false. It is in this context that the Christian confession that Jesus of Nazareth is the Word made flesh (John 1:14), and thus himself no less than God (John 1:1), takes on particular significance. For if Jesus is in truth Emmanuel, or "God with us" (cf. Matt. 1:23; Isa. 7:14), then he is not simply another prophet proclaiming the promise of God's kingdom, but (in the words of Origen of Alexandria) the *autobasileia*—the kingdom in person—in whom the reality of life with God is realized and all God's promises correspondingly fulfilled (2 Cor. 1:20; cf. Matt. 5:17).[15] It is on this basis that Scripture can declare that Jesus *is* "our hope" (1 Tim. 1:1).[16]

Yet this assertion can only be sustained if Jesus' life can plausibly be construed as hopeful. In addressing this question, the claim that Jesus was raised from the dead is obviously crucial, but it cannot be considered decisive in itself. For while Jesus' resurrection is undoubtedly good news for him, whether it is similarly good news for the rest of us depends on the kind of life that was raised (the news that Hitler or Stalin had risen would hardly be cause for celebration). If to be redeemed is to be called by God to a life with Christ so intimate that it can be described as becoming a member of his body, then it becomes crucial to know the defining characteristics of his life, since it can only be judged worthy of hope if it is a life in which I both want to share myself and can in good conscience encourage others to share. The basis for making such an assessment cannot simply be Jesus' teaching, healing and the like, since they are particular to his particular vocation as Messiah and therefore are not activities in which all will share (cf. 1 Cor. 12:29–31). The features of his life that ground Christian hope will instead be the patterns of solidarity he exhibits, since these will display those features of life in communion with him that may be shared across the full range of human vocations. Three such patterns stand out in the Gospels: solidarity with Israel, solidarity with sinners, and solidarity with the poor in spirit. Let us consider each of them in turn.

---

15. Origen of Alexandria, *Commentary on Matthew* 14.7; in *Origen, Spirit and Fire: A Thematic Anthology of His Writings*, ed. Hans Urs von Balthasar, trans. Robert J. Daly, SJ (Washington, DC: Catholic University of America Press, 1984 [1938]), 362.

16. The fact that Christians view Jesus as the answer to the charge that Israel's hope has proved false does not preclude the possibility of other, non-Christian answers. Both rabbinic Judaism and Islam may be taken as alternative accounts of how God's promise to Abraham—and thus Israel's hope—remain credible in spite of the fall of the Davidic kingdom and the subsequent dispersion of the Jewish people.

Solidarity with Israel

Jesus was a Jew; and one is a Jew (that is, a member of the people of Israel) by birth, not by subsequent discernment or decision.[17] Jesus was therefore a Jew quite simply and irrevocably because, as a biological descendant of Jacob, he was "born under the law" (Gal. 4:4; cf. Matt. 1:2–16; Luke 3:23–34; Rom. 9:5). Yet insofar as he is also Israel's promised Messiah, his Jewishness is integral to his vocation: he is not simply any Jew, but the "son of David" (Matt. 1:1; 9:27; 15:22; 20:30–31; 21:9, and pars.; Rom. 1:4), who, as such, is called specifically to "save his people from their sins" (Matt. 1:21) and to "reign over the house of Jacob forever" (Luke 1:33). In other words, to be "born under the law" is not something that is true of Jesus only incidentally (as is the case, for example, with his height or his hair color), but crucial to his identity as Savior (Luke 2:11), since, as he himself teaches, "salvation is from the Jews" (John 4:22; cf. Gen.12:3; 28:14).

It is a further feature of Jesus' vocation that he not only is a Jew but also actively lives the life of a Jew: that is, he is not simply "born under the law," but actively keeps it. Luke is careful to note that even as an infant Jesus' life unfolds in accordance with the law's precepts (1:21–24), and Jesus himself insists that he has come not "to abolish the Law or the Prophets . . . but to fulfill. For truly I tell you, until heaven and earth pass away, not one letter, not one stroke of a letter, will pass from the law until all is accomplished" (Matt. 5:17–18; cf. 4:1–11 and par.). In line with this perspective, the evangelists report that Jesus understood the whole course of life as the fulfillment of Israel's Scriptures (Matt. 26:24; Luke 22:37; 24:44), and they themselves are keen to interpret the defining events of his life in these same terms (Matt. 1:22–23; 2:14–18, 23; 4:13–16; 13:34–35; 21:1–5; John 2:13–17; 12:37–38; 19:31–36; cf. 1 Cor. 15:3–4). Indeed, according to Matthew, Jesus was sufficiently convinced of the specifically Jewish character of his vocation as to insist that his earthly ministry was directed exclusively to Israel (Matt. 15:24; cf. 10:1–6; John 1:31; Acts 3:26).

Given Jesus' frequent conflicts with Israel's religious authorities (e.g., Matt. 5:20; 9:34; 12:1–4 and pars.; 12:22–28 and par.; 15:1–14; 21:12–13, 45–46; 22:15–33 and pars.; 23:1–36 and par.; Mark 2:1–11 and par.; John 7:32–34; 8:12–18; 11:45–50), culminating in his condemnation by the Sanhedrin (Matt. 26:57–66 and pars.), his solidarity with Israel can hardly be viewed in terms of ethnic pride or chauvinistic nationalism.[18] At the same time, neither will it do to go to the opposite extreme and interpret Jesus' relationship with Israel contrastively, as though his perfect Messianic obedience simply stood over against the collective faithlessness of all other Jews.[19] Admittedly, the evangelists report that at

---

17. To be sure, it is possible for a Gentile to convert to Judaism and thereby become a Jew (Jesus himself refers to the practice in Matt. 23:15), but this act is dependent on the existence of Jews who are physical descendants of Abraham. Jewishness is first of all and fundamentally a congenital identity, and only derivatively a chosen one.

18. Contrast this with Paul, who, in spite of the fact that he conceives his ministry as directed specifically to Gentiles (Gal. 2:2, 7–9), seems far more conscious than Jesus of his own dignity as an Israelite (Rom. 11:1; Phil. 3:4–6; cf. Rom. 9:4–5).

19. Eugene Rogers critiques Karl Barth's theology of Israel on the grounds that it does just this. See Eugene F. Rogers Jr., *Sexuality and the Christian Body: Their Way into the Triune God* (Oxford: Blackwell, 1999), chs. 6–7; see especially p. 149: "Barth throws up a conceptual screen onto which he can at once *project* a partial abstraction ('Israel') and *hide* actual human beings ('the Jews') behind it."

70 *The Hope of Glory*

certain points Jesus' evaluation of his compatriots was extremely harsh (Matt. 12:34–42 and par.; 23:37–38 and par.; John 8:39–47), but such passages in no way justify the conclusion that Israel has in any sense been displaced as the object of God's love.[20] Apart from a handful of (admittedly striking) encounters with Gentiles and Samaritans, Jesus' ministry takes place entirely among Jews, so that if his opponents are Jewish, so are his followers; and between these two more or less well-defined extremes stand a mass of other Jews ("the crowds") whose attitude toward him ranges from adulation (Matt. 21:6–11 and pars.; cf. John 6:14–15) to bemusement (John 6:24–66) to overt hostility (Matt. 26:15–23 and pars.; cf. Mark 3:19–22)—with all three reactions capable of arising in the course of a single episode (Luke 4:16–30).[21]

In light of this evidence, Jesus' relation to Israel cannot be characterized as either uncritical affirmation or as wholesale rejection. Instead, it needs to be understood as reflecting the conviction that there is no encountering (and thus no knowing) the true God, whether in judgment or in blessing, apart from Israel. For the Creator God is omnipresent, but precisely as such invisible: active everywhere and in everything, but neither known nor knowable in that activity. Instead, this God is known only in the gracious divine decision to be known by assuming perceptible form within the world of time and space—and God has done this concretely in the election of Israel. For this God to have been incarnate in anything other than Jewish flesh, or, having been born a Jew, to deny or marginalize his Jewish identity, would therefore amount to God's denying God's own self as the one who has determined to be known by (and thereby to bless) humankind through Israel. For although God calls all human beings individually (that is, after all, what it means to say that every person has a vocation), God calls them precisely to become part of the history of God with this people, whether as shoots that have sprung naturally from the Abrahamic trunk (Jews) or as branches from other nations that have been grafted into it (Gentiles; see Rom. 11:16–18).

This pattern of solidarity sustains hope because it demonstrates God's faithfulness. In the first instance and most immediately, God is faithful to Israel as the people whom God promised both to give the blessing of redemption and to be the means by which that blessing would be extended to the whole creation. But this faithfulness to Israel also signals a broader faithfulness to the material order as a whole, which God established as one of radical interdependence, in which the flourishing of any one creature depends on its various relationships with myriad others. Within the human sphere, this interdependence is exhibited in the fact that is only in learning from—and thus placing ourselves in a position of trust in and vulnerability to—others that we come to know what is

---

20. Jesus also stands in solidarity with sinners (see below), but that is different from his solidarity with Israel. Matthew 9:13 ("I have not come to call the righteous but sinners") and Matthew 15:24 ("I was sent only to the lost sheep of the house of Israel") are provocatively similar, but they are not synonymous.

21. Even the distinction between Jesus' Jewish followers and opponents is not always clear-cut: one of his disciples betrays him (Matt. 26:14–16 and pars.; cf. John 6:71), another denies him (Matt. 26:69–75 and pars.), and all desert him (Matt. 26:56 and par.); contrariwise, the Gospels testify that there are some among the Jewish leadership who are sympathetic to his message, including Nicodemus (John 3:1; 7:50–51; 19:39), Joseph of Arimathea (Mark 15:43 and pars.), and at least one unnamed scribe (Mark 12:28–34; cf. John 12:42; Acts 6:7).

3. *"Jesus Our Hope"* 71

true, right, and necessary for our well-being. In this context, Thomas Paine's complaint that in a matter as consequential as divine revelation "the proof and evidence of it should be equal to all, and universal" gets it precisely wrong.[22] The mode of knowing he envisions here is that of angels, each of whom (at least according to one significant strand of theological speculation) receives its knowledge of God directly from God, and thus as a matter of immediate certainty.[23] Among human beings, by contrast, knowledge—whether of God or anything else—is dependent on an ongoing process of listening to and speaking with other humans, in full recognition that such dependence renders all our claims to knowledge (including those derived from divine revelation) contingent, relative, and always only partial.

In this way, solidarity with Israel is hopeful because it testifies to God's commitment to the integrity of created being. In redeeming creatures, God honors their character as creatures, in line with the principle that grace perfects nature rather than destroying it.[24] That we come to know God through (and thus in dependence upon) other people reflects God's commitment to blessing us as the creatures we are. To add to this the recognition that there is and can be no blessing for Gentiles (which is what most Christians are) apart from God's blessing of the Jews simply reflects the particular way God has determined for the divine word of blessing to be heard within the realm of time and space.[25] To confess that Jesus, as the Christ, is first of all the Savior of Israel, and only then (and on that basis) the Savior of the nations as well, is thus simply to acknowledge the concrete form by which God realizes the divine intention that in this life the supernatural blessing of redemption no less than the natural blessings of created existence should be mediated to creatures by way of other creatures.

Solidarity with Sinners

Jesus was a Jew. He was not a sinner (Heb. 4:15; 1 Pet. 2:22; cf. Matt. 3:13–15). At the same time, because God "made the one who knew no sin to be sin, so that in him we might become the righteousness of God" (2 Cor. 5:21), his life was one of solidarity with sinners no less than one of solidarity with Israel. Yet the basis for this solidarity is different in the two cases. Jesus was a Jew because he was born a Jew; he had no choice in the matter (or, better, the choice was made long before his birth, when God chose the seed of Abraham to be the means by which all the earth's families were to be blessed). Unlike all other human beings, however, Jesus was not born a sinner.[26] That he nevertheless chose to stand with sinners by giving his life as a ransom for them (Matt. 20:28 and par.)

---

22. Thomas Paine, *The Age of Reason: Being an Investigation of True and of Fabulous Theology* (Cambridge: Cambridge University Press, 2013 [1794]), 6.

23. See Aquinas, *ST* 1.56.3, 60 vols., Blackfriars ed. (London: Eyre & Spottiswood, 1964–81).

24. *Gratia non tollit naturam, sed perficit.* Aquinas, *ST*, 1.1.8.2.

25. Importantly, this demand for Christian solidarity with Jews does not entail support for the nation-state of Israel (any more than it required Jesus to adopt the nationalist political program of the Zealots), nor does it require endorsement of the beliefs or practices of any particular Jewish religious group (again, Jesus' interactions with various Jewish religious leaders of his day make this clear).

26. Although Adam and Eve were not *created* sinners, they also were not *born*, and so do not constitute an exception to this rule. Christians who subscribe to the doctrine of the Immaculate Conception will count Jesus' mother as an exception, though they will also concede that her congenital sinlessness is dependent on Jesus' redemptive activity as Jesus' sinlessness is not.

72   *The Hope of Glory*

therefore entailed a commitment to people who are fundamentally unlike him, as his solidarity with Israel did not.

Another significant difference between these two forms of solidarity is that Jesus' sinlessness was not evident to his contemporaries in the way that his Jewishness was. Indeed, in raising the specter of guilt by association, Jesus' habit of socializing with those whose sins were especially obvious and noteworthy cast doubt on his credibility as a religious teacher (Matt. 9:10–11 and pars.; cf. Luke 7:36–50). Yet as much as Jesus insists that he came "to call not the righteous but sinners" (Matt. 9:13 and pars.), he at no point suggested that his solidarity with sinners entailed overlooking (let alone endorsing) their sin; on the contrary, he explicitly instructs them to sin no more (John 5:14; 8:11). He associates with sinners in order to call them away from their sin, in a way that is consistent in substance with (though, as he himself notes in Matt. 11:19 and par., different in form from) the message of repentance proclaimed by John the Baptist (see Matt. 3:2; 4:17; cf. Mark 1:4, 15). Thus, when asked why he eats with sinners, he responds, "Those who are well have no need of a physician but those who are sick" (Mark 2:17; cf. Luke 19:10). Nevertheless, the fact that Jesus' calling of sinners included his assuming the divine prerogative of actually declaring their sins forgiven led him to be viewed as guilty of the worst sin of all: blasphemy (Mark 2:5–7 and pars.; Luke 7:48–49; cf. John 10:31–33; Matt. 26:64–65 and pars.).

Jesus was crucified by the Roman governor of Judea on the charge of political sedition, not blasphemy (see Matt. 27:37 and pars.; cf. Luke 23:2; John 19:12–16); but it is a deep-seated conviction of Christians that whatever the formal reasons for his execution, his death is an integral part of his mission to "save his people from their sins" (Matt. 1:21; cf. John 11:48–52), and thus as a further (and, indeed, climactic) manifestation of his earthly declarations of forgiveness (1 Cor. 15:3; Gal. 1:4; 1 John 2:2). Thus, when Paul writes that God "made the one who knew no sin to be sin, so that in him we might become the righteousness of God" (2 Cor. 5:21), he seems to have had Jesus' crucifixion in mind: "Christ redeemed us from the curse of the law by becoming a curse for us—for it is written, 'Cursed is everyone who hangs on a tree'" (Gal. 3:13; cf. Deut. 21:23). Exactly how Christ's taking on this curse frees the rest of sinful humanity from the law's condemnation is not spelled out by Paul or any other biblical author. Indeed, since the New Testament refers to Jesus' saving work using a wide range of metaphors, including ransom (Matt. 20:28 and par.; 1 Tim. 2:6), conquest (Col. 2:14–15; cf. John 16:33), sacrifice (Eph. 5:2; Heb. 10:12), and condemnation (Rom. 8:3; cf. John 16:11), it seems unlikely that the biblical authors intended to identify the particular mechanism by which redemption was accomplished.[27] But this variety does not obscure the fundamental witness of the New Testament that in taking flesh as Jesus, God has linked the divine life to that of humanity so profoundly that their destiny has become inseparable, to the extent that even "if we are faithless, he remains faithful—for he cannot deny himself" (2 Tim. 2:13 alt.).

---

27. A striking example of the open-endedness of the biblical witness on this question is seen in the fact that Jesus' identification with Isaiah's suffering servant (Isa. 53:4–6) is interpreted by different writers in different ways, with one writer referring to it as Jesus' active ministry of healing the sick (Matt. 8:16–17) and another to passive endurance of suffering on the cross (1 Pet. 2:24–25).

3. "Jesus Our Hope"

Yet Jesus' solidarity with sinners is more than (though it most certainly also includes) his solidarity with humanity as such. For though not even the most pious Pharisee or priest would claim to be without sin (after all, much of the liturgical life of Israel, including especially the temple cult, was concerned with confessing and atoning for sin), they would draw a distinction between sin that is unintentional and sin that is flagrant (see Num. 15:27–30; cf. John 8:4). Their complaint about Jesus was that his practice of seemingly indiscriminate table fellowship suggested (among other things) a disregard for this distinction. Yet Jesus' response to his critics—that he had "come to call not the righteous but sinners to repentance"—implies that he was perfectly well aware of the differences among various forms of sin, and that his association with (notorious) sinners derived precisely from his recognition of their greater need.[28]

The significance of this form of solidarity for Christian hope is clear: there is no sin is so serious as to exceed God's capacity to forgive.[29] This does not mean taking sin less seriously; on the contrary, Jesus' tendency is arguably to take sin *more* seriously than those who seek to stress different gradations of sin, as shown in the antitheses of the Sermon on the Mount, where anger is judged no less culpable than murder, and the lustful glance as damnable as adultery (Matt. 5:21–22, 27–28). Granted, practically speaking the consequences of murder are far graver than name-calling, and it is with such practical effects in mind that the New Testament shows no hesitation in instructing Christians to break fellowship with those whose sinning is flagrant (see 1 Cor. 5:11; 2 John 9–11). And yet even in these cases, when a person has so violated the conditions of communion that they can only be regarded "as a gentile and a tax collector" (Matt. 18:17), Jesus' own practice toward just these categories of people suggests that the appropriate course of action is to engage with rather than simply to abandon them (see, e.g., Matt. 8:5–13; 9:9)—albeit while recognizing that under such circumstances the conditions of fellowship must be reestablished rather than presupposed.[30] In this way, Jesus' solidarity with sinners allows

28. Jesus could also turn the charge of failing to recognize the relative seriousness of sins against his critics: "Woe to you, scribes and Pharisees, hypocrites! For you tithe mint, dill, and cumin and have neglected the weightier matters of the law: justice and mercy and faith. It is these you ought to have practiced without neglecting the others" (Matt. 23:23; cf. 15:1–6 and pars.).

29. At this point it is necessary to address some biblical passages that seemingly run counter to the claim that no sin is beyond the reach of God's forgiveness: "Whoever speaks a word against the Son of Man will be forgiven, but whoever speaks against the Holy Spirit will not be forgiven, either in this age or in the age to come" (Matt. 12:32 and pars.); "For it is impossible to restore again to repentance those who have once been enlightened and have tasted the heavenly gift and have shared in the Holy Spirit and have tasted the goodness of the word of God and the powers of the age to come and then have fallen away, since they are crucifying again the Son of God to their own harm and are holding him up to contempt" (Heb. 6:4–6); and "If you see your brother or sister committing what is not a deadly sin, you will ask, and God will give life to such a one—to those whose sin is not deadly. There is sin that is deadly; I do not say that you should pray about that" (1 John 5:16). Recognizing the particular meaning of "falling away" in Hebrews and the "deadly sin" of 1 John are obscure, it is crucial to note that in the Gospel text Jesus' warning is directed to those who reject his commitment to bring salvation to the lost, suggesting that the only sin that is beyond forgiveness is the one that refuses to acknowledge and receive the gospel itself (i.e., the "unforgivable sin" is not a particular, arbitrarily defined transgression, but rather analytic to the content of the gospel itself: the rejection of the forgiveness Jesus offers). Cf. James Cone: "the sin against the Holy Spirit . . . is unforgiveable because it is never recognized." James H. Cone, *Black Theology and Black Power* (New York: Seabury, 1969), 72.

30. That the terms of Christian engagement with the neighbor are contingent upon the neighbor's status as an ecclesial insider or outsider is clear in Paul's instructions for addressing sexual immorality in Corinth: "I wrote to you in my letter not to associate with sexually immoral persons—not at all meaning the sexually immoral of this world, or the greedy and swindlers, or idolaters, since you

74   *The Hope of Glory*

Christians to take sin—both their own and their neighbor's—with all due seriousness without losing hope for themselves or their neighbor. On the contrary, their hope can be strengthened in the knowledge that no one's deeds place them beyond the reach of grace.

Solidarity with the Poor in Spirit

"Blessed are the poor in spirit, for theirs is the kingdom of heaven" (Matt. 5:3). These words from Matthew's Gospel are often viewed as a watered-down version of the Lukan "Blessed are you who are poor" (Luke 6:20), which is taken to be the more original form of the saying.[31] While recent scholarship has called into question the historical-critical basis for that judgment,[32] at first blush it does seem that Matthew's "poor in spirit" (*ptōchoi tōi pneumati*) constitutes a more nebulous (and correspondingly less challenging) category than the seemingly more straightforward commitment to the dispossessed found in Luke, where the emphasis on physical poverty is highlighted by Jesus' parallel pronouncement of "woe" on the rich (6:24). And yet the shape of Jesus' ministry suggests that the Matthean phrasing better reflects the breadth of his concern. For while the Gospels certainly show Jesus attentive to the destitute (see, e.g., Mark 10:46–52; 12:41–44; John 9:1–8; cf. Matt. 11:5 and par.), his focus is by no means limited to those whose need and vulnerability are reducible to economic distress (see, e.g., Matt. 8:14–15; 9:2–7; 12:9–13; Luke 8:1–3; 13:10–13; 19:1–10; John 8:2–10).[33] It would be more accurate to say that his ministry is characterized by solidarity with those suffering from any form of social marginalization, whatever its cause. Insofar as Matthew's "poor in spirit" connotes persons who for whatever reason lack a sense of their own integrity as creatures of God—those whose condition is one of chronic "deflation" or having "the wind knocked out of them" (to draw on colloquial English to bring out the sense of the Greek *pneuma*, which can mean "breath" as well as "spirit")—it reflects Jesus' vision of the kingdom more fully than does the Lukan parallel.[34]

---

would then need to go out of the world. But now I am writing to you not to associate with anyone who bears the name of brother or sister who is sexually immoral or greedy or an idolater, reviler, drunkard, or swindler" (1 Cor. 5:9–11). Again, the point is not to write the sinner off, but to acknowledge frankly the rupture that has occurred as the context for the possibility of genuine restoration of fellowship (cf. 1 Cor. 5:5; Matt. 18:21–22). That the ecclesial discipline of excommunication has just this restorative function is a central feature of William Cavanaugh's argument in *Torture and Eucharist: Theology, Politics, and the Body of Christ* (Malden, MA: Blackwell, 1998), especially 234–52.

31. See, e.g., Joseph A. Fitzmyer, SJ, *The Gospel according to Luke I–X: A New Translation with Introduction and Commentary* (New York: Doubleday, 1981), 632.

32. The claim for the Lukan form being more original is bound up with the hypothesis that in these passages Matthew and Luke are both drawing on "Q," a now lost collection of dominical sayings. Absent the increasingly questioned assumption that this putative source ever existed, the natural alternative is to see Matthew as providing the earlier form of the saying, which was then adapted by Luke for his own rhetorical and theological ends. See Marc Goodacre, *The Case against Q: Studies in Markan Priority and the Synoptic Problem* (Harrisburg, PA: Continuum, 2002); cf. Francis Watson, *Gospel Writing: A Canonical Perspective* (Grand Rapids: William B. Eerdmans, 2013), 160–65.

33. In this context, it is worth noting that although the Hebrew term '*ănāwîm* (which by scholarly consensus underlies the Greek *ptōchoi* in both Matthew and Luke) "was used originally to denote the physically poor . . . in time it came to be applied to people in Israel who were unfortunate, lowly, sick, downtrodden. Their opposites were not simply the rich, but included the proud, the arrogant, those who felt no need of God" (Fitzmyer, *The Gospel according to Luke I–IX*, 361).

34. In addition to "poor in spirit" other designations Jesus uses for people in such circumstances are "little ones" (see Matt. 10:42; 18:6–7, 10–14 and pars.) and "the least of these" (Matt. 25:40, 45).

3. "Jesus Our Hope" 75

This third form of Jesus' solidarity is also the most distinctive. As a Jew who understood himself to be the Messiah, Jesus' solidarity with Israel is axiomatic; and given that his foundational message is a universal call for repentance (Matt. 4:17 and pars.), Jesus could hardly exercise this form of ministry at all without standing in solidarity with sinners. By contrast, the decision to live in solidarity with the "poor in spirit" stands out more strikingly as a choice, since Jesus might have aligned with the more vigorous and self-respecting among his contemporaries without thereby diminishing his solidarity with Israel or even (as a form of noblesse oblige) with sinners. According to the Gospel accounts one of the key reasons for opposition to Jesus was his association with people whose condition made it impossible for them to participate fully in the life of the covenant community—not only "tax collectors and sinners," but also the ritually unclean (e.g., the leper of Matt. 8:2–3 and pars. and the woman with the hemorrhage of Matt. 9:20–22 and pars.).[35]

In light of the fact that Jesus felt it necessary to offer such people healing and forgiveness (as well as the fact that these same people were aware enough of their need to seek it out), it is evident that he did not differ from the Pharisees in his assessment of the needs of the marginalized, but rather in his understandings of their significance for the life of God's people. According to the Gospels they were for Jesus' religious opponents a problem: a scandal or embarrassment to be kept at arms' length as a means of preserving the distinctiveness of Israel as the people of God. By contrast, for Jesus God's kingdom is meant precisely for those who don't seem to belong and so is defined by its inclusion of such people (Matt. 11:2–5 and par.), to the extent that the promise of life with Jesus is inseparable from life with them (Matt. 25:31–46). The fact that Jesus promises the kingdom to "poor in spirit" thus reflects the kingdom's character as a divine gift rather than a human achievement—and therefore as something that can be received only by those who recognize that they have no claim to it.[36]

In this way, Jesus' solidarity with the poor in spirit speaks especially to those who suffer. To be a Jew or a sinner is not necessarily to suffer; to be poor in spirit, by contrast, is to live a life characterized by lack, by the daily experience

---

Under whatever description, however, this dimension of Jesus' vocation is equivalent to what Latin American liberation theologians have described as a "preferential option for the poor" (see especially Gustavo Gutiérrez, *A Theology of Liberation: History, Politics, and Salvation,* ed. and trans. Sister Caridad Inda and John Eagleson [Maryknoll, NY: Orbis, 1973]. In his encyclical *Centesimus annus* (1991), Pope John Paul II affirmed this language, while clarifying that the "option is not limited to material poverty, since . . . there are many other forms of poverty," noting in particular the "different forms of poverty . . . experienced by groups which live on the margins of society, by the elderly and the sick, by the victims of consumerism, and even more immediately by so many refugees and migrants" (§57). Pope John Paul II, *Centesimus annus,* 1991, https://www.vatican.va/content/john-paul-ii/en/encyclicals /documents/hf_jp-ii_enc_01051991_centesimus-annus.html.

35. In this context, the distinction between "tax collector" and "sinner" in the Gospels is important: while tax collectors might sin by taking more than was prescribed for them (see Luke 3:13), their primary offense in the eyes of their fellow Jews was collaboration with the Roman occupation.

36. Jesus observed that it was precisely "the tax collectors and the prostitutes" (Matt. 21:32) rather than the conventionally pious who had "acknowledged the justice of God" (Luke 7:29) by responding to John the Baptist's call for repentance. This same focus on dependence underlies Jesus' claim that "whoever does not receive the kingdom of God as a little child will never enter it" (Mark 10:15; cf. Matt. 19:14 and pars.): his point is not that a putative state of childhood innocence (a thoroughly modern concept) makes a person worthy of the kingdom, but rather that the kingdom can only be received by those who admit their lives are as bereft of objective merit—and correspondingly dependent on the good will and gifts of others—as is a child's.

76   *The Hope of Glory*

of vulnerability to forces that threaten to overwhelm one. It therefore rounds out the different forms of solidarity that characterize Jesus' life by situating hope squarely in the context of suffering. Importantly, the claim that the hoped-for kingdom belongs to the poor in spirit does not mean that it is a reward for suffering; it reflects rather the conviction that suffering does not have the last word, because God has determined to end it and is working even now to bring it to an end. Thus, if solidarity with Israel is the foundation of life with God in Christ, and solidarity with sinners the context within which this life is lived out, then solidarity with the poor in spirit reflects its goal: the drawing of all people to Christ (John 12:32) that takes the form of bestowing the enjoyment of life's blessings on those who in the present order are excluded from it.

Enacting Hope

It is because Jesus' resurrection from the dead is the vindication of a life shaped by these commitments that he can be proclaimed by Christians as a fit object for their and the whole world's hope. This is not to say that the story of Jesus by itself discloses the content of the hoped-for future, whether on a cosmic scale or at the level of the individual. The incarnation does not change the principle that "hope that is seen is not hope" but only secures the narrative framework within which it becomes possible to "wait for it with patience" (Rom. 8:24–25). As the theologian Hans Frei once put it,

> The past cannot be an absolute clue to the future, if the future is a genuinely open one. Not even the event of Jesus Christ can be such an absolute clue. The providential action of God over and in his creation is not that of a mechanical fate to be read off of one occasion. God's work is mysteriously, abidingly mysteriously, coexistent with the contingency of events. The history of his providence is one that must be narrated. There is no scientific rule to describe it . . . . That is why Christians, precisely because they believe in providence, know far less than certain ideological groups about the shape of the future.[37]

Our ignorance of the future's shape makes hope difficult to sustain in the face of historical currents that seem to block the possibility of its realization. Scripture itself bears witness to this when it reports that the immediate result of Moses' declaration to the Israelites that God would liberate them from slavery was that their situation actually became worse:

> That same day Pharaoh commanded the taskmasters of the people, as well as their supervisors, "You shall no longer give the people straw to make bricks, as before; let them go and gather straw for themselves. But you shall require of them the same quantity of bricks as they have made previously; do not diminish it, for they are lazy; that is why they cry, 'Let us go and offer sacrifice to our God.' Let heavier work be laid on them; then they will pay attention to it and not to deceptive words." . . . Then the Israelite supervisors came to Pharaoh and cried, "Why do you treat your servants like this? No straw

---

37. Hans W. Frei, *The Identity of Jesus Christ: The Hermeneutical Bases of Dogmatic Theology* (Eugene, OR: Wipf and Stock, 1997 [1975]), 67.

3. *"Jesus Our Hope"* 77

is given to your servants, yet they say to us, 'Make bricks!' Look how your servants are beaten! But the fault is with you." He said, "You are lazy, lazy; that is why you say, 'Let us go and sacrifice to the LORD.' Go now and work; for no straw shall be given you, but you shall still deliver the same number of bricks." (Exod. 5:6–9, 15–18)

In response to these developments, Moses complains to God (Exod. 5:22–23), who repeats the divine promises (Exod. 6:1–8); but the Israelites are not consoled: "they would not listen to Moses, because of their broken spirit and their cruel slavery" (Exod. 6:9).

This story serves as a reminder that no vision of the future, however attractive in itself, can sustain hope in the face of adversity if it does not find some resonance in people's present circumstances. If the vision is to remain a matter of hope, it will be no more than resonance, for the Christian's task is not to build the kingdom, but rather to bear witness to its advent, which happens "he does not know how" (Mark 4:27). It is therefore an important feature of Jesus' ministry from the beginning that he not only displays himself a particular set of commitments, but also calls others to share them. When he proclaims, "Repent, for the kingdom of heaven is at hand" (Matt. 4:17 and pars. alt.), he is calling his listeners to undergo a change of mind (the literal meaning of the Greek verb translated "repent"), a profound adjustment of their dispositions and actions in light of the new reality that is knocking at the door (cf. Rev. 3:20). To hope in the kingdom that Jesus proclaims is to respond to his call by taking up a new form of life that is one of following him.

For this reason, a Christian's vocation will always correspond to the form of life revealed in Jesus, but correspondence is not the same as identity. Here again the Pauline imagery of the body is helpful in emphasizing the diversity of Christian vocations: the foot is not the same as the hand, nor the ear the same as the eye, even though both are recognizably part of the same body (cf. 1 Cor. 12:14–20). As Luther says, we are to be Christs to one another by bearing each other's burdens (see Gal. 6:2); but the way in which that is accomplished in any given case will be specific to every individual's vocation, which will be as distinctive from all others as the various parts of the body are from one another (see 1 Cor. 12:27–30).[38] To be a Christ to one's neighbor is thus quite different from trying to be a second Jesus, whose vocation was particular to himself and belongs to no one else.[39] And if the discernment of vocation is first and foremost a matter of finding the place where one "fits" within the body of Christ, then one obvious place to look is at the callings Jesus himself issued to

---

38. "Hence, as our heavenly Father has freely come to our aid, we also ought freely to help our neighbor through our body and its works, and each one should become as it were a Christ to the other that we may be Christs to one another and Christ may be the same in all." Martin Luther, *The Freedom of a Christian*, in *Career of the Reformer I*, vol. 31 of *Luther's Works*, American ed., ed. Harold J. Grimm (Philadelphia: Fortress Press, 1957), 367–68.

39. The question "What would Jesus do?" therefore has no place in Christian discipleship. What Jesus would do, he has already done (viz., to be born of the Virgin Mary, suffer under Pontius Pilate, endure crucifixion, die, be buried, and rise again on the third day). The question for the Christian is "What should I do, as a disciple of Jesus called to my own vocation in this time and place?" Thus, when Paul counsels the Corinthians to be "imitators of me, as I am of Christ" (1 Cor. 11:1), he certainly is not encouraging slavish repetition, as should be evident from the fact that his own vocation was to bring the gospel to the Gentiles (Acts 9:15; 22:21; cf. Gal. 2:7–8), while Jesus preached only to Israel (Matt. 15:24).

78   *The Hope of Glory*

his contemporaries during his earthly ministry. The result of such an investigation will certainly not be a comprehensive checklist of Christian callings, for the subsequent history of the church in the context of the ever-evolving character of human society counsels a good deal of modesty when it comes to venturing *a priori* judgments about which forms of life have a place in the body of Christ. Evaluating putative vocations will always be inseparable from *a posteriori* reflection on their effect on the life of the body: specifically, do they build it up or not?[40] Thus, while the number of callings depicted in the Gospels is small, attending to the kinds of demands Jesus made of his contemporaries does provide a basis for further reflection on the basic character and limits of Christian vocation. We will examine briefly three accounts of Jesus calling persons to a new form of life, each of which also reflects in a particular way the patterns of solidarity that define Jesus as the object of Christian hope.

Peter the Jew (Matt. 4:18–20)

Not only was Jesus a Jew, but so also were his closest disciples, giving concrete form to the principle that the world's salvation both begins with and is mediated through the people of Israel. If Gentiles are called to the kingdom, it is only because Jews have been called first; and the calling of the Jew Simon Peter in particular has near iconic status, for a number of reasons. Most obviously, all four Gospels place it at the very beginning of Jesus' public ministry (albeit with significant differences between the Synoptic and Johannine accounts), and the Matthean version is undeniably dramatic:

> As [Jesus] walked by the Sea of Galilee, he saw two brothers, Simon, who is called Peter, and Andrew his brother, casting a net into the sea—for they were fishers. And he said to them, "Follow me, and I will make you fishers of people." Immediately they left their nets and followed him. (Matt. 4:18–20; cf. Mark 1:16–18)[41]

To be sure, the form of Peter's call is by no means unique. All four evangelists tie it closely with that of his brother Andrew, and the first three join it to that of James and John, their fishermen colleagues, as well (see Matt. 4:21–22 and pars.). Later on in the Gospel story, the tax collector Matthew is reported to have responded to an equally imperious summons (Matt. 9:9).[42] But Peter's status as the most prominent of the Twelve (indicated by his being listed first among them in Matt. 10:2; 17:1 and pars., as well as in passages like Matt. 16:18;

---

40. "'All things are permitted,' but not all things are beneficial. 'All things are permitted,' but not all things build up" (1 Cor. 10:23; cf. 14:12; Eph. 4:12; 1 Thess. 5:11).

41. In contrast to the suddenness of the call in Matthew and Mark, both Luke and John provide more context, which has the effect of making Peter's decision to follow Jesus seem less sudden: in Luke Jesus only calls Peter after teaching from his boat and helping him to a miraculous catch of fish (5:1–11), while in John Peter's call is actually mediated through his brother Andrew, who was already a follower of John the Baptist and started following Jesus before Peter did (1:35–42).

42. While all three Synoptic Gospels report Jesus' calling of a tax collector in similarly arresting terms, only the first evangelist names him Matthew and includes him among the Twelve (see Matt. 10:3). Mark and Luke give his name as Levi (Mark 2:14; Luke 5:27–28) and do not identify him with the "Matthew" they list among the Twelve (whom they also do not describe as a tax collector; cf. Mark 3:18; Luke 6:15).

3. "Jesus Our Hope"

Luke 22:31–32; John 6:67–69; Acts 1:15–22; Gal. 1:18) make it natural that the biblical account of his vocation should assume special prominence.

Like the rest of the Twelve, Peter is sent out already during Jesus' lifetime to undertake the same ministry of teaching, healing, and exorcism practiced by Jesus himself (Matt. 10:1, 5–8; cf. Mark 3:14–15; Luke 10:1–9). But he is also treated by the evangelists (for better or worse) as the spokesperson for all the disciples (e.g., Matt. 15:15; 17:4 and pars.; 18:21–22 and pars.). Both these aspects of Peter's ministry continue after Jesus' ascension (see, e.g., Acts 1:15–22; 2:14–40; 3:1–10; 5:14–16; 9:32–41), after which Peter's missionary focus on the Jews mirrors Jesus' own (cf. Gal. 2:7–8 and Matt. 15:24). Whether or not he ever had a formal position of leadership in the church at Rome, Peter was clearly a figure of authority in the early church: one of the "acknowledged pillars" (Gal. 2:9), who by tradition also suffered death by crucifixion.[43]

All the same, it is by no means the case that the Gospels portray Peter in a uniformly positive light. Like the rest of Jesus' closest disciples, he is often obtuse (see, e.g., Matt. 16:5–12 and pars.; Mark 6:51–52). When Jesus summons him to walk on the water, his fear causes him to sink, earning him a dominical rebuke (Matt. 14:26–31). And if Peter is praised for recognizing Jesus' status as the Christ (Matt. 16:17–19), his objection to the prospect that this role would lead to suffering and death leads almost immediately to Jesus upbraiding him in the harshest possible terms: "Get behind me, Satan! You are a stumbling block to me" (Matt. 16:23 alt.).[44] He is unable to stay awake with Jesus in Gethsemane (Matt. 26:36–46 and pars.), and, along with the rest of the disciples, flees at his arrest (Matt. 26:56b and pars.). Worst of all, when challenged to acknowledge Jesus—the very act that Jesus himself had elsewhere said would be the criterion of a person's inclusion in the kingdom (Matt. 10:32–33)—Peter denies him not just once, but three times (Matt. 26:69–75 and pars.). Nor does this pattern stop after Easter: in spite of his status as a "pillar," Peter remains capable of hypocritical behavior that in one case leads to a public dressing down by Paul (Gal. 2:11–14).

The upshot of all this is that Peter is a genuinely ambivalent figure. He is widely recognized as a leader of the early Christian movement. Yet although the shape of his own vocation seems to involve as direct an imitation of Jesus' ministry as any possibly could, he cuts a very different figure: enthusiastic, but often unreliable and seemingly ever unaware of his own shortcomings—as

---

43. The tradition that Peter was martyred at Rome is very early, and it stands to reason that someone of his prominence would exercise a position of influence among the Christians of any city where he lived. At the same time, evidence of a monarchical episcopacy at Rome before the latter half of the second century is notable for its absence: there is no hint of such a figure in 1 *Clement* (whose eponymous author seems more secretary than pope, since the salutation describes the letter not as from him but rather from "the church of God . . . in Rome [Prologue]," and its original title seems to have been simply "The Letter of the Romans to the Corinthians"), in the letters of Ignatius of Antioch (who was not only familiar with but also a staunch supporter of the episcopal office), or in the writings of Justin Martyr (who was a member of the Roman church). For the text of 1 *Clement*, see *Early Christian Fathers*, ed. Cyril C. Richardson (New York: Macmillan, 1970), 43, 73.

44. The only other person in the Gospels whom Jesus calls "Satan" is Satan himself (Matt. 4:10). While Jesus can call his opponents "hypocrites" (Matt. 15:7 and par.; 22:18; 23:13, 15, 23, 25, 27, 29; Luke 12:56; 13:15), "brood of vipers" (Matt. 12:34; 23:33), and even the devil's children (John 8:44), Peter is the only one he explicitly identifies with the devil (though cf. John 6:70–71).

80   *The Hope of Glory*

Jesus himself is ruthless in pointing out (see Matt. 26:33–34 and pars.).[45] And yet for all that Jesus rebukes him, he never abandons him; quite the contrary, in the wake of his disciples' collective failure to remain faithful, Jesus assigns Peter in particular the task of strengthening his companions (Luke 22:31–32; cf. John 21:15–19). We also learn that despite Peter's own missionary focus on the Jews, he was not only instrumental in extending the church's mission to the Gentiles but also had the courage to defend this initially controversial practice before the Jerusalem church (Acts 10; 15:1–11). His designation as "the rock" (the meaning of his Greek nickname *petros*; see Matt. 16:18) is therefore not ironic, or at least not finally so: for Peter is the one on whom Jesus builds the church precisely as someone who can and does persevere not by his own strength or merit, but solely by the faithfulness of the God of Israel—and thus as a Jew (Rom. 4:13–16).

Zacchaeus the Sinner (Luke 19:1–10)

The reader is told that Zacchaeus is a rich man, certainly far more prosperous than Peter. Like Peter, he, too, is a Jew, though as a tax collector he would have been shunned by his coreligionists as a collaborator with the occupying power of Rome. And if that were not bad enough, he is also a sinner who exploits his position for personal gain (or so we may surmise from what he himself eventually discloses about himself). As already noted, Jesus had a reputation of being a friend to tax collectors and sinners alike, but the text suggests that initially the only thing drawing Zacchaeus to Jesus was idle curiosity: he wanted "to see who Jesus was" (v. 3). Being short, he could not see over the heads of the crowd, so he ran ahead and climbed a sycamore tree to get a better view (v. 4).

It is from this perch that Jesus calls him: "Zacchaeus, hurry and come down, for I must stay at your house today" (v. 5). And Zacchaeus obeys: with all the alacrity shown by Peter at the seashore, "he hurried down and was happy to welcome him" (v. 6). Admittedly, Jesus demands of Zacchaeus much less than he had asked of Peter (or of that other tax collector, Matthew)—nothing more than an evening's hospitality. Yet Zacchaeus commits himself to much more than that: "Look, half of my possessions, Lord, I will give to the poor; and if I have defrauded anyone of anything, I will pay back four times as much" (v. 8). And in response to this unsolicited pledge, Jesus makes an equally startling declaration unique in the Gospels: "Today salvation has come to this house, because he, too, is a son of Abraham" (v. 9).[46]

And that is all. The episode comes to an end, the narrative moves on, and the figure of Zacchaeus drops out of view, never to resurface, either in Luke's Gospel or anywhere else in the New Testament. There is no suggestion that

---

45. At the same time, if the account of Papias, according to which the second Gospel is the reminiscences of Peter as recorded by Mark, who "took especial care, not to omit anything he had heard, and not to put anything fictitious into the statements," then Peter should be accorded the highest marks for honesty in giving such a full account of his own faults. For Papias, see *Fragments of Papias*, in *The Apostolic Fathers, with Justin Martyr and Irenaeus*, vol. 1 of *The Ante-Nicene Fathers*, ed. Alexander Roberts and James Donaldson (Grand Rapids: William B. Eerdmans Publishing Co., 1985 [1885]), 155.

46. Elsewhere Jesus says to individuals, "Your faith has saved [*sesōken*] you" (Matt. 9:22 and pars.; Luke 7:50; 18:42), but these are all in response to particular sins or illnesses; the story of Zacchaeus is the only place where Jesus offers a comprehensive declaration of salvation [*sōtēria*] with respect to an individual and his household.

3. "Jesus Our Hope"

his call resulted in a change of career. Jesus does not ask him to give up his current occupation to follow him on the road. Presumably, he went back to his tax collecting, albeit with an implied commitment to share with the poor and to refrain from extortion (cf. Luke 3:12–13). Although Jesus' call to him is as explicit as any described in the Gospels, its effects at first glance seem notably less dramatic, however practically beneficial we may imagine Zacchaeus's reformed character might prove for his fellow citizens in Jericho.

And yet given that it is only here in the Gospels that Jesus declares that salvation has already come to a person answering his call, there is evidently more to Zacchaeus's vocation than a conversion to more responsible public service. For if with respect to its effect on his immediate situation the calling of Zacchaeus is less dramatic than that of Peter, who leaves everything to follow Jesus, it stands out for the fact that the shape of his vocation is evidently discerned from within rather than dictated from without. Jesus tells Peter to follow him, but Zacchaeus is not told to do anything other than to come down from the tree. Jesus states his intention to come to Zacchaeus's house, but according to Luke the tax collector's change of heart happened while "Zacchaeus stood there" and thus before Jesus ever went under his roof. Remarkably, Zacchaeus manages to articulate the implications of Jesus' calling him without Jesus giving him any direct instruction about what he should do. Even as a tax collector, a way of life seemingly without hope because in every way remote from Jesus' vision of God's reign (see especially Matt. 17:24–27), Zacchaeus discerns a way to bear witness to the kingdom's presence and power—and thereby receives the good news of salvation.

The Gerasene Outcast (Mark 5:1–20)

The central figure in this story is typically described as "the Gerasene demoniac," and his story is generally characterized as an exorcism. Yet there is much to be gained from framing this story less as a tale of miraculous healing (though it is certainly also that) than of vocation, in which a person utterly alienated from society finds a new place and purpose within it. The outcast is an obscure figure. Like Zacchaeus, he appears only in this one episode in the New Testament, but we know much less about him than we know about the short, corrupt tax collector from Jericho. None of his words are recorded: all the direct speech that Mark reports coming from his lips is evidently to be ascribed to the unclean spirits within him (see vv. 6–12). We are not told his ethnicity or where he is from (though we learn in v. 1 that Jesus encounters him in "the region of the Gerasenes," part of the predominantly Gentile region known as the Decapolis).[47] We are given no information about any sins he may have committed. Indeed, we do not even know his name. What we do know is that (in contrast to Peter, whose situation prior to meeting Jesus appears to have been one of modest but settled prosperity, or Zacchaeus, who, however much an

---

47. Matthew (8:28–33) associates this story with Gadara, another city of the Decapolis, but closer to the Sea of Galilee than Gerasa.

object of opprobrium, was both wealthy and secure) he was a person in truly desperate straits: out of his mind, exiled from society to dwell among the dead, an object of fear who "had often been restrained with shackles and chains" (v. 4), and whose misery is summed up with the report that "Night and day among the tombs and on the mountains he was always howling and bruising himself with stones" (v. 5).

Jesus responds to his need by casting out the demons who possess him, sending them into a herd of swine who, immediately set raving, stampede down the hill and plunge into the Sea of Galilee, where they drown. For a Jewish audience the account of demons begging to be sent into (unclean) pigs and then drowning in a lake would doubtless have had a humorous dimension; but this graphic illustration of the number of spirits exorcised also highlights the terrible plight of the demoniac. Moreover, it is important to note that the immediate effect of Jesus' exorcism on the man's situation was not as positive as one might expect. The evangelist reports that in response to the mad dash of the pigs, the swineherds ran off to report what had happened, with the result that a great crowd assembled: "They came to Jesus and saw the man possessed by demons sitting there, clothed and in his right mind, the very man who had had the legion; and they became frightened" (v. 15). The man was healed—no longer raving or harming himself—but he is not welcomed back into society; instead, he remains an object of fear.

It is at this point that the matter of vocation arises. The crowd begs Jesus to leave their territory, and we are told that the following transpired:

> As [Jesus] was getting into the boat, the man who had been possessed by demons begged him that he might be with him. But Jesus refused, and said to him, "Go home to your own people, and tell them how much the Lord has done for you and what mercy he has shown you." And he went away and began to proclaim in the Decapolis how much Jesus had done for him, and everyone was amazed. (vv. 18–20)

Given the local population's lack of enthusiasm over his recovery, it is perhaps not surprising that the man wants to follow Jesus in much the same way Peter had done. But Jesus rejects his advances. Instead, he calls him to a different task: "Go home to your own people, and tell them how much the Lord has done for you and what mercy he has shown you." His vocation, too, is one of bearing witness to Jesus, but at a distance. Still more significantly, in light of Jesus' focus on proclaiming the gospel to Israel, we are told that the healed demoniac fulfilled his calling by speaking in the Decapolis—that is, among the non-Jewish, Greco-Roman colonial cities of the Levant (one of which was Gerasa itself).

In this episode Jesus' calling reaches into the depths of human misery—the poorest of the "poor in spirit." Given the demoniac's level of social marginalization and helplessness prior to his being healed, one might expect that he would subsequently exhibit a far greater degree of ongoing dependence on Jesus than the former fisherman Peter. And yet Jesus calls him to a life of significant independence by sending him away to tell the story of God's mercy in his life unsupervised, without (as far as we know) any subsequent contact with Jesus or his inner circle. Of course, he remains dependent upon Jesus as

3. *"Jesus Our Hope"* 83

the one who gave him the command to go and tell his story. But this passage nevertheless serves as a powerful reminder that although vocation is rooted in divine address, God's aim in calling people is not to undermine their integrity as responsible agents, but rather to empower them: freeing them from captivity to forces that diminish and destroy in order to enable them to witness to the coming of God's kingdom into the world. In this way, a central message of this story is that part of what it means to be called is to be trusted to live out that call, as Jesus trusts the demoniac, in spite of his past incapacities, to operate on his own, using his own judgment to carry out the work to which he has been called—with the result that "everyone was amazed."

❖❖❖❖❖❖❖❖❖

These three examples are hardly exhaustive of the range of Christian vocations, even within the relatively narrow compass of Scripture. But they do give a sense of how vocation is both dependent on and able to sustain hope in this life. Because to be called is to be addressed by God, calling exemplifies the shift in the divine economy from the grace of creation to the grace of redemption. In creation God shapes identity in a hidden manner, through the complex interactions between a person's intrinsic qualities ("nature") and various external environmental factors ("nurture"); in redemption God, while still making use of the created elements that shape every human life both within and without, summons the individual to take on a particular form of existence that may diverge sharply from the possibilities suggested by their native endowments and context. Because all things were made through the Word (John 1:3), human life is no less shaped by God in creation than in redemption, but in redemption the shaping is direct: by calling us to a particular form of life, God discloses to us the mystery of who we are as creatures destined for glory.

And yet there are plenty of examples of human beings finding themselves drawn to a radically new way of life without their ascribing this to an encounter with the God of Israel (the Buddha in the ancient world and Gandhi in the modern come to mind). And even within the church, the discernment of vocation is rarely the product of the sort of direct encounter with the *viva vox Dei* experienced by Abraham or Paul. It tends to be a rather slow, laborious, and uncertain process, in which the immediate reference points are the weighing of one's own perceived abilities on the one hand, and the possibilities afforded by one's immediate environment (including especially expressions of encouragement or dissuasion by one's neighbors) on the other; and the result in the overwhelming majority of cases is a form of life that in its basic features does not look all that different from that of people who have no sense of their having a vocation in the theological sense of that term.

All the same—and for all the various ways in which the church has in practice done as much to stifle as to enhance individuals' efforts to respond faithfully to God's call—vocation is not an empty concept. That God's call is typically mediated through other creatures should come as no surprise when it is remembered that in redemption God seeks precisely to honor our being as creatures, and thus to engage us using creaturely means. Again, this commitment to creaturely being is intrinsic to the logic of the incarnation itself,

84   *The Hope of Glory*

as exemplified by the fact that Peter, Zacchaeus, and the Gerasene demoniac (in contrast to Abraham and Paul) were not called by a disembodied heavenly voice, but by a Palestinian Jew whose appearance was in many ways decidedly unexceptional (cf. Mark 6:3; Luke 4:23–24). Moreover, the point of a vocation is not to extract a person from the world, but rather to place her more firmly in it by giving her the assurance that her future, while certainly shaped by her own peculiar combination of character and circumstance, is secured through (and, often enough, in spite of) these factors by God's own word. In this way, to affirm the reality of vocation is to believe that all Abraham's children also receive Abraham's promise: "Do not be afraid. . . . I am your shield; your reward shall be very great" (Gen. 15:1).

Such assurance provides the basis for continuing to pursue one's vocation even when the prospects look dim. For to hope—to hold to what cannot be seen but which has been promised—is to refuse to reduce the possibilities of the future to the results of present calculation. After all, to say that we hope for that which we do not see is to confess that hope always subsists in the context of lack—the recognition that our current condition is one in which we do not possess and cannot guarantee hope's fulfillment. Thus, it certainly can happen that for a person the experience of suffering overwhelms a commitment to hope, there is no inherent incompatibility between the two.[48] Indeed, just to the extent that the co-existence of suffering and hope is taken seriously, genuine hope will never be fanciful. If Peter, for example, continued on his path, it was not because he has any illusions about his earthly future, for Jesus had explicitly warned him, "when you were younger, you used to fasten your own belt and to go wherever you wished. But when you grow old, you will stretch out your hands, and someone else will fasten a belt around you and take you where you do not wish to go" (John 21:18). Lest there be any doubt as to what this means, the evangelist immediately adds that Jesus "said this to indicate the kind of death by which [Peter] would glorify God," and yet the verse continues: "After this [Jesus] said to him, 'Follow me'" (John 21:19). And Peter followed.

Christian hope is for an ultimate vindication that cannot be measured by worldly success, as Jesus himself makes clear: "In the world you face persecution, but take courage: I have conquered the world" (John 16:33). This doesn't mean that the Christian hope is for some other world—the deferred gratification of "pie in the sky when you die." That would just return us to the problem of false hope in which present suffering has no significance beyond that of a (highly variable) price of admission to future glory. We see this already in Jesus, whose resurrection and ascension do not mean transportation to an alternative timeline on some higher ontological plane. After all, Jesus can rise only because he has died, and death marks the end of his life, which is defined by the period extending from Christmas to Good Friday. Indeed, if Jesus' life were to have any further extension beyond that timespan (let alone one of infinite extent),

---

48. As Thomas Joseph White notes, the combination of the expectation and non-possession of hope's object renders hope "a complex virtue" in which "the states of desire, sadness, deprivation, and agony can and often do coexist." In this context, the fact that Jesus suffers on the cross does not count against his hope, but rather displays sharply the fact that hope subsists under the sign of its contradiction. See Thomas Joseph White, OP, *The Incarnate Lord: A Thomistic Study in Christology* (Washington, DC: Catholic University of America Press, 2015), 319 (with reference to Aquinas, *ST* 3.46.7–8).

3. "Jesus Our Hope"

then he could not be our hope, for we would have to entertain the possibility that what followed after his departure might qualify or even completely reverse the message of his earthly ministry.[49] The resurrection is good news because it is the vindication of Jesus' earthly life as the fullness of God's life (Col. 1:19; 2:9); and just as Christians do not hope for any Jesus other than the one whose life began in Bethlehem and ended on a Roman cross, so they do not hope for life that replaces the one they live now. Quite the contrary, because Jesus is our hope, we hope that our lives will be joined to his, and thus affirmed in their this-worldly reality. In short, that for which Christians hope in Christ is the glorification of their *present* lives, that life on earth—with all its failures and limits and loss—should somehow be confirmed as a thing capable of bearing an eternal weight of glory (2 Cor. 4:17).[50]

But how can this be? How can our lives now, which to a greater or lesser extent are all marked by suffering, be glorified without thereby glorifying suffering? Or, alternatively, how can one vindicate sinners without also vindicating their sin? At one level, this is just to ask how human life, which in our this-worldly experience can be sustained only amid countless and often conflicting interactions with other creatures, can be sustained solely by God's word, alongside of but no longer either constrained by or constraining the lives of other creatures. At another, it is to ask how there can be such a thing as forgiveness. For in both cases it strains credulity to suppose that the truth about human persons can be separated from the past relationships that constitute— irreversibly—their history. And here, once again, the claim that "hope that is seen is not hope" is at once both the only possible response and a genuine problem, because if for Christians Jesus discloses God's irrevocable will for life in the face of suffering and evil, he does not thereby render any less mysterious the presence of suffering and evil in a world founded and sustained by a God who is confessed to be at once all-powerful and infinitely good. Before talking about the glory that God promises, it is therefore worth pausing to explore the implications of the mystery of evil for Christian talk about hope.

---

49. See p. 7 above.

50. In this context, the point of evangelization is not rightly conceived as "saving" people in the sense of guaranteeing them a spot in another world (whether conceived "horizontally" as in the future or "vertically" up in heaven), because any such framing of the gospel reduces the present life to a means toward a kingdom that is fundamentally elsewhere, which is inconsistent with Jesus' message that the kingdom is "at hand" and, indeed, "among you" (Luke 17:21b). If the Spirit is truly active in people's lives now, then the task of the Christian preaching is to help people discern what place God is calling them to in the kingdom now, in the conviction that God saves people not by removing them from this life, but rather by claiming their lives here and now as fit objects of glorification. "Being saved has to do with the part we are playing *now* in God's story and therefore with the question whether we have understood the story rightly." Lesslie Newbigin, *The Gospel in a Pluralist Society* (London: SPCK, 1989), 179 (emphasis added).

Interlude

4. The Mystery of Evil and the Limits of Eschatology

Christians claim that Jesus is the incarnation of God's Word, and because this Word was with God "in the beginning," they confess that he is God (John 1:1), of the very same substance as the one he called "Father." It is on the grounds of his being identified with God in this way that Jesus may be proclaimed as the one in whom "the whole fullness of deity dwells bodily" (Col. 2:9; cf. 1:19). Likewise, Jesus can be called Savior on the basis of the conviction that in encountering him and hearing his words, we encounter the presence and hear the words of none other than God. For only the God who created all things from nothing, and whose will for the fulfillment of creation can therefore be impeded by nothing, can be trusted to save creatures from every conceivable threat to their well-being. Therefore, only if Jesus is God is it possible to defend the claim that "there is no other name under heaven given among mortals by which we must be saved" (Acts 4:12).

But just here, at the heart of the Christian confession of Jesus as the one who brings salvation, stands a problem. For the very fact that creatures need saving indicates that their well-being is under threat, and this seemingly cannot be the case if the world as a whole and in every part is as utterly dependent on God's will as the Christian doctrine of creation teaches. For since Christians teach that God, being goodness itself, wills only the good, it follows (in line with the teaching of Gen. 1:31) that everything God wills to exist is good. But since it is also Christian teaching that nothing exists except by virtue of God's willing that it should, then it is seemingly impossible that anything could arise to threaten the well-being of creation. And yet something does.

"Evil" is the name given to this something. As that which threatens what God has willed to be, it may be defined as that which is counter to God's will. And yet just because God wills only the good, and because nothing can exist except by God's will, there is and can be no accounting for evil—no explanation of how there might exist any state of affairs that is counter to God's will. Evil is therefore a mystery, but it is not an illusion. Evil is real enough for God to hate it (Zech. 8:17; cf. Amos 5:15; Rom. 12:9); and it acquires this reality through sin, which may be defined as those actions of creatures in and through which they oppose God's will and so pervert God's intentions for creation.[1] But to locate

---

1. At the same time, it must be acknowledged that Scripture seems to view the reality of sin and evil as in some respect prior to and independent of human actions, such that sinful actions do not arise spontaneously in the human will but rather are incited by external forces. This certainly is the implication of the role of the serpent in Eden (Gen. 3:1–7), as well as of God's warning to Cain that "sin

90   The Hope of Glory

the source of evil in this way does not render it any more explicable. For the creature's dependence on God is so complete that its least action is only possible as God wills it to act, and it is a sheer contradiction to suppose that God might will it to act counter to God's own will. Indeed, the problem of contradiction arises even if sin is considered solely from the perspective of the creature, whose absolute dependence on God means that resistance to God's will constitutes a rejection of the very conditions of its own existence that amounts to an act of self-destruction. And the mystery is only deepened when it is recognized that even as the creature undermines the conditions of its own existence by sinning, the fact that it nevertheless continues to exist (since it can sin only if it exists) shows that God wills otherwise. In this way, even the mystery by which an omnipotent God somehow "permits" sin and the evil that follows from it serves as a strange witness to God's resistance to it.[2]

Yet however seemingly impossible it is that evil should succeed in thwarting God's will that creatures should be and flourish, it is Christian teaching that the sinner's rejection of God, if uncorrected, will inevitably find its fulfillment in a state of final and irreversible estrangement from God traditionally referred to as death and damnation. Since God wills that the sinner should live and not die (Ezek. 33:11), this outcome, too, can only be described as evil—indeed, as the ultimate evil, the final defeat of God's will for creation. Yet while evil's reality is seemingly demonstrated precisely by God's willing that it should *not* be even in the midst of the devastation it wreaks on the created order, the fact that nothing can exist unless God wills that it *should* be means that the *kind* of reality evil has is not clear.

The question may be put as follows: If God's will is the cause of all reality other than God, and if God does not will evil, is it possible to say that evil is real for God? That is, granted that sin is the creature's refusal to live in communion with God (since such communion is precisely the content of the divine will that the creature opposes in sinning), does this refusal block God's ability to live with the creature? The witness of Scripture is ambiguous. On the one hand, the fact that it speaks of God reconciling the sinful world to God's self and not the other way round (2 Cor. 5:19) implies that the answer to this question is no: since it is the creature—and not God—who needs to be reconciled, it would seem to follow that sin and evil have no effect on God's love for (and thus on God's ability to *be* for) creatures. On the other hand, the Bible's frequent references to God's condemnation of sinners suggest that evil and sin *are* real for God, in the sense that even amid the patience whereby God sustains the existence of sinners, God also pronounces judgment against them, and in so doing wills their (eventual) destruction (Rom. 2:5–10; 3:5–6; cf. 2 Thess. 2:11–12).

Nor does the revelation of God in Jesus resolve this tension; for however true it may be that Jesus came into the world to save rather than to judge

---

is lurking at the door; its desire is for you, but you must master it" (Gen. 4:7); but both passages also imply that these external forces (whatever their origin may be) are unable to give rise to the worldly effects that are the object of God's hatred until and unless human beings give into them.

2. See pp. 48–49 above for a more detailed discussion of the language of divine permission.

4. The Mystery of Evil and the Limits of Eschatology 91

(John 3:17; 12:47), it is nevertheless the case that judgment has been given to him (John 5:22, 27), and the biblical witness is insistent that he will exercise it when he comes again in glory (Matt. 25:31–46; cf. Acts 10:42; 2 Tim. 4:1). This ambiguity poses a significant challenge to Christian claims about Jesus and the God whose will he reveals. For if in Jesus the fullness of God's will for creation is disclosed, and this will is for the world's salvation (see, e.g., 1 Tim. 2:3–4), then how can evil be viewed as having any claim on—and therefore to constitute any real threat to—any creature's ultimate well-being? And yet if evil is so insubstantial that its threat is ultimately illusory, then what need is there for us to be saved from it—let alone at the cost of God's own life on the cross?

This ambiguity points to the limits of eschatology. Of course, eschatology is not the only place where theology faces limits. What Søren Kierkegaard famously called the "infinite qualitative difference" between Creator and creation dictates that all human talk about God, conditioned as is by our location within the world, will necessarily fall short when applied to the One who transcends the world.[3] But the way in which the question of evil's reality constrains our ability to talk about our future with God, and thus of the Christian hope, illustrates theology's limits in a very particular way. For the question of evil's reality for God allows for only two mutually exclusive answers: either evil is real for God, or it isn't. And the answer one chooses defines two equally exclusive theological alternatives: for if evil is real for God, then Christian hope seems necessarily qualified by the threat evil poses; but if it is not, then the very grammar of salvation (i.e., the claim that there is a life-threatening situation from which we need to be saved) seems compromised. In the first case Christian hope must be refused as finally unequal to the reality of evil that stands in the way of its fulfillment; and in the second case hope is unnecessary, since evil is merely an illusion and therefore not a genuine problem that needs to be overcome.

If the biblical commendation of a hope that does not disappoint means that it is not possible for the church to accept either of these options, then this only serves to highlight once again eschatology's limits, for the choice between the ultimate reality or unreality of evil appears to be both exhaustive and mutually exclusive. The problem is all the more serious in that a theologically compelling case can be made for each of these two mutually exclusive positions, as I will try to show by comparing two texts in which the question of the reality of evil for God is engaged with particular clarity and power: Julian of Norwich's *Showings* and Martin Luther's *Bondage of the Will*. There are, of course, other differences between these two texts that have nothing to do with their respective stances on the reality of evil. Julian's book is a tightly focused set of meditations on a series of visions, over which she reflected for many years before committing them to paper in the final form known as the "Long Text."[4] By contrast,

---

3. See Søren Kierkegaard, *Training in Christianity and the Edifying Discourse Which "Accompanied" It*, trans. Walter Lowrie (Princeton, NJ: Princeton University Press, 1944), 139.

4. Julian states that it took her "twenty yere after the tyme of the shewing, save thre monthys" for her to acquire sufficient confidence in her understanding of the famous parable of the lord and the servant (about which more below) to set it down. Julian of Norwich, *The Showings of Julian of Norwich*, ed. Denise N. Baker (New York: W. W. Norton, 2005), 72 (ch. 51).

92   *The Hope of Glory*

Luther's treatise is a sprawling theological polemic that was written quickly and in the heat of controversy.[5] Moreover, conventional readings of both texts tend to magnify the substantive differences between them in unproductive ways, with Julian cast as a dogmatic universalist and Luther as a defender of a rigid scheme of double predestination. Not only are both of these characterizations incorrect, but they obscure the significant amount of common ground the two theologians share. This is certainly not to deny the very real differences between the two texts—it is just their differences that I wish to highlight—but it is to argue that these differences are combined with a shared sense of the difficulty of reckoning with eschatology's limits that is far more profound than casual readings might suggest.

Indeed, it is precisely the clarity with which these two treatises bring Julian's and Luther's *shared* commitments to the fore that makes comparative examination of them theologically productive. For the two authors not only sketch out their own (contrasting) positions on the question of the reality of evil for God with great care, but also draw attention to the theologically troublesome consequences of their respective stances. Thus, if the two treatises illustrate different views on the question of evil's reality for God, this comes out of their authors' struggle with the same fundamental problem: how the conviction that Jesus Christ represents the definitive revelation of God's will for the world is to be reconciled with the acknowledgment that what has been revealed in Jesus does not resolve the problem of evil—and thus does not disclose everything about God's ways with the world.

Of course, it would be hard to name a Christian theologian of any standing who does not wrestle with the relationship between what of God is revealed and what remains hidden. The treatments found in *Showings* and *Bondage of the Will* stand out because in them Julian and Luther both take great care to keep these two contrasting dimensions of Christian belief in equipoise. But because in the quest to communicate the essence of the good news of Jesus Christ the question of the reality of sin and evil for God cannot be avoided, their efforts at maintaining this balance cannot hold, and the different judgments they make on this point cause their theologies to crystallize in strikingly different—and divergent—ways.

When read carelessly, each text can all too easily seem to convict its author of theological overreach—of presuming to say more about God than the biblical evidence warrants. As already noted, Julian may be criticized for leaving no place for judgment, and Luther for allowing the prospect of judgment to overwhelm the promise of the gospel. But careful reading shows that such charges are misplaced.[6] For while it is true that neither writer is inclined to prevaricate when it comes to declaring what they hold to be the fundamental truth about

---

5. In a letter written soon after completing *Bondage of the Will*, Luther describes it as having been written "as best I could in a short time and in a hurry" ("To Michael Stifel," in *Luther's Works* [hereafter *LW*] 49, 140). Still, Luther clearly retained a personal fondness for this text: in a letter from 1537, he pairs it with his *Small Catechism* as the only of his writings worth keeping in print (see "To Wolfgang Capito," in *LW* 50, 172–73).

6. For prominent rebuttals of these caricatures, see, e.g., Denys Turner, *Julian of Norwich, Theologian* (New Haven, CT: Yale University Press, 2011); and Gerhard O. Forde, *The Captivation of the Will: Luther vs. Erasmus on Freedom and Bondage*, ed. Stephen Paulson (Grand Rapids: William B. Eerdmans, 2005).

4. The Mystery of Evil and the Limits of Eschatology   93

God and God's ways with the world, for both this forthrightness is coupled with an explicit (and repeated) recognition of the limits of their ability to speak about God: convinced that Christ reveals God's response to sin and evil, they nevertheless recognize that Christ does not reveal why God permits either to arise in the first place—and thus precisely what either means for God. It is the fact that this shared commitment nevertheless gives rise to sharply divergent judgments about the nature of the threat evil poses for creation that renders consideration of their work instructive for Christian eschatology.

The Case of Julian

In the case of Julian of Norwich, talk of a writer having a theological "vision" is not simply metaphorical. It is not just that her writing is explicitly based on the series of sixteen visions that she had on May 13, 1373, but that she strictly delimits her theological reflections to the content of what she saw on that day, in the wake of being shown a crucifix and instructed, "Looke ther upon and comfort thee ther with."[7] While not all of the revelations that followed have the crucified Jesus (or, for that matter, any corporeal form) as their object, nevertheless the "bodely sight" of Jesus' suffering remains the focal point of Julian's experience, "in which all the shewynges that foloweth be groundide and joined."[8] Not surprisingly, the theology that results is radically christocentric, to the extent that she refuses to contemplate God at all except in and through Jesus:

> Then had I a profyr [proposal] in my reason, as it had ben frendely seyde to me, "Loke uppe to hevyn to hys [Jesus'] Father." And than sawe I wele with the feyth that I felt that ther was nothing betwene the crosse and hevyn that myght have dysseyde [troubled] me. Here . . . I answeryd inwardly with alle the myght of my soule and sayd, "Nay, I may nott, for thou art my hevyn. . . ." Thus was I lernyd to chese Jhesu for my hevyn. . . . And that hath ben a lernyng to me that I shulde evyr more do so, to chese Jhesu only to be my hevyn in wele and in woe.[9]

Because Jesus is God, Julian reasons, he is not to be treated simply as a means to some putatively higher experience of divinity; rather, to see Jesus is to see the Father (cf. John 12:45; 14:9), such that to presume to look for the Father above or beyond him is precisely to have failed to understand who Jesus is. For Julian there just is no God but the one who is revealed—and thus seen—in Jesus.

And yet neither does Julian understand the fullness of God to be exhausted by Jesus. On the contrary, it is just her vision of Jesus that testifies to the fact that God is not simply reducible to him, but is Trinity: Father and Spirit as well

7. Julian, *Showings*, 7 (ch. 3).
8. Julian, *Showings*, 3 (ch. 1). Direct ("bodily") vision of Jesus' wounded body is the content of Revelations I, II, IV, VIII, and X. By contrast, Julian describes Revelation XI as a "ghostly [spiritual] shewing" of Mary (4, ch. 1) that she explicitly contrasts with bodily vision: "Often tymes I preyed . . . to have seen her in bodily lykyng, but I saw her not so." Instead, "Jhesu . . . shewyd me a gostly syght of her" (38, ch. 25). The relationship between physical ("bodily") and spiritual ("gostly") vision in Julian's thought is complex, as seen in her description of the "shewyng" of the lord and the servant, where she contrasts one part "shewed gostly in bodely lycknesse" with another "more gostly withoute bodely lycknes" (70, ch. 51).
9. Julian, *Showings*, 31 (ch. 19).

94 *The Hope of Glory*

as Son.[10] Nevertheless, precisely because what Julian finds revealed in Jesus is nothing less than God's triune identity, she also insists that she has no resource for talking about God other than what she sees in Jesus. Again, to suppose otherwise would be to deny the significance of Jesus as the revelation of the one God.

Because of Julian's restriction of her theological conclusions to that which she can derive from her vision of Christ, where those visions do not touch on established church teachings, Julian's response is not to reject those teachings, but simply to note that she only speaks of what she has seen. For example, early on in the text, having affirmed that her vision of God's goodness as revealed in Christ must be a source of comfort to all that have need of it, she adds a double qualification: first, "I speke of them that shalle be savyd, for in this tyme God shewde me no nother"; and then the additional assurance that "in all thing I believe as holy chyrch prechyth and techyth . . . wyllyng and meanyng never to receyve ony thyng that might be contrary ther to."[11] In short, while she speaks (and speaks with absolute conviction) of what she has seen, she acknowledges that there is other Christian teaching, affirmed by the church, to which her visions do not speak, but which she also accepts as true.[12]

The problem is that the more Julian reflects on what she has seen, the more her theological conclusions appear not just different from official church teaching, but opposed to it. Thus, although she clearly states that what she sees of God's mercy pertains only to those who are saved, as the content of her visions unfolds, one cannot avoid asking how, if what she has seen is true, any will *not* be saved. The tension here builds to the breaking point when Julian concludes on the basis of what she has seen that the very possibility that God might be wrathful with human beings at any point—let alone eternally—is simply excluded:

> we be synners and do many evylles . . . wherefore we deserve payne, blame, and wrath. And nott withstondyng alle this, I saw verily that oure Lorde was nevyr wroth nor nevyr shall. For I saw truly that it is agaynst the propyrte of hys myght to be wroth, and agaynst the propyrte of hys wisdom, and agaynst the propyrte of hys goodness.[13]

---

10. "The Trinitie is our endlesse joy and our bleisse by our Lord Jesu Christ and in our Lord Jesu Christ . . . for where Jhesu appireth the blessed Trinitie is understand as to my sight." Julian, *Showings*, 8 (ch. 4); cf. 89 (ch. 57): "the Trynyte is comprehendyd in Christ."

11. Julian, *Showings*, 16 (ch. 9). So generally thereafter Julian uses locutions like "all that be under hevyn whych shall come theder" (77, ch. 51), or "all the soulys that shalle be savyd" (84, ch. 53; cf. 85, ch. 55; 88, ch. 56), thereby indicating that her conclusions refer to those who will be saved, while leaving open the possibility that some may not be. But cf. ch. 63: "I understode that *all* his blessyd chyldren whych be come out of hym by kynd shulde be brought agayne in to hym by grace" (*Showings*, 99; emphasis added).

12. Another example comes in chapter 80, where she writes: "I beleve and understonde the mynystracion of holy angelys, as clarkes telle, but it was not shewed me." Julian, *Showings*, 120.

13. Julian, *Showings*, 64 (ch. 46). At the same time, it is important to note that Julian seems able in at least one instance to join confession of her inability to see any wrath in God with the idea that some people are not saved: "But in God may be no wrath as to my syght. For our good Lorde endelessly havyng regard to his awne worshyppe and to the profyghte of all them that shalbe savyd, with myght and ryght he withstondyth the reprovyd, the which of malice and of shrewdness besye them to contrary and do against Goddes wyll" (*Showings*, 23; ch. 13). Because the text on either side of this short paragraph speaks of God's resistance to the work of the devil, it is possible that she intends "the reprovyd" to refer to the demonic host rather than to human beings; but given that these and all other

4. The Mystery of Evil and the Limits of Eschatology   95

Julian's conclusion here follows a clear chain of theological argument. She begins by defining wrath as "nott ells but a frowerdnes and a contraryoudnes to pees and to love. And eyther it comyth of feylyng of might, or of feylyyng of wisdom, or of feylyng of goodnesse."[14] But, she reasons, the ontology of creation itself dictates that there cannot be any such failing of power, wisdom, or goodness in God:

> For truly . . . yf God myght be wroth for a whyle, we shuld neyther have lyfe ne stede ne being. For as verely as we have oure being of the endles myght of God, and of the endlesse wysdom, and of the endlesse goodnesse, also verely we have oure kepyng in the endles myght of God, and in the endlesse wysdom, and in the endlesse goodnesse.[15]

In short, because creatures can exist only as they are continually upheld by God's power, wisdom, and goodness, even the least interruption in God's exercise of any of those attributes (which divine wrath would entail) would lead to the creature's immediate destruction. And since creation evidently persists in spite of human sin, Julian concludes that divine wrath is simply "unpossible."[16]

Importantly, the tension that emerges at this point between the content of Julian's visions and the teaching of the church does not relate to the question of universalism (the population of hell is not a question Julian addresses directly at any point in the *Showings*[17]), but rather to the reality of divine forgiveness of sin. Julian rightly sees the latter as bound up with God's wrath, with the result that her inability to see divine wrath entails a concomitant inability to see divine forgiveness: "I toke [based on church teaching] that the forgevenesse of his wrath shulde be one of the pryncypall poyntes of [God's] mercy. But for oughte that I might beholde and desyer, I culde nott see this point in all the shewyng."[18] In light of this apparent conflict with church teaching, Julian posits two separate assessments ("domes") of the human situation before God:

> The furst dome, which is of Goddes rightfulness . . . is that feyer, swete dome that was showed in alle the feyer revelation in which I saw hym assignys to us no maner of blame. And though theyse were swete and delectable, yytt only in the beholding of this I culde not be fulle esyd. And that was for the dome of holy chyrch. . . . [For] by this dome me thought that me behovyth nedys to

---

references to demonic agency in *Showings* are in the singular, the possibility that "the reprovyd" refers to a class of human beings distinct from "all them that shalbe savyd" cannot be ruled out.

14. Julian, *Showings*, 66 (ch. 48).

15. Julian, *Showings*, 67 (ch. 49).

16. Julian, *Showings*, 67 (ch. 49): "For this was shewed: that oure lyfe is alle grounded and totyd in love, and without love we may nott lyve. And therfor to the soule that of his special grace seeth so ferforth of the hye, marvelous goodnesse of God . . . it is the most unpossible that may be that God shulde be wrath."

17. See Julian, *Showings*, 22 (ch. 12): "Beholde and see the vertu of this precious plenty of his dereworthy blode! It descended downe into helle and brak her bondes and deliverd them, all that were there which belong to the courte of heven." So Christ's blood releases from hell those "that were there which belong to the courte of heven," but the size of that class of persons is not specified.

18. Julian, *Showings*, 65 (ch. 47): cf. 64 (ch. 46), where she writes that God with respect to "hym selfe may not forgeve, for he may not be wroth." It is important to note that Julian operates throughout with a distinction between *forgiveness* (which she sees as a removal of divine wrath and therefore inapplicable) and *mercy* (which refers to God's general disposition of love). See especially *Showings*, 48–49 (ch. 35): "marcy is a werkyng that comyth of the goodness of God, and it shalle last . . . as long as synne is sufferyd to persew ryghtfulle soules."

96   *The Hope of Glory*

know my selfe a sinner. And by the same dome I understode that synners be sometyme wurthy blame and wrath, and theyse two culde I nott see in God. And therefore my advyce and desyer was more than I can or may telle. For the higher dome God shewed hym selfe in the same tyme, and therefore we behovyd nedys to take it. And the lower dome was lernyd me before tyme in holy chyrche, and therefore I might nott by no weye leve the lower dome.[19]

On the one hand, she is convinced enough of the truth of her vision that she has no hesitation in insisting that "we behovyd nedys to take it" as true. On the other, she confesses that she "culde not be fulle esyd" in this conclusion, because it contradicts "the dome of holy chyrch," according to which "me behovyth nedys to know my selfe a sinner" and thus "wurthy [of] blame and wrath."

Julian's designation of the two "domes" as "higher" and "lower" should not be taken as implying the simple subordination of one to the other. Such a reading would simply dissolve the tension between them, and that is precisely the route Julian refuses to take.[20] The language of "higher" and "lower" rather reflects Julian's anthropology, according to which the human soul has a higher and a lower part. The higher ("oure kyndely substance") is "evyr kepte one in [God], hole and safe without ende," while the lower ("oure chaungeable sensualyte") is the locus of the blindness and instability that causes us to turn away from God and thus to feel in our own sight worthy of condemnation.[21] The contrast between high and low is thus rooted in human ontology, such that there is no basis for the conclusion that established church teaching (and the personal experience of the sinner with which it conforms) is simply trumped by what Julian has seen in her revelations. On the contrary, Julian states that her desire was precisely to see "in what manner . . . the dome of holy chyrch here in erth is tru in his [God's] syght."[22] The tension between the two must therefore be allowed to stand.[23]

Even as she introduces the topic of the two "domes," however, Julian reports that she was given something of an answer as to how they might "both be savyd" in the parable of the Lord and the Servant.[24] Interestingly, after first

19. Julian, *Showings*, 62 (ch. 45).
20. Cf. David Bentley Hart's claim that the New Testament describes "two distinct eschatological horizons, one enclosed within the other. . . . One set of images marks the furthest limits of the imminent course of history, and the division therein . . . between those who have surrendered to God's love and those who have not; and the other set refers to that final horizon of all horizons. . . . Each horizon is, of course, absolute within its own sphere: one is the final verdict on the totality of human history, the other the final verdict on the eternal purpose of God." David Bentley Hart, *That All Shall Be Saved: Heaven, Hell and Universal Salvation* (New Haven, CT: Yale University Press, 2019), 103–4; cf. 120. Although this language echoes Julian's doctrine of two "domes," where Julian refuses to collapse the tension between the domes, Hart has no such hesitations and simply allows the higher to trump the lower (though on p. 109 of his text he does acknowledge that "Rev. 21:8 seems to place a major limit on the extent" of the reconciliation in that final horizon).
21. Julian, *Showings*, 62 (ch. 45); cf. ch. 53 for a more extended discussion of Julian's anthropology.
22. Julian, *Showings*, 63 (ch. 45).
23. "For alle hevynly thynges and alle erthely thynges that long to hevyn be comprehendyd in theyse ii domes. And the more knowing and understanding by the gracious ledyng of the Holy Gost that we have of these ii domes, the more we shalle see and knowe oure felynges." Julian, *Showings*, 63 (ch. 45).
24. Julian, *Showings*, 63 (ch. 45). In light of Julian's words here (as well as her subsequent exposition of the parable in ch. 5), I differ from Karen Kilby, who is reluctant to ascribe to the parable of the Lord and the Servant a "unifying vision"—though I agree with her that it would be a mistake to suppose

4. The Mystery of Evil and the Limits of Eschatology

alluding to this parable, she defers actually reporting its content for a further five chapters—a fact suggesting that its interpretation requires special care.[25] Nevertheless, for all the challenges connected with the proper interpretation of the parable, its storyline is very simple:

> The lorde sytteth solempnely in rest and in pees. The servaunt stondyth before his lorde, reverently redy to do his lords wylle. The lorde lokyth uppon his servaunt full lovely and swetly and mekely. He sendyth hym to a certeyne place to do his wyll. The servaunt . . . rynnyth in grett hast for love to do his lordes wylle. And anon he fallyth in a slade [valley] and takyth ful grett sorow. And than he gronyth and monyth and wallowyth and wryeth, but he may nott ryse nor helpe hym selfe by no manner of weye.[26]

That the lord stands for God is clear and remains a fixed point in Julian's subsequent reflections on the parable's meaning. The question of the servant's identity is less straightforward. The resonances between the parable and the story of the fall make it natural to identify the servant with Adam; but that immediately raises a problem, since such an identification would make of the fall the result of an eagerness to obey God's command rather than (as Genesis clearly teaches) of disobedience to it.[27] A straightforward identification of the servant with Adam would thus fail to offer the promised reconciliation of the two "domes" by virtue of its incompatibility with church teaching. "For," as Julian puts it, "in the servaunt that was shewed for Adam . . . I sawe many dyverse properteys that myght by no manner be derecte to syngell Adam."[28]

It was thus clear to Julian from the outset that the "obvious" meaning of the parable could not be correct. This is not to say that the identification of the servant with Adam was wrong, but only that it was incomplete. The breakthrough came when Julian came to realize that the servant, precisely as Adam, must be understood to represent not only humankind in general, but also Jesus in particular:

> In the servaunt is comprehendyd the Seconde Person of the Trynyte, and in the servaunt is comprehendyd Adam, that is to sey, all men. And therefore, when I sey the Sonne, it menyth the Godhed, whych is evyn with the Fader. And when I sey the servaunt, it menyth Crystes manhode, whych is ryghtfull Adam. By the nerehede of the servaunt is understand the Sonne, and by the stondyng of the lyft syde [of the lord] is understond Adam. The lorde is God the Father, the servant is the Sonne Jesu Cryst, the Holy Gost is the . . . love whych is in them both.[29]

---

that this vision is such as to dissolve the mystery of sin and evil. As I hope is evident, my claim is that Julian and Luther alike cannot help but move toward some sort of unifying vision, though both take care that this vision not be totalizing. See Karen Kilby, "Julian of Norwich, Hans Urs von Balthasar, and the Status of Suffering in Christian Theology," *New Blackfriars* 99, no. 1081 (May 2018): 309, especially n. 32.

25. Both when she first mentions the parable in chapter 45 and when she actually reports it in chapter 51, Julian avers that it was revealed to her "full mystely," which Baker suggests should be rendered as "very obscurely and figuratively." *Showings*, 63, n. 3; 70, n. 6.

26. *Showings*, 70 (ch. 51).

27. In the vision the lord insists that the servant's fall was entirely "for my love, yea, and for his good wylle," thus calling for reward rather than punishment. Julian, *Showings*, 71 (ch. 51).

28. Julian, *Showings*, 71 (ch. 51). One may surmise that it was because she had not yet resolved this problem that Julian did not include the parable in the "Short Text," her first account of her visions.

29. Julian, *Showings*, 75–76 (ch. 51).

98   *The Hope of Glory*

It is this identification of the servant with the incarnate Son that constitutes the framework within which the promised reconciliation of the two "domes" can be understood. Because of this identification, Julian can affirm that "[w]hen Adam felle, Goddes Sonne fell . . . with Adam in to the slade [hollow] of the meyden's womb . . . for to excuse Adam from blame in hevyn and in erth; and myghtely he fechyd hym out of hell."[30] In this way, it is possible for Julian to affirm God's unmitigated love for us in the divine Son, while also affirming the reality of blame that we experience in Adam.

And yet as much as Julian understands the parable to be a means of reconciling the two "domes," it is hard to avoid the conclusion that her explication renders the "higher dome" triumphant, since it discloses *God's* view of the human situation. The force of the equation of Jesus and Adam, after all, is that from God's point of view we are seen only in Christ, because we are human beings at all only insofar as we are in Christ. It would seem to follow that the sense of alienation that we experience in our fallen state derives from our ignorance of how God sees us: as with the servant in the parable, our perception of abandonment (and thus of wrath) is due to the fact that we do not discern God's true disposition, and not to any objective wrath on God's part. And while the suffering we experience as a result is certainly real, because that suffering lacks any objective ground in God (whose disposition toward us remains always a single, fixed, and unchanging one of favor), it cannot be lasting. At one level there remains genuine drama in salvation in that the Son, in taking flesh, shares the pain of human existence in order to save us from the state of abandonment we would experience without his identifying with us in this way.[31] And yet precisely to the extent that Christ is identified with Adam, there is and in the final analysis can be no "work" of redemption (i.e., no genuine transformation of the relationship between God and ourselves), "but only one hye love and mervelous joy, in whych mervelous joy all paynes be holy dystroyed."[32]

In short, it seems difficult to see on Julian's view how it is possible to speak of Jesus *saving* human beings, since fundamentally human beings have no need of being saved. Again, this is not to say that for Julian human beings do not experience genuine fear about their status before God—that is precisely their experience as "Adam" in the pit—but that fear is fundamentally unfounded, *so that to be saved is not so much to be taken out of the pit as to realize that the pit itself is an illusion*, since in fact one has never been severed from the love and joy of God's favor and presence.[33] Thus, as much as Julian never backtracks on

---

30. Julian, *Showings*, 76 (ch. 51), which goes on as follows: "For in alle this oure good Lorde shewed his ownr Son and Adam but one man. The vertu and the goodnesse that we have is of Jesu Crist, the feblenesse and blyndnesse that we have is of Adam, which two were shewed in the servant."

31. So it is that "we have mater of morning, for oure synne is cause of Cristes paynes." Julian, *Showings*, 80–81 (ch. 52).

32. Julian, *Showings*, 82 (ch. 52). Immediately prior to these words, Julian explains that what we *experience* as redemption—"payns and passions, ruthis and pyttes, mercis and forgevenesse and such other"—pertain only to the soul's "lower perty," so that while they may be "profitable" as part of the process whereby we are awakened to the reality of God's love for us, they do not reflect any genuine alteration in our state before God.

33. See Julian's fascinating account of sin in *Showings*, 111 (ch. 73): "For some of us beleve that God is allmyghty and may do alle. . . . But that he is alle love and will do alle, there we fayle.

"And this unknowing it is that most lettysh [hinders] Goddes lovers as to my sight. For whan we begynne to hate synne and amend us by the ordynaunce of holy chyrch, yet ther dwellyth a drede that lettyth [blocks] us, by the beholldyng of our selfe and of oure synne afore done. . . . And thys drede

4. The Mystery of Evil and the Limits of Eschatology

her acknowledgment that there remains much that is hidden in God, by virtue of the power of her account of God's love for us in Christ, this acknowledgment of divine hiddenness is simply overwhelmed by her insistence of our essential union with God in love. Julian's emphasis on oneness with Christ, which is the basis for our assurance of salvation, makes it hard to see how within her vision the Bible's witness to divine judgment and wrath, as well as to divine forgiveness, can be affirmed as the word of God.[34] Again, Julian has powerful theological arguments underpinning this conclusion: because the doctrine of creation teaches that "oure lyfe is alle grounded and rotyd in love, and without love we may nott lyve," and that, since "wrath and frenschyppe be two contrarioese," it follows "yf God might be wroth a whyle, we shuld neyther have lyfe ne stede ne beyng."[35] This is anything but a trivial argument; on the contrary, it follows the venerable tradition of viewing evil as the privation of being, and thus as having no ontological status.[36] But in its very comprehensiveness it seems to claim too much: stressing evil's nonexistence to the extent that it risks being reduced to an illusion, so that the forgiveness of sins, which the church (as Julian herself notes) places at the heart of the gospel, can only be affirmed with qualification. Thus, while Julian recognizes the need for the theologian to acknowledge both what is revealed and what remains hidden of God, in her vision the former risks eclipsing the latter.

The Case of Luther

In *The Bondage of the Will* Luther, too, seeks to balance the hidden and the revealed. Moreover, he is no less insistent than Julian on God's comprehensive sovereignty; indeed, insistence on divine sovereignty is arguably the *leitmotif* of the treatise, hammered home again and again in response to Erasmus's efforts to render God's actions contingent on the decisions of human willing.[37] Erasmus's concern is that unless it is possible to affirm that human beings possess freedom of the will, human action loses its point.[38] With his eye firmly fixed on soteriology, however, it is precisely the pointlessness of human action on which Luther wants to insist. For, he argues, if our ultimate destiny is contingent upon our behavior (that is, if human action has a "point" with respect to our salvation), then our situation is miserable, since we can never be sure (and, indeed,

---

we take some tyme for a mekenes, but it is a foule blyndnes and a wyckydnesse. . . . For ryght as by the curtesy of God he forgetyth oure synne after the tyme that we repent us, so wylle he that we forget oure synne as against oure unskylfulle hevynesse and oure doughtfulle dredes."

34. "For wrath is not ells but a frowerdness and a contraryousnes to pees and to love…whych felyng is nott in God, but it is in oure party." Julian, *Showings*, 66 (ch. 48).

35. Julian, *Showings*, 67 (ch. 49).

36. This is the upshot of Kilby's reading of Julian in the article cited in note 24 above.

37. In this respect, Robert Kolb is correct to summarize the thesis of *Bondage of the Will* as, "Let God be God." See Robert Kolb, *Bound Choice, Election, and Wittenberg Theological Method: From Martin Luther to the Formula of Concord* (Grand Rapids: William B. Eerdmans, 2005), 32. Cf. Philip S. Watson's classic study of Luther's thought, *Let God Be God: An Interpretation of the Theology of Martin Luther* (Philadelphia: Fortress, 1947).

38. "Why, you will say, grant anything free choice? In order to have something to impute justly to the wicked who have voluntarily come short of the grace of God, in order that the calumny of cruelty and injustice may be excluded from God, that despair may be kept away from us, that complacency may be excluded also, and that we may be incited to endeavor." Desiderius Erasmus, *On the Freedom of the Will*, in *Luther and Erasmus: Free Will and Salvation*, ed. E. Gordon Rupp and Philip S. Watson (Philadelphia: Westminster, 1969), 96.

100   *The Hope of Glory*

must, if we are honest about our situation as fallen, sinful beings, always doubt) that our actions are pleasing to God. Luther thus rejects absolutely the idea that God's work is in any way contingent on human activity, insisting rather that God "foresees and purposes and does all things by his immutable, eternal, and infallible will."[39] "For," he goes on to argue, "if you doubt or disdain to know that God foreknows all things . . . necessarily and immutably, how can you believe his promises and place a sure trust and reliance on them?"[40] Crucially, according to this line of argument, belief in God's omniscience and omnipotence is not the starting point of theological reflection, but rather a necessary implication of the Christian conviction that God's promises (specifically, the promise of salvation in Christ) can be trusted absolutely and without reservation.[41]

The difference between the two positions could not be starker. Erasmus is concerned that if people are told that God does all things, they will both cease any efforts at moral improvement and (in light of the experience of evil in the world) come to doubt the love of God.[42] But for Luther this is just the point: because we are congenitally sinful and perverse, none of us is able either to love God or to trust that God loves us by our own efforts, but only by the gift of grace that brings faith: "Who will believe, you say, that he is loved by God? I answer: No man will or can believe this; but the elect will believe while the rest perish in unbelief."[43] In short, to ask how people can come to a life of faith apart from free will is precisely to have failed to understand that the life of faith is not something to which *we* come, but rather that which comes *to us*; it is a gift of the Holy Spirit, not a matter of human effort. Through this gift human beings love God willingly, even as they willingly do evil in the Spirit's absence; but the will is for Luther fundamentally determined rather than determining, always following rather than generating its own inclination, whether that be to sin apart from grace or to live in faith and love with it.[44]

Now, when stated in these terms, the claim that God gives grace to some and not to others appears to be simply a brute fact: a truth about how the world works as inexorable but also as existentially meaningless as the law of gravity. But for Luther to understand God in this way, as an all-determining and ultimately inscrutable force, is to have failed to understand God at all, because God is not a phenomenon (like gravity or any other feature of the natural

---

39. Martin Luther, *On the Bondage of the Will*, in *Luther and Erasmus: Free Will and Salvation*, ed. E. Gordon Rupp and Philip S. Watson (Philadelphia: Westminster, 1969), 118.

40. Luther, *Bondage*, 122.

41. "We do not have to do with an abstract God of fate nor with a frozen 'first principle' but with a God who makes promises and keeps them and will not surrender them. What can we do about such a God? Listen to him!" Gerhard O. Forde, *The Captivation of the Will: Luther vs. Erasmus on Freedom and Bondage*, ed. Stephen Paulson (Grand Rapids: William B. Eerdmans, 2005), 68–69.

42. "What evildoer will take pains to correct life? Who will be able to bring himself to love God with all his heart when He created hell seething with eternal torments in order to punish his victims as though he took delight in human torments?" Erasmus, *Freedom*, 41.

43. Luther, *Bondage*, 136; cf. 138: "If . . . I could by any means comprehend how this God can be merciful and just who displays so much wrath and iniquity, there would be no need of faith."

44. ". . . when a man is without the Spirit of God he does not do evil against his will, as if he were taken by the scruff of the neck and forced to it . . . but he does it of his own accord and with a ready will." Luther, *Bondage*, 139; cf. 140: "By contrast, if God works in us, the will is changed, and being gently breathed upon by the Spirit of God, it again wills and acts from a pure willingness and inclination and of its own accord, not compulsion." Thus, ". . . in relation to God, or in matters pertaining to salvation or damnation, a man has no free choice, but is a captive, subject and slave either of the will of God or the will of Satan." Luther, *Bondage*, 143.

4. The Mystery of Evil and the Limits of Eschatology   101

world) that we either do or can encounter by way of our general experience of the world, but rather the one who encounters us in Jesus above and beyond every and any effort on our part. For, as already noted, the confession of God's all-determining power is for Luther not theology's starting point, but rather a deduction from the prior conviction that God's promises are a fit object of our trust, upon which we may rely unconditionally. We know God, in short, only as we are addressed by God in Christ; and the divine address is designed precisely to persuade us that God's attitude toward us, far from being indifferent, arbitrary, or pointless (on the model of a law of nature), is one of undeviating grace and favor.[45]

To be sure, the mode by which God communicates this favor is not altogether straightforward. According to Luther, human beings in their fallen state have a natural resistance to grace; indeed, that is just what it means to be fallen: to imagine that we have some capacity for securing our righteousness—that is, our status as worthy to stand before God—independently of the God who, as our Creator, is the only possible guarantor of our worth. Therefore, before we are prepared to accept the good news of God's promises, we need to be disabused of this illusion:

> God has assuredly promised his grace to the humble, that is, to those who lament and despair of themselves. But no man can be thoroughly humbled until he knows that his salvation is utterly beyond his own powers, devices, endeavors, will, and works, and depends entirely on the choice, will, and work of another, namely, of God alone . . . [For] when a man has no doubt that everything depends on the will of God, then he completely despairs of himself and . . . waits for God to work; then he has come close to grace, and can be saved.[46]

Luther contends that God uses the law to school us in our helplessness, so that the point of the law's commands is not to instruct us on how we can achieve salvation, but rather "to lead us . . . to a knowledge of our own impotence," so that we may rely for our salvation upon God's gracious promises alone.[47] Thus, while for Julian God's love leaves no room for wrath, for Luther our fallen state means that we cannot experience God's love apart from a vivid appreciation of divine wrath: we know God's love concretely in the word of forgiveness that comes to us unmerited, just as and because through the law we recognize that we stand under God's just condemnation.[48]

---

45. Cf. Martin Luther, *Lectures on Genesis*, in *LW* 5, 45: "For God did not come down from heaven to make you uncertain about predestination, to teach you to despise the sacraments, absolution, and the rest of the divine ordinances. Indeed, he instituted them to make you completely certain and remove the disease of doubt from your heart."

46. Luther, *Bondage*, 137; cf. 196: "by the command to love we are shown the essential shape of the law and what we ought to do, but not the power of the will or what we are able to do, but rather what we are not able to do, and the same is shown by all other expressions of demand."

47. Luther, *Bondage*, 185; cf. 218–19, where Luther argues that Paul's aim in Romans "is to lead the ungodly and the proud by means of those threatenings [of the law] to knowledge of themselves and their own impotence, so as to humble them by the knowledge of sin and thus prepare them for grace."

48. "Those . . . who have not yet experienced the office of the law, and neither recognize sin nor feel death, have no use for the mercy promised by the word." Luther, *Bondage*, 200. Cf. Dietrich Bonhoeffer, *Ethics*, vol. 6 of *Dietrich Bonhoeffer Works*, ed. Clifford J. Green, trans. Reinhard Kraus, Charles C. West, and Douglas W. Stott (Minneapolis: Fortress, 2005), 151: "Justification presupposes the creature became guilty."

102   *The Hope of Glory*

And yet it is just in this insistence on divine judgment and wrath that Luther's perspective runs into theological problems. Luther does not understand sin is as a feature of the "lower part" of the human soul, but on the contrary, as a product of willing—the highest of human faculties.[49] Thus, in contrast to Julian (for whom human beings are in their true, "higher" nature never severed from God), for Luther human separation from God, and the condemnation that righty follows from it, are real. Whereas for Julian the incarnation reveals the primordial and indissoluble unity of Christ and Adam in which there is and can be neither wrath, judgment, or forgiveness, for Luther the distinction between "Adam" and Christ is crucial, in that our salvation is secured precisely by the "happy exchange" (*fröhliche Wechsel*) of properties between Christ and fallen humanity, in which Christ receives the judgment we deserve and we are ascribed the righteousness that he alone has earned.[50] It follows that as much as Luther characterizes the law as a pedagogical device designed to drive us to the promise of forgiveness proclaimed by Christ, it is and cannot be only that; rather, for the gospel truly to be one of forgiveness, Luther cannot avoid the conclusion that its proclamation is inseparable from acknowledgment of a divine wrath that brings judgment. Moreover, insofar as the God of judgment is the same God who promises, and therefore who works all things inexorably and irresistibly according to the divine will, God is as much the author of damnation as of salvation.

Importantly, Luther himself at no point suggests that Christians should proclaim this wrathful God. Quite the contrary, he insists that insofar as Christians have been commissioned to proclaim the gospel of Jesus Christ alone, they neither can nor should have anything to do with the God of wrath: "we have to argue in one way about God . . . as preached, revealed, offered, and worshiped [in Christ], and in another way about God as he is not preached, not revealed, not offered, not worshiped," because to "the extent that God hides himself and wills to be unknown to us, it is no business of ours."[51] In this way, Luther insists, the God of wrath and judgment simply falls outside of the compass of Christian theology. This God must rather "be left to himself in his own majesty, for in this regard we have nothing to do with him, nor has he willed that we should have anything to do with him. But we have something to do with him insofar as he is clothed and set forth in his Word."[52] If this last point is stressed in a way that Luther himself does not, it is possible to see that even as Julian does not foreclose the possibility that some people are in fact damned, Luther's position allows that the possibility of damnation is never in fact realized. But in just the same way as it is hard to see how the actuality of damnation can be squared with Julian's vision of a God without wrath, so it is difficult to understand how

49. "For if what is most excellent in man is not ungodly and lost or damned, but only the flesh, or the lower and grosser desires, what sort of redeemer do you think we shall make Christ out to be? . . . Choose which you please: if the higher part of man is sound, it does not need Christ as its redeemer. . . . Then the kingdom of Satan, too, will be as nothing, since it will rule only over the lower part of man." Luther, *Bondage*, 276.
50. For this idea of exchange in Luther's works, see *Operationes in Psalmos*, in the Weimarer Ausgabe (hereafter WA) 5, 608; *Lectures on Galatians*, in *LW* 26, 284; cf. *Two Kinds of Righteousness*, in *LW* 31, 297; *The Freedom of a Christian*, *LW* 31, 351.
51. Luther, *Bondage*, 200–201.
52. Luther, *Bondage*, 201.

4. The Mystery of Evil and the Limits of Eschatology 103

wrath and judgment can be viewed as proper to God in the way that Luther maintains if their effects are never definitely actualized.

It is tempting to charge Luther with inconsistency when in spite of his own warnings about the illegitimacy of presuming to speak about this hidden God, he seems to do just that, as when, for example, he draws a distinction "between the word of God and God himself," such that God "does not will the death of a sinner, according to his word; but he wills it according to that inscrutable will of his."[53] Yet however jarring Luther's rhetoric at this point may be, it is not simply inconsistent. For if Julian's vision of divine love—in which she can see no wrath, judgment, or forgiveness—puts her in a (logical) position where she can only remain silent about that which is hidden in God, Luther's insistence on the reality of forgiveness does not allow him (logically) the same silence. For if God's forgiveness is real, then so, too, must be the condemnation under which we lie apart from it.[54] The specter of the hidden God cannot, correspondingly, be dismissed as a macabre but ultimately inconsequential backdrop to the gospel of forgiveness, but must be accepted as a condition of its very possibility; for there can be no mercy, no forgiveness, and thus no salvation where there is no judgment, wrath, or damnation—that is, where there is no recognition of a God who "hidden in his majesty neither deplores nor takes away death."[55]

It is vital to remember here that in all this Luther is not presuming to explain *how* judgment and mercy can coexist in God, in the manner of a modern theodicy. On the contrary, he flatly admits that "how things can be good in God's sight which are evil to us only God knows."[56] His aim, no less than Julian's, is precisely to stress that in the present age whatever resolution there may be to the mystery of sin and evil (since it is just this mystery which seems to set God's love and justice against each other) remains hidden in God. What differentiates him from Julian is that this mystery has to do not simply with how it is that evil comes about (viz., "how things can be good in God's sight which are evil to us") but also with God's response to evil: the implacable divine "no" to that which contradicts God's will for the flourishing of creatures.[57] His point is that Christians have to acknowledge this "no"—the divine wrath and judgment— as corollary to their convictions regarding the "yes" of God's mercy and forgiveness. But because it is the latter and not the former that is the content of the

---

53. Luther, *Bondage*, 201.

54. "As to your saying that the window is opened for impiety by these dogmas [viz., that God wills all necessarily, including the death of the unbelieving], let it be so. . . . Nevertheless, by these same dogmas there is opened at the same time a door to righteousness, and entrance to heaven and a way to God for the godly and the elect. But if, as you advise, we left these dogmas alone and concealed the Word of God from men . . . then we might very well have closed your window, but in its place we should be opening for ourselves and all men floodgates . . . not only to impiety, but to the depths of hell." Luther, *Bondage*, 136–37.

55. Luther, *Bondage*, 201.

56. Luther, *Bondage*, 231.

57. See Luther's comments near the end of the treatise: "Let us take it that there are three lights—the light of nature, the light of grace, and the light of glory. . . . By the light of nature it is an insoluble problem how it can be just that the good man should suffer and a bad man prosper [the 'problem of evil' in its typical sense]; but this problem is solved by the light of grace [viz., with its revelation of postmortem punishment and reward]. By the light of grace it is an insoluble problem how God can damn one who is unable by any power of his own to do anything but sin and be guilty. Here both the light of nature and the light of grace tell us that it is not the fault of the unhappy man, but of an unjust God. . . . But the light of glory . . . will show us hereafter that the God whose judgment here is one of incomprehensible righteousness is a God of most perfect and manifest righteousness."

104   *The Hope of Glory*

gospel message, he insists that the church's (and, therefore, the theologian's) focus should be squarely on God's mercy as revealed in Christ, in relation to which the divine judgment is simply the reflex or shadow and not properly an object of theological interest in its own right.[58]

To fail to observe this rule—to attend to the shadow rather than the light—is for Luther (as for Julian) the heart of sin.[59] And yet he fully well recognizes the difficulty of walking this line. Indeed, it is just at this point that his theology of law and gospel comes into its own: not as a theoretical solution to a problem that will only be resolved in the light of glory, but as a means of making sense of the experience of divine judgment pastorally. Within the context of the gospel, he can insist that the law (that is, God's word of command that can only be heard by fallen human beings as a word of judgment, wrath, and condemnation) is the means whereby God seeks to bring human beings to receive the good news of God's gracious favor as the utterly unconditional declaration that it is.[60] As God's (hidden) work of judgment comes to be understood as an instrument for furthering God's (revealed) work of mercy in this way, its terror is relativized. And yet as much as Luther seeks to guard against the believer's heart and mind fixating on the hidden God, the shadow persists. Because the very terms in which the revealed God is proclaimed (viz., as the one who forgives sin) are logically inseparable from what remains hidden (viz., the will by which God works death and damnation), the latter risks overwhelming the former.[61]

Evaluation

Appreciation of the theological principles Julian and Luther hold in common makes the divergences between them all the more striking. Both confess that God is uniquely and unsurpassably revealed in Christ, who must therefore be placed at the center of Christian theology as the constant reference point for all claims about what God wills and does; but both also concede that the mystery of evil means that what has been revealed in Christ is not all there is to know of

---

58. "[T]he secret will of the Divine Majesty is not a matter for debate, and the human temerity which with continual perversity is always neglecting necessary things in its eagerness to probe this one, must be called off and restrained from busying itself with the investigation of these secrets of God's majesty. . . . Let it occupy itself instead with God incarnate . . . for through him it is furnished abundantly with what it ought to know and ought not to know." Luther, *Bondage*, 206.

59. "[T]he offense of unbelief lies precisely in having doubts about the favour of God, who wishes us to believe with the utmost possible certainty that he is favourable." Luther, *Bondage*, 309.

60. See especially Luther's discussion of his own struggles with the experience of God's judgment in *Bondage*, 244: "And who would not be offended [at the idea that 'God by his own sheer will should abandon, harden, and damn men']? I myself was offended more than once, and brought to the very depth and abyss of despair, so that I wished I had never been created a man, before I realized how salutary this despair was, and how near to grace."

61. "Theodicy is not, as Leibniz thought, to be brought before the forum of reason, which can understand and judge, so that one can dispute or reflect *about* God; as Job experienced it, it is much more about dispute *with* God . . . one appeals to God against God. The only speech that is legitimate is the careful form of speech that recognizes that there are boundaries and that concerns the experience of the terrifying hiddenness of God. . . . Only through Christ does the Holy Spirit let one see into the heart of God the Father. . . . But to turn this understanding into a theological principle would make it a form of enthusiasm, which impatiently does away with the difference between faith and seeing." Oswald Bayer, *Martin Luther's Theology: A Contemporary Interpretation*, trans. Thomas H. Trapp (Grand Rapids: William B. Eerdmans, 2008 [2007]), 213.

4. The Mystery of Evil and the Limits of Eschatology 105

God. Needless to say, for neither theologian does it follow from conceding that the mystery of sin and evil lies hidden in God that God is responsible for sin or evil. Instead, for Julian and Luther alike acknowledgment of divine hiddenness functions as a means of affirming that God's love for humanity, revealed in Christ, overcomes sin (along with the divine wrath and judgment that sin calls forth) without accounting for it. Yet while neither thinker seeks to account for sin (again, that is just what it means for both of them to insist that the resolution of sin's evident inexplicability lies hidden in God), they cannot help but situate sin in the story they tell of God's saving work in Christ. It is at this point that their positions diverge—and in a way that is instructive insofar as it seems doubtful that any theologian who faces the problem of sin and evil seriously can finally avoid following either one or the other of them.

On the one hand, one may adopt with Julian what might be called a view "from above" that is resolutely focused on the unstinting generosity and love by which God brought the world into being and sustains it in being at every point of its existence. Within this perspective there is no place for divine wrath or condemnation: sin is real, but the alienation from God to which it gives rise exists entirely and exclusively on the human side, such that however serious a problem it may appear (and Julian has no interest whatsoever in minimizing its seriousness), it does not reflect any alienation on God's side. Consequently, the incarnation does not change anything in God's relation to the world; it simply reveals God's unbreakable love for human beings, which has never been severed and never can be. The theology underlying this position is in one fundamental respect unimpeachable, for it is grounded in the principle that no creature could exist for an instant if God's love for it were interrupted, since any such interruption would, *eo ipso*, cause the creature (which is sustained by nothing except that love) to fall out of existence. In this way of telling the Christian story, sin is an absolute nullity and thus cannot finally be considered a factor in God's relationship to human beings—nothing that could give rise to wrath or condemnation on God's part. And yet by insisting on the unbroken character of God's love in this way, Julian has difficulty giving forgiveness the place in God's ways with human beings that the New Testament seems to require.

To avoid this problem, the theologian may adopt with Luther a view "from below" that focuses precisely on the human experience of divine forgiveness: the release from the condemnation to which human beings would justly be consigned apart from God's gracious determination to meet their refusal of life under God with forbearance and mercy. Yet this perspective's emphasis on the transformation of the sinner's situation before God effected by Jesus' ministry carries with it, as its presupposition and shadow, the conviction that the alienation from God produced by sin is not restricted to the human side, but is a rupture for God as well, such that the same God who promises life to those who receive divine grace also intends the destruction of those who refuse it. Thus, however much Luther may insist that God uses the proclamation of the law and its message of divine judgment to lead us to Jesus, and that human beings should therefore focus their theological attention exclusively on the will of God as revealed in Jesus (and it would be difficult to overstate his insistence on both these points), the "hidden God" of wrath, judgment, and damnation remains the background, and thus—as with any background—invariably comes to

106   *The Hope of Glory*

appear as the more fundamental reality, from the specter of which the believer cannot turn away in spite (and indeed precisely because) of its inseparability from the confession of Christ as the one who saves from wrath and judgment. The logic of this perspective, too, is unimpeachable on its own terms, since speaking a word of forgiveness presupposes the presence of a genuine fault that requires forgiveness; and yet in emphasizing the reality of God's wrath, Luther seems foredoomed to rob the good news on which he so vehemently insists of its essential presupposition: that God is in no respect other than God shows God's self to be in Jesus.

Both Julian and Luther recognize that their accounts of the character and significance of God's work in Jesus Christ inevitably fall short, owing to the deep and unfathomable mystery of God's relation to sin and evil. To the extent that each nevertheless pursues a central insight into what *has* been revealed to us of God's will in Christ, both accounts are at once profoundly compelling and burdened with implications that are theologically troubling. In Julian's case, her theological vision of the invariant and unbroken character of God's love for all humankind shown forth in Christ cuts against the gospel message that Jesus came to secure the forgiveness of sins (Matt. 26:28; cf. Luke 24:27; Acts 5:31; Col. 1:14) and thereby to deliver human beings from God's wrath (1 Thess. 1:10; cf. Col. 3:6; Rev. 14:9–11). On the other hand, Luther's contrasting focus on Christ as the agent of forgiveness who saves us from divine wrath ends up driving a wedge between God and God's word that contradicts the biblical claim that God's word *is* God (John 1:1; cf. Col. 2:9) and thereby undermines the conviction that what God reveals in Jesus Christ is precisely the divine intention that all people be saved (1 Tim. 2:3–4; cf. Rom. 11:32; Titus 2:11).

The seriousness of the problem here can be seen in noting that as striking as the difference in outcome of Julian's and Luther's respective theological visions is, the precise point at which they diverge from one another is remarkably subtle. Again, both thinkers are resolutely christocentric, viewing Jesus as the touchstone of all proper Christian talk about God. Even as both maintain that in Jesus is the revelation of the one, true God, however, both also find themselves compelled to acknowledge that there remain things hidden in God that are *not* revealed in Jesus, so that although *in Jesus* we see only divine forgiveness and mercy, we have to allow that in Jesus we do not see *everything* about God. And yet this does not mean for either writer that there exists any source of knowledge of God other than Jesus, since for both it is just the revelation of God's love for us in Christ that defines the content of what remains hidden: namely, the mystery of evil, death, and damnation.[62]

---

62. At first blush, it might seem that Julian and Luther *do* view the experience of divine judgment on human sin as independent of and, indeed, having priority over the revelation of God's love in Christ. After all, for Julian the identification of the fallen servant with Adam precedes the recognition that he is also Christ; and Luther likewise views the good news of Jesus precisely as balm to the soul already aware of its sinfulness. But this appearance is misleading, since it remains the case for both Julian and Luther that the knowledge of God as distant and wrathful is at bottom a false knowledge that derives precisely from the failure to know that God has made God's self known in Jesus. As such, it cannot be viewed as having any independent significance for Christian faith and practice; rather, it can truly be known only as that which is hidden—precisely as that which has *not* been made known in Christ and thus no part of what has been revealed of God. In this context, it is important to stress that the relation between what is revealed and hidden in God at the center of Julian's and Luther's struggles is not the problem of the relation between the *Deus absconditus* and *Deus revelatus* that animated Karl

4. The Mystery of Evil and the Limits of Eschatology 107

In his own account of the mystery of evil, Karl Barth famously suggested that it should be rated "as low as possible in relation to God and as high as possible in relation to ourselves."[63] This seems to me exactly right, and it is a sentiment that both Julian and Luther implicitly endorse in the way they seek to give appropriate attention both to that which is revealed of and to that which remains hidden in God. If the foregoing analysis has any merit, the fact that neither is finally successful is significant because it suggests that in this matter success is simply not within the theologian's grasp. The problem, in short, is not that Julian has not thought sufficiently hard about the mystery of suffering and evil or that Luther has not given sufficient attention to God's love as revealed in Christ. Indeed, it would be better to say that the experiences of evil and grace are, respectively, Julian's and Luther's starting points in the *Showings* and *Bondage of the Will*. The difficulty derives rather from their shared conviction both that God is revealed in Christ and that even this revelation does not render all God's ways transparent. For both theologians the picture of God we have in Christ is *full* (such that to look for God elsewhere than in Christ is inevitably not to see God at all) but not *fully transparent* (such that the light of glory in which all will be made plain at the end of the age is not reducible without remainder to what can be seen in the light of grace). This is not because the one who will be revealed as the Lord of glory will be anyone other than Jesus Christ, but simply because so long as the final revelation of that lordship remains outstanding, we do not now see face-to-face, but only in a mirror, dimly.

Of course, both Julian and Luther believe that there will come a day when our vision will no longer be so partial, and that we will then know fully, even as we have been fully known.[64] But the admission that this resolution remains outstanding does not solve the problem of bearing faithful witness to Christian hope now. The ability to identify the shortcomings in the two theologians' respective positions provides no clue as to how one might arrive at a more satisfactory solution to the challenge of reconciling God's revelation of the defeat of sin and evil in Jesus with the experience of their enduring power in the present. After all, although both theologians show themselves fully aware of their own inability to resolve this problem, neither can avoid taking a stand on the question of whether sin and evil are real for God, and thus whether judgment, wrath, and condemnation can be ascribed to God. Both theologians seek to preserve the tension between the hidden and the revealed: Julian at no point rejects the witness of church teaching (as well as her own quotidian experience) regarding the death-dealing power of sin; and Luther insists that we should

---

Barth's theological project. That is, their problem is not reconciling the fullness of God's revelation in Christ with the freedom of that revelation (i.e., the problem of whether confession of the graciousness of God's revelation in Christ does not imply an unknown—and unknowable—divinity hidden behind the God revealed in Jesus). It is rather the recognition that the fullness of God's revelation in Christ—and thus the definitive disclosure of the divine will for humankind that both theologians believe it represents—does not address the problem of evil. In other words, strictly speaking what remains hidden is not anything about *God*, but rather about that which God *opposes*.

63. Karl Barth, *Church Dogmatics* III/3, ed. G. W. Bromiley and T. F. Torrance (Edinburgh: T&T Clark, 1960), 295. It is important to note that Barth was, of course, critical of Luther (and his own Reformed tradition) on the matter of the *Deus absconditus*, so I do not mean to claim here that Barth would see Luther as giving a proper estimation of evil within the divine economy; my point is simply that Luther's insistence that we regard only Christ's righteousness and not our own was his way of trying to get at Barth's point—not that it is a fully satisfactory solution to the problem.

64. See, e.g., note 57 above.

108   *The Hope of Glory*

not have anything to do with God except as God has revealed God's self in Christ. And yet in spite of these qualifications, there is no mistaking in either case the theological upshot of their respective accounts. The caricatures according to which Julian defends a Pollyanna universalism and Luther rigid double predestination are wrong, but they are not simply crazy; rather, they reflect an over-reading of theological tendencies that are genuinely present within the two texts—tendencies that follow from the distinctive ways Julian and Luther address the mystery of sin and evil.

And it is just the fact that neither of their positions is finally satisfactory that highlights the limits of Christian eschatology—and thus of the claims I will make about the content of Christian hope in the second part of this book. For if Christians believe that all will be made clear with Christ's return, and that this clarity will both reveal and vindicate the fullness of God's goodness and glory, they cannot say how this will be. And yet since (as far as I can see) it is not possible to say anything now about the content of the Christian hope without taking a position on the question of the reality of sin and evil for God that veers either toward Julian or toward Luther, and since both positions run in distinctive ways against the fundamental grain of the faith, it follows that the truth that will be revealed at the eschaton will show that the content of the following chapters is not simply incomplete, but in some fundamental respect incorrect.

Of course, if my analysis of the theological challenge posed by the theologies of Julian and Luther is accurate, a correct account cannot be given on this side of the eschaton, so that any alternative proposal I might devise would be equally (if differently) wrong. Moreover, the recognition that error here is unavoidable does not rob me of the conviction that it is nevertheless possible to write something that has the capacity both to counter other sorts of errors that have proven particularly harmful to the church's witness to the promise of the world's redemption, and to provide at least a sense of why the vision of the future that Christians defend is a hopeful one. It is that conviction that prompts me to write in the first place.

And yet there is no avoiding the fact that eschatology has limits not shared with any other doctrine. I am sure that there is plenty wrong with what I have written on other theological topics (some of which has already been identified by readers), but of no other topic is it the case that I wrote knowing as I wrote that what I wrote was wrong and, indeed, where it is wrong (for I myself incline toward the position of Luther, the problems with which I have noted above). Again, all talk of God invariably falls short of the fullness of the divine, so that any correspondence between a theologian's claims and God's reality entails the recognition of a still greater lack of correspondence.[65] But my claim here is that where eschatology is concerned, this lack of correspondence is not simply a falling short, but necessarily includes also a movement in the wrong direction, and thus a witness that is unavoidably (though, I trust, not totally or irredeemably) false.

But because one cannot speak honestly of the Christ who has come without also attempting to explain what it means to confess that he "will come again in

---

65. So the Fourth Lateran Council: *"inter creatorem et creaturam non potest tanta similitudo notari, quin sit semper major dissimilitudo notanda."* DH §806.

4. The Mystery of Evil and the Limits of Eschatology 109

glory to judge the living and the dead" to inaugurate a kingdom that "will have no end," the venture must be made. So if the first half of this book attempted to defend the basic coherence of Christian hope by distinguishing it from the temptations of false hope and hope's refusal, and tying hope's present *form* to the person of Jesus, the second half seeks to give witness to hope's future *content*. The challenge is easily defined but difficult of execution: to say what is necessary in order to give "an accounting for the hope" that grounds the church's life, and yet to "do it with gentleness and respect" (1 Pet. 3:15–16), knowing full well that "no eye has seen, nor ear heard, nor the human heart conceived, what God has prepared for those who love him" (1 Cor. 2:9).

Part 2

Glory

5. Jesus, the Lord of Glory

At one level there is no difference for Christians between hope's present form and future content: both are defined by Jesus of Nazareth, the Word made flesh.[1] For at the heart of the Christian faith lies the belief that the one who *will* come again in glory is the same as the one who already *has* come in the form of a slave (Phil. 2:7): Jesus of Nazareth, who was born of the Virgin Mary and put to death on Good Friday, but who also rose from the dead and ascended into heaven to sit at the right hand of the Father. It is for just this reason—because the one we "wait for" is none other than he "who gave himself for us that he might redeem us from all iniquity" (Titus 2:13–14)—that Scripture calls Jesus "our hope" (1 Tim. 1:1).

The resurrection is the guarantee of this continuity in identity between the one who was and the one who is to come, for it is precisely God's vindication of Jesus of Nazareth as "Lord and Christ" (Acts 2:36 alt.), and thus the affirmation that it is he—the child of Mary who was crucified under Pontius Pilate—who will "come again in glory to judge the living and the dead." As argued in the introduction, it is important in this context to distinguish resurrection from resuscitation: in being raised from the dead, Jesus is not just temporarily restored to earthly life in a way that would leave him subject to death at a later date, like Lazarus or Jairus's daughter. But (and more controversially) it is equally necessary to understand that neither is resurrection a continuation of life, as though the risen Jesus carries on living as he did before, only in a new, heavenly location. For in taking flesh as a human being, the Word assumes the conditions and characteristics of human life, which is finite in time as well as in space, bounded not only physically by the contours of the body but also temporally by the limits of birth and death.[2] It follows that for Jesus to be resurrected is not for his life to continue, whether on earth or in heaven, as though his death were merely one more in the series of events that constitute his life rather than

---

1. "[T]he fundamental content of Christian eschatology is the personal identity of the one who was and is and is to come. . . . Its core is not the elaboration of a scheme of historical purposes, but the coming of Jesus Christ." John Webster, *Word and Church: Essays in Christian Dogmatics* (Edinburgh: T&T Clark, 2001), 274. Cf. James H. Cone, *God of the Oppressed* (San Francisco: Harper & Row, 1974), 126: "The meaning of Jesus Christ for us today is not limited to his past and present existence. Jesus Christ is who he will be. He is not only the Crucified and Risen One but also the Lord of the future who is coming again to fully consummate the liberation already happening in our present."
2. "He who had once decided to share our humanity had to experience all that belongs to our nature. Now human life is encompassed within two limits, and if he had passed through one and not touched the other, he would only have half fulfilled his purpose, having failed to reach the other limit proper to our nature." Gregory of Nyssa, "An Address on Religious Instruction," in *Christology of the Later Fathers*, ed. Edward R. Hardy (Philadelphia: Westminster Press, 1954), 309–10.

113

114 *The Hope of Glory*

the termination of that series. Easter does not change the fact that Jesus' death marks the end of his human life.[3] To confess that Jesus has been raised from the dead means instead to affirm that his human life, as defined by the timespan that runs from his birth in Bethlehem to his death on Golgotha, is sustained in its completeness beyond the perils and possibilities of this world. Only so is it the case that "Christ, being raised from the dead, will never die again," since the reason "death no longer has dominion over him" (Rom. 6:9) is that he has already died, which means that his life has run its course and thereby achieved its full and final shape. In short, the reason that his life is no longer under threat is that it is indeed *finished* (John 19:30). As resurrected, Jesus indeed lives, but on new and different terms than he did before: no longer "according to the flesh" (2 Cor. 5:16 alt.), within the realm of narratable, spatio-temporal interactions and the potential for growth and decline that go with them; instead, "the life he lives, he lives to God" (Rom. 6:10; cf. 2 Cor. 13:4), in glory, and thus beyond time and its vicissitudes.

The further claim that Jesus has (in the words of the Nicene Creed) "ascended into heaven and is seated at the right hand of the Father" adds more to the picture by confirming that the risen one is no less than God, for to sit at God's right hand is to exercise God's own power as the one who, in the words of Paul, has been given "the name that is above every other name" (Phil. 2:9; cf. John 5:19–23)—the divine name that belongs to God alone (Exod. 3:15). Thus, if the resurrection is the vindication of Jesus' human life as sustained by God on the far side (and thus beyond the reach) of death, the ascension confirms that the life thereby vindicated is no less than God's own—that of the eternal Word, who "was in the beginning with God" (John 1:2). Moreover, because the life he now lives before God is not properly conceived as an ongoing series of events, resurrection and ascension should not be viewed as two separate, sequential postmortem occurrences, but rather as two different perspectives on the same reality: the definitive divine affirmation of Jesus as the Son of God (cf. Rom. 1:4), who lives and reigns with the one he calls Father in the unity of the Holy Spirit.[4]

To view Jesus' risen life otherwise, as though his mode of existence between Easter and advent included any sort of continuation of his life beyond its eternal affirmation would imply the possibility of the development of dimensions of his character that were not revealed during his earthly ministry. And against that supposition stand not only the basic principles of biblical anthropology, according to which human life is a finite span bounded by the limits of birth

---

3. "However we wish to interpret dying physically or metaphysically . . . one thing is certain, that then there happens the last action that can happen in creaturely existence. Whatever may happen beyond death must at least be something different than the continuation of this life. Death really means the *end*." Karl Barth, *Dogmatics in Outline*, trans. G. T. Thompson (New York: Harper & Row, 1959), 117.

4. "Thus the resurrection and ascension of Jesus Christ add to what He was and is and to what took place in Him . . . only the new fact that in this event He was to be seen and was actually seen as the One He was and is. He did not become different in this event." Karl Barth, *Church Dogmatics* [hereafter *CD*], 13 vols., ed. G. W. Bromiley and T. F. Torrance (Edinburgh: T&T Clark, 1956–1974), IV/2, 133. That Scripture has no stake in seeing resurrection and ascension as temporally distinct occurrences is suggested by the fact that the third evangelist evidently felt no compunction about dating the ascension forty days after Easter in Acts 1:3–9, notwithstanding having earlier dated it on Easter Sunday in Luke 24:1–51.

5. Jesus, the Lord of Glory

and death, but also specifically soteriological considerations. For if Jesus' post-resurrection life did entail such development, then it would be impossible to view the revelation of God's will in Jesus' earthly life as definitive, since in a context where Jesus continued to live (especially in a sphere that is inherently invisible to us) our knowledge of his story, and thus of its significance for our well-being, would be incomplete, and the proclamation of Christ crucified as the sum of the gospel correspondingly false.[5] But it is central to Christian belief that with Jesus' resurrection and ascension, God's definitive word to and for the world has been spoken once for all (cf. Heb. 7:27; 9:12, 26; 10:10). And this word is sure and certain: that God has determined creation for life in communion with God by irrevocably binding the creation to God's own life in Jesus. In short, Jesus' life is our life—but this is only good news if in his flesh we have indeed seen "the eternal life that was with the Father" (1 John 1:2; cf. John 1:14).

And yet if God's final word has been spoken, the fact that the present order continues—with its undeniable blessings of wisdom, compassion, and courage, but also with its all but unendurable torrent of stupidity, cruelty, and violence—shows that God has not yet finished speaking it. Although Christians confess that the Jesus who will come again in glory is none other than the one who died on the cross, and that the will of God already revealed in Jesus' earthly life is the same to be revealed at the last trumpet, nevertheless the precise contours of the latter cannot simply be read off of the former, because Jesus' life was lived in history, where the place of evil—and thus its final significance before God and for us—remains opaque. In light of the resurrection, Christians confess that evil's ultimate defeat is not in doubt, but it remains an open question whether its destruction includes that of at least some creatures as well. As argued in the previous chapter, eschatology reaches its limits when faced with this question. Thus, as much as the claim that Jesus will come again is a defining conviction of the Christian faith, exactly what that coming will portend for the world and its inhabitants remains beyond present sight (1 Pet. 4:17). There is an unfathomable difference between what Christians now experience and that for which they hope. And yet so long as Christians remain committed to the confession that the Jesus who has come is the object of their hope, they must be prepared to venture some claims about what will transpire upon his return.

In the great Scholastic theologies of the post-Reformation period, such claims took the form of an exposition of the "four last things": death, judgment, heaven, and hell. Since the turn of the twentieth century, the recovery of a vibrant sense of the eschatological character of Jesus' preaching and early Christian expectation of his imminent return (1 Cor. 16:22; Heb. 10:37; Rev. 22:7; cf. Matt. 26:64 and pars.) has led to an eclipse of that rather formulaic scheme in favor of approaches that stress Jesus' own insistence that the kingdom of God is genuinely "at hand" (Matt. 4:17 and pars., RSV) and even "among you (Luke

---

5. For further discussion of this point, see Ian A. McFarland, *The Word Made Flesh: A Theology of the Incarnation* (Louisville, KY: Westminster John Knox Press, 2019), 159–76. Cf. Ingolf U. Dalferth, *Crucified and Resurrected: Restructuring the Grammar of Christology*, trans. Jo Bennett (Grand Rapids: Baker Academic, 2015), 79: "The resurrection of Jesus by God . . . is not a historical fact, however incomparable its uniqueness. . . . The resurrection of the crucified does not mean that he came back to the life in the world that he had left on the cross: what God did for the crucified Jesus resulted in new life, not in a new version of the old life."

116   *The Hope of Glory*

17:21). Yet although the traditional list of "last things" is associated with a style of eschatology at once more pat in tone and otherworldly in focus than is consistent with the apocalyptic urgency of the gospel, the sequence reflects a clear and compelling logic, in which each topic lays the conceptual groundwork for what follows. I will therefore deploy it in this chapter, with one exception: the substitution of advent for death. The reason for this exception is simply that death is not in fact one of the "last things." Paul is very explicit on this point: "We will *not* all die, though we will all be changed" (1 Cor. 15:51). In the light of Easter, Christians affirm that it is encounter with the Lord, not death, that defines the final boundary of human life.

Advent

If Jesus' death on Good Friday marks the end of his life, then his coming again can no more be regarded as a further event in his life story than can his resurrection and ascension. Instead, his Parousia, or advent, should be understood as a third—public—dimension of the one eschatological event that is his vindication by God as Lord and Savior.[6] Thus, if the resurrection is God's vindication of Jesus' human life, and the ascension confirms that the human being thereby vindicated is none other than the divine Son, then advent is the universal disclosure of this vindication.[7] It is consistent with this view that the Nicene Creed describes this disclosure in terms of Jesus' coming "in glory," for because glory is proper to God alone, for Jesus to appear at the right hand of the Father can be nothing less than his revelation as the "Lord of glory" (1 Cor. 2:8; cf. Jas. 2:1) with a clarity and finality that will cause "every knee" to "bend . . . and every tongue" to "confess that Jesus Christ is Lord, to the glory of God the Father" (Phil. 2:10–11).[8]

Because the Parousia is not to be conceived as a separate event in Jesus' life, it should no more be conceived as a physical descent from heaven to earth than

---

6. Based on its use in biblical passages like Matt. 24:3, 27, 37, 39; 1 Cor. 15:23; 1 Thess. 2:19; 3:13; 4:15; 5:23; 2 Thess. 1:8; Jas. 5:7–8; 2 Pet. 3:4; and 1 John 2:28, the Greek word *parousia* has been appropriated in English to refer to Jesus' return. The fact that etymologically the word refers not to motion but instead to presence serves as a reminder that Jesus' return is not the culmination of a journey from a distant location (and thus a further event in his life), but rather the universal disclosure or appearing of the crucified and risen Lord.

7. See McFarland, *The Word Made Flesh*, 159–60. I thus differ from Wolfhart Pannenberg, who includes the incarnation together with resurrection and return as from "the standpoint of eternity . . . one and the same event," on the grounds that all three constitute "the inbreaking of the future of God" (*Systematic Theology*, vol. 3, trans. Geoffrey W. Bromiley [Grand Rapids: William B. Eerdmans, 1998, [1993]], 627). While resurrection, ascension, and return can indeed be described the same "event" (viz., different aspects of God's vindication of Jesus as Lord), since they take place outside the bounds of Jesus' life in time and so can only be viewed "from the standpoint of eternity," Jesus' birth is a distinct and properly temporal event that inaugurates the whole series of events that constitute his earthly life as a series of events which, taken as a whole, are the object of the vindication variously described in terms of resurrection, ascension, and return.

8. Stephen's vision of "the heavens opened and the Son of Man standing at the right hand of God" (Acts 7:56) can be understood as a private anticipation of what will be experienced by all.

5. Jesus, the Lord of Glory 117

the ascension should be understood as a relocation from earth to heaven.[9] And if Jesus' coming again cannot be understood as a further event in *his* life, neither is it a new event in the lives of the creatures to whom he appears. It is rather the end of their lives, the terminal boundary of their existence in space and time. And in this respect, the traditional identification of death as the first of the "last things" has some justification, since the vast majority of human beings who have existed will not be alive at the time of Jesus' return, and for them death is the point at which they come into the presence of the living Lord.[10] In other words, if Jesus' second coming defines the end—and thus the essential finitude—of the material creation as a whole, death is an anticipatory sign of this finitude at the level of the individual human life. To be human is not to live forever (see Gen. 6:1–3; cf. 3:22; Ps. 90:10), but to be granted a definite lifespan, the end of which, whether in death or at the Parousia, is marked by an encounter with Jesus, the Lord.

Nevertheless, although the facts of human demographics suggest that death will be the occasion of this encounter for the vast majority of human beings, from a theological perspective it should not be understood as normative. In his first letter to the Thessalonians (the earliest Christian document we possess), Paul clearly views the Christian experience of death as anomalous. His claim that "we who are alive, who are left until the coming of the Lord, will by no means precede those who have died" (1 Thess. 4:15) indicates that (at least at this point in his ministry) Paul did not envision either himself or most of his fellow believers dying before Jesus returned (cf. 2 Thess. 2:1). While this assumption was obviously mistaken as a matter of historical fact, it nevertheless rightly indicates the character of the Christian hope; for although death may be the point at which most human beings encounter Jesus, strictly speaking that which defines the end of human life is not death, but advent: Christians do not look forward to dying (for death is "the last enemy" according to 1 Cor. 15:26), but to meeting the one who lives.[11]

9. This is not to deny that the New Testament narrates the ascension as a historical event—and in so doing draws a parallel with the Parousia (Acts 1:11). But the fact that, as with the resurrection appearances (and in sharp contrast to the biblical accounts of Jesus' arrest, trial, and execution), the Gospel accounts of the ascension—even within the single-authored corpus of Luke–Acts (see p. 114, n. 4 above)—are characterized by narrative disarray (as opposed to the simple disagreement between the Synoptic and Johannine datings of the crucifixion) cautions against thinking of it as an event in space-time.

10. It is estimated that around 117 billion people have been born over the 50,000 years or so since our species, *Homo sapiens*, first emerged in Africa; of these 117 billion approximately 8 billion were alive in 2024. Thus, unless the earth's human population were to grow to unimaginable levels, the number of people alive at any given time in the future will never exceed the number of those who have died. See Toshiko Kaneda and Carl Haub, "How Many People Have Ever Lived on Earth," Population Reference Bureau, updated November 15, 2022, https://www.prb.org/articles/how-many-people-have-ever-lived-on-earth/.

11. A more serious theological problem posed by 1 Thessalonians 4 is that the text does not clearly indicate that "those who have died" have already encountered Jesus. Indeed, the fact that Paul uses the euphemism "to fall asleep" (*koimasthai*; cf. John 11:11–14) rather than the normal Greek word for dying (*apothanein*) to refer to the dead might be taken to suggest that he understands death as a state of unconsciousness rather than encounter. To be sure, Paul elsewhere does explicitly state that to die is to "be with Christ" (Phil. 1:23), but the prevalence of biblical language that describes death and resurrection in terms of sleep and waking (e.g., Dan. 12:2; Matt. 27:52) raises questions over the status of the dead prior to Jesus' return. In the Western church the idea that the dead exist in a state of unconsciousness prior to the general resurrection ("soul sleep") was definitively rejected in the papal bull *Benedictus Deus* (1336); a similar position was defended by John Calvin in his first theological treatise, *Vivere apud Christum non dormire animis sanctos, qui in fide Christi decedunt* (1542; later translated

118   *The Hope of Glory*

It is for this reason that coming into Jesus' presence—seeing him face-to-face (1 Cor. 13:12; cf. 1 John 3:2)—is the most appropriate designation for the first of the "last things" that form the content of Christian hope.[12] It is first, because, in making clear that human life is temporally bounded, it is the presupposition and ground of the other three. Paul's insistence that not all will die serves as a reminder that the fact that human life comes to an end is not simply a by-product of sin, as though human beings would have lived forever apart from their violation of God's primordial commandment in Eden (see Gen. 2:16–17; 3:22). It is certainly true that in the wake of sin death has acquired the additional, negative significance of exclusion from God's presence (see, e.g., Ps. 6:5; Isa. 38:18–19; cf. Eccl. 9:5) and is therefore rightly named "the last enemy" (1 Cor. 15:26; cf. Rev. 20:14). But while death in this latter sense is not a defining feature of created existence, temporal finitude (viz., "death" in the purely neutral sense seen, e.g., in passages like Gen. 6:3; Eccl. 3:2; or Isa. 65:20) most certainly is: for human life to come to an end is not in itself a result of sin, but inherent to humans' (and all worldly beings') condition as creatures.[13] To encounter Jesus, the Word through whom all things came into being (John 1:3), at life's end is simply to be confronted with the fact of one's status as a creature: a being whose existence is in every respect rooted, upheld, and bounded by God, and whose ultimate destiny is therefore in God's hands alone. To identify advent as the first of the "last things" is thus to confess that the ultimate fate of human beings, whether good or ill, depends entirely on the One in whom "we live and move and have our being" (Acts 17:28).

If advent is the theologically normative way of understanding that coming into Jesus' presence that is the destiny of all mortal creatures, how is it to be conceived? Scripture's language is dramatic and has given rise to vivid depictions of the event (most famously, perhaps, in Michaelangelo's *The Last Judgment* in the Sistine Chapel). The tone is set by Jesus' own words in the Gospels, which echo those of Daniel and speak of the Son of Man "coming on the clouds of heaven" (Matt. 26:64 and pars.; cf. Dan. 7:13-14; 1 Thess. 4:16–17). Rhetorically, this language highlights the contrast between the universal revelation of Jesus' lordship and its current hiddenness: in ascending to heaven, Jesus moves beyond the powers of earthly sight, whereas in his return he will again be seen (see Acts 1:11; Rev. 1:7). But, again, this sequence of departure and return is not

---

into French with the title *Psychopannychie*). For further discussion of the so-called intermediate state between death and resurrection, see pp. 141–42 below.

12. "It is advisable and even indispensable to realise that dying is in fact only one form of the end, confronted in free superiority by the very different form of departing to be with Christ, because only on this basis and in this association can we really see the meaning of death as the end which overtakes us. If death is the more obvious and apprehensible and relevant form of the end, we must set alongside it the fact that the coming of Jesus Christ Himself . . . may bring and be the same end, namely, the end which is also the goal and therewith the beginning without end, the resurrection of the flesh, eternal life in eternal life." Barth, *CD* IV/3.2, 926.

13. See the Catholic Mariological dogmas, which teach that Mary was without original sin, but that—at least according to Pope John Paul II—she nevertheless experienced death (viz., a termination of physiological function) prior to her bodily assumption into heaven. Since Mary was sinless, such death cannot be ascribed any punitive dimension and so must be viewed in purely neutral terms as simply marking the terminus of her life. See Pope John Paul II, "General Audience, Wednesday, 25 June 1997," §§3–5, https://www.vatican.va/content/john-paul-ii/en/audiences/1997/documents/hf_jp-ii_aud_25061997.html. Cf. Augustine's idea (*The City of God against the Pagans* 14.10) that in the absence of sin, Adam and Eve would have lived a fixed amount of time in Eden and then been translated to a state of glory.

5. Jesus, the Lord of Glory 119

properly interpreted in spatial terms as a matter of Jesus physically going and coming between earth and heaven, because heaven is not a "place" alongside other places. After all, to affirm that God is "in heaven" is not to provide directions on where to direct one's attention in order to locate God (as is the case with, e.g., "Smith is in the office"), but precisely to deny that God—apart from the period of Jesus' earthly life—can be located by reference to spatio-temporal coordinates.[14] And so while the image of Jesus coming on clouds is an effective means of communicating both the suddenness and the universality of his appearing (and thus the contrast between the eschatological revelation of Jesus' lordship and its present hiddenness), the language cannot be taken literally, for it suggests that Jesus' second coming is akin to an extraterrestrial invasion: the intrusion of a new and alien power, through the arrival of someone who has been absent. But it is not Christian faith that Jesus will be Lord only in some more or less distant future, but that he is Lord even now (Acts 10:36; Rom. 10:9; Phil. 2:9–11; cf. 1 Cor. 12:3).

Because the one who will one day be revealed in glory is hidden in the present, there is a real contrast between our current experience and the eschaton. There can be no denial of this difference: faith is not sight, and we do not hope for what we now see. And yet it is vital to remember that the one who is hidden in the present is the same as the one who will one day come, and therefore that he does not come as one unknown and to be feared. For when he comes it will not be to take up his authority, but to reveal that he—Jesus Christ, "the same yesterday and today and forever" (Heb. 13:8)—has always ruled, and that the kingdom, the power, and the glory have always been his (cf. John 17:5). In this way, the glory with which Jesus will come does not signify the returning Jesus' *difference* from the crucified, but rather the universal disclosure of the crucified as Lord (Rev. 1:7; cf. Acts 2:36). If Jesus' followers are instructed to "stand up and raise your heads" at the coming of the Son of Man, it is precisely because they know the One who is coming and therefore know that his coming has but a single meaning: "your redemption is drawing near" (Luke 21:28).

It must be stressed that Jesus' hiddenness in the present is not an absence. We are reminded of this in the Eucharist, which is an encounter with Jesus in the present that, in light of his own association of the kingdom with feasting (see Matt. 8:11; 22:1–10; 26:29 and pars.), may be viewed as the sacrament of his promised advent. That the Eucharist is reserved to those who have "been buried with [Jesus] by baptism into death" (Rom. 6:4) points to the fact that our meeting him at the table anticipates our encounter with him at the end of our lives—and thereby looks to his coming (1 Cor. 11:26). Admittedly, the Eucharist is not the same as that final encounter, any more than baptism is the same as physiological death. Our earthly lives have not come to an end, and so we do not see the Lord "face to face" (1 Cor. 13:12) in the sacrament, but only as hidden under the bread and the wine. But in meeting him there, we are reminded forcefully that the one who is coming one day in glory as Lord of all is the one who already meets us now as Lord of all. In the sacrament we experience his advent proleptically, by anticipation. We are confronted by Jesus in the elements, and we hear the words that define his relationship to us both now and

---

14. For a more extended discussion of heaven, see pp. 125–29 below.

120   *The Hope of Glory*

when he comes in glory: "This is my body that is for you" (1 Cor. 11:24). Jesus' meeting us in the supper is not the same as his meeting us at the end, but it is a training up for it, for it presents us now with the one whom we will meet then; and the form of that presentation reminds us that he will come as one who may be tasted and seen, and with words of grace.

Judgment

But will it bring only words of grace? Does not the creed link Jesus' coming with judgment—indeed, does it not speak of judgment as the very purpose of his coming ("He will come again in glory *to judge the living and the dead*")—and does not judgment raise the possibility of a negative no less than a favorable verdict? The answer to all these questions is yes, and this, too, is anticipated in the Eucharist, as Paul notes:

> Whoever, therefore, eats the bread or drinks the cup of the Lord in an unworthy manner will be answerable for the body and blood of the Lord. Examine yourselves, and only then eat of the bread and drink of the cup. For all who eat and drink without discerning the body eat and drink judgment against themselves. For this reason many of you are weak and ill, and some have died. But if we judged ourselves, we would not be judged. But when we are judged by the Lord, we are disciplined so that we may not be condemned along with the world. (1 Cor. 11:27–32)

The words that define encounter with Jesus in the Eucharist—"This is my body that is for you"—are words of grace. Yet Paul describes a situation where these words do not give life, but rather judgment that issues in weakness, illness, and death. How can this be? Paul ascribes it to a failure to discern the body. Obviously, he is not referring to a discernment of vision, for Jesus' body is not visible in the eucharistic elements in human form. It is rather a failure to recognize Jesus' invisible presence in the sacrament, and thus to treat the bread and wine merely as an occasion for filling one's belly ("When you come together, it is not really to eat the Lord's supper. For when the time comes to eat, each of you goes ahead with your own supper," 1 Cor. 11:20–21).[15] Paul's proffered solution to this threat is therefore not a closer inspection of the elements (as though a more attentive eye would perceive Jesus' body in the bread), but rather self-examination, since "if we judged ourselves, we would not be judged." But in what does this self-examination consist? It is, seemingly, to submit ourselves to the judgment of the Lord whose body is given for us. For although the flow of the argument seems initially to suggest that the alternative to "judging ourselves" now is to be "judged"—and, presumably, condemned—"by the Lord" in the future, Paul goes on to say that the result of the Lord's judgment, too, is

---

15. Note the parallel between Paul's indictment of the Corinthians here and Jesus' judgment of the crowd at Capernaum (at the beginning of a discourse with clear eucharistic reference): "Very truly, I tell you, you are looking for me, not because you saw signs, but because you ate your fill of the loaves" (John 6:26).

5. Jesus, the Lord of Glory 121

that "we may *not* be condemned."[16] But how does this kind of divine judgment square with Paul's implicit claim that the sickness and death experienced in the congregation are also the result of being judged by the Lord?

Before trying to answer this question, some preliminary remarks are in order. First of all, judgment's status as the second of the traditional "last things" makes good logical sense, since it is only once a life has run its full course and come to an end that it can be judged. It likewise makes sense that God should be the one to give judgment, since only the Creator who has sustained the creature throughout every moment of its existence and in all its myriad relationships with other creatures is in a position to provide a truly comprehensive assessment of its life. Finally, that the task of judgment should be given to the Second Person of the Trinity in particular follows from the fact that it is just this person who has assumed flesh and is therefore able to have the kind of personal encounter with the creature that judgment (as opposed to the operation of impersonal forces like fate or karma) entails.[17] Taken together, these principles provide the conceptual framework within which to interpret the biblical teaching that "all of us must appear before the judgment seat of Christ, so that each may receive due recompense for actions done in the body, whether good or evil" (2 Cor. 5:10; cf. Acts 10:42; 17:31; Rom. 14:10).

But what are the mode and timing of this appearance before Christ's judgment seat? As Paul suggests, the Eucharist may be understood to provide a proleptic experience of this judgment, grounded in the individual's encounter with the judge in the elements. But the biblical witness points to a "Last Judgment" that is universal in scope and follows immediately upon Jesus' return: the biblical "day of the Lord," when "the Son of Man . . . will sit on the throne of his glory," and "[a]ll the nations will be gathered before him, and he will separate people one from another as a shepherd separates the sheep from the goats" (Matt. 25:31–32; cf. Rev. 20:11–12). According to this picture, individual judgment takes place in the context of the judgment of all. But even as death replaced Parousia as the moment of encounter with Jesus in the imagination of most Christians after the earliest generations, so the judgment associated with that encounter came to be conceived as a highly individualized experience that followed immediately upon death, in line with the papal decree *Benedictus Deus* (1336), which taught that the souls of the blessed "immediately after death . . . have been, are and will be with Christ in heaven."[18] Yet because there can only be one judgment—one definitive verdict on a person's life—if judgment occurs for the majority of human beings immediately upon death, then a universal Last Judgment would seem to be superfluous for all but the comparative few "who are left until the coming of the Lord" (1 Thess. 4:15).

---

16. The NRSV's use of strong adversative conjunctions to characterize the relationship between these three judgments ("For this reason many of you are weak and ill. . . . *But* if we judged ourselves . . . *But* when we are judged by the Lord . . .") thus posits much more of a contrast among (as though they were clearly defined alternatives) than the flow of Paul's argument warrants, failing to capture the ambiguities of the relationship between them and over-translating the particle *de*. Better would be, "Now if we judged ourselves . . . And when we are judged by the Lord. . . ."

17. Cf. the witness of John 5:27 that the Father "has given [the Son] authority to execute judgment, *because* he is the Son of Man" (cf. 5:22).

18. *Benedictus Deus*, in *Compendium of Creeds, Definitions, and Declarations on Matters of Faith and Morals*, ed. Heinrich Denzinger, Peter Hünermann, et al., 43rd ed. (San Francisco: Ignatius Press, 2012), §1000.

122   *The Hope of Glory*

A little further reflection, however, shows that the expectation of an imme-diate postmortem encounter with Jesus does not render the prospect of the Last Judgment redundant. Indeed, even Christian anthropology demands that advent rather than death be regarded as the theologically normative way of conceiving of the end of human life, so, too, the Last Judgment should be regarded as prior in significance even if its placement at history's end means that it comes later in time.[19] The basis for this claim is not simply the Bible's own emphasis on the significance of the "day of the Lord," but also because the myr-iad lines of relationship that connect every human being with countless others across space and time alike mean that a definitive assessment of any individual life cannot be made apart from consideration of the whole course of human his-tory. For only when all the repercussions of a person's words and deeds have played out fully is it possible to assess the proper "recompense for what has been done in the body," and that ongoing history of effects will only terminate when Jesus' coming brings all history to an end.[20] At the same time, the recogni-tion that the full and final accounting of a person's life can only be known at the end of time does not negate the significance of the individual's encounter with Jesus upon death. The difference between the two may be stated as follows: if one's encounter with Jesus at death reveals *that* one is saved, only the Last Judgment reveals *what it means* to have been saved. That is, in light of the incal-culable effects of even the most seemingly trivial sin, only when the full tally of each person's errors is manifest will the magnitude of God's grace likewise be disclosed—and with it the meaning of the biblical principle that it is *only* by God's word that we live (Matt. 4:4 and par.; Deut. 8:3).

But will encounter with the judge in fact mean salvation? It is at this point that we return to the basic question of the character of eschatological judgment, irrespective of whether that judgment is experienced immediately upon death or only at Jesus' return. The problem here is simply stated: if eschatology is fundamentally the doctrine of Christian hope, it would seem to follow that eschatological judgment must necessarily result in salvation, but at first glance the evidence of Scripture seems to count strongly against viewing the judgment associated with the eschatological "day of the LORD" in hopeful terms. Isaiah is typical:

> Wail, for the day of the LORD is near;
>   it will come like destruction from the Almighty!
> Therefore all hands will be feeble,
>   and every human heart will melt,

---

19. Strictly speaking, the phrase "later in time" here refers only to the perspective of those who are still alive, for whom Jesus' return can only be regarded as temporally subsequent to all deaths that have occurred. For a discussion of what it might mean for the Last Judgment to be experienced as "later" by those who have died (i.e., the problem of the "intermediate state"), see pp. 141–42 below.

20. "Even though the definitive truth of an individual is fixed in the moment of death, something new is contributed when the world's guilt has been suffered through to the bitter end. It is at this point that one's final place in the whole is exhaustively determined: after what one might call the solidifica-tion in their finished state of all the effects to which one has given rise." Joseph Ratzinger, *Eschatology: Death and Eternal Life*, 2nd ed. (Washington, DC: Catholic University of America Press, 1988), 207. Cf. John E. Thiel, *Icons of Hope: The "Last Things" in Catholic Imagination* (Notre Dame, IN: University of Notre Dame Press, 2013), 149: "The doctrine of the Last Judgment affirms the social nature of judg-ment, an appreciation for the myriad ways that all our lives are bound together across time and space that elude individual perception."

5. Jesus, the Lord of Glory

> and they will be terrified.
> Pangs and agony will seize them;
>> they will be in anguish like a woman in labor.
> They will look aghast at one another;
>> their faces will be aflame.
> See, the day of the LORD is coming,
>> cruel, with wrath and fierce anger,
> to make the earth a desolation,
>> and to destroy its sinners from it.
>> *(Isa. 13:6–9; cf. Jer. 46:10)*

If that prospect were not dismal enough, Amos specifically rebukes those who would make the day of the Lord an object of hope:

> Woe to you who desire the day of the LORD!
>> Why do you want the day of the LORD?
> It is darkness, not light;
>> as if someone fled from a lion,
>> and was met by a bear;
> or went into the house and rested a hand against the wall,
>> and was bitten by a snake.
> Is not the day of the LORD darkness, not light,
>> and gloom with no brightness in it?
>> *(Amos 5:18–20)*

To be sure, not all will be consumed by the fire of divine wrath on that day. The eschatological separation of people described in Matthew 25 includes the assurance that the judge will say to some, "Come, you who are blessed by my Father, inherit the kingdom prepared for you from the foundation of the world" (v. 34; cf. John 5:29); but even here, the fact that the saved no less than the damned are evidently surprised by the results of this final assize (see Matt. 25:37–38, 44) would seem to cast a pall of uncertainty and dread over the whole process (cf. 1 Pet. 4:17). Against this background, it is hard to see how anyone—especially Christians, whose belief includes a profound consciousness of the depth of their weakness and failure (Ps. 51:3–5)—could regard the prospect of just judgment with equanimity, let alone with the confidence Jesus commends to his disciples in Luke 21:28.

There is no denying that divine judgment not only reveals the fact of human sin, but also the devastating truth that the weight of this sin is incompatible with life in communion with God (Ps. 130:3). For this reason, the confession that Jesus will come as *judge* can seem to cast doubt on the claim that the one who once came in humility preaching the gospel of the forgiveness of sins and the one who is to come "'on the clouds of heaven' with power" (Matt. 24:30; cf. Dan. 7:13) are identical. Can the one who "will come in glory to judge the living and the dead" really be the same as the one who during his earthly life declared, "I came not to judge the world, but to save the world" (John 12:47; but cf. 5:22–27; 8:15–16; 9:39)? Given that even in the Gospels the images associated with the coming of the Son of Man are typically far from consoling (see especially Matt. 13:40–42, 49–50; 25:31–33, 41–43; Luke 13:23–28; cf. 2 Thess. 1:6–9; Rev. 20:14–15), it is important to recognize that it is not simply modern

124   *The Hope of Glory*

dispensationalist premillennialists who posit a strong contrast between the disposition of the Jesus who walked in first-century Palestine and the Jesus who will return in judgment.[21] Already in Christianity's first millennium Pope Gregory I felt compelled to warn that "he who was mild at his ascent will be terrible at his return."[22]

And yet elsewhere the contrast between Jesus' first and second comings is described in rather different terms: "Christ, having been offered once to bear the sins of many, will appear a second time, not to deal with sin [*chōris hamartias*], but to save those who are eagerly waiting for him" (Heb. 9:28). The purpose of the second coming is not to deal with sin, because sin has already been dealt with in Christ's earthly ministry, with the result that the ruler of the world has *already* been judged (John 16:11; cf. 12:31; Luke 10:18) and the destructive power of sin already confronted. This is not to say that the Last Judgment does not address sin, but only the way it does so is by confirming and fully revealing the condemnation of sin that was made already in Jesus' earthly ministry.[23] Importantly, the fact that sin has already been dealt with means that "if we willfully persist in sin after having received the knowledge of the truth, there no longer remains a sacrifice for sins but a fearful prospect of judgment" (Heb 10:26–27). But, objectively speaking, such persistence is not a possibility, because, as Paul insists, those who been claimed by Jesus have already undergone the judgment of sin with him, and "How can we who died to sin go on living in it?" (Rom. 6:2). Because sin and its wages are in the past, the prospect of judgment offers no other possibility for believers than to "stand up and raise your heads, because your redemption is drawing near."[24]

And yet in almost the same breath that he affirms the objective impossibility of believers continuing in sin, Paul immediately goes on to say that his own life is marked by just such ongoing captivity to sin:

> So I find it to be a law that, when I want to do what is good, evil lies close at hand. For I delight in the law of God in my inmost self, but I see in my members another law at war with the law of my mind, making me captive to the law of sin that dwells in my members. Wretched person that I am! Who will rescue me from this body of death? (Rom. 7:21–24)

Once again, in the face of the sheer, inexplicable fact of human sin, a favorable outcome seems hopeless. Paul has indeed "judged himself," and what he finds is that he is utterly unworthy—"captive to the law of sin." Nevertheless, it turns out that his situation is *not* hopeless, because the answer to his final

---

21. See pp. 24–25 above.

22. "Homily 29," in Gregory the Great, *Forty Gospel Homilies*, trans. David Hurst (Collegeville, MN: Cistercian Press, 1990), 234.

23. Thus, in the same way that the Last Judgment reveals fully what it means to be saved for those who have already received Christ's words of grace at their death, so, too, it discloses what it means to have been judged to those who "have been condemned already" (John 3:18).

24. "Those who hope in Him cannot possibly droop or shake their heads; they can only lift them up. No spark of presumption can pervert the expectation of those who hope in Him, for whence could they derive it in this hope? Nor can any spark of resigned anxiety of anxious resignation disturb it, for how could such be possible or permissible in this hope? If they hope in Him, as they may and should in their moving toward this Judge, then it is He Himself, the Subject of this hope, who lives and thinks and speaks and acts in it. It is He Himself, the Judge towards whose fiery, purifying and sifting, yet gracious judgment they look and move." Barth, *CD* IV/3.2, 922–23.

5. Jesus, the Lord of Glory

question—"Who will rescue me from this body of death?"—is ready to hand: "Thanks be to God through Jesus Christ our Lord!" (Rom. 7:25), for in spite of the fact that even the believer must confess that "with my flesh I am enslaved to the law of sin" (Rom. 7:25), "Therefore there is now no condemnation for those who are in Christ Jesus" (Rom. 8:1).[25] And this, at last, provides us a way of understanding Paul's words in 1 Corinthians 11 surrounding the dynamics of judgment in the reception of the Eucharist. In the face of the apparent incompatibility between judging oneself and being judged by the Lord, it turns out that the gospel has eliminated the possibility of self-judgment, in the sense of evaluating oneself apart from Jesus and according to one's own merits, because to receive the gospel is to recognize that as a member of the body of Christ, one does not exist apart from Jesus. The self as considered apart from Jesus has died and been raised with him, so that even now our lives are "hidden with Christ in God" (Col. 3:3; cf. Gal. 2:20).

None of this, of course, changes the fact that all of us, like Paul, are in our flesh slaves to the law of sin. Indeed, we do not now truly understand how much this is the case. Only the final judgment will reveal fully the unfathomable gravity of human sin, and thus the fact that no one, Christian or not, can stand by their own righteousness. And so only then will we be able to say with full understanding, "Who will rescue me from this body of death?" But at that very point the answer will be given, not as a proposition to be believed, but as a reality present and visible to all: "Thanks be to God through Jesus Christ our Lord!" The warnings of Amos and Isaiah are therefore perfectly justified, for the burden of our sinfulness is such that if we are saved, it can and will be "only as through fire" (1 Cor. 3:15), in the full, agonizing realization of our unworthiness and our inability to stand before God. And yet it remains the case that we *are* saved, because the God before whom we can only be judged as ungodly is precisely the one "who justifies the ungodly" (Rom. 4:5; cf. 5:6). It is in this way that the Last Judgment is a proper object of Christian hope, not because we deserve to escape condemnation in light of the accounting that will then be made, but because the judge has made his life surety for our own. For what judgment will finally reveal is that "where sin abounded, grace did much more abound" (Rom. 5:20, KJV).

Heaven and Hell

To be saved in just this way—solely by the grace of Jesus Christ—is to enjoy life with God, which is the focus of the third of the traditional "last things": heaven. But what is heaven? When *Benedictus Deus* declares that the blessed dead "have been, are and will be with Christ in heaven," the image evoked is that of a parallel realm best described in spatial terms as *above* this world, rather than Jesus' language of "the kingdom of heaven" as a power breaking in on the present from a time *ahead* of us. This tension between heaven as present

---

25. The fact that Paul makes the confession, "So then, with my mind I am enslaved to the law of God, but with my flesh I am enslaved to the law of sin" (Rom. 7:26) *after* he has given thanks for Jesus Christ (Rom. 7:25) would seem to count against the idea that Paul is in these verses describing his situation before hearing the gospel.

126   *The Hope of Glory*

reality above and future state ahead is rooted in the biblical texts themselves. For while in the Bible "heaven" can mean simply the sky (e.g., Gen. 7:11; 1 Chr. 21:16; Dan. 5:21; Mal. 3:10), elsewhere it clearly refers to a transcendent realm located beyond the physical heavens (1 Kgs. 22:19; Ps. 103:19; Isa. 66:1; cf. Matt. 5:34; 2 Cor. 12:2), as reflected in the Nicene Creed's troping of "heaven and earth" as demarcating the realms of the invisible and the visible.[26] In this context (and as already noted), heaven is arguably best defined as the created sphere where God dwells, and where creatures therefore experience God's presence continually.[27]

And yet if there is on these grounds an appropriate contrast between heaven and earth as present realities referring to those spheres of creation where God is and is not immediately present to creatures, respectively, considered eschatologically, reference to "heaven" must be interpreted as a synecdoche, for the Christian hope is not for heaven alone, but rather for a "new heavens *and* a new earth, where righteousness is at home" (2 Pet. 3:13; cf. Isa. 65:17; 66:22; Rev. 21:1).[28] Indeed, far from looking to a future in which life with God means that we "fly away" from earth *up* to some distant plane, the Bible's climactic eschatological vision is that of "the holy city, the new Jerusalem, coming *down*" from heaven to earth, accompanied by the divine declaration that "the home of God is among mortals" (Rev. 21:2–3).[29] That this state of cosmic renewal in which the current "distance" between earth and heaven collapses should be named as "heaven" reflects again the principle implicit in the third petition of the Lord's Prayer: that heaven refers to that realm where God's will is done immediately and transparently.[30] With Christ's coming, this realm (viz., "the kingdom of

---

26. The invisibility of heaven differs from that of, e.g., oxygen, subatomic particles, or dark matter, in that in the present age human ingenuity cannot penetrate it apart from an act of special divine revelation (see 2 Cor. 12:1–4).

27. This slippage between "above" and "ahead" is also visible in Galatians 4, where Paul contrasts "the present [viz., earthly] Jerusalem" (v. 25) with "the Jerusalem above" (v. 26); cf. Rev. 21:2, where by virtue of its heavenly descent, "the Jerusalem above" becomes the future Jerusalem on earth. Cf. Markus Mühling's distinction between eschatologies "from ahead" and "from above" referenced on p. 1, n. 1 above.

28. The witness to the new heavens and earth in 2 Peter is preceded by a twofold prediction that with the day of the Lord "the heavens will pass away with a loud noise, and the elements will be destroyed with fire" (2 Pet. 3:10; cf. 12), which was traditionally interpreted within the Lutheran tradition in particular as implying "[n]ot a transformation of the world, but an absolute annihilation of its substance" (see Heinrich Schmid, *The Doctrinal Theology of the Evangelical Lutheran Church*, 3rd ed., trans. Charles A. Hay and Henry E. Jacobs [Minneapolis: Augsburg, 1961], 656). Here it must be admitted that the Reformed tradition has proven more insightful. See, e.g., Charles Hodge, *Systematic Theology*, IV.iv.3.2 (Grand Rapids: William B. Eerdmans, 1940 [1872]): "The destruction here foretold [in 2 Pet. 3:6–13] is not annihilation. (*a*.) The world is to be burnt up; but combustion is not a destruction of substance. It is merely a change of state or condition. (*b*.) The destruction of the world by water and its destruction by fire are analogous events; the former was not annihilation, therefore the second is not. (*c*.) The destruction spoken of is elsewhere called a παλιγγενεσία, regeneration (Matt. xix. 28); an ἀποκατάστασις, a restoration (Acts iii. 21); a deliverance from the bondage of corruption (Rom. viii. 21). The Apostle teaches that our vile bodies are to be fashioned like unto the glorious body of Christ, and that a similar change is to take place in the world we inhabit. There are to be new heavens and a new earth, just as we are to have new bodies. Our bodies are not to be annihilated, but changed. (*d*.) There is no evidence, either from Scripture or experience, that any substance has ever been annihilated."

29. As Christopher Morse has noted, heaven "is less about a place we go to than one that comes to us." Christopher L. Morse, *The Difference Heaven Makes: Rehearsing the Gospel as News* (London: T&T Clark International, 2010), 7.

30. It follows from the confession of God as the one who creates from nothing that God's will is always done even now, insofar as nothing—on earth no less than in heaven—is outside the compass of the divine will. Thus, the Lord's Prayer does not contrast heaven and earth as realms where God's will

5. Jesus, the Lord of Glory

heaven") will encompass the whole created order, which will thus no longer be divided between the visible and the invisible (see Rev. 21:22–23).[31] In this sense the millenarian insistence that the Christian hope not be consigned to an otherworldly sphere is fully justified, even if the idea of Christ returning to reign on earth within history (following a literal reading of Rev. 20:4–6) has rightly been rejected by most Eastern and Western church traditions as failing to recognize that even as Christ's individual lifespan ends with his death, so the lifespan of the world of which he is Lord ends with his return.

Importantly, however, whether conceived as "above" or "ahead," heaven, in its distinction from "earth" (i.e., the whole of the material cosmos, including the terrestrial sky and interstellar space), is not a place. That is, because it is not part of the physical universe, it cannot be located in terms of space-time coordinates and should not be conceived as occupying space within or even alongside the space we inhabit that emerged with the big bang.[32] It is rather a completely sui generis sphere that is independent of "earthly" cosmology. Yet this does not mean that references to heaven are completely devoid of topographical significance. Heaven, no less than earth, is created; but, again, it is that portion of creation where God is immediately present to creatures, and thus where not only God but also creatures may be said to dwell. The creatures that dwell in heaven include pre-eminently and from the beginning "angels," a collective term used in Christian theology to designate that indeterminately large, varied, and mysterious group of supernatural beings who populate God's heavenly court (see, e.g., 1 Kgs. 22:19–20; Isa. 6:1–3; Rev. 4:2–8; 5:11–12).[33] Ultimately, however, heaven, understood fundamentally as the sphere of life in God's presence, is the destiny of all creatures by virtue of the eschatological descent of the heavenly city to earth. In this way, "heaven," precisely as the term for that

---

is and is not done, respectively, but rather in terms of *how* God's will is done in both spheres. In heaven God's will is done transparently, corresponding to God's immediate presence to creatures; on earth prior to the eschaton the way in which God's will is accomplished amid those realities (sin and evil) that by definition do not correspond to God's will is hidden, corresponding to the present hiddenness of God's agency on earth in general (miracles and the incarnation excepted).

31. In this context, it is important to note that the eschatological promise of a "new heaven" does not refer to the created sphere where God dwells, since that heaven, as the realm where God's will is already perfectly accomplished, does not need to be created anew. It refers rather to the physical heavens, which form part of the earthly (i.e., visible) sphere of creation that does require renewal. See, e.g., 2 Pet. 3:12–13, where the claim that "the heavens will be set ablaze and dissolve" immediately precedes the promise of "a new heavens and a new earth."

32. According to some versions of big bang cosmology, a primordial period of inflation gave rise to distinct and mutually incommunicable "spaces," each evolving independently of all the others, so that a different region of the resultant "multiverse" could not be mapped in terms of coordinates in our region of space-time. "Heaven" is not rightly conceived as a region within such a multiverse, since that would, again, simply make it parallel to and thus ontologically of the same species as "earth."

33. These beings are referred to by a range of designations in Hebrew, including the ṣᵉbā haššāmayim ("host of heaven," 1 Kgs. 22:19), each of whom is a rūaḥ ("spirit," 1 Kgs. 22:21), sᵊrāphîm ("seraphim," Isa. 6:2), and kᵊrubîm ("cherubim," Ezek. 10:1), as well as malākîm ("angels," i.e., messengers, Gen. 28:12; Job 4:18; Pss. 103:20; 148:2). To these the New Testament (specifically, Rom. 8:38 and Col. 1:16) adds the Greek terms *archai* ("rulers"), *dynameis* ("powers"), *thronoi* ("thrones"), *kyriotētes* ("dominions"), and *exousiai* ("authorities"). In subsequent theology Thomas Aquinas offered a maximalist understanding of angelic diversity, arguing that since matter is what differentiates individual members of a species, and since angels are immaterial, each angel must constitute its own species (see his *Summa Theologiae* 1.50.4, 60 vols., Blackfriars ed. [London: Eyre & Spottiswood, 1964–1981]). Yet even if one maintains with others in the Christian tradition (e.g., Gregory of Nyssa, Dionysius the Areopagite, and John Duns Scotus) that angelic species include multiple members, the biblical evidence points to the angelic hosts as unimaginably extensive, both quantitatively and qualitatively.

128   *The Hope of Glory*

sphere where creatures dwell immediately in God's presence, is finally not to be understood in terms of contrast or opposition to earth and its creatures but rather as the goal or fulfillment of God's intentions for the whole of creation, in light of which God's status as "Lord of heaven and earth" (Acts 17:24) will be fully and finally vindicated.

Prior to this final vindication, heaven also defines "the direction from which God is said to act in relation to the earth."[34] In this respect there is an analogy between the physical heavens and the heaven of God's dwelling that justifies the use of the same term for both, in that each in its own way may be said to overarch the earth and to shape its destiny.[35] Scripture speaks of God hearing earthly prayers in heaven and acting from heaven to direct the course of human events (1 Kgs. 8:30–43; 2 Chr. 7:13–14; Neh. 9:28; cf. Pss. 57:3; 80:14; Isa. 63:15; 2 Pet. 1:17–18). Indeed, the use of "angels" as the generic term for heaven's permanent residents reflects the fact that their primary function is that of "messengers" (Greek *angeloi*) charged with communicating God's heaven-determined intentions to the earth.[36] And if through most of history this movement from heaven to earth is perceived by human beings only episodically, at those pivotal points in the divine economy where God invites human beings to participate in enacting God's redemptive purposes (see, e.g., Gen. 12:1–3; 17:1–8; Exod. 3:1–12; Judg. 13:1–20; Luke 1:26–38), its eschatological culmination is both comprehensive and public in the descent of the heavenly city described in Revelation 21. Against the charge that the promise of heaven (or, more accurately, of the comprehensive renewal of creation described in Scripture as a "new heaven and a new earth") is an opiate that only serves to defer indefinitely demands for justice in the present, it is vital to stress that heaven is best understood not as an otherworldly realm, but rather the power of God supervening on and overcoming the limitations of earthly existence, in line with the vision of the descent of the heavenly Jerusalem.[37] It is in this context that Jesus's famous statement to Pilate—that his kingdom "does not belong to this world" (John 18:36)—is to be understood: not that his kingdom is located elsewhere, but that its source is rooted in the power of God rather than in the possibilities and potentials of worldly existence. To hope for heaven is to look forward to the time when the

---

34. "References to heaven as God's dwelling place emphasize not a state of confinement but the direction from which God is said to act in relation to the earth." Morse, *The Difference Heaven Makes*, 10. It is worth noting that this understanding of heaven holds whether it is conceived as "above" or "ahead."

35. In the premodern period there were a range of astrological theories that affirmed the influence of the motions of heavenly bodies on earthly events; contemporary science would describe such influences in more general terms (e.g., the ways in which stellar lifecycles, gravity, various forms of electromagnetic radiation, and the forces of cosmic expansion, including as yet little understood features like dark energy, condition the evolution and continuation of life on earth).

36. Claus Westermann maintained that in the Old Testament there is a clear distinction between God's messengers ("angels" in the etymological sense) and the heavenly creatures who comprise God's court (e.g., the cherubim and seraphim) and who "are not messengers of God, but are in the message of the messenger" (Claus Westermann, *God's Angels Need No Wings*, trans. D. L. Scheidt [Philadelphia: Fortress Press, 1979], 23). In the New Testament, however, it would seem that any such distinction falls away, as Gabriel, identifying himself to Zechariah in Luke 1:19, combines the two: "I am Gabriel. I stand in the presence of God, *and* I have been sent to speak to you and to bring you this good news."

37. "For black slaves . . . heaven meant that the eternal God had made a decision about their humanity that could not be destroyed by white masters." James H. Cone, *The Spirituals and the Blues* (New York: Seabury Press, 1972), 91.

5. Jesus, the Lord of Glory

divine glory which shines there eternally becomes visible with equal clarity and permanence on earth, which will then "be full of the knowledge of the Lord as the waters cover the sea" (Isa. 11:9).

And yet this vision of heaven joined with earth in a city illumined by the light of God and the Lamb is not quite final. For no sooner has John finished describing his vision of the heavenly Jerusalem coming down to earth than he hears the following, more ambiguous account of the last things:

> It is done! I am the Alpha and the Omega, the Beginning and the End. To the thirsty I will give water as a gift from the spring of the water of life. Those who conquer will inherit these things, and I will be their God, and they will be my children. But as for the cowardly, the faithless, the polluted, the murderers, the sexually immoral, the sorcerers, the idolaters, and all liars, their portion will be in the lake that burns with fire and sulfur, which is the second death. (Rev. 21:6–8, translation altered)[38]

These words suggest that not all are included in the eschatological union of heaven and earth, and this apparent proviso brings us to the fourth and final topic in the traditional list of "last things": hell, defined as "a place of torment, in which [the damned] suffer, according to the degree of their ungodliness, in bodily and spiritual pains, for their sins, eternally."[39] That the Bible (and, more specifically, Jesus) speaks of a place of postmortem torment for the wicked is undeniable (e.g., Matt. 13:49–50; 25:41–46; Mark 9:47–48; cf. Dan. 12:2; Rev. 20:10, 14; 21:8). But it does not do so consistently. Paul, for example, nowhere speaks of eternal torment, but rather seems to envision the resurrection as limited to believers (1 Cor. 15:42–44; Phil. 3:11; 1 Thess. 4:13–17) and, correspondingly, to view the punishment of the wicked as consisting in their destruction (see Phil. 3:19; 2 Thess. 1:9; but cf. Rom. 2:8–9), a position that has come to be known in the modern period as "annihilationism."[40] And the situation is further complicated by the fact that still other biblical passages appear to support the idea that all people are saved (Rom. 5:18; 11:32; 1 Tim. 4:10; Titus 2:11; cf. 1 Cor. 4:5; 1 Tim. 2:4; 2 Pet. 3:9): the doctrine of universalism or *apokatastasis* (the Greek word for "restoration").[41]

---

38. The NRSVue translates the latter part of v. 8, "But as for the cowardly . . . their *place* will be in the lake that burns with fire." As explained in the following paragraph, there are good theological reasons for denying hell the status of place; moreover, the Greek word used here is *meros*, which is better translated "portion" or "lot."

39. Heinrich Schmid, *Doctrinal Theology of the Evangelical Lutheran Church*, §67, 3rd ed., trans. Charles A. Hay and Henry E. Jacobs (Minneapolis: Augsburg, 1961 [1899]), 656. While this definition is taken from a Lutheran text, there would be no appreciable difference were the definition to be drawn from Reformed or Catholic sources.

40. The author of 2 Peter may also be read as holding such views, since his (admittedly sketchy) eschatological reflections speak of the rebellious angels being kept in hell "until" (*eis*) the judgment, but, seemingly, not beyond it (2 Pet. 2:4, 9)—an interpretation reinforced by the writer's later reference to "the present heavens and earth . . . being kept until the day of judgment and destruction of the godless" (2 Pet. 3:7; cf. 2:6, 12).

41. The word *apokatastasis* occurs once in the Greek New Testament, when Luke records Peter teaching that Jesus "must remain in heaven until the time of universal restoration [*apokatastaseōs pantōn*] that God announced long ago through his holy prophets" (Acts 3:21). While the sentence is certainly patient of interpretation in a universalist sense, it is less explicit in support of universal salvation than passages like 1 Timothy 4:10 that speak directly of salvation extended to all people.

130 *The Hope of Glory*

The exegetical debates over the proper interpretation of these passages remain unresolved and are probably unresolvable.[42] Equally unsatisfactory are efforts to decide the question in terms of comparative evaluations of the power of God's mercy on the one hand, and the requirements of God's justice on the other, as such approaches tend to trade on general moral sensibilities unmoored from specifically Christian theological considerations. Given these ambiguities, and in light of the confidence with which the topic is often treated in the pulpit as well as in dogmatic writing, the first note to be sounded in any theological reflection on hell is the need for caution.[43] For example, although the habit of speaking of "heaven and hell" together, as though they were parallel realities, is thoroughly entrenched in the tradition, it is not at all biblical. As noted in the previous paragraphs, Scripture pairs heaven with *earth*, not hell. Heaven and earth are complementary realities, distinct spheres of God's creative activity, each with its own characteristic richness and beauty, and, as such (in accord with John's vision of the descent of the heavenly Jerusalem), are destined to be united in glory. Hell has no such status. It forms no part of the order of creation, as reflected in Revelation's teaching that "Hades" is destined for destruction together with death in the eschatological lake of fire (20:14).[44]

In this same vein, it is important to stress that hell, like heaven, is not properly conceived of as a place, though for importantly different reasons. Heaven is not a place because it constitutes a different sphere of created reality than earth. In the realm of the visible, "place" designates a specific location within space-time; but God, as the Creator of the space-time continuum, cannot be located within it (except during the period of the earthly ministry of the incarnate Word).[45] Heaven is the realm of God's immediate, glorious presence, in distinction from earth, where God's power is no less active in sustaining creaturely existence, but where perception of divine presence (i.e., the sight of God's glory) will only be realized after the end of time, when the earth is to

42. Something of the futility of these debates is evident in the often-tortured character of arguments on both sides. Among universalists, for example, much energy is spent trying to show that the post-mortem torment of which Jesus warns is not eternal. This effort is often centered on interpretation of the Greek word *aiōnios*, which, though rendered "eternal" in most English translations, literally means "of an age," and so might be taken to suggest a long but nevertheless limited period; but such arguments face the difficulty that in passages like Matthew 25:46 the threat of *aiōnios* punishment occurs in parallel with the promise of *aiōnios* life—and no one suggests that the latter is anything other than everlasting (though see David Bentley Hart's suggestion that the term should be understood qualitatively rather than referring to duration in *The New Testament: A Translation* [New Haven, CT: Yale University Press; 2017], 537). Contrariwise, those who reject universal salvation must resort to fairly tendentious exegesis to explain how in the various passages that speak of all people being saved, "all" does not really mean all, but only some human beings.

43. Hans Urs von Balthasar describes this legacy of inordinate confidence in both directions as a "double *praesumptio*." See Hans Urs von Balthasar, *Dare We Hope "That All Men Be Saved"? with a Short Discourse on Hell*, trans. Dr. David Kipp and Rev. Lothar Krauth (San Francisco: Ignatius, 1988), 28.

44. To be sure, "Hades" seems here to be equivalent to the Old Testament Sheol, that is, the abode of the dead, which is not as such a place of torment, in contrast to the Gehenna of Matt. 5: 22, 29–30 and *passim*, as well as Revelation's lake of fire. But it is part of the mystery of biblical accounts of "hell" that "Hades" should be consigned to "Gehenna."

45. Although heaven is also created, another reason for denying that it is a place is the absurdity of affirming that God is contained in it, as would follow were it conceived as a place in which God could be located (see 1 Kgs. 8:27). God transcends heaven no less than earth, but in such a way that in heaven God's transcendence is (so to speak) "visible" insofar as to be in heaven is to dwell in God's presence. If one wishes to use the language of place in relation to heaven, it would be least misleading to say that heaven is the "place" where God is our place.

5. Jesus, the Lord of Glory
131

be created anew on a different basis than the current order of things (see Isa. 65:17; 66:22; 2 Pet. 3:13; Rev. 21:1). By contrast, hell is not a place because, unlike either heaven or earth, it is defined by God's *absence* (see Isa. 38:18; cf. Ps. 6:5; Eccl. 9:10), and that from which God is absent can have no proper reality—and thus no "place"—because all that is real comes from God and so cannot continue in existence apart from God's power.[46] Thus, whereas both heaven and earth, in their own particular ways, are realms characterized by vitality, hell is ultimately powerless and, in this sense, empty, whatever one's views on the question of universal salvation (see Matt. 16:18–19).

But clearly this last question—whether all are in fact saved, such that hell's nullity means that it proves to be empty in every sense—cannot be avoided. As that from which God is absent, hell may be understood as encompassing all to which God says a final and irrevocable no. That death and Hades, those forces that stand in the way of creaturely life in God's presence, should receive this definitive condemnation is one thing; but that creatures—not only those human beings who are cowardly, faithless, polluted, and idolatrous, but even the beast, the false prophet, and the devil himself (insofar as the terms are taken to refer to beings created by God and so by definition essentially good)— should be subject to this fate (see Rev. 19:20; 20:10) seems to fly in the face of God's will (which, in Christian belief, cannot ultimately be defeated) that all should be saved (2 Tim. 2:4; cf. Matt. 18:14). From this perspective, there seems good reason to distinguish God's love for the sinner from God's hatred for the sin, and to argue that this distinction implies that in the course of eschatological judgment the sin that is condemned both can and must be separated from the sinner, who is saved (see 1 Cor. 3:15).[47] To suppose otherwise would seem to raise the appalling specter of a God who is love (1 John 4:8, 16) consigning creatures who are in their essence good (Gen. 1:31) to a destiny of eternal torment. One might cite Hebrews 12:7–11, which distinguishes divine from human punishment precisely on the grounds that the former serves to benefit us (see especially v. 10: "he disciplines us for our good, in order that we may share his holiness"). Although this passage is referring to earthly trials rather than postmortem destiny, the principles of divine activity here described seem hard to reconcile with God's submitting any creature to an eternity of torture.

The question of how a God who is at once all-good (and thus ineluctably committed to creaturely well-being) and all-powerful (and so able to overcome every form of resistance to the divine will) could will the eternal suffering of some creatures is a variation on the broader problem of theodicy, or the problem

---

46. To be sure, Job 26:6; Ps. 139:8; and Amos 9:2 proclaim that God's power extends even to Sheol, but the point in these passages seems to be poetic exaltation of the comprehensive character of God's sovereignty rather than literal description.

47. So Balthasar: "Hell would be what is finally condemned by God; what is left in it is sin, which has been separated from the sinner by the work of the Cross." Hans Urs von Balthasar, *The Last Act*, vol. 5 of *Theo-Drama: Theological Dramatic Theory*, trans. Graham Harrison (San Francisco: Ignatius, 1998 [1983]), 314; cf. 321, where he links this to Ambrose's statement *Idem homo et salvatur ex parte, et condemnatur ex parte* (*In Ps.* 118, serm. 20, 58; *PL* 15:1502): "Hope can only cling blindly to the miracle that has taken place in the Cross of Christ. . . . What is damnable in him has been separated from him and thrown out with the usable residue that is incinerated outside the gates." A further variation on this idea is found in the work of Pavel Florensky, who argues that while the self will be saved in judgment, a person's sinful "'work,' his self-consciousness will become a pure illusion, eternally burning, eternally perishing." Pavel Florensky, *The Pillar and Ground of the Truth: An Essay in Orthodox Theodicy in Twelve Letters*, trans. Boris Jakim (Princeton, NJ: Princeton University Press, 2004), 171.

132   *The Hope of Glory*

of evil. For the most part Christians have addressed this "problem" by qualifying the degree to which evil can be considered real, arguing (for example) that evil is best understood as a privation of the good, and thus as lacking any proper being (unlike creatures, who, by virtue of having been created by a good God, are real and so, following Genesis 1:31, inherently good).[48] At the same time, they have generally taken care to distinguish this position from the idea that evil is simply an illusion, for fear of failing to take the threat it poses to creaturely well-being sufficiently seriously.[49] David Bentley Hart, however, seems to come close to this latter position when he argues that from the perspective of eternity evil will ultimately count as zero (i.e., as no obstacle to creaturely communion with God), drawing on the story from *The Brothers Karamazov* of the man who after an absurdly long and tortuous postmortem journey finally enters into paradise and declares it worth the trouble. According to Hart, the upshot of the story is that whatever one's vision of final perfection may be, no such vision can finally be compelling "unless . . . eternity reduce the price of evil to absolutely nothing."[50]

There is real power in this view. Superficially, it may seem similar to compensatory theodicies, in which the experience of evil in this life could be quantified and then balanced out by a greater quantity of good in the next. That sort of approach, in which the experience of, say, five hundred units of evil now would be trumped by a thousand of good in glory fails to grapple with the character of the human experience of evil, which is not uniform and fungible across individuals and their circumstances.[51] But to speak of the reduction of evil to zero is not to hypothesize a process of overbalancing in this sense, for if evil is reduced to zero, then it isn't the case that the blessings of glory compensate for it. To say that evil ultimately doesn't count at all is not to argue that it is outweighed by good, but rather that it is revealed as a nullity before it. Finally, it *is* an illusion.

In many respects, this position is similar to that of Julian of Norwich as described in the previous chapter, though it lacks Julian's concomitant insistence that the church's teaching on judgment and damnation must be held firm alongside her vision of unbroken divine love. And this difference seems to me decisive, for Hart's reduction of evil to zero ventures a claim that Christians cannot make, if God's opposition to evil is real and (as discussed in the previous chapter) the forgiveness of sins correspondingly significant for Christian life. If forgiveness matters, then God's judgment—and the evil against which it is exercised—can't simply reduce to nothing. Moreover, such a reduction

---

48. To give the classic example, the evil that is represented by the rotting of an apple is a deficiency or lack of being in the apple (i.e., a situation where the apple is not what an apple should be), such that when the rot consumes the apple completely, not only the (good) apple, but also the (evil) rot cease to exist. As privation, evil "exists" only as something parasitic on the good and therefore has no "being" of its own.

49. As discussed in chapter 2 (see pp. 50–56 above), there are, of course, alternative assessments: process theologians address the problem of evil by qualifying God's omnipotence, and so-called protest theodicies hold that the gravity of evil calls God's goodness into question. But both are very much minority positions in both the Jewish and Christian traditions.

50. David Bentley Hart, "The Devil's March: *Creatio ex nihilo*, the Problem of Evil, and a Few Dostoyevskian Meditations," in *Creation* ex nihilo: *Origins, Development, Contemporary Challenges*, ed. Gary A. Anderson and Markus Bockmuehl (Notre Dame, IN: University of Notre Dame Press, 2018), 317.

51. See Rowan Williams, "Redeeming Sorrows: Marilyn McCord Adams and the Defeat of Evil," in *Wrestling with Angels: Conversations in Modern Theology*, ed. Mike Higton (Grand Rapids: William B. Eerdmans, 2007), especially 256–59.

5. Jesus, the Lord of Glory 133

carries problematic implications for evil's victims, for if the guilt of the sinner is finally nothing, then so, too, must be the harm suffered by those sinned against. And if the point of glorification is precisely the affirmation of the lives that have been lived in this world (rather than a vision of their ever-increasing insignificance in the face of an eternity in the presence of divine glory), then the idea that evil comes to zero ultimately fails to honor the texture of human life here and now.[52]

Following again the line of argument in the previous chapter, this does not mean that universalism is false, but rather that—in line with the ambiguity of the biblical evidence—there are insufficient theological resources to decide unequivocally in favor of either damnation or *apokatastasis*. Whatever surprises the eschaton may hold, however, dogmatically speaking hell is best conceived not as an independent theologoumenon, but rather as what might best be described as a background or "reflex" doctrine of the church. It arises because Christians teach that God forgives sin. If the forgiveness means something, then it presupposes genuinely righteous wrath and judgment against the sin, to which I would be justly subject absent this forgiveness; for insofar as God's holiness is absolute, it would seem to follow that the divine rejection of transgression would be equally uncompromising.[53] In this sense, hell is indispensable, not as an object of theological interest in its own right, but as background to the gospel of forgiveness.[54] And yet though this prioritization of forgiveness makes it difficult to conceive how hell should ultimately turn out to be anything other than empty, it does not justify the judgment that the concept is theologically (because morally) incoherent. It does, however, justify the position that hell is known only as that which has been utterly undone by the power of God. And this means that hell cannot be deployed to make any claim about the possible fate of other people. To do so is to mistake hell's place in Christian discourse. Christians do not proclaim hell; they proclaim the gospel, and hell emerges from that proclamation, again, only by reflex and not as an independent teaching.[55]

---

52. The problem of loss is central to Hart's defense of universalism, as evident from his claim that "if anything were to be eternally lost—the least little thing—then the goodness of creation could never be more in the end than a purely conditional goodness, a mere relative evaluation, rather than an essential truth" (David Bentley Hart, *That All Shall Be Saved: Heaven, Hell and Universal Salvation* [New Haven, CT: Yale University Press, 2019], 317). My point is that this (quite appropriate) concern about the loss of any creature ends up creating other sorts of loss. For if the point of glorification is the affirmation of the lives that have been lived in this world, then the idea that evil comes to zero risks nullifying defining features of creaturely lives—all the more so if the gospel entails that our most fundamental identity is that of forgiven sinners, and thus creatures for whom our sin is an irreversible (though not irredeemable) part of our histories.

53. This is the *particula veri* in Anselm of Canterbury's insistence that the gravity of sin requires the most radical of divine countermeasures (*nondum consideravisse pondus peccati*): not that some counterbalancing act of justice is required a priori (viz., *remoto Christo*) in order for God to be able to forgive, but that the fact of divine forgiveness presupposes that in the absence of God's forgiving, the consequences of sin (viz., death and damnation) would define human destiny.

54. The fact that hell is not prominent in the Old Testament is theologically salient, since in the same way that the gravity of sin is known only as it is forgiven, so the specter of hell emerges with clarity only in the light of the clear proclamation of the gospel of forgiveness of sins.

55. I have considerable sympathy with Hart's view that in any thorough discussion of the problem, evil "must prove to be either all or nothing" (see *That All Shall Be Saved*, 67). The difference is that while he feels obliged under those circumstances to opt for nothing, it seems to me that any final dogmatic decision for one or the other leads to insurmountable theological difficulties. At the same time, I concede that in practice one will necessarily list toward one or the other alternative.

Hell can be viewed as an object of hope, and thus as having a legitimate place in Christian eschatology, insofar as hell stands for God's final and irrevocable rejection of sin and death. For Christians cannot help but regard with hope the prospect that all those things that keep creatures from life with God should be completely and definitively overcome. But hell is certainly not an object of hope insofar as it includes the possibility of the ultimate rejection of any of those creatures for whom God, in the very act of creating them, intended abundant life. If God wishes all to be saved, then Christians can neither hope for nor, indeed, expect another creature's damnation.[56] In this respect, hell's place as the final topic in the old eschatological treatises is appropriate, for it is best regarded not as a "last thing" in its own right, but rather as a limit on our ability to speak definitively about the last things. As that topic which emerges in connection with the final resolution of the mystery of evil, hell defines a boundary to eschatological speech beyond which we cannot pass without presuming to occupy the state of glory that remains before us. In the meanwhile, the concept of hell can be confronted only as at once inconceivable (insofar as it is inconsistent with God's unbreakable love for all that God has made) and unavoidable (insofar as the possibility of damnation is intrinsic to the gospel's logic of forgiveness). In short, Christians cannot avoid speaking of hell, but they should do so only to look away from it.

For that to which Christians are to look is Jesus, the Lord of glory, such that any truly Christian account of the last things—and thus of what glory means— must be defined by reference to him. And in this context, Gregory the Great's dictum that "he who was mild at his ascent will be terrible at his return" must be viewed as fundamentally mistaken. For glory is not a property that can be understood or defined independently of Jesus, as though it were an attribute whose content could be known on other grounds and then applied to Jesus as a sign of his singular importance and authority. A vision of Jesus' glory in that sense—as a compensatory reward for his earthly suffering that will allow him at his return to exercise the kind of brute force used against him in Palestine only on an unimaginably vaster scale—deforms Christian hope to an exercise in Nietzschean *ressentiment*: a fantasy of terror and vengeance that is born of frustration, self-loathing, and despair. But the glory of Christ is different. It is the glory of the cross. And that means for Jesus to return in glory is (in line with the angel's words in Acts 1:11) for him to return in exactly the same way that he ascended: as the one who, "[h]aving loved his own who were in the world . . . loved them to the end" (John 13:1) and, indeed, beyond it. In this way only is Jesus the Lord of glory.

---

56. As indicated above, even the hope for the devil's damnation is seemingly inconsistent with Christian belief, if the devil is viewed (as in the majority tradition) as a creature of God, and thus as essentially good. In this context, Karl Barth's refusal to identify the realm of the demonic with fallen angels (i.e., creatures) provides a framework within which the promise of Satan's damnation is more consistent with other fundamental convictions of the Christian faith; see Barth, CD III/3, 519–30. For an explanation of how the redemption of fallen angels might be conceived as ontologically impossible, given their particular creaturely ontology, see Eugene F. Rogers Jr., *Sexuality and the Christian Body: Their Way into the Triune God* (Oxford: Blackwell, 1999), 229–30.

6. The Transformation of the Self

As argued in the previous chapter, the primary and essential content of "the hope of glory" is Jesus, since his return in glory (that is, when he will manifest fully his divinity as the eternal Word whose kingdom "will have no end") is the first and decisive of the "last things" of Christian eschatology. Indeed, the items in the traditional list of eschatological topics—death/judgment, heaven, and hell—are just particular specifications of what Jesus' return entails: the disclosure of the final truth of every creature's existence, the experience of life in God's presence, and the definitive rejection of everything that stands in the way of God's will to dwell with human beings in a renewed creation, respectively. In this way, Christians place their hope in Jesus not simply as the one who proclaims the kingdom, but (as noted earlier) as the *autobasileia*: the one in whom the promise of the kingdom—that "the home of God is among mortals" (Rev. 21:3; cf. Matt. 1:23)—is realized. Life in the kingdom is simply life with Jesus.[1]

But what does the promise of such life mean concretely for individual human beings? Scripture is clear that the glory with which Jesus comes is not for him alone, but will be shared with all those called to be God's children (1 Pet. 5:4; cf. Heb. 2:7, 9) and, through them, with the whole creation (Rom. 8:21).[2] Yet life in glory has a particular character, which, as already noted, is not resuscitation and thus is not rightly understood merely as the extension

---

1. Note that from this perspective the question of whether it is possible to be saved apart from Jesus must be answered in the negative, since if salvation is life *with* Jesus, then it is impossible *per definitionem* to experience it *apart from* Jesus. At the same time, asserting that salvation is impossible apart from Jesus is very different from claiming that it is impossible unless one is a Christian, for, as emphasized in the previous chapter, it is intrinsic to Christian eschatology that *everyone* will encounter Jesus (2 Cor. 5:10), and there is nothing in Scripture to suggest that the outcome of that encounter is determined exclusively by a person's confessional status during their lives. Paul displays a noteworthy agnosticism on this point when he writes of unconverted Gentiles that "their conflicting thoughts will accuse or perhaps excuse them on the day when, according to my gospel, God, through Christ Jesus judges the secret thoughts of all" (Rom. 2:15–16).

2. Given the long Christian tradition that views angels along with human beings as members of Christ's body, the enormous diversity that obtains among human beings (so that, e.g., many we would recognize as human do not have the textbook definition of 46 chromosomes), as well as the possibility of extraterrestrial life forms to whom it might seem appropriate to preach the gospel, it seems wise to refrain from any precipitous judgments about defining too sharply the line between "those called to be God's children" and the rest of creation. In this context, Paul Griffiths seems to offer a prudent way forward: "the second person of the Trinity takes flesh and dies for all sinners, and they are also the ones to whom . . . the offer of redemption is made. The term *homo* can, on this view, be understood as a placeholder for 'enfleshed animate creature in the LORD's image and likeness.' . . . It need not be understood as a placeholder for 'member of the species *Homo sapiens sapiens.*'" Paul Griffiths, *Decreation: The Last Things of All Creatures* (Waco, TX: Baylor University Press, 2014), 270.

135

136   *The Hope of Glory*

of a person's earthly life in a new location. It is rather life reconstituted on a completely different basis, for to speak as the New Testament does of the life of the kingdom in terms of a new heaven and a new earth is to point to a novel context of creaturely existence in which "everything old has passed away" (2 Cor. 5:17). As if to drive home the point, Paul insists that "flesh and blood cannot inherit the kingdom of God" (1 Cor. 15:50), thereby raising the question of how we, who are indisputably creatures of flesh and blood (see Gen. 3:19), can possibly have any part in the kingdom. If the coming of the kingdom truly means that *everything* old has passed away, then what sense can be given to the idea that we, whose lives are defined by their place amid the flesh-and-blood realities of the present creation, are destined for glory?

That Paul thinks such participation is possible in spite of these considerations is clear from the fact that he speaks of the passing away of everything old not as a future prospect, but as present reality. Already *now*, he writes, it is the case that "if anyone is in Christ, there is a new creation: everything old has passed away; look, everything has become new!" (2 Cor. 5:17 alt.). But this would only seem to deepen the problem, for it does not take particularly keen perception to see that Christians (i.e., those who identify themselves as being "in Christ") continue to bear the marks of the old, not merely in their physical constitution as flesh-and-blood human beings but also in their behavior. Indeed, much of the content of Paul's correspondence with the Corinthian church is taken up with rebuking its members on just these grounds. To be sure, Paul also declares that the Corinthians, in spite of their shortcomings, are even now "the temple of the living God" (2 Cor. 6:16). Yet the question remains of how, given the ambivalent character of Christians' lives, the relation between the old and the new in them is to be understood. Paul maintains that our lives are not reducible to mere "flesh and blood," since

> we know that if our tent-like earthly house is destroyed, we have a building from God, a house not made with hands, eternal in the heavens. For in this tent we groan, longing to be further clothed with our heavenly dwelling, for surely when we have taken it off we will not be found naked. (2 Cor. 5:1–3; translation altered)

He thus draws a clear distinction here between our lives now and our lives in glory: in the present we dwell in an "earthly house like a tent" (*epigeios oikia tou skēnous*) that is subject to destruction (the specification "like a tent" is presumably added to stress its temporary character); in glory we will inhabit "a building from God" (*oikodomēn ek theou*) that is eternal. But given that our earthly living is structured entirely by the flesh-and-blood material components of our bodies (so that even what we might think of as "spiritual" activities like thinking, willing, and loving are vulnerable to the effects of chemicals, heatstroke, and physical trauma to the brain), what exactly is the "we" that is left once our "earthly house" has been destroyed? In other words, how can we be found other than "naked"—without any identity at all—once our material substance is taken away? In order to answer this question, which is crucial to understanding what it might mean to live by God's word alone (i.e., freed from dependence on and corresponding vulnerability to material entities, both living and nonliving), it is necessary to examine what the destruction of our present lives

6. The Transformation of the Self   137

(and thus the passing away of everything old) entails; and this brings us once again to the topic of death.

Death

According to Scripture, death, whether defined medically as the irreversible cessation of biological function or in a more traditionally theological idiom as the separation of soul and body, is not intrinsic to human existence. As Paul taught, we shall not all die (1 Cor. 15:51), and the list of people who do not includes not only those who will be alive at the time of Jesus' return, but also Enoch and Elijah, who according to biblical tradition were taken up to heaven without dying (Gen. 5:24; 2 Kings 2:11). What *is* intrinsic to human existence is temporal finitude, such that our lives are defined by a beginning and end in time.[3] Death is the way in which the vast majority of people will experience this end, but that which defines it as an end is not death, but rather encounter with Jesus, which may occur either at death or at Jesus' return.[4] That this encounter marks the completion and thereby defines the final shape of every individual human life is reflected in the belief that it is an occasion of judgment (see Heb. 9:27): the definitive verdict on a person's life, given by the One who, as Creator, is alone in a position to assess what that life has been in comparison with what it was meant to be. Such a final and comprehensive judgment is simply not possible so long as a person still has an outstanding future lying ahead of them.[5]

Yet if death is not an inherent feature of human existence as such, it has particular theological significance in light of the fact that it is the way in which most human lives come to an end. According to Scripture the fact that human beings die is the result of sin. Although human lives were always intended to be temporally finite (Gen. 6:3), that this finitude is now experienced as death— the dissolution of our earthly bodies—is the consequence of humankind's primordial disobedience to God (Rom. 5:12, 17; cf. Gen. 2:16–17 and 3:17–19). Understood in this way, death is not neutral, but punitive; and in this context it is important to note that in the Old Testament, death is not understood as the occasion for encounter with God, but quite the opposite: as a state of where such encounter—and thus the hope of relationship that follows from

3. Angels, too, are creatures and therefore are also finite, but their finitude does not take temporal form. Although the traditional angelologies of both the Eastern and Western churches hold that angels do have a history constituted by their primordial decision to turn to or away from God, this history, located as it is in heaven, does not take time. Still, this framework means that angelic lives have their own form of completeness, defined by their confirmation in grace. For further discussion, see Ian A. McFarland, "When Time Is of the Essence: Aquinas and the *Imago Dei*," *New Blackfriars* 82, no. 963 (May 2001): 208–23.

4. The question of how Enoch and Elijah encountered Jesus at the point of their respective translations admits of no ready explanation, beyond stressing once again that because heaven is not part of the world of space and time, the issue cannot be settled simply by observing that the Word had not yet become incarnate at the time of their translations: heavenly realities are not constrained by earthly time (see 2 Pet. 3:8).

5. Karl Rahner argued that the end of life (and the possibility of judgment that comes with it) is intrinsic to the dignity of human life on the grounds that "freedom precisely does not consist in a quest to achieve ever fresh changes at will. Rather it is of its very nature the event of a real and definitive finality which cannot be conceived otherwise than something that is freely achieved once for all." Karl Rahner, "Ideas for a Theology of Death," in *Theology, Anthropology, Christology*, vol. 13 of *Theological Investigations*, trans. David Bourke (New York: Seabury, 1975), 186.

138   *The Hope of Glory*

it—is impossible (Ps. 6:5; cf. Job 7:9; Eccl. 9:10).[6] Apart from the good news of God's incarnation, death is not the occasion for hope (see Isa. 38:18), but *only* the end: the line drawn under all that a person has accomplished and failed to accomplish, and nothing more.[7]

This understanding is modified in later texts in the Old Testament (most explicitly, Dan. 12:2–3) that bear witness to an eschatological hope for the resurrection of the dead. Seemingly emerging in the post-exilic period, by the time of Jesus this belief had come to be accepted by many Jews, and he himself explicitly endorsed it (see especially Matt. 22:23–33 and pars.). Insofar as the resurrection is understood as the occasion for a final and definitive divine judgment that includes both reward and punishment on the far side of death, it gives rise to a conceptual framework where death itself need no longer appear as only (or even primarily) punitive. Instead, death marks the end of human life as lived amid the pain and confusion of the present time in such a way as to provide the possibility for the ultimate vindication of God's purposes for creation.[8]

The possibility that death might not be as final as it appears is, however, made actual only in Jesus' resurrection from the dead, since the fact that the one raised is none other than the one who was crucified implies that there is

6. Importantly, this does not mean that death poses a barrier to relationship from *God's* side, as though God were constrained by it (see 1 Sam. 2:6; Prov. 15:11; cf. Job 26:6; Ps. 139:8; Amos 9:2), but that from the human side death is experienced as a state of exclusion from God's presence (Job 17:13–16; Ps. 49:13–14).

7. In other words (and in line with the discussion in the previous chapter), only in light of the gospel can the prospect of encounter with the Lord (and the judgment that entails) be regarded as an occasion for hope, not fear (see Phil. 1:23; 2 Tim. 4:8). To know that in dying one will be judged can bring only joy when it is known that the one judging is Jesus: "there can be no doubt that those who know Him will look and move forward to His judgment, fire and testing, not with hesitant but with assured unequivocally positive and therefore joyful expectation. . . . If they wait for His righteousness, as is inevitable since it is His coming which is expected, they wait for the righteousness of His grace." Karl Barth, *Church Dogmatics* [hereafter *CD*], 13 vols., ed. G. W. Bromiley and T. F. Torrance (Edinburgh: T&T Clark, 1956–1974), IV/3.2, 922.

8. On similar grounds, later Christian writers would go so far as to interpret God's sentencing of human beings to mortality through their expulsion from the garden of Eden and access to its tree of life as an act of mercy, since it provided a guarantee that the life without hope to which human beings had consigned themselves through their disobedience will come to an end, thereby leaving open the possibility that by God's grace it might be reconstituted on an entirely new and different basis. Thus, Gregory of Nyssa interprets God's clothing of Adam and Eve in "garments of skin" (Gen. 3:21) as signifying the gift of mortality: "In my opinion we are not bound to take these skins in their literal meaning. For to what sort of slain and flayed animals did this clothing devised for these humanities belong? But since all skin, after it is separated from the animal, is dead, I am certainly of opinion that He Who is the healer of our sinfulness, of His foresight invested man subsequently with that capacity of dying which had been the special attribute of the brute creation. Not that it was to last for ever; for a coat is something external put on us, lending itself to the body for a time, but not indigenous to its nature. This liability to death, then, taken from the brute creation, was, provisionally, made to envelope the nature created for immortality. It enwrapped it externally, but not internally. It grasped the sentient part of man; but laid no hold upon the Divine image. This sentient part, however, does not disappear, but is dissolved. Disappearance is the passing away into non-existence, but dissolution is the dispersion again into those constituent elements of the world of which it was composed. But that which is contained in them perishes not, though it escapes the cognisance of our Senses. . . . [And so] the maker of our vessel, now that wickedness has intermingled with our sentient part, I mean that connected with the body, will dissolve the material which has received the evil, and, re-moulding it again by the Resurrection without any admixture of the contrary matter, will recombine the elements into the vessel in its original beauty." Gregory of Nyssa, *The Great Catechism*, 8, in *Gregory of Nyssa: Dogmatic Treatises, Etc.*, vol. 5 of *Nicene and Post-Nicene Fathers*, 2nd series, ed. Philip Schaff and Henry Wace (Boston: Hendrickson, 1995 [1893]), 897–98. Cf. Dietrich Bonhoeffer, *Creation and Fall: A Theological Analysis of Genesis 1–3/Temptation* (New York: Macmillan, 1959), 86: "Death, this having to return to dust, which burdens man as the ultimate, the most terrible curse, is now to man who lives in merciful preservation, a promise of the God of grace."

6. The Transformation of the Self

genuine continuity between the life that is subject to the judgment of death and that which is vindicated in glory. At the same time, it is not immediately clear what sort of continuity this could be. In line with the principle that there can be no future for the sinful human being other than destruction (since existence apart from God, which is what sin means, is an ontological impossibility), Paul writes that "our old self was crucified with [Christ] so that the body of sin might be destroyed, so we might no longer be enslaved to sin" (Rom. 6:6). In other words, there is more to our substance than "the body of sin," so that somehow (to recall Paul's language in 2 Corinthians 5) it remains possible even after the dissolution of our bodies to speak of a "we" who are not found "naked" when our present, "earthly house" is destroyed. And yet what more could there be, if when all is said and done, we are but "dust" (Gen. 3:19; cf. 18:27; Job 10:9; 34:15; Ps. 90:3; 103:14; Eccl. 3:20; 12:7)?

One possible answer would be that what remains after death is the soul, understood as an indestructible kernel of human nature beneath the perishable husk of our bodily existence; but this will not do, since Paul explicitly links the soul with our flesh as a feature of life in the present age, arguing that it is precisely the "soulish" (*psychikon*) body that must die in order to be raised a "spiritual" (*pneumatikon*) body (1 Cor. 15:44).[9] The contrast Paul seems to be drawing here is between our present, earthly state as bodies animated by souls with a future one in which we will have bodies animated directly by God's Spirit.[10] And this, in turn, suggests that no part of our created substance, body or soul, survives the catastrophe of death.[11] At this point, however, it is vital to insist that *who* we are is not defined by *what* we are (viz., our created substance), or, to revert to the technical language of the Council of Chalcedon, a person's hypostasis is not reducible to their nature. Even if it is also true that a human hypostasis cannot be said properly to subsist apart from human nature (since a hypostasis is just a particular instantiation of that nature: Mary in distinction from Peter or Paul, for example), it is nevertheless the case that what is true of the prophet Jeremiah is true of all human beings: that God knew us—that is,

---

9. The whole verse is properly translated, "It is sown a soulish body, it is raised a spiritual body. If there is a soulish body, there is also a spiritual body." Importantly, there is no reason to interpret Paul as teaching that in the resurrection the soul is removed and replaced by the spirit, but only that the spirit supervenes on the soul to become the active principle animating human life. This is certainly the way in which he was understood by Irenaeus of Lyon: "when the spirit . . . blended with the soul is united to [God's] handiwork, the man is rendered spiritual and perfect because of the outpouring of the Spirit. . . . But if the Spirit be wanting to the soul, he who is such is indeed of an animal nature, and being left carnal, shall be an imperfect being. . . . Those, then, are perfect who have had the Spirit of God remaining in them, and have preserved their souls and bodies blameless." Irenaeus of Lyon, *Against Heresies* 5.6, in *The Apostolic Fathers with Justin Martyr and Irenaeus*, vol. 1 of the *Ante-Nicene Fathers*, American ed., ed. Alexander Roberts and James Donaldson (Grand Rapids: William B. Eerdmans, 1985 [1885]), 532.

10. See N. T. Wright, *The Resurrection of the Son of God* (London: SPCK, 2003), 350.

11. Jesus' warning, "Do not fear those who kill the body but cannot kill the soul; rather fear him who can destroy both soul and body in hell" (Matt. 10:28), would seem to count against this claim. But since this is the only text in the New Testament that contrasts body (*sōma*) and soul (*psychē*) in this way (indeed, in the only other verse where the two words are found together, 1 Thess. 5:23, the focus is on their constituting a unity, along with "spirit") and since in virtually all other instances *psychē* functions (in parallel to the Old Testament Hebrew *nepeš*) as simply a synonym for "life" (see, e.g., Matt. 11:29; Luke 21:19; John 12:27; Heb. 6:19; Jas. 1:21; 1 Pet. 1:9; Rev. 18:13), Jesus' words are best interpreted along the lines I propose: as referring to the distinction between the "what" and the "who" of human being (viz., nature and hypostasis) rather than teaching that human nature is a composite of distinct mortal and immortal substances.

140   *The Hope of Glory*

had identified us as the particular persons or hypostases we were to be—even before we were formed in the womb (Jer. 1:5; cf. Ps. 139:15–16). In other words, prior to our having any substance at all, God already knew us and, indeed, had already, prior to our living as ensouled bodies through which we could accomplish anything, predestined us "to be conformed to the image of his Son" (Rom. 8:29), so that it is exclusively God's determination that we should be so conformed, and not any bodily performance (or soulish virtue) we might claim for ourselves, that defines who we are. Only as those whom God had foreknown and foreordained before we had bodies does God call, justify, and glorify us in the body. Thus, although in this life we inhabit bodies of death (Rom. 7:24), we can be and are rescued from the death that afflicts our bodies by the one who knew us before those bodies took form, and who therefore can and does acknowledge us even when those bodies have returned to dust: Christ Jesus our Lord (Rom. 8:39).

In this way, to die is to be confronted fully and finally with the hard but saving truth that we live by God's grace alone (i.e., the divine word) and not by our works ("bread"). The God who has known us even before we took shape in our mothers' wombs, and who calls us by name throughout our earthly lives, can uphold our identities even in the face of the destruction of our earthly bodies.[12] Nor, importantly, is this promise of life in the face of death merely a future prospect, as though the actual experience of grace were a matter of deferred gratification, requiring us to endure patiently the futility of our sinful, earthly lives until the time when death will bring them to an end. On the contrary, because in Christ "one has died for all" it is *already* the case that "all have died" (2 Cor. 5:14; cf. Gal. 2:20; Col. 3:3)—including those who have not experienced biological death. The baptized are those who through their response to the gospel are conscious of their status as those who have died; for although they still subsist in time and space and thus continue to be sustained in their earthly existence by "bread," because they have been "buried with [Christ] by baptism into death" (Rom. 6:4; cf. Col. 2:12), even apart from the experience of physical dissolution they already hear the judgment that comes to every person in death: that human beings live not by virtue of their deeds but solely because of God's gracious call.[13] And so it is that even now, in spite of their continuing to inhabit this "earthly house," human beings are able to live lives that are not subject to futility, for "our old self was crucified with him so that the body of sin might be destroyed, and we might no longer be enslaved to sin" (Rom. 6:6). It is on this basis that Paul enjoins the Christians of Rome—and us—to "present yourselves to God as those who have been brought from death to life" (Rom. 6:13; cf. 2 Cor. 4:10).

---

12. The parallel between the human situation after death and the human situation before birth is not exact, because those who have not yet been born have been foreknown only and so have not yet existed, whereas those who have died have already existed—and therefore (following the *ordo salutis* of Romans 8) are known by God as those who *have been* called and justified rather than as persons who *are yet to be* called and justified.

13. Christ "grants a perfect redemption not only to the nature which he assumed from us in unbreakable union, but to *each* of those who believe in him. . . . To that end he instituted holy baptism. . . . It is not the nature only, but the hypostasis of each believer that receives baptism." Gregory Palamas, Homily 5, *PG* 151:64D; cited in John Meyendorff, *A Study of Gregory Palamas*, trans. George Lawrence (Crestwood, NY: St. Vladimir's Seminary Press, 1964), 159.

6. The Transformation of the Self   141

The proleptic experience of death in baptism thus establishes a solidarity among the living and the dead that is a genuine *novum* in comparison to the Old Testament vision of death as cutting off those who have died from communion with the living (see, e.g., Job 7:9; Ps. 6:5; Eccl. 9:10; Isa. 38:18; cf. Num. 16:33). By contrast, the New Testament insists that the faithful dead surround the living as a "great . . . cloud of witnesses" (Heb. 12:1). Paul's insistence that at Christ's coming "we who are alive . . . will by no means precede those who have died" (1 Thess. 4:15) likewise reflects an understanding of the essential solidarity between those who have died in Christ and believers who are still alive: because both groups have proleptically died with Jesus in baptism, his return means life for both without distinction (cf. 1 Thess. 5:10). Moreover, the claim that on either side of biological death the baptized person, rescued from the "body of death" (Rom. 7:24) but not yet raised a "spiritual body" (1 Cor. 15:46), is upheld by God's word of promise also sheds light on the vexed question of the "intermediate state" of those who experience biological death prior to Jesus' return. Although the lives of all the baptized are suspended on God's word of promise, this state of suspension is actually *more* extreme for those whose earthly lives have come to an end, since, unlike the living, they no longer live in any sense under their own steam (viz., as "soulish bodies"), since in death they have undergone the destruction of their entire substance, body and soul. They are reduced entirely to their hypostatic identity, known and upheld by God entirely apart from their created human substance. At the same time, unlike the living who in their ongoing earthly existence are "away from the Lord" (2 Cor. 5:6), those who have died encounter Jesus directly and so even now may be said to be "with the Lord" (2 Cor. 5:8; cf. Phil. 1:23; see also Luke 23:43), in line with traditional Western teaching that the blessed dead do not wait to enjoy the vision of God. Moreover, because their earthly lives have ended, they no longer exist in the flow of time; instead, they are suspended on God's word outside of time and thus have no experience of "waiting" for the Parousia (even if in the unconscious state of "soul sleep").[14] Yet they no less than the living still await the resurrection of the body, and because human life is embodied life, so long as they have yet to put on immortality in the resurrection, they cannot be said to live in glory.[15]

---

14. "[D]eath is in *this* sense the absolute *end* of the temporal dimension of a being of the kind to which man belongs. What takes place after death is not something new in a temporal sense, or something that is constantly changing" (Rahner, "Ideas for a Theology of Death," 174). It is just at this point that the chief conceptual difficulty with the Catholic doctrine of purgatory arises, for if all who have died in Christ are sustained by Christ's word outside of time, then the question arises of the difference between the postmortem-but-not-yet-resurrected condition of those saints envisioned in *Benedictus Deus* who do not need purification and those who do. One might affirm that something about the experience of being upheld by Christ's word differs in some way for the two groups (cf. 1 Cor. 3:13–15), but only so long as purgatorial "experience" is not understood to entail the kind of temporal succession that would depict postmortem existence as a continuation of this life; yet to specify such a condition would seem to conflict with Catholic teaching on indulgences, which specifically refers to purgatorial punishments as "temporal." See the *Catechism of the Catholic Church*, 2nd ed. (Vatican City: Libreria Editrice Vaticana, 1997), §§1472, 1479; cf. 1030–32.

15. It is hard to know what to make of the enigmatic report in Matthew's passion narrative that at the moment of Jesus' death, "The tombs also were opened, and many bodies of the saints who had fallen asleep were raised. After his resurrection they came out of the tombs and entered the holy city and appeared to many" (27:52–53). On the one hand, the evangelist does not seem to be referring to a Lazarus-like resuscitation to earthly life; on the other hand, the fact that this "resurrection" is restricted to a small number of human beings ("many"—but seemingly not all—of the saints) whose

142   *The Hope of Glory*

It might seem that this claim that even the blessed dead do not live in glory conflicts with Jesus' defense of the resurrection in response to the Sadducees: "the fact that the dead are raised Moses himself showed, in the story about the bush, where he speaks of the Lord as the God of Abraham, the God of Isaac, and the God of Jacob. Now he is God not of the dead but of the living; for to him all of them are alive" (Luke 20:37–38 and pars.). Yet the patriarchs are evidently not alive in the sense of having already been resurrected, since according to the Gospels Jesus viewed the resurrection as a future event (e.g., Luke 14:14; John 6:40, 54; cf. 2 Tim. 2:18); instead, they are presumably to be understood as "alive" insofar as their lives are upheld by God in view of the resurrection (though, again, since this state is outside of time, it must not be conceived as entailing any experience of delay or waiting). Thus, although the blessed dead are confronted with God's word of grace with a directness and immediacy lacking for the baptized who are still living, even they do not yet fully *live* by that word, because to live a fully human life requires a body, and prior to the resurrection the dead have no bodies.[16]

Resurrection

The Christian understanding of human salvation necessarily includes the resurrection, because human beings were created as embodied beings (Gen. 2:7). For it is precisely as human beings who have lived on earth in time that we are called to life with God in eternity, and since our earthly lives are defined at every point by our bodily relations with other created bodies, there can be no vindication of our earthly lives apart from our bodies. Importantly, the *cause* of our salvation is exclusively God's word spoken to us apart from any (bodily) activity on our part; only so can salvation be confessed as an unconditional gift of blessing rather than a reward for services rendered (see Rom. 4:4–5). But God's call does not exhaust salvation's *content*, in which our participation as creatures is essential, since salvation takes the form of our living in relationship with God, in which we are active participants as those who "will know fully, even as [we] have been fully known" (1 Cor. 13:12). Indeed, having been reborn as God's children through God's call (John 1:12; 3:8; cf. 1 Pet. 1:23), we

---

risen life is confined to a temporally limited set of appearances in the earthly Jerusalem clearly distinguishes it from the final resurrection. What seems to be involved is a sign for the living (along with the darkness, the rending of the temple veil, and the earthquake) of the eschatological significance of Jesus' death rather than a partial realization of the final resurrection. Calvin, for example, views the story simply as testimony to the fact that the Old Testament patriarchs are included in the promise of future life. John Calvin, *Institutes of the Christian Religion* 2.11.23, ed. John T. McNeill, trans. Ford Lewis Battles (Philadelphia: Westminster, 1960), 448–49.

16. This point is crucial in order to make the bodily resurrection for the blessed dead more than the mere theological appendix to the postmortem existence of the saints that it often appears to be in many accounts. While Dante, for example, is entirely orthodox in his affirmation that the life of the blessed will not be complete until they are reunited with their bodies, his depiction of the bliss of heavenly existence prior to the resurrection in the *Paradiso* makes it difficult to imagine what meaningful difference the addition of a body will make. It is worth noting, however, that Thomas's view of the blessedness of the disembodied souls of the saints in *Summa Theologiae* 3.82.2 does suggest a more restricted sense of the beatific vision prior to the resurrection than Dante's portrayal would suggest. Thomas Aquinas, *Summa Theologiae* [hereafter *ST*], 60 vols., Blackfriars ed. (London: Eyre & Spottiswood, 1964–81).

6. The Transformation of the Self

are already empowered by the Holy Spirit to join Jesus in calling God "Father" (Rom. 8:15–17; Gal. 4:4–7; cf. John 20:17) and caught up into the activity of mutual glorification that characterizes the life of the Trinity from all eternity (John 17:1–5) so as to become "participants of the divine nature" (2 Pet. 1:4).[17] Any thought that this participation might be conceived in disembodied terms is foreclosed by the recognition that our incorporation into the divine life as Jesus' sisters and brothers is the product of God having bound the divine life to ours by assuming the fullness of flesh-and-blood existence in Jesus (Heb. 2:17): for if it is by taking a body that God lives with us, then it is only as embodied that we, in turn, can live with God.[18]

And yet at this point we run into a problem, for our bodies of flesh and blood are destroyed in death; and according to Paul this destruction is necessary, because "flesh and blood *cannot* inherit the kingdom of God, nor does the perishable inherit the imperishable" (1 Cor. 15:50). Furthermore, because our status as fleshy creatures "formed . . . from the dust of the ground" (Gen. 2:7; cf. Eccl. 12:7; 1 Cor. 15:47) precedes the fall, the incapacity of flesh and blood to inherit the kingdom cannot be interpreted only as a consequence of sin.[19] It rather derives from the fact that the flesh-and-blood composition of our bodies means our earthly lives are tied to—and thus dependent on—all the other creatures, both human and non-human, that make up our terrestrial (and, indeed, cosmic) environment; this state of interdependence is just what it means to live by "bread" rather than by God's word alone.[20] There is nothing wrong with life lived on these terms, as should be clear from the fact that it is just this earthly life that is vindicated in being raised from the dead. But it is vindicated precisely as finite: bounded in time by a beginning (birth) and an end (typically, though not necessarily, death) and therefore able to be regarded—and glorified—*as* a

---

17. For a compelling account of salvation as humanity being caught up into the mutual glorification of the divine persons, see Khaled Anatolios, *Deification through the Cross: An Eastern Christian Theology of Salvation* (Grand Rapids: William B. Eerdmans, 2021).

18. See Joseph Ratzinger, *Eschatology: Death and Eternal Life*, 2nd ed. (Washington, DC: Catholic University of America Press, 1988), 115: "Communion with God, which is the native place of life indestructible, finds its concrete form in sharing the body of Christ. . . . Faith in the resurrection is not part of some speculation in cosmology or the theology of history but is bound up with a person, with God in Christ." Cf. Thomas Aquinas, who argues (citing 1 Cor. 15:20–21) that Christ's resurrection is the cause of our own: "Consequently, the Word of God first bestows immortal life upon that body which is naturally united with Himself, and through it works the resurrection in all other bodies." Aquinas, *ST* 3.56.

19. This matter is not so clear in the Greek theological tradition, where the "garments of skin" God provides Adam and Eve in Genesis 3:21 have typically been interpreted as referring to human beings' current biological existence as mortal creatures of flesh and blood. For an extended discussion of the patristic tradition and its appropriation in modern Orthodox thought, see Panayiotis Nellas, *Deification in Christ: The Nature of the Human Person*, trans. Norman Russell (Crestwood, NY: St. Vladimir's Seminary Press, 1997), ch. 2. Augustine sets the tone for the Western Christian tradition in explicitly rejecting this view: "we are not to suppose that Adam had a spiritual body before he sinned, and that this was changed into an animal body as a punishment for sin." Augustine, *The City of God against the Pagans* 13.23, ed. and trans. R. W. Dyson (Cambridge: Cambridge University Press, 1998), 573.

20. "For while our present life is active amongst a variety of multiform conditions, and the things we have relations with are numerous, for instance, time, air, locality, food and drink, clothing, sunlight, lamplight, and other necessities of life, none of which . . . are God,—that blessed state which we hope for is in need of none of these things, but the Divine Being will become all, and instead of all, to us, distributing Himself proportionately to every need of that existence." Gregory of Nyssa, *On the Soul and the Resurrection*, in *Dogmatic Treatises, Etc.*, vol. 5 of *Nicene and Post-Nicene Fathers*, 2nd series, ed. Philip Schaff and Henry Wace (Boston: Hendrickson, 1995 [1893]), 452.

144   *The Hope of Glory*

whole.[21] In short, the reason that flesh and blood cannot inherit the kingdom is simply that life in the kingdom is the eternal vindication of one's flesh-and-blood existence *as that which has come to an end*, and which therefore can no longer be lived on flesh-and-blood terms (viz., by means of ongoing interactions with other creatures in time).

In this context, it is crucial to remember that resurrection, unlike resuscitation, is not a reversal of death. The reason that the risen Jesus and those who share his resurrection will "never die again" (Rom. 6:9) is because they have already died, and their deaths mark the definitive end of their earthly lives, which are now behind them (Luke 20:36). Rather than a reversal of death, resurrection is the revelation that the possibilities of human life in communion with God are not (as had previously seemed to be the case; see, e.g., Ps. 115:17) foreclosed by death: "The death he died, he died to sin once for all; but the life he lives, he lives to God" (Rom. 6:10)—that is, a life that is sustained by God's word alone.

As already noted, Paul describes this transition from earthly to risen life in terms of a shift from life in a "soulish" (*psychikon*) body to a "spiritual" (*pneumatikon*) one (1 Cor. 15:44, 46), so that the difference between earthly life and life in glory is not between life with a body and life without one, but rather between two distinct modes of bodily existence. In the present realm of time and space our bodies are animated by the soul, understood as that feature of human nature that constitutes human beings as living bodies rather than inanimate ones (see Gen. 2:7).[22] In this context, the point of the transition from the soulish to the spiritual body in glory is not that in being resurrected a person ceases to have a soul (however the latter is understood), but rather that the soul ceases to be the animating principle of human life; instead, the whole of the individual's life, body and soul together, is sustained directly by God's word (i.e., in Christ, by the power of the Holy Spirit).[23] Moreover, this transition from the soulish to the spiritual is not based in any intrinsic properties or capacities of human nature. In its created form as earthly flesh and blood, human life has no natural orientation to glory: its destiny is maturation through infancy through childhood and adolescence to adulthood—but then on to senescence, death, and dissolution back into the elements from which it was composed, in line with God's word to Adam: "you are dust, and to dust you shall return" (Gen. 3:19; cf. 1 Cor. 15:50). The hope of resurrection is therefore secured by

---

21. Cf. Augustine's view that although apart from sin human beings would not have died, their earthly existence would have remained temporally finite, concluding with a translation "to the company of the angels and . . . a blessed immortality without end." Augustine, *City of God* 12.22 (533); cf. 13.23 (570): "Adam, had he not sinned . . . could have retained [life] perpetually in Paradise, albeit only in an animal body until it should have been made spiritual as a reward for his obedience."

22. From this perspective, it is of no theological importance whether the earthly body's animating principle (or "soul") is understood with Plato as a distinct substance, with Aristotle as a substantial form, or in some other way.

23. "After death, the only powers of life our bodies have are God's own powers of life via the life-giving humanity of Christ in the power of the Spirit." Kathryn Tanner, *Jesus, Humanity and the Trinity: A Brief Systematic Theology* (Edinburgh: T&T Clark, 2001), 109. Cf. Matthias Scheeben: "The Holy Spirit animates and moves the spiritual man otherwise than he vitalizes and moves merely natural beings. In the latter He evokes their own proper life; but in His sanctifying work He communicates His own proper life." Matthias Joseph Scheeben, *Nature and Grace*, trans. Cyril Vollert, SJ (New York: Herder, 1954), 190.

6. The Transformation of the Self 145

God's promise alone, and not by any inherent human teleology.[24] Immortality is not native to the human condition, whether in whole or in part, but is rather something that must be "put on" (1 Cor. 15:53) through resurrection, which, in reconstituting life on the far side of death, is rightly understood as a divine overruling of natural processes rather than their fulfillment.[25]

In this context, it is entirely appropriate that Paul, in describing God as the one who "who gives life to the dead and calls into existence the things that do not exist" (Rom. 4:17), draws a parallel between resurrection and creation. No more than creation is resurrection grounded in any preexisting potential or possibility in the creature. The same point is reflected in Paul's description of the life in Christ (which, according to 1 Cor. 15:22–23, is the basis of the hope of future resurrection) as a "new creation" (2 Cor. 5:17). For in resurrection and creation alike, God brings life where there is no life, nor even the promise of life. In biblical perspective death is at no point the door to a new or transformed existence—let alone to life with God. It is rather the "last enemy" (1 Cor. 15:26) that is from a human point of view the supreme and seemingly insuperable obstacle to such life (see, again, Ps. 6:5; Isa. 38:18).

And yet the parallel between creation and resurrection is not absolute. If it were, then it would not be possible for Paul to insist that it is just "*this* mortal body," which determines the contours of our earthly lives in time and space, that will "put on immortality" in glory (1 Cor. 15:52). As shown explicitly by the visibility of Jesus' wounds on his risen body (Luke 24:40; John 20:24–27), there is continuity between the human being who dies and the one who is raised that distinguishes resurrection from the original work of creation, which entails no reference to any antecedent reality other than God. And yet in what does the continuity lie, if death really does mean the dissolution of the body back into its earthly elements? Paul speaks in terms of a seed sown in the ground, but in using this image he is not identifying a point of physical continuity between the present body and the risen body but denying that any such point exists:

> What you sow does not come to life unless it dies. And as for what you sow, you do not sow the body that is to be but a bare seed, perhaps of wheat or of some other grain. But God gives it a body as he has chosen and to each kind of seed its own body. Not all flesh is alike, but there is one flesh for humans, another for animals, another for birds, and another for fish. There are both heavenly bodies and earthly bodies, but the glory of the heavenly is one thing, and that of the earthly is another. (1 Cor. 15:36–40)

According to Paul, what is sown is not the body, but that which is to be given a body by God, which new body, by virtue of its being imperishable, is distinct

---

24. "Just as in Christ's case the continuity through death was not due to Christ himself but to 'the glory of the Father,' so too in our case the continuity from the old to the new life is not to be sought in anything in our lives but exclusively in the saving activity of God." Ingolf U. Dalferth, *Creatures of Possibility: The Theological Basis of Human Freedom* (Grand Rapids: Baker Academic, 2016 [2011]), xviii.

25. For a classic treatment of the contrast between resurrection and belief in immortality, see Oscar Cullmann, *The Immortality of the Soul or the Resurrection of the Dead: The Witness of the New Testament* (London: Epworth, 1964). It may also be noted that it is perfectly appropriate to describe resurrection as "supernatural," if the term is understood to refer to an action by which God brings about an effect in the creaturely realm by means other than the divine *concursus* (i.e., the intrahistorical form of divine providential activity whereby God effects an outcome through empowering the natural capacities of a created nature).

146   *The Hope of Glory*

from the earthly body that has died (1 Cor. 15:42). Precisely because "flesh and blood cannot inherit the kingdom of God," the continuity between our earthly and heavenly bodies is not material.[26] For what makes a human body *this* body—mine as opposed to Jesus' or Sappho's or Napoleon's—is not its material content (which is always in flux), but its identification with my particular hypostasis. As indicated in the previous section, that which perdures through death is simply my hypostasis, or the sheer fact of my identity as known by God, which is indeed a "bare seed": not a substance at all, but more like a dimensionless mathematical point marking the "whoness" of a human life entirely apart from any consideration of the "whatness" of its created substance. Thus, for a human being to be raised from the dead is for a hypostasis whose life has come to an end to be reconstituted as a fully human life by being given again a body that can be identified as that of a particular person by virtue of the fact that it bears the marks (e.g., the wounds of the crucifixion in Jesus' case) of the life that person lived. Indeed, because resurrection is precisely the vindication of earthly life rather than its extension, it cannot be abstracted from the concrete bodily features that are the accumulated precipitate of its interactions with other creatures.[27]

The significance of the risen body is thus supremely personal, in that to be raised is to receive back one's life in its completeness from God so as to make possible life with God as a child of God—that is, a life in which God's love for us may be answered by our love for God, and which therefore takes the form of participation in the perichoretic cycle of mutual glorification that constitutes the life of the Trinity itself. And yet the significance of the risen body is not simply personal; or, rather, one's identity as a person is not reducible to one's individual relationship with God. For the characteristics that define the risen body as that of a particular person are the precipitate of its interactions with other creatures, by which it is constituted through every moment of its existence from birth to death (again, Jesus' wounds are a signal example). Precisely as risen and glorified, therefore, one is not a person in isolation, but only in the context of one's relations with other creatures, human and nonhuman, whose embodied histories are mutually constituting and, as such, inextricably intertwined.

The fact that human embodiment means that it is impossible to separate the story of any individual human life from the totality of other created bodies provides further grounds for the claim that people are not raised at the time of their death, but only as part of the final eschatological renewal of creation as a whole. Here the principle that the author of Hebrews applies to the saints of

26. The difficulties in supposing otherwise—already evident in the premodern era in theological puzzlement over the destiny of bodies that had been eaten by other animals (whether human or nonhuman)—is only magnified by current scientific understanding, according to which the material composition of the body turns over wholly every seven to ten years. If there is no material continuity to our existence that clearly demarcates our bodies from the rest of the material order even in this life, what sense can it make to posit such continuity across the line of death?

27. Admittedly, this point by itself tells us very little about what a risen body will look like (e.g., whether it will correspond to a person's appearance at death)—a point perhaps reflected in the fact that the risen Jesus is frequently not recognized by his followers immediately (see Luke 24:15–16; John 20:14–15; 21:4; cf. Matt. 28:17, with its notation that when the disciples were met by the risen Jesus in Galilee, "some doubted"). Nevertheless, the principle that the vindication of earthly life is inseparable from the form of the earthly body means that I side with the Latin rather than the Greek tradition in affirming that sexual identity is preserved rather than transcended in glory (cf., e.g., Gregory of Nyssa, *Homily 7 on the Song of Songs*, and Augustine, *City of God* 22.17).

6. The Transformation of the Self 147

the Old Testament pertains equally to those of the present age: "though they were commended for their faith, [they] did not receive what was promised . . . so that they would not, apart from us, be made perfect" (11:39–40).[28] While this passage highlights the way in which human lives are bound up with one another, the character of bodily existence is such that these interconnections are limited to members of our own species. We are dependent on a nonhuman environment throughout our earthly lives, and this dependence includes cosmological processes that long antedate not only our individual births, but also the emergence of our species: the dynamics of cosmic evolution that gave rise to second-generation stellar systems like our own, as well as the physical, chemical, and biological processes that provide the earth with an oxygenated atmosphere that both sustains and is sustained by myriad diverse ecologies of mutually interdependent organisms. Nor are our somatic connections with other creatures merely external: within our own bodies there are as many bacterial as human cells, and the presence of these nonhuman biota is integral to our ability to live as human beings.[29] In short, because we are not and cannot be specifically human bodies in the absence of the full range of other bodies, personal resurrection (individual eschatology) is inseparable from the renewal of the whole of material creation (cosmic eschatology), in line with Paul's insistence that "the creation itself will be set free from its enslavement to decay and will obtain the freedom of the glory of the children of God" (Rom. 8:21).

And yet, once again, the recognition that the resurrection of the body is inseparable from the hope for the glorification of all creation does not mean that risen life is simply an extension of the present form of human existence under improved circumstances. As with Jesus, so with the rest of us, to confess the resurrection of the *dead* is to affirm that the only life that can be resurrected is a life that has come to a definitive end. It follows that in being raised from the dead we do not so much go on living (i.e., having further experiences that extend our biographies indefinitely into the future) as we find the lives we have lived (and which have come to an end) given eternal and imperishable validation.[30] Indeed, for the resurrection to be understood the continuation of earthly life would necessarily imply the ultimate insignificance of the latter, which would,

---

28. "History would be deprived of its seriousness, if resurrection occurred at the moment of death," since no human being "can be said to have reached his fulfilment and destiny [viz., resurrection] so long as others suffer on account of him." Ratzinger, *Eschatology*, 184, 187. While recognizing the difficulty of relating the time of resurrection to historical time, both Karl Rahner and Hans Urs von Balthasar maintain that human beings are raised at the moment of death in order to avoid the implication that people are judged twice (viz., once at death and then again at the Parousia). See Karl Rahner, "The Intermediate State," in *Jesus, Man, and the Church*, vol. 17 of *Theological Investigations*, trans. Margaret Kohl (New York: Crossroad, 1981), 115; and Hans Urs von Balthasar, *The Last Act*, vol. 5 of *Theo-Drama: Theological Dramatic Theory* (San Francisco: Ignatius, 1998), 356–60; cf. 377. For a conceptual solution to the problem of a double judgment, see the discussion on pp. 121–22 above.

29. While some earlier studies had suggested ratios of bacterial to human cells in the human body as high as 3:1, the best current estimates suggest a proportion of 1:1, with the bacterial component accounting for around 0.3 percent of total body weight. See Ron Sender, Shai Fuchs, and Ron Milo, "Revised Estimates for the Number of Human and Bacteria Cells in the Body," *PLoS Biology* 14, no. 8 (August 2016): e1002533.

30. Cf. Wolfhart Pannenberg, *Systematic Theology*, vol. 3, trans. Geoffrey W. Bromiley (Grand Rapids: William B. Eerdmans, 1998), 561: "The finitude of the perfected . . . will no longer have the form of a sequence of separated moments of time but will represent the *totality* of our earthly existence."

148   *The Hope of Glory*

in the face of the unending accumulation of further experiences in heaven, be reduced to an infinitesimal (and correspondingly trivial) fraction of the whole.[31]

And yet to deny that life in glory takes the form of an ongoing sequence of *temporal* experiences is not to imply that it does not include subjective experience at all, as though resurrection were the equivalent of being preserved in God's memory like an insect in amber. After all, though God's eternal life is not composed of a series of temporally sequential experiences, it does not follow that God, who is love (1 John 4:8, 16), lacks experience; on the contrary, as the eternal one God is supremely living (see, e.g., Jer. 10:10; Dan. 6:26), the source of temporal life (Neh. 9:6), and thus the one to whom all are alive (Luke 20:38).[32] To live by God's word alone rather than by "bread" means no longer to live by the processes of material give-and-take that define created life in space and time, for where all are upheld by God's word alone, our relationships with other creatures are no longer a matter of need, in which our dependence on other creatures (both human and non-human) renders us vulnerable to damage and destruction when those relationships are disrupted.[33] But if resurrection life is no longer sustained by these inter-creaturely relationships, that does not mean that they are absent. Scripture is clear that the kingdom of God is populated by all manner of creatures, each with its distinct nature: not only angels and human beings (Rev. 5:11; 7:9), but also a wide diversity of other created beings from trees (Rev. 22:2) to gold and precious stones (Rev. 21:21) that constitute the biblical vision of a new heaven and a new earth (cf. Isa. 65:25).[34] In the new Jerusalem God is not all that is seen; quite the contrary, God is the light in which we are able to see and enjoy the whole of the renewed creation (Rev. 22:5; cf. 21:23). Rather than creatures mediating our relationship to God, as is the case in this life, in glory it is God who will mediate our relationship with

---

31. Likewise, the notion of risen life as a continuation of earthly life would make nonsense of the idea that the record of one's earthly life (which would amount to a vanishingly small fraction of an individual's entire ante-plus-postmortem existence) could be decisive for one's eternal destiny; such a prospect would make no more sense than the idea that the significance of an individual's earthly life could be assessed based on the first minute after birth.

32. Maximus the Confessor argues that while God does not undergo motion (which entails temporal sequence), it does not follow that God is unmoving in the sense of being static: "God neither moves nor is stationary (for these are properties of naturally finite beings, who have a beginning and an end). . . . He is beyond all motion and rest." Maximus the Confessor, *Ambiguum* 15 (*PG* 91:1221A), in Maximos the Confessor, *On Difficulties in the Church Fathers: The Ambigua*, 2 vols., ed. and trans. Nicholas Constas (Cambridge, MA: Harvard University Press, 2014), 1:375–76. The character of God's life as complete and yet endlessly rich thus suggests an alternative to accounts of glory in which "[e]ither personal experience is retained, in which case the series of actual occasions constituting the self continue, and change is still possible, or personal experience is abandoned in favor of permanency, in which case immortality can only consist in a completed and non-experiencing self." Robert B. Mellert, *What Is Process Theology?* (New York: Paulist Press, 1975), 125. See pp. 175–76 below for Maximus's account of glory as a state of "ever-moving rest."

33. When Jesus says there is no marrying in heaven, but that the resurrected will be like angels (Matt. 22:30 and pars.), he may be taken to be stressing the fact that human beings will receive their existence directly from God. While in many respects they will be unlike angels (for example, they will have bodies and the earthly histories those bodies reflect behind them), the promise that they will live by God's will alone means that the fate of the species will no longer depend on the vagaries of secondary causes ("bread"), including those of biological reproduction.

34. The assertion that in the renewed creation there will be no sea (Rev. 21:1) should be interpreted in terms of the conventions of ancient Near Eastern cosmology, according to which oceanic waters symbolize the forces of chaos and destruction surrounding and threatening creation (see Gen. 1:2, 6–9; 7:11; cf. Job 26:8–12; Ps. 89:9), and not as a denial that the aquatic realm is a genuinely "good" feature of creation (Gen. 1:21; cf. Ps. 104:24–26).

6. The Transformation of the Self

other creatures, who, in God, will be immediately present to us in a way we cannot imagine, but which will fulfill the promise of "the freedom of the glory of the children of God" (Rom. 8:21).

To be sustained by God's word alone therefore does not mean to be alone with God's word. For if one's earthly life is constituted at every moment from birth to death by relationships with other creatures (including both those who died before one's birth and those affected by the consequences of one's actions after one's death), then one cannot know and therefore be oneself apart from those others. Indeed, it is only with the final resurrection, when the tally of history has come to an end and one's relationships with all those others are fully visible in the light of glory, that a person can know fully who they are, and therefore can truly be the person she is.[35] Because the form and content of my life are inseparable from all those creatures with and through whom my life has been lived, it is impossible for God to love me without God's also loving them—and correspondingly impossible for me to love God, as the one who through them gave me my life, without my loving them. In this way, belief in the resurrection of the dead and the promise of a new heaven and a new earth are inseparable.

Life Everlasting

In Scripture and the creeds, resurrection is the gateway to eternal life (see, e.g., Matt. 25:46; John 6:40, 54; Rom. 6:22–23). Yet although life everlasting is the culmination of Christian hope (Titus 1:2), the Bible says very little about its content. The closest thing to a definition is found in Jesus' so-called farewell discourse in the Fourth Gospel: "this is eternal life, that they may know you, the only true God, and Jesus Christ, whom you have sent" (John 17:3). Evidently, such knowledge, though beginning in the present, can only be consummated outside of the limitations of earthly existence, when, being at last "with Christ" (Phil. 1:23), we "will know fully, even as [we] have been fully known" (1 Cor. 13:12). Apart from this one statement of Jesus, however, biblical accounts of eternal life are largely symbolic. Paul writes that "there is reserved for me the crown of righteousness, which the Lord, the righteous judge, will give to me on that day, and not only to me but also to all who have longed for his appearing" (2 Tim. 4:8; cf. 1 Pet. 5:4; Rev. 2:10; 3:11), but this language simply reaffirms the character of resurrection as vindication without any account of what follows. Some content seems to be provided when Jesus, in keeping with the theme of abundant life (John 10:10), describes life in the kingdom using the image of a banquet (Matt. 8:11 and par.; 22:1–14; cf. Isa. 25:6); but in a context where eating is no longer necessary, such imagery is evidently metaphorical. And while

---

35. "No earthly moment can be fully exhausted. . . . Whatever eternal content it contains—and our temporal existence cannot bring it forth out of the depths—is 'laid up' for us in heaven: in heaven we shall live the full eternal content of what on earth was present only as a transcendent, unsatisfiable longing. This is at least *one* aspect of heavenly life. In heaven . . . our earthly existence . . . will be present in an unimaginable and unimaginably true manner." Hans Urs von Balthasar, *The Last Act*, 413. The same point is implicit in the refrain of the old spiritual, "O, nobody knows who I am, a-who I am, till the Judgement morning" (https://www.negrospirituals.com/songs/nobody_knows_who_i_am.htm).

150   *The Hope of Glory*

the book of Revelation gives a stunning depiction of the heavenly Jerusalem, it is limited to an account of its physical features: although we are told that it is a place into which people *"will* bring . . . the glory and honor of the nations" (21:26), and where they *"will* worship the Lamb" (22:3), they do not do so yet: we are presented a magnificent stage on which the actors have yet to appear.

Of course, given that the life of glory is outside of time and space, such reticence is perfectly appropriate, for any biblical account of life with God would inevitably describe it in terms of a sequence of temporal experiences; our conceptual and linguistic resources are simply not able to talk about life in any other terms. As already noted, we can affirm on the basis of the confession that God's life is love, that the life we are promised in glory need not be tied to an ongoing succession of temporal events, but we have no inkling of what it would be like to experience life in this way. Thus, while it seems entirely proper to affirm that the infinity of the divine nature will render our life with God one of inexhaustible richness (as Gregory of Nyssa sought to emphasize in his doctrine of *epektasis*, or endless spiritual progress[36]), that does not make it any easier for us now to imagine such life apart from the experience of novelty and change that defines life in this world, but which is incompatible with an understanding of resurrection as the completion rather than the continuation of that life.[37]

And yet this understanding of resurrection poses a challenge to Christian hope that is far more serious than that posed by our inability to conceive of or describe life outside of space and time. To understand resurrection as the vindication of earthly life means that the hope of life everlasting is not about leaving earthly life behind, but rather believing that the life we have lived here will be forever upheld and celebrated by God. But given that earthly life is often profoundly wretched, if the hope of risen life is the eternal affirmation of life as it has been lived here below, then it would seem to be not much of a hope. After all, whatever the problems with "pie in the sky when you die" theology, it does at least take seriously the misery that marks so much of earthly existence for so many. Moreover, we have already seen that there seems to be strong biblical support for contrasting life everlasting with life as lived here and now, not least in Paul's insistence that, "If for this life only we have hoped in Christ, we are of all people most to be pitied" (1 Cor. 15:19), and his corresponding conviction that "the sufferings of this present time are not worth comparing with the glory about to be revealed to us" (Rom. 8:18; cf. 2 Cor. 4:17). Even if such passages cannot be taken to support a straightforward endorsement of suffering as good in itself, a plausible eschatological account of the Christian hope must explain how it is that the guilt and suffering that so deeply mark our earthly lives are not eternalized (which seems rather to describe what Christians mean by damnation), and thus how it is that in glory we escape the weight of sin—whether committed by us or against us—that mars our existence now.

36. "This truly is the vision of God: never to be satisfied in the desire to see him. . . . Thus, no limit would interrupt growth in the ascent to God, since no limit to the Good can be found nor is the increasing of desire for the good brought to an end because it is satisfied." Gregory of Nyssa, *The Life of Moses* 2.239, trans. Abraham J. Malherbe and Everett Ferguson (New York: Paulist, 1979), 116.

37. "Resurrection means not the continuation of this life, but life's completion. . . . The Christian hope does not lead us away from this life; it is rather the uncovering of the truth in which God sees our life." Karl Barth, *Dogmatics in Outline*, trans. G. T. Thompson (New York: Harper & Row, 1959), 154.

6. The Transformation of the Self   151

In light of this challenge, it is not surprising that the Christian eschatological imagination has often included some qualification of the degree to which
earthly experience is preserved in glory.[38] While claims that sin and evil are
simply forgotten are rare, the idea is often present implicitly even when it is
not explicitly taught.[39] For example, compensatory eschatologies, in which the
blessedness of glory simply outweighs the pain of earthly existence, trade on
an overwhelming experience of the good that implies a forgetting of evil.[40] As
noted in the previous chapter, one significant difficulty with such accounts is
that they trade on a problematic conception of the character of earthly life, as
though experiences of evil could be demarcated as discrete episodes capable
of being tallied up and bracketed out from a person's biography.[41] But if one
has a robust understanding of human fallenness (as found, for example, in the
Lutheran characterization of the Christian as *simul justus et peccator*), the prospect of making a clear distinction between good and bad deeds in a human life
is simply impossible: our every action is too much bound up with the power of
sin (both our own and that which presses upon us from without) to allow *any*
part of our lives to be singled out as worthy of glorification.

Nor is this the only problem, for even if a sequestration of sin and evil were
possible, it would seem to compromise personal identity. Granted that our
identities are secured by God's grace apart from anything we have done or
failed to do, nevertheless that grace comes to us as creatures whose lives take

---

38. See the discussion of the forgetfulness implicit in both escapist and titanist eschatologies on pp.
32–37 above. One striking exception to this tendency is found in the work of John Thiel, whose efforts
to take seriously the eternal significance of earthly life lead him precisely to eternalize the sinfulness
of human beings, which, he holds, is never finally healed, because even the blessed dead, as "persons
broken by their sin and the sin of others," must continue "to engage in the virtuous work of forgiveness that is as never ending as the effects of sin in resurrected life," and, indeed, "to be busy in heavenly life at the work of redemption." It is hard to see how this vision, in which heaven is scene of the
(evidently eternal) work of redemption rather than redemption's fruit is consistent with the Christian
hope, but it is, in any case, a vision of glory in which the resurrected do not live by God's word (viz.,
grace) alone, but rather a form of life that though "largely [!] a work of God's grace," nevertheless
"continues to transpire by grace and works." John E. Thiel, *Icons of Hope: The "Last Things" in Catholic
Imagination* (Notre Dame, IN: University of Notre Dame Press, 2013), 53–54; cf. 146–47, 168–69.

39. The most straightforward account of eschatological forgetting is found in Dante, for whom the
final stage of purgation in *Purgatorio* XXXI entails submersion in the River Lethe, which (as demonstrated two cantos later in *Purgatorio* XXXIII.91–99) removes all memory of sin. In recent theology
Miroslav Volf has offered the most explicit argument that glorified existence includes the forgetting of
earthly sin and suffering, though he is careful to note that the "forgetting" he has in mind should not
be understood (as seemingly in Dante) as the erasure of memory, but rather as a "non-remembrance"
or "not coming to mind." Miroslav Volf, *The End of Memory: Remembering Rightly in a Violent World*
(Grand Rapids: William B. Eerdmans, 2006), 145.

40. For perhaps the most sophisticated recent example of such a compensatory account, in which
the "great good" that God will provide in heaven will outweigh all sufferings experienced on earth,
see Marilyn McCord Adams, *Horrendous Evils and the Goodness of God* (Ithaca, NY: Cornell University
Press, 1999); and *Christ and Horrors: The Coherence of Christology* (Cambridge: Cambridge University
Press, 2006). As noted in ch. 5 above, David Bentley Hart takes a different tack when he argues that
from the perspective of eternity evil turns out to be simply nothing: not outweighed by a greater
quantity of good, but revealed ultimately to have no quantity at all. But the upshot is the same: though
Hart's intent is to affirm that in glory nothing is forgotten (because "if anything were to be eternally
lost—the least little thing—then the goodness of creation could never be more in the end than a purely
conditional goodness"), he can achieve this end only by reducing evil to the status of an illusion,
which can therefore be "forgotten" in much the same way as a bad dream: falling out of remembrance
as ultimately unreal. David Bentley Hart, "The Devil's March: *Creatio ex nihilo*, the Problem of Evil,
and a Few Dostoyevskian Meditations," in *Creation ex nihilo: Origins, Development, Contemporary Challenges*, ed. Gary A. Anderson and Markus Bockmuehl (Notre Dame, IN: University of Notre Dame
Press, 2018), 317.

41. See p. 132 above.

152   *The Hope of Glory*

shape in time and space as a story (that is, a narrative with a dramatic shape), so that it is as the one who was born, grew, labored, and loved in myriad relationships with other creatures, both human and nonhuman, that I am glorified. Moreover, insofar as a—if not the—defining feature of personal identity in Christian perspective is our status as those whom God blesses in spite of what we have done or what has been done to us, it is hard to see how the knowledge of the sins we have committed or that have been committed against us could fall out of remembrance without undermining our self-understanding as children of the God "who justifies the ungodly" (Rom. 4:5).[42]

The obvious alternative to the idea that our experience of evil is simply forgotten in glory is to affirm that it is redeemed. But how can one claim that such experiences will be redeemed without more or less explicitly suggesting that they were perhaps not so terrible after all? A promising approach to this difficult question is found in Jonathan Tran's suggestion that redemption might be conceived in terms of what Toni Morrison called the "rememory" of suffering.[43] Morrison characterizes rememory as the process of "reconstituting and recollecting a usable past" that recognizes simultaneously "the stress of remembering, its inevitability, the chances for liberation that lie within the process."[44] To speak of rememory is thus to recognize that not every event in one's life is recalled with equal vividness or is to be regarded as of equal significance, still less that everything remembered is good. Evil is not simply forgotten, nor is its status as evil in any way mitigated, and yet there is a kind of vindication of the worth of the life that evil has afflicted. To the extent that the rememory of evil in the present might be taken as a clue to the experience of redemption in glory, it is important to note that there is no reason to suppose it will be easy: it is most certainly not so for Morrison's characters, whose struggles to recover a usable past more nearly resemble Paul's talk of being saved "as through fire" (1 Cor. 3:15) than by way of any sort of natural or progressive revelation of wholeness.[45]

"Rememory" is not compensatory, as though it involved a conviction that evil experiences are ultimately outweighed by the good; there is no presumption of tallying up and balancing out different forms of experience. Nor does it involve a postmortem accumulation of additional experiences that might create a surplus of the good, since implicit in the eschatological invocation of

---

42. Even Volf concedes that "[m]uch would be lost if the self simply discarded its past and abandoned it in favor of 'being in God.'" Volf, *The End of Memory*, 201.

43. Jonathan Tran, *The Vietnam War and Theologies of Memory: Time and Eternity in the Far Country* (Oxford: Wiley-Blackwell, 2010), 136.

44. Toni Morrison, "Rememory," in *The Source of Self-Regard: Selected Essays, Speeches, and Meditations* (New York: Alfred A. Knopf, 2019), 324. Cf. her use of the term in Toni Morrison, *Beloved* (New York: Alfred A. Knopf, 1998), 43, 116, 189, 222, 238.

45. David Kelsey observes "what 'redemption' concretely means for Christians is relative to the concrete particularities of the situation and events that cry out for redemption." David H. Kelsey, *Imagining Redemption* (Louisville, KY: Westminster John Knox, 2005), 2. Thus, what it will mean concretely for a life to be "rememoried" may be expected to vary enormously across different individual cases. In this context, I find particularly arresting these words of JoAnne Terrell: "I believe that anyone's death has salvific significance if we learn continuously from the life that preceded it," in its insistence on ongoing attending to the life as a whole over against summary judgments of its worth or lack of worth based on particular incidents within it. JoAnne Marie Terrell, "Our Mothers' Gardens: Rethinking Sacrifice," in *Cross Examination: Readings on the Meaning of the Cross Today*, ed. Marit Trelstad (Minneapolis: Fortress), 37–38.

6. The Transformation of the Self
153

rememory is that one's life is a completed whole to which no new experiences may be added. The point is thus not that the effect of evil experiences is diluted by a greater quantity of good ones, but that they are integrated into a narrative—most immediately of an individual life and ultimately of creation in its entirety—that allows the whole of a person's life to be seen as a product of God's will that it should *be*, and thus that it is *good*. Again, this does not entail that the evil one has suffered or committed is ultimately reinterpreted as something good or meaningful, or even that it is seen to have been the occasion for the emergence of goodness or meaning (as in Gen. 50:20, or Augustine's notorious simile of the dark patch in a beautiful painting). There is nothing glorious in the rememory of evil as such; and to drive home this point, Tran insists that if the integration of experiences in rememory is removed from the concrete realities of this-worldly encounter, then the process "shrivels into solipsistic . . . fantasizing."[46]

The doctrine of resurrection proves helpful as a means of ensuring that these concrete realities stay in view, because the example of Jesus shows that the body that is raised carries the wounds or scars acquired during earthly life, and these serve as a potent sign of its various this-worldly encounters that check any pollyannaish accounts of a person's life story. As a creation of God, the body is good all the time in all its parts. If sin and evil are a privation—a lack of being—they form no part of the body and so are neither resurrected nor glorified. That the effects of sin and evil on the body remain in glory in the form of scars is thus not a sign of *evil's* ultimate goodness, but rather of the goodness *of the body* as that which has endured evil and, in being raised, resisted its assaults.[47] The presence of a scar is proof that evil is not simply nothing, that it has real and calamitous effects; but the scar itself is not itself evil, but rather a mark of the body's resistance to evil; and it is that resistance, as given concrete form by and in the body, that is glorified.[48] The integrity of life as constructed via rememory is thus inseparable from the eschatological integrity of the body, which is, as it were, the precipitate of all one's encounters with other creatures over the course of one's earthly existence and thus the concrete substance of one's life. In this way, the upshot of belief in resurrection is not the glorification of evil, but rather that the body that has borne and resisted the evil—a bearing and

---

46. Tran, *The Vietnam War*, 165.

47. Jesus' side wound might seem to pose a problem here, in that although he explicitly speaks of it as an identifying mark (John 20:27), it was only inflicted after death (John 19:33–34) and therefore seemingly cannot be viewed as a sign of the body's resistance to evil. In response I would merely note that insofar as it is part of the story of the crucifixion (i.e., of how Jesus was put to death) rather than the story of his burial (i.e., how his corpse was disposed of after taken down from the cross), it is appropriately viewed as part of his life story and thus rightly assimilated with the wounds in his hands and feet. One might note in this context the convention of portraying martyred saints with the wounds produced by their martyrdom, without worrying about whether any particular wound (e.g., the many arrows shot at St. Sebastian) were inflicted before or after death.

48. In this context, one might accept Luther's point that "sin . . . is swallowed up by [Christ's] resurrection," and yet deny his inference that Christ's wounds do not remain on his risen body, since the wounds are not a sign of sin, but of the body's resistance to sin. See Martin Luther, *A Meditation on Christ's Passion*, trans. M. Bertram, in *Devotional Writings I*, vol. 42 of *Luther's Works*, American ed. (Philadelphia: Fortress, 1969), 12. For a review of the history of Christian reflection on the risen Christ's wounds through the early modern period, see Peter Widdicombe, "The Wounds and the Ascended Body: The Marks of Crucifixion in the Glorified Christ from Justin Martyr to John Calvin," *Laval théologique et philosophique* 59, no. 1 (February 2003): 137–54.

154 The Hope of Glory

resistance evident in scars both physical and psychological—is nevertheless by the power of God vindicated as good and therefore capable of bearing the weight of glory.[49]

How it is that this life, in which for every person (albeit in vastly different ways) experiences of love, joy, and confidence are inseparable from sin and suffering, will be glorified—that is, how we will actually experience a redemption in which the perishable inherits the imperishable—is beyond our present capacity to fathom, not least because (as Paul puts it in response to just this question), what is sown "does not come to life unless it dies" (1 Cor. 15:36), and so long as we can ask such questions we are evidently still alive and therefore without access to the life to come. And yet if we understand life in glory to be nothing other than the vindication (rather than the displacement or indefinite extension) of this life, we can nevertheless affirm that the content of life everlasting is being determined now, such that to seek the kingdom is not to look beyond the present life, but precisely to seek to discern the shape of one's vocation within it as one who has already now been called by God to life with God.

For although the fullness of life in glory comes only with the resurrection (1 Cor. 15:42–43; cf. 2 Cor. 4:17), it is also the case that Jesus claims to have given his disciples glory already (John 17:22; cf. Rom. 8:30). As noted above, this present gift of glory takes concrete form in the fact that although all people continue to live by means of "bread" during their earthly lives, those who have heard the gospel understand their identities to be defined by who God calls them to be rather than by what they have done or has been done to them. In light of this understanding, the experience of life in glory begins with living out one's earthly vocation as the framework for cultivating now those relationships that will be part of the story of who one is eternally. This certainly does not entail the presumption that one will bring about the kingdom by one's actions in this world, for precisely as that which is realized beyond time rather than within it, the kingdom "is not coming with things that can be observed," such that it will at any point in time be possible to say, "'Look, here it is!' or 'There it is!'" Nevertheless, it can be said that the kingdom is "among you" (Luke 17:20–21) insofar as life everlasting is nothing other than earthly life—the life we live now—that has been redeemed and glorified.

In short, to conceive eternal life in terms of the resurrection of the body is to be directed to life lived in the present as the place where the kingdom's contours are to be discerned. The kingdom, after all, is simply life in the presence of God, sustained solely by the power of God's word; and to have been called and justified is to be conscious already of living in this way. It follows that any theologically serious effort to address the question of what life will be like in the kingdom of God cannot take the form of speculation about existence in some otherworldly context, but rather must be built on discernment of what life should look like on earth. For an individual to believe the gospel is (inter alia) to confess, "*I* will be raised from the dead to live in God's presence." But

---

49. "After you have suffered for a little while, the God of all grace, who has called you to his eternal glory in Christ, will himself restore, support, strengthen, and establish you" (1 Pet. 5:10).

6. The Transformation of the Self   155

because the "I" who makes this confession is living in this world, and because the life that is to be raised is just this earthly life that I am now living, the only possible reference point for the shape of one's life in glory is the commitments that define one's life in the present.

This principle is illustrated in the parable of the Last Judgment in Matthew 25. Often this parable interpreted as describing the connection between individuals' risen lives and their this-worldly actions as a simple matter of postmortem reward and punishment, such that every person's tally of good or bad deeds performed on earth becomes the basis on which they enter into a new—and completely distinct—stage of life that is characterized by either joy or torment. But given that such a purely transactional understanding of glory as payment for services rendered on earth is completely inconsistent with the teaching that no human being can merit glory ("since all have sinned and fall short of the glory of God," Rom. 3:23), the parable is more plausibly read as reflecting the principle that resurrection life is not a supplement to earthly life, but precisely its eternal validation. All the people gathered before the throne have hoped for life in God's presence; what they learn in the judgment is that they have *already* been living in God's presence, such that "just as you did it to one of the least of these brothers and sisters of mine, you did it to me" (Matt. 25:40). In this way, the surprise experienced by the saved and the condemned alike in the parable derives from the discovery that the life to come is *not* a further stage of existence that follows upon their earthly lives, but rather the revelation of their earthly lives' ultimate significance.

Admittedly, there is nothing especially revolutionary about the idea that we pursue works of justice and mercy in the present because that is consistent with the life in Christ into which we have already been called. It only makes sense (as Paul long ago pointed out) that we who claim to live by the Spirit should be guided by the Spirit in our day-to-day living (Gal. 5:25). As opposed to accounts that interpret this shift to Spirit-infused existence in terms of an act of divine justification that leads to a progressive process of human sanctification, however, Jesus' language in Matthew 25 implies that such works are not so much preparatory for future life with Christ as constituting the very substance of that life. For to say that the life to which we have been called in Christ begins now is not to imply that it then it ends somewhere else. Indeed, far from providing an occasion for speculation about some otherworldly, postmortem paradise, it points to the fact that it is just the person who has lived *this* earthly life, which begins and ends in time, who is raised from the dead. To receive the gospel is thus to recognize that the kingdom of God is "at hand" (Matt. 4:17 alt.) and, indeed, "among you" (Luke 17:21), such that life in the kingdom is to be engaged as present reality rather than an exclusively future prospect.

It follows, then, that our sanctification is a function of our vocation, meaning that it is to be understood not as a general process of moral improvement culminating in some ideal endpoint (e.g., "entire sanctification"), but rather as the individual's living out the concrete form of the life before God to which they have been called. Vocation—God's calling of a person—defines who a person is, and so who they will be in glory, as a member of Christ's body, and therefore

156 *The Hope of Glory*

also what sanctification (i.e., their own particular form of being "set apart" in holiness) will mean for them in particular.[50] As Scripture teaches, to be called is to recognize that each of us has been "created in Christ Jesus" to live out a form of existence that is unique and unsubstitutable, such that the "good works" we are to do are just those "which God prepared beforehand so that we may walk in them" (Eph. 2:10). It is vital to insist on this understanding of vocation over against bastardized versions that would reduce calling to a practical means of acquiring "bread" in this life in anticipation of a more fulsome existence hereafter. Unlike classical pagan notions of an "afterlife" in the mode of Valhalla or the Elysian Fields, the Christian belief in the resurrection of the dead rejects the reduction of earthly life to a temporal means to an eternal end. Quite the contrary, to hope in the resurrection is to understand oneself as living already now in and by the power of God's word, in the knowledge that for us no less than Jesus it is precisely *this* life with its joys and its scars that will be raised to glory.[51]

As Paul cautions, it is not that we "have already obtained this or have already reached the goal" (Phil. 3:12). After all, it is a defining feature of vocation that both God's call and the kingdom to which it summons us break in upon time and space rather than being built up from the world's—or our own—natural capacities. In this respect it is absolutely true that "here we have no lasting city, but are looking for a city that is to come" (Heb. 13:14). Both our sin and finitude pose inherent limits on our capacity to live into the reality of the kingdom in this life; that is why we and the world need to be redeemed (Rom. 8:23). To be sure, in John 11 Jesus, when confronted by the resolutely futurist perspective on eschatology offered by Martha in the face of her brother Lazarus's death ("I know that he will rise again in the resurrection on the last day," v. 24), responds, "I am the resurrection and the life. Those who believe in me, even though they die, will live, and everyone who lives and believes in me will never die" (vv. 25–26). But in the event Lazarus is only temporarily resuscitated rather than resurrected in the eschatological sense, reflecting the fact that even the Johannine Jesus recognizes a difference between life now and resurrection on "the last day" (see John 6:39, 40, 44, 54). And yet it remains the case that to believe in Jesus is to understand that life in God begins now and not in some more or less distant future; for although it is certainly true that "the *form* of this world is passing away" (1 Cor. 7:31 alt.), the promise of the gospel is that its *substance* is held eternally before God. For "God did not send the Son into the world to condemn the world but in order that the world might be saved through him" (John 3:17).

---

50. For a more detailed discussion of the relationship between vocation, justification, and sanctification, see Ian A. McFarland, *In Adam's Fall: A Meditation on the Doctrine of Original Sin* (Malden, MA: Wiley-Blackwell, 2010), 205–12.

51. Thus, although there is in the New Testament no illusion about the fact that life on earth is still constrained by the vulnerabilities associated with the human need for "bread," the point remains that the disciple's life is to be defined by the exigencies of God's call: "Therefore do not worry, saying, 'What will we eat?' or 'What will we drink?' or 'What will we wear?' For it is the gentiles who strive for all these things; and indeed your heavenly Father knows that you need all these things. But seek first the kingdom of God and his righteousness, and all these things will be given to you as well" (Matt. 6:31–33).

6. The Transformation of the Self   157

It follows that to hope for life everlasting is not to look away from the contours of earthly existence, but precisely to see it as the object of God's redemptive activity—which means to commit oneself to its flourishing now. The next chapter explores some of the contours of this combined discipline of perceiving and committing oneself to God's eschatological kingdom in relation to the divine promise for the renewal not just of individual human beings, but of the cosmos as a whole.

7. The Transformation of the World

Christian eschatology's focus on the return of Jesus to judgment, the resurrection of the dead, and eternal life seems at first glance to push the horizon of hope entirely beyond the present world. How else, after all, is it possible to think of a mode of existence not accessible to flesh and blood (1 Cor. 15:50)—in which our current weak, perishable, earthly body is transformed into an imperishable and glorified spiritual body (1 Cor. 15:42–44), and where death, mourning, crying, and pain will be no more (Rev. 21:4), so that we are "like the angels in heaven" (Matt. 22:30 and pars.)—than in terms of complete contrast with life here and now? And yet I have argued that careful reflection on the implications of belief in the resurrection of the dead checks the temptation to displace the church's attention from life in the present to an otherworldly future. In contrast to belief systems for which some part of the self survives death (whether to be reincarnated in another earthly form or translated to existence on an otherworldly plane), the Christian doctrine of resurrection takes death seriously as the end of life. To confess the resurrection of the dead is certainly to deny that death is triumphant (1 Cor. 15:55; cf. Rom. 8:24–25), but the ultimate victory of life over death does not mean that any part of the self escapes the effects of death; the point is rather that in spite of the fact that we have died "once for all" (Rom. 6:9; cf. Heb. 9:27), we nevertheless live by the power of God.

In short, if it is *this* earthly life that is raised from the dead, then there is no *content* to the life for which we hope beyond that which we experience now. This is certainly not to say that life now is identical with life in glory. The fact that earthly life is afflicted by the devastating power of sin, suffering, and sorrow requires that the present form of the world pass away (1 Cor. 7:31) so that our lives may be redeemed from the patterns of sin and suffering with which they are afflicted in the present. That is part of what it means to say that in order to experience life in glory we must put on imperishability and immortality: the ambiguity of our present existence must be brought into God's light and thereby become light (Eph. 5:13–14). Because "what we will be has not yet been revealed" (1 John 3:2), we do not know what our redeemed state will look like. But because the promise of redemption applies precisely to our *bodies* (Rom. 8:23)—that is, to our lives as shaped by our present existence on earth—its form is not only something for which we wait, but also that which, however obscurely, we are working out in the present (Phil. 2:12).

Yet because our lives as embodied beings take shape in and through our relationships with myriad other creatures, both human and nonhuman, and because these relationships extend from the present back to the most remote

160   *The Hope of Glory*

reaches of the past, the promise of eternal life cannot be viewed in individu-
alistic terms, but must be seen as inseparable from the renewal of the created
order in its entirety.[1] The hope of glory thus includes the whole of creation,
which "waits with eager longing for the revealing of the children of God, for
the creation was subjected to futility, not of its own will, but by the will of the
one who subjected it, in hope that the creation itself will be set free from its
enslavement to decay and will obtain the freedom of the glory of the children
of God" (Rom. 8:19–21). In this vision human beings retain a distinctive place:
it is their redemption ("the revealing of the children of God") upon which the
redemption of the nonhuman creation depends. Why this should be the case is
not immediately clear. One might suppose that because it was human disobedience that disrupted the original harmony of the created order (Gen. 3:14–19), it
is appropriate that the restoration of creation as a whole should be contingent
upon the redemption of human beings in particular. But Paul gives no explanation of why creation "was subjected to futility" beyond God's mysterious will,
and since our current knowledge of natural history shows that pain, suffering, and death were features of creaturely existence long before human beings
appeared on earth, they cannot plausibly be explained as the result of human
malfeasance.

Whatever the reason for God's assigning this pivotal role in the drama of
salvation to human beings, it is in the incarnation that it is played out: because
God united the divine life to creation through a human being, it is by way of
the redemption of human nature that all created nature is brought into God's
presence. Maximus the Confessor illustrates this point by describing the cosmic
scope of God's redemptive work in just such incarnational terms:

> And with us and for us [the Word] encompassed the extremes of the whole
> creation . . . as His own parts, and He joined them around Himself, each with
> the other, tightly and indissolubly: paradise and the inhabited world, heaven
> and earth, the sensible and the intelligible, since like us He possesses a body,
> sense perception, soul, and intellect.[2]

Because his humanity includes all the extremes of created being, in bringing
his human nature to God's right hand in the ascension, Jesus also brings the

---

1. "The fulness . . . of the time allotted to each of us (our life-time), that which when we have lived
our lives will be before God and in His judgment, is our history. *Our* history? It is ours only as we
have lived and experienced and actualised and suffered it together with others, in the stretch of time
which is theirs, too." Karl Barth, *Church Dogmatics* [hereafter *CD*], 13 vols., ed. G. W. Bromiley and
T. F. Torrance (Edinburgh: T&T Clark, 1956–1974) IV/2, 444 (emphasis original). Although Barth is
only referring to other human beings here, the logic of his analysis extends to the nonhuman realm.

2. Maximos the Confessor, *Ambiguum* 41, in *On Difficulties in the Church Fathers: The Ambigua*, 2 vols.,
ed and trans. Nicholas Constas (Cambridge, MA: Harvard University Press, 2014), 2:115. Whether
Maximus held a supralapsarian account of the incarnation (i.e., one in which Jesus would have
become incarnate even apart from the fall) is open to debate. The fact that earlier in the same treatise
Maximus describes Jesus' work as fulfilling what human beings (described as "possessing by nature
the full potential to draw all the extremes [of creation] into unity," 2:105) ought to have done but failed
to do suggests an infralapsarian view (cf. *Ambiguum* 3, where the salvation of humankind is described
as "the sole reason for his birth in the flesh," 1:19). Yet since elsewhere he argues "that it is for the sake
of Christ"—that is, the Word made flesh—"that all the ages and the beings existing within the ages
received their beginning and end in Christ," it seems possible to argue that for him the task of overcoming creation's polarities would always have been realized in Christ even if Adam had not sinned.
See St. Maximos the Confessor, *On Difficulties in Sacred Scripture: The Responses to Thalassios*, 60, trans.
Maximos Constas (Washington, DC: Catholic University of America Press, 2018), 429.

7. The Transformation of the World 161

whole of creation with him.[3] In his resurrection Jesus is thus the "first fruits" (1 Cor. 15:20) of a comprehensive renewal of the whole creation, the completion of which awaits the definitive "revealing of the children of God" at Jesus' return (Rom. 8:19; cf. 1 Cor. 15:23–24; 1 John 3:2).[4]

Signs and Portents

The fact that Jesus is the ground of creation's renewal does not mean that his resurrection is the only anticipation of that future in the present. It is true that because only Jesus has risen from the dead, he alone can be described as "the first fruits of those who have died" (1 Cor. 15:20); but those who receive the gospel (and thus begin even now to experience something of what it means to live by God's word alone) are also called "a kind of first fruits of his creatures" (Jas. 1:18) "through sanctification by the Spirit and through belief in the truth" (2 Thess. 2:13). And insofar as believers remain dependent on relationships with other creatures for their day-to-day existence, it should come as no surprise that they should encounter examples of the first fruits of the kingdom in the nonhuman realm as well. Indeed, Scripture makes it clear that the "belief in the truth" that renders Christians themselves first fruits is bound up with their encountering irruptions of future glory in the created order more broadly.

The most striking examples of such irruptions are the extraordinary events conventionally called miracles and described in the New Testament as "signs" (*sēmeia*; see, e.g., Matt. 12:39 and pars.; John 2:11; 4:54; 6:2; 20:30; Acts 2:43; 4:22; Rom. 15:18–19; Heb. 2:4). The Gospels report Jesus himself affirming that the wonderful works he does bear witness to the advent of the kingdom (Matt. 12:28 and par.; cf. John 10:25).[5] And yet precisely because miracles are proleptic signs of the inbreaking of the eschatological order of glory, they cannot be identified simply by reference to their extraordinary character. After all, the devil, too, can work wonders (2 Thess. 2:9; Rev. 13:11–13; 16:14; 19:20); but even leaving that consideration aside, to equate the miraculous with the unusual renders it relative to the experience of the observer and thus a matter of purely subjective judgment rather than the distinct kind of event that could count as a proleptic manifestation of eschatological glory.[6] As Thomas Aquinas put it,

3. For not even "the most ignoble among [created] beings [is] completely destitute or devoid of a natural share in the general relationship to the most honored beings." Maximos the Confessor, "*Ambiguum* 41," 2:117.

4. For an account of the cosmological significance of the incarnation developed in classical Chalcedonian terms, see Rebecca L. Copeland, *Created Being: Expanding Creedal Christology* (Waco, TX: Baylor University Press, 2020), especially chapter 4.

5. At the same time, it is also worth noting that the same Jesus can at other times chastise those who follow him for their focus on his miraculous deeds: "Unless you see signs and wonders you will not believe" (John 4:48).

6. Admittedly, some theologians have been happy to define miracles in purely subjective terms. In perhaps the most extreme case, Friedrich Schleiermacher wrote, "'Miracle' is merely the religious name for an event, every one of which, even the most natural and usual, is a miracle as soon as it adapts itself to the fact that the religious view of it can be the dominant one" (*On Religion: Speeches to Its Cultured Despisers*, ed. and trans. Richard Crouter [Cambridge: Cambridge University Press, 1996], 49). Yet Augustine, too, was inclined to view the miraculous as a matter of perspective, arguing that "we give the name nature to the usual common course of nature; and whatever God does contrary to

162   *The Hope of Glory*

"the same thing may be wondered at by the one and not by the other. . . . But the word 'miracle' connotes something altogether wondrous [*quasi admirationem plenum*], i.e., having its cause hidden absolutely and from everyone."[7] And, Thomas goes on to note, the only cause that is hidden in this way is God.[8] By contrast, "whatever an angel or any other created thing does by its own power takes place in accordance with the ordinary processes of nature" (since "nature" refers precisely to the intrinsic powers of creatures as made by God) "and so is not miraculous" by definition.[9] In short, miracles are created effects caused directly by God rather than indirectly through the operation of other created (viz., natural or secondary) causes.

Of course, precisely because the cause of a miracle cannot be perceived, it is impossible to prove that any given event is a miracle: one may concede that no secondary cause can be identified for a particular event, but that evidently falls short of proving that such a cause does not exist.[10] Thus, a miracle is not subject to demonstration, though (and not unimportantly) it is open to disproof if a plausible natural cause can be identified. And yet belief in miracles is nevertheless arguably integral to Christian faith precisely because it reflects a conviction that the destiny of the world and its creatures is not reducible to the operation of created causes. Because the gospel itself makes this very same claim—that by virtue of the forgiveness of sins, the significance of a human life is not reducible either to what one has done or to what one has suffered—it would seem entirely appropriate that God should confirm this message by means of such accompanying signs (see Mark 16:17–20).[11] Thus, although the experience of miracles cannot ground Christian hope (since, again, miracles cannot in their nature count as proof of divine activity), they can strengthen it by providing

---

this, we call . . . a miracle," so that "[c]ontrary to nature is here used in the sense of contrary to human experience of the course of nature; as that a wild olive engrafted in a good olive should bring forth the fatness of the olive instead of wild berries. But God, the Author and Creator of all natures, does nothing contrary to nature; for whatever is done by Him who appoints all natural order and measure and proportion must be natural in every case." Augustine, *Reply to Faustus the Manichaean* 26.3, in *St. Augustin: The Writings against the Manichaeans and against the Donatists*, vol. 4 of *Nicene and Post-Nicene Fathers*, 1st series, ed. Philip Schaff (Grand Rapids: William B. Eerdmans, 1984 [1887]), 548.

7. Thomas Aquinas, *Summa Theologiae* [hereafter *ST*] 1.105.8, 60 vols., Blackfriars ed. (London: Eyre & Spottiswood, 1964–81); translation altered.

8. "[T]he cause absolutely hidden to every man is God, inasmuch as no man in this life can mentally grasp the essence of God." Thomas Aquinas, *Of God and His Creatures: An Annotated Translation (with Some Abridgement) of the* Summa Contra Gentiles *of St. Thomas Aquinas* 3.101, trans. Joseph Rickaby, SJ (London: Burns and Oates, 1905), 474.

9. Aquinas, *ST* 1.110.4; cf. 1.110.4.1, where Aquinas clarifies that this still allows God to make creatures (whether angels or humans) ministers of miraculous deeds through the power of the Spirit (see, e.g., Ezek. 37:1–14).

10. This understanding is reflected in the Catholic Church's procedure for adjudicating miracles in the context of the canonization of saints: in order for an alleged miracle of healing (the predominant type in such cases) to be judged genuine, at least two-thirds of the medical commission investigating the case have to certify that the healing cannot be assigned a natural cause. "Regolamento della Consulta Medica della Congregazione delle Cause dei Santi, 23.09.2016," §15. https://press.vatican.va/content/salastampa/it/bollettino/pubblico/2016/09/23/0666/01504.html.

11. "Jesus accompanies his words with many 'mighty works and wonders and signs,' which manifest that the kingdom is present in him and attest that he was the promised Messiah. The signs worked by Jesus attest that the Father has sent him. They invite belief in him. To those who turn to him in faith, he grants what they ask. So miracles strengthen faith in the One who does his Father's works; they bear witness that he is the Son of God." *Catechism of the Catholic Church*, 2nd ed. (New York: Doubleday, 1997), §§547–48.

7. The Transformation of the World 163

tangible instances of God's will for the flourishing of creatures in the midst of seemingly hopeless situations.[12]

And yet as significant as miracles may be for an individual's life of faith, their rarity, unpredictability, and openness to contestation invariably render their impact on believers uneven: a person who has been blessed by miraculous healing will have an experience of miracles quite different from someone who knows of them only by report. By contrast, the Eucharist is a this-worldly irruption of the kingdom that is given equally to all the faithful as a means whereby they, having died and been buried with Christ in baptism, can experience the first fruits of the renewed creation in the present. For just as human beings experience the first fruits of glory through the good news that their identity as a child of God is determined by God's word alone rather than by "works" (i.e., either what they have done or what has been done to them), so the Eucharist's status as first fruits of the eschatological renewal of the whole creation rests on the conviction that here, too, creaturely identity (in this case, that of the consecrated elements) is defined by God's word rather than by their physical properties as products of human agriculture. This does not mean that by virtue of their consecration the eucharistic elements cease to be bread and wine, any more than baptized human beings on this side of the eschaton cease to be creatures of flesh and blood. Rather, in the sacrament Christ is present in, with, and under these material elements, such that what they are—the body and blood of Christ given and shed for the life of the world—is determined not by what they have been but by what they have been called to be: a concrete manifestation of divine presence, and thus a means of grace.

The present experience of the sacrament of the altar can in this way be understood as a proleptic manifestation of how every creature will exist in the new creation, because it is central to the Christian hope for a renewed creation that with the consummation all creatures will be perceived as manifestations of divine glory.[13] For even as we do not see worldly light directly, but only as it either radiates from or is reflected off of creaturely bodies, so in the heavenly Jerusalem, where "the glory of God is its light, and its lamp is the Lamb" (Rev. 21:23; cf. 22:5), our perception of the divine glory will be bound up with our perception of creatures, whether that glory is seen radiating from the body of the Lamb or reflected from the myriad surfaces of the creatures that will populate the new heaven and earth. In the meantime, the sacramental economy provides a foretaste of glorified existence, in that God confirms through it that the reception of the divine word that secures human redemption is inseparable

---

12. It is important to distinguish signs of the kingdom from the various signs of the end of the present age described in the apocalyptic passages of the Synoptic Gospels (Matt. 24:1–30 and pars.). While the former are proleptic examples of the economy of the consummation (viz., according to which creatures are sustained directly by God's word rather than by created causes), the latter are part of the order of creation. Indeed, because the signs of the end described in the New Testament (e.g., wars, famines, earthquakes, and the like) reflect the permanent condition of life in the present age, they are better conceived as a perpetual summons to watchfulness rather than a means of calculating the time of Jesus' return. See Joseph Ratzinger, *Eschatology: Death and Eternal Life*, 2nd ed. (Washington, DC: Catholic University of America Press, 1988), 198.

13. Even now the world displays God's glory to those who have eyes to see, but because "most people, immersed in their own errors, are struck blind in such a dazzling theatre . . . however much the glory of God shines forth [now], scarcely one man in a hundred is a true spectator of it." John Calvin, *Institutes of the Christian Religion*, 2 vols., ed. John T. McNeill, trans. Ford Lewis Battles (Philadelphia: Westminster, 1960), 1.61 (I.v.8).

164 *The Hope of Glory*

from the renewal of the nonhuman creation, even as, conversely, the renewal of creation in the sacraments serves "the revealing of the children of God" through the gospel.

The Eucharist thus exemplifies the inseparability of human and cosmic redemption, with the former initiating the latter by way of God's assumption of human flesh in Christ, and the latter confirming the former through the same Christ's presence in the nonhuman substance of bread and wine. The sacrament also points to the way in which the transition from creation to consummation transforms creaturely existence from an economy where human life is sustained by God indirectly, through the mediation of other creatures (viz., "bread" in its worldly sense) to one where it is upheld directly by God (through the eucharistic bread, which is none other than "my body, given for you"). As Augustine noted, this shift establishes a new relationship between what is eaten and the one who eats it: "you will not change me into you like the food your flesh eats, but you will be changed into me."[14] In other words, in the Eucharist we no longer are sustained by metabolizing other created substances into our own substance; rather, God's word draws us directly into God's life, in which we become participants just by virtue of the fact that we live by God's power (viz., the divine word, which takes visible form in the consecrated elements) rather than our own.[15]

In summary, if miracles are signs of the kingdom whose occurrence is utterly unpredictable, the Eucharist is God's provision of a regular opportunity of receiving a foretaste of what it means to live not "by bread alone, but by every word that comes from the mouth of God."[16] In both cases, however, the form of the irruption of the power of God's kingdom in the present is entirely a matter of divine determination: human beings may be the instruments through whom God acts, but it is God alone—whether through the unpredictability of miracle or the established provisions of the eucharistic liturgy—who is responsible for its shape. There is, however, a third category of signs of the kingdom that derives from human activity—not the "first fruits" represented by the lives of believers themselves noted at the beginning of this section, but the results of that activity in the world. Here, too, Christians will appeal to God as the ground of their actions, in line with Paul's assessment that in his own ministry "it was not I, but the grace of God that is with me" (1 Cor. 15:10; cf. Gal. 2:20); but the effects of Paul's actions, understood as a function of Paul's particular vocation (see Rom. 1:1; 1 Cor. 1:1; Gal. 1:15; cf. Gal. 2:1–14; Phil. 1:12–14) is for that reason inseparable from Paul's own discernment of the proper form

14. Saint Augustine, *Confessions* 7.10.16, trans. Henry Chadwick (Oxford: Oxford University Press, 1991), 124.

15. The description of the sacraments as "visible words" (*verba visibilia*) comes from Augustine's *Contra Faustum*, where Augustine describes the difference between the "sacraments" of the Old Testament (e.g., circumcision) and the New as analogous to the change in form associated with conjugating verbs in different tenses: "For if in language the form of the verb changes in the number of letters and syllables according to the tense, as *done* signifies the past, and *to be done* the future, why should not the symbols which declare Christ's death and resurrection to be accomplished, differ from those which predicted their accomplishment?" See Augustine, *Reply to Faustus the Manichaean* 19.16, 418 (emphasis added).

16. Thus for Aquinas the Eucharist is also a miracle, but of a different sort than the "signs" of the New Testament: "some miracles are themselves matters of faith [*fides*] as, for example, the virgin birth, the Lord's resurrection, the Sacrament of the Altar. . . . The purpose of other miracles, however, is to confirm our faith [*ad fidei comprobationem*]." Aquinas, *ST* 3.29.1.2; translation altered.

7. The Transformation of the World

his witness should take at any given point in time. This involvement of the Christian's own agency means that such actions are not miraculous in the technical sense (viz., performed by God apart from the mediation of secondary causes), but they nevertheless anticipate the kingdom insofar as their results in the world serve as portents of the kingdom.[17] Prompted by the love by which Jesus says "everyone will know that you are my disciples" (John 13:35; cf. Gal. 5:14), as well as the further fruits of the Spirit described by Paul—"joy, peace, patience, kindness, generosity, faithfulness, gentleness, and self-control" (Gal. 5:22–23)—these actions take form in the struggle against "the rulers, against the authorities, against the cosmic powers of this present darkness, against the spiritual forces of evil" (Eph. 6:12). And they have as their result hospitality shown to the outcast (Luke 14:13; cf. Jas. 2:1–7), caring for the sick (Matt. 10:8), resources shared with the poor (Matt. 25:34–40; Jas. 1:27; cf. Rom. 15:26; Gal. 2:10), and the liberation of the oppressed (Luke 4:18; cf. Acts 10:38).

It is in this context that the idea of the millennium—that is, the earthly, intra-historical manifestation of the kingdom of God described in Revelation 20:4–6—both can and must be affirmed as having a place in Christian belief rather than dismissed as merely a "Jewish opinion."[18] The rejection of premillennial teaching is justified insofar as the latter includes belief in a perfect fulfillment of the kingdom within history, during which "the ungodly are suppressed everywhere."[19] For according to Revelation the very fact that the millennium is limited in time to a thousand years is a function of the fact that the reign of Christ and the saints it entails is evidently not so universal or final as to prevent the rise of Gog and Magog (Rev. 20:8)—and thus of the need for further struggle against the forces of evil within history. But if it follows that the millennium cannot be understood to mean that God's intentions for creation are consummated within history, it nevertheless does point to the possibility of a real, if limited, fulfillment of those intentions in this age. Because even apart from the destructive effects of sin, life in space and time poses physical limits to the possibility of the simultaneous flourishing of all creatures, such intra-historical fulfillment can only be partial; but it would be inconsistent both with Christian confession of the essential goodness of the old creation (Gen. 1:31) and with the conviction that in Christ everything has already become new (2 Cor. 5:17) to view the present age as nothing more than a vale of tears.[20] Granted that those

---

17. This category of portents of the kingdom may also be reflected in Jesus' words, "If I am not doing the works of my Father, then do not believe me. But if I do them, even though you do not believe me, believe the works" (John 10:37–38; cf. 14:11). While the reference to works (*erga*) rather than signs (*sēmeia*) does not present a contrast with the miraculous (after all, among the "works" presumably on Jesus' mind is his healing of the blind man in the previous chapter, which had just been mentioned by some members of his audience in v. 21), it does suggest that what is at stake is less the extraordinary character of Jesus' deeds than their bearing witness to the Father's will that people "may have life, and have it abundantly" (John 10:10). See also Matt. 11:4–5, where Jesus answers John the Baptist's question regarding his status by saying, "Go and tell John what you hear and see: the blind receive their sight, the lame walk, those with a skin disease are cleansed, the deaf hear, the dead are raised, *and the poor have good news brought to them*." Cf., too, the sermon in Nazareth of Luke 4:18, where Jesus (citing Isaiah) characterizes his ministry as including "good news to the poor" and "release to the captives" as well as "recovery of sight to the blind."

18. Augsburg Confession (Latin Text), Article XVII, in *The Book of Concord: The Confessions of the Evangelical Lutheran Church*, ed. Robert Kolb and Timothy J. Wengert (Minneapolis: Fortress Press, 2000), 51.

19. Augsburg Confession (Latin Text), Article XVII, 51.

20. "The idea of an earthly paradise remains inadmissible. But this does not do away with the Christian hope that even here, on earth, a ray of the transfiguration can shine and that the fullness of the

166   *The Hope of Glory*

who look to Christ's second coming rightly conceive themselves as "exiles" (1 Pet. 1:1; 2:11) who in the present age "have no lasting city, but . . . are looking for the city that is to come" (Heb. 13:14), they nevertheless have every reason to remember God's word to Israel and "seek the welfare of the city where I have sent you into exile, and pray to the LORD on its behalf, for in its welfare you will find your welfare" (Jer. 29:7). For though whatever "welfare" achieved in this age can never be more than a sign of the life to come, where "mourning and crying and pain will be no more" (Rev. 21:4), it is yet the very nature of a sign to point to a reality other than itself and on which it depends. And because the reality, as that to which the sign refers, is logically prior to the sign, Christians will interpret the worldly effects of even non-miraculous works of human love and justice as anticipatory signs of eschatological glory—and thus of the hope of a renewed creation—breaking in on the present.

A New Heaven and a New Earth

But is this hope for a final, comprehensive renewal of creation credible? If the persistence of the power of sin even in the light of the promised millennium rules out the claim that history has an "arc" that ultimately "bends toward justice," is not the promise of a new heaven and earth rightly dismissed as wishful thinking—and the signs thought to presage it as so much whistling in the dark?[21] This problem seems to be particularly acute given that modern science shows that the world does not exist in a steady state. Such a perspective represents a sharp shift from the common view throughout most of the church's history, for which the forms and structures of the created order were understood to be fixed and invariant between the time of the world's origination and the Last Judgment (cf. Gen. 2:1–3; 9:22; and Matt. 24:29–31). This view is no longer tenable, as it is now clear that our present experience of creation is only a brief moment within an expansive cosmic history, in which periods both previous and subsequent to our own differ radically from current arrangements. Notwithstanding the acrimony with which some Christians regard scientific claims about the age of the earth, the fact that long before the emergence of modern science Christians were open to reading the chronology of Genesis's opening chapters loosely suggests the shape of earlier periods of cosmic history does not pose any particular problems with respect to Christian beliefs about creation.[22] By contrast, Christian hope for the future of creation would seem

---

kingdom of God is attainable. And who can say what this fullness and its achievement will be like? If an enervating dreaminess is reprehensible, a Christian dream is still admissible, and this dream is given a place in Revelation." Sergius Bulgakov, *The Sophiology of Death: Essays on Eschatology: Personal, Political, Universal,* trans. Robert J. De La Noval (Eugene, OR: Cascade, 2021), 27.

21. The claim that "the arc of history bends toward justice" are quite properly associated with Martin Luther King Jr., who used them often, but always in quotation marks, because they come from Theodore Parker, "Of Justice and the Conscience," in *Ten Sermons of Religion* (Boston: Crosby, Nichols, and Company, 1853), 84–85: "I do not pretend to understand the moral universe. The arc is a long one. My eye reaches but little ways. I cannot calculate the curve and complete the figure by experience of sight. I can divine it by conscience. And from what I see I am sure it bends toward justice."

22. See, e.g., Saint Augustine, *Confessions,* XII, especially xviii (27)–xxv (34), trans. Henry Chadwick (New York: Oxford University Press, 1991), 258–65. Of course, other aspects of Christian teaching— most especially the fall and original sin—do seem at first glance to be far more dependent on a literal reading of Genesis, to the extent that Augustine himself became rather more insistent in emphasizing

7. The Transformation of the World 167

to be more difficult to affirm if they involve a radical deviation from what the inherent dynamics of the created order suggest that future will be: it is, after all, one thing to speak (as Scripture seems to) of God bringing to an end a worldly history that has no intrinsic terminus, but quite another to argue for a Christian hope for the future that is seemingly inconsistent with the outcome of natural processes that God has established in creating the world to begin with—all the more so given that there are at least three levels where such a mismatch between worldly processes and Christian hope is in evidence.

The first level is that of the universe as a whole. There is a broad consensus among cosmologists that the universe began some 13.7 billion years ago with the rapid expansion of space-time known colloquially as the "big bang." Although the subsequent eons have seen the clustering of matter into galaxies, stars, and planets, the universe continues to expand under the impulse of that initial event. There is less consensus about how this process will continue into the future. Calculations based the total mass of the universe and the current rate of expansion have tended to throw doubt on the idea that the expansion will slow and eventually reverse, leading to a terminal collapse of the universe on itself in a "big crunch." A more likely alternative is that the rate of the universe's expansion will continue to accelerate under the influence of the mysterious force known as dark energy, leading (around twenty billion years from now) to a "big rip," in which the force of expansion will tear the universe apart beginning with galaxies, then stellar systems and planets, and proceeding down to the level of atoms. Still another possibility is that the current process of expansion will continue indefinitely, so that the universe becomes ever more diffuse, culminating in the unimaginably distant future (around 10^{32}—or, if it turns out that protons decay, 10^{100}—years from now) in a universe reduced to a thin soup of widely scattered subatomic particles: a cold and dark "big chill."[23]

Turning to the level of the solar system, the dynamics of stellar evolution will render earth incapable of sustaining life long before the universe as a whole comes to an end.[24] As the sun depletes the hydrogen that fuels its thermonuclear engine, it will grow ever brighter, leading to steadily increasing terrestrial surface temperatures. About 500 million years from now this process will deplete the supply of atmospheric carbon dioxide sufficiently to suppress photosynthesis and kill off plant life. In a further 500 million years, the increasing heat will cause the oceans to evaporate into space, with the loss of surface water leading to the extinction of all multicellular life and eventually even of bacteria. In a further four to five billion years, the sun, having finally exhausted

---

the historicity of Genesis 2–3 as he found himself defending the doctrine of original sin in the course of the Pelagian controversy (see, e.g., *The Literal Meaning of Genesis*, especially VIII.1–12, in *On Genesis*, ed. John E. Rotelle, OSA, trans. Edmund Hill, OP [Hyde Park, NY: New City Press, 2002], 346–54; cf. *The City of God against the Pagans*, XIII.21, ed. and trans. R. W. Dyson [Cambridge: Cambridge University Press, 1998], 567–69). Modern theology has seen a variety of attempts to decouple this doctrine from a literal reading of the biblical account; see Ian A. McFarland, *In Adam's Fall: A Meditation on the Christian Doctrine of Original Sin* (Malden, MA: Wiley Blackwell, 2010), 39–45, 154–61.

23. For an accessible discussion, see Chris Impey, *How It Ends: From You to the Universe* (New York: W. W. Norton & Company, 2010), 261–70; cf. Paul Halpern and Paul Wesson, *Brave New Universe: Illuminating the Darkest Secrets of the Cosmos* (Washington, DC: Joseph Henry Press, 2006), 113–17, 142–46.

24. For the material in this paragraph, see Peter D. Ward and Donald Brownlee, *The Life and Death of Planet Earth: How the New Science of Astrobiology Charts the Ultimate Fate of Our World* (New York: Times Books, 2003), chs. 6–9.

168   *The Hope of Glory*

its hydrogen supply, will swell to over 100 times its current size and scorch the earth to a cinder—though by that time the earth will long since have reached a future that looks rather like its most distant past: hot, dry, and barren.[25]

If we move to the third level of the future of the human species itself, there is good reason to doubt that any of its members will be alive by the time the earth's capacity to sustain life begins to be compromised. It is possible that human extinction could prove to be our own doing: our pollution of the biosphere (which would rise to catastrophic levels if augmented by nuclear war) constitutes an ongoing threat to human survival; and if in the long term it is loss of atmospheric carbon dioxide that will reduce the earth's biological carrying capacity, in the short term the burning of fossil fuels is increasing carbon dioxide levels to an extent that threatens rapid and catastrophic climate change.[26] But even apart from considerations of the harmful effects of our own activity on our future survival, it is a basic fact of the paleontological record that species no less than individuals have finite lifespans of varying lengths. In the current (Cenozoic) geological era, for example, bivalve mollusk species (oysters, clams, mussels, and the like) survive for around ten million years; by contrast, mammalian species like ourselves last only one or two million years.[27] While it is a common conceit that human brain power renders us masters over our biology, there is in fact no reason to suppose that any amount of cultural evolution will allow us to float free of our wider environment in a way that would make us evolutionary exceptions to this norm.[28]

In short, the human story seems likely to last no longer than 10^6 years on a planet that will exist for around 10^{10} years, and which is, in turn, a tiny fragment of a universe that may not cease evolving for perhaps 10^{100} years. To get at least some sense of what this means concretely, consider that if the whole twelve-billion-year anticipated history of the earth were mapped on to a 24-hour clock, animals would have come and gone between 8 and 10 a.m., and within that time the entire history of humankind (assuming it were to last as long as a million years) would come to a mere 7.2 seconds. And given that the history of the earth is an even smaller fraction (viz., 1/1,000,000,000,000,000,000,000,000,

---

25. "All scientific models predict a gradual return to a hot world where life becomes less diverse, less complicated, and less abundant through time, until the last life looks much like the first life—a single-celled bacterium, last survivor and descendant of all that came before." Ward and Brownlee, *Life and Death of Planet Earth*, 19. It is worth adding that these features of terrestrial evolution render highly doubtful scenarios that imagine humans surviving the death of the sun by colonizing other stellar systems. Even leaving aside the technological challenges posed by the enormous distances that would have to be traversed in order to reach another stellar system, the odds of finding there a planet capable of supporting human life diminish significantly when it is recognized that such planets are habitable for less than 10 percent of the total history of their existence. See Ward and Brownlee, *Life and Death of Planet Earth*, 109; cf. their earlier book, *Rare Earth: Why Complex Life Is Unusual in the Universe* (New York: Copernicus Books, 2000).

26. See, e.g., *Climate Change 2022: Impacts, Adaptation and Vulnerability*, the Working Group II contribution to the Sixth Assessment Report of the Intergovernmental Panel on Climate Change, https://www.ipcc.ch/report/ar6/wg2/.

27. See David Raup and Steven M. Stanley, *Principles of Paleontology*, 2nd ed. (New York: W. H. Freeman, 1978), 318. Of course, because species are defined by constant morphology over time, their lifespans are not characterized by the sorts of morphological changes that mark the development of individual organisms from juvenile to adult forms.

28. Although transhumanism banks on our capacity to transcend our biological limits, many of its proponents' visions of the human future depend on questionable anthropological assumption. See p. 29 above.

7. The Transformation of the World 169

000,000,000,000,000,000,000,000,000,000,000,000,000,000,000,000,000,000,000,000,000,
000,000) of the history of the universe, the whole human venture amounts to
an inconceivably brief episode, followed by unfathomably long ages in which
every trace of it will have been completely obliterated.[29] In this context, to speak
of the hope of a new creation anticipated by present signs and portents seems
frankly delusional.

This judgment can be resisted by appealing to a parallel between the Christian hope for the transformation of the world and the transformation of the
individual. In the case of the individual the promise of life sustained by God's
word alone is anticipated in this life by the gospel of forgiveness, which is simply God's assurance that one's identity is not determined by (even though it is
not separable from) one's "works"—that is, the totality of what one has done
and endured in relation to other creatures over the course of one's existence
in space and time (viz., on the basis of "blood or . . . the will of the flesh or . . .
the will of man," John 1:13)—but solely by God's call. This promise does not
change the fact that one's earthly life continues to be sustained by (and correspondingly vulnerable to) relationships with other creatures, still less that
this life will come to an end. Quite the contrary, because the life that is raised is
precisely that which is finished, the hope of resurrection is inseparable from the
understanding of human life as essentially finite—and this precisely because
it is bound up with other creatures. Again, resurrection is not more life, in the
sense of the continuation of one's earthly story in a new location, but rather the
vindication of that story as finished.

So understood, the significance of resurrection is completely independent of
the length of a person's earthly life, whether considered in itself or in relation to
the broader sweep of human history. Indeed, that point is the upshot of Paul's
assurance to the Thessalonians that "we who are alive, who are left until the coming of the Lord, will by no means precede those who have died" (1 Thess. 4:15):
precisely because risen life with God is outside of the realm of space and time, its
quality (let alone its reality) bears no relation to the location of a person's life in
the space-time continuum. That human history should continue for a mere few
decades or countless millennia after one's death is irrelevant to one's status as a
child of God. Along similar lines, one might argue that whether the universe continues for a short or long time after the passing of the human species or the earth
on which it finds a home is of no import for the hope of a new creation, because
that hope, too, is not a calculation based on the possibilities and potentials inherent in the current order, but precisely an anticipation of the supervening of God's
power on it. That is, again, just what it means to live "not by bread alone, but by
every word that comes from the mouth of God."

Still, one might grant all this and still ask whether the promise of Jesus' second coming—that is, the universal and public disclosure of his status as Lord
and Savior—makes any sense apart from there still being human beings alive
to witness it. To be sure, the confession that Jesus "will come again in glory to

---

29. Even though humans may launch spacecraft that escape the destruction of the solar system (e.g.,
the two late twentieth-century Voyager probes have already crossed the heliopause into interstellar
space), no such devices will survive the eventual dissolution of baryonic matter predicted in both the
"big rip" and "big chill" scenarios; and even apart from that consideration, the sheer vastness of space
renders odds that any putative extraterrestrial civilizations will come upon them negligible.

170   *The Hope of Glory*

judge the living and the dead" does not logically entail that there should be anyone left among the living at his coming, but in such a scenario his return would seem to be somewhat anticlimactic—a revelation without an audience.[30] If considerations like these suggest that the delay of the Parousia to a posthuman future is not credible, then we are back at the problem of a hoped-for future that runs against the natural course of events in a way that both smacks of wishful thinking and implies that the grace of redemption subverts creation rather than perfecting it. Nor can this problem be avoided by identifying Christ's return with the end of the natural history of the universe (whether by way of the drama of the "big rip" or the somber heat death of the "big chill"), since that approach errs in the opposite direction by effectively making the Parousia the culmination of natural processes rather than an act of supernatural grace.[31]

A more effective counter to these worries is to note that they all rest on an understanding of the Parousia as a further event in Jesus' life following on his resurrection and ascension and thus as one (albeit climactic) historical event alongside others. As already argued, however, confession of Jesus' full humanity entails that his lifespan is defined by his birth in Bethlehem and his death on Golgotha, since the idea that his life extends beyond his crucifixion subverts the belief that the fullness of the Godhead is revealed in his life (Col. 1:19; 2:9).[32] Because the risen Lord no longer lives in time and space, no experience of him as alive after his death can be understood as the product of spatio-temporal relations; that is, one cannot explain the appearance of Jesus—whether on Easter morning or at the eschaton—in the same way that one might have explained his appearance in the temple or by the Sea of Galilee during his life (viz., as the product of a temporal sequence of cause and effect). It is neither the case that the observer can bring such experiences about (in the way that someone living in the first century could have in principle arranged to meet Jesus during his earthly life), nor can their occurrence be predicted: appearances of the risen Jesus, past or future, are miraculous and, as such, beyond our control and simply to be received with thanks when they are given. It follows that the experience of a new heaven and a new earth that comes with Jesus' return can no more be understood as a historical event than can the resurrection, all the more so since that promise is really nothing else than the application of "resurrection"—that is, the translation from existence sustained through created causes to existence sustained directly by God's word—to the nonhuman creation. Considered in these terms, the return of Christ is not to be identified

---

30. The problem is accentuated by the fact that biblical predictions of the Parousia are connected with a series of specifically human precursors in passages like 1 Thess. 2:1–8; 1 John 3:18–19; cf. Matt. 24:14. Likewise, Paul's claim that not all shall die, though all shall be changed (1 Cor. 15:51) evidently presupposes that there remain human beings alive on earth when Jesus returns.

31. Note that another version of this same problem arises in light of the argument that the reason the general resurrection must await the Parousia is that one's redemption cannot be final until the full extent of what it means to have been redeemed (viz., the entire accounting of the effects of one's sins) is revealed (see p. 122 above). For if that is the case, then the end of the human species would seem to constitute a *terminus ad quem* for Christ's return, since at that point any further downstream effects of one's sins on one's neighbor will cease (and, of course, the same problem arises even if one were to extend the timeline by including nonhuman life as also the victim of human sin).

32. See pp. 114–15 above.

7. The Transformation of the World   171

with some more or less distant future point in time, for (as Jesus himself makes clear) "the kingdom of God is not coming with things that can be observed" (Luke 17:20); that is, it is not a spatio-temporal event, but rather the sublation of all such events.[33]

Like the resurrection, then, the promise of a comprehensive renewal of creation is not a claim about the future of the world and therefore not to be conceived in terms of any sort of intra-historical development. Because the renewal of creation bespeaks a shift from the realm of time and space to that of eternity, it cannot be located on a historical timeline: even as the fact that the life of Jesus ends on the cross means that his resurrection cannot be conceived as a further event in his life, so the coming of the new creation cannot be conceived as one more historical event succeeding previous ones. Belief in the resurrection, whether on the individual or the cosmic scale, is rather a belief about the eternal significance of the temporal and for this reason refers to a mode of existence outside of time in which the creation lives by the word of God and not by its own powers.[34]

In this way, to speak of the new creation as the end of history is misleading to the extent that such language suggests a terminal point on a narrative timeline. The equation of the advent of Jesus—and thus of the new heaven and the new earth that he brings—with the end of history can be defended insofar as the promise of a new creation refers to that state where there is nothing more to be redeemed and thus to the completion of the divine economy. In this sense resurrection takes the temporal finitude of creatures seriously: that which is saved and renewed in glory has ended its earthly history; there is no more content to be added; what remains is rather the illumination of that story from the perspective of God's eternal and indefeasible purposes for it. Arguably, the proper biblical idiom for this state is not "end," which suggests coming to a stop, and thus a blunt cessation of activity that implies something closer to death than renewed life. A better choice is rather Sabbath, insofar as this term connotes rest, and thus not so much termination of life as its transposition to a new key.

Sabbath

Genesis reports that God finished creating the heavens and the earth "and all their multitude" in six days, "and he rested on the seventh day from all the

---

33. As already discussed (see note 12 above), when Jesus does refer to spatio-temporal events in relation to the eschaton, it is not to provide the basis for calculation. Quite the contrary, he concludes his discussion by emphasizing that no such calculation is possible: "But about that day and hour no one knows, neither the angels of heaven, nor the Son, but only the Father. For as the days of Noah were, so will be the coming of the Son of Man. For as in those days before the flood they were eating and drinking, marrying and giving in marriage, until the day Noah entered the ark, and they knew nothing until the flood came and swept them all away, so too will be the coming of the Son of Man. . . . Keep awake therefore, for you do not know on what day your Lord is coming" (Matt. 24:36–39, 42 and pars.).

34. "For if eternity limits and sets an end to time as such, it does indeed establish it thus as finite, but also establishes it. Whoever realises this is relieved from the temptation to confuse the end of history with a closing passage of history, however staggering and splendid it may be. Of the real end of history it may be said at any time: The end is near!" Karl Barth, *The Resurrection of the Dead*, trans. H. J. Stenning (Eugene, OR: Wipf and Stock, 2003 [1933]), 112.

172   *The Hope of Glory*

work that he had done" (Gen. 2:1–2). At first blush, it might seem that these verses are superfluous: once God had finished creating, then by definition God would have "rested" (i.e., ceased to create). There would thus seem to be no need to make an explicit statement of the point—especially in light of the belief that God is not one to become fatigued by creating (see Isa. 40:28). The fact that the narration includes this detail thus suggests that the divine resting (Hebrew *šābat*) is not simply cessation from activity (i.e., a purely privative concept), but itself a form of activity, something God *does* with as much intentionality as the explicitly creative work of the first six days.[35] And yet this resting is evidently not the kind of activity that has an observable product distinct from itself. Unlike God's creative utterances, "Let there be light" (Gen. 1:3), or, "Let the waters under the sky be gathered together into one place" (Gen. 1:9), God's resting does not result either in any new creature coming into being or in the rearrangement of already existing creatures. Neither God nor the world are visibly transformed by the divine resting. And yet God's resting does have consequences: "God blessed the seventh day and hallowed it, because on it God rested from all the work that he had done in creation" (Gen. 2:3). The consequence of God's resting is that the seventh day is set apart from the other six with respect to the way in which God relates to it. On the first six days God actively transforms the world so that it becomes the reality that God intends; on the seventh day God celebrates that reality as it has come to be.

This pattern can be understood as an anticipation within the present age of the transformation from creation to new creation. God's rest on the seventh day does not mean that creation ceases to be upheld through secondary causes and is instead sustained by God's word alone, as will be the case in glory; but the distinction between the six days and the Sabbath nevertheless points to a distinction between the world in process, taking shape through time both in its myriad creaturely parts and as a whole, and the world considered in its completed fullness, which, though not yet realized, may be affirmed as the goal of God's creative work. In short, the Sabbath may be seen as a reminder, built into the structure of creation itself, that creation has a significance that is not exhausted (even if it is structured) by history. In history individual creatures and the creation as a whole become what they are over the course of a more or less extended temporal span; but whether considered individually or as a whole, the essential truth of creation's being is not defined by these intraworldly processes (works), but rather by the sheer fact of God's delight in it (grace).

Of course, to speak of the Sabbath as a reminder of creation's ultimate significance does not mean that God needs such reminding, any more than God stands in need of rest after the work of creation. The Sabbath, like all God's other works, is rather to be understood as ordered to the creature. God's resting on the seventh day establishes a pattern that God's people are to observe:

---

35. The Hebrew *šābat* can simply mean "cease" or "desist." Indeed, the same form of the verb found in Gen. 2:2 (*yišbōt*) occurs with just that meaning elsewhere in the Old Testament (Hos. 7:4; Prov. 22:10). But that minimalist interpretation is precluded in Genesis 2 by the fact that there God's resting from the work of creation is distinguished from God's having finished (*kālāh*) it, as indicated by the subsequent explanation that it is God's resting from (rather than simply having finished) the work of creation that is the occasion for the divine blessing of the seventh day.

7. The Transformation of the World 173

> Remember the sabbath day and keep it holy. Six days you shall labor and do all your work. But the seventh day is a sabbath to the LORD your God; you shall not do any work—you, your son or your daughter, your male or female slave, your livestock, or the alien resident in your towns. For in six days the LORD made heaven and earth, the sea, and all that is in them, but rested the seventh day; therefore the LORD blessed the Sabbath day and consecrated it. (Exod. 20:8–11)

In the case of human beings and livestock, the command to rest also has a practical function, because animals, unlike God, do get tired and require time to be refreshed and restored. Indeed, in Deuteronomy the institution of the Sabbath is explained in just these terms, by reference to the Israelites' bondage in Egypt rather than to God's rest after creation: "Remember that you were a slave in the land of Egypt, and the LORD your God brought you out from there with a mighty hand and an outstretched arm; therefore the LORD your God commanded you to keep the Sabbath day" (Deut. 5:15). And the same logic undergirds the expansion of Sabbath practice in the Levitical Holiness Code:

> When you enter the land that I am giving you, the land shall observe a Sabbath for the LORD. Six years you shall sow your field, and six years you shall prune your vineyard and gather in their yield; but in the seventh year there shall be a Sabbath of complete rest for the land, a Sabbath for the LORD: you shall not sow your field or prune your vineyard. You shall not reap the aftergrowth of your harvest or gather the grapes of your unpruned vine: it shall be a year of complete rest for the land. You may eat what the land yields during its Sabbath. (Lev. 25:2–6)

Here the Sabbath respite extends not just to human beings and animals but to the land itself. And the final instantiation of the same principle is constituted by a further extension of the pattern from seven years to forty-nine years (or "seven weeks of years" according to Lev. 25:8), with the fiftieth year constituting a "year of jubilee" (Lev. 25:13), in which the normal provision of giving rest to the land is augmented by the restoration of property to its ancestral owners and the liberation of (Hebrew) slaves. The reasoning behind these last two provisions—that "land shall not be sold in perpetuity, for the land is mine" (Lev. 25:23), and likewise that Israelites are not to be kept in bondage because "they are my servants, whom I brought out of the land of Egypt" (Lev. 25:42)—reflect the underlying principle that a creature's status is not determined either by what it has accomplished by itself or by what it has suffered at the hands of others, but solely by God's judgment: no creature lives by bread alone, but by every word that comes from the mouth of God.

In this context, it should come as no surprise that by the time of the exile one of the prophets should have explicitly conflated the jubilee principle of Sabbath rest and restoration ("the year of the LORD's favor," Isa. 61:2) with the promise of God's eschatological redemption of Israel ("I will make you majestic forever, a joy from age to age," Isa. 60:15; "everlasting joy shall be theirs," Isa. 61:7). And in the wake of this interpretation of the cyclical celebration of Sabbaths (whether in their weekly, septennial, or quinquagenarian forms) as an anticipation of the final realization of God's kingdom, it is entirely to be expected that

174   *The Hope of Glory*

in his first recorded public sermon, Jesus, as God's kingdom in person (the *auto-basileia*), should proclaim the fulfillment of this same prophecy in his ministry (Luke 4:16-21).[36] Yet, as Jesus' conflicts with his contemporaries over Sabbath observance indicate, the content of Sabbath rest—precisely because of its rootedness in the restfulness of God—cannot be taken as self-evident. Indeed, the fact that our understanding of Sabbath rest takes its cue from God's rest rules out its being understood in terms of the creaturely distinction between activity and inactivity. As the one who creates from nothing (i.e., such that the creation is entirely gift), God is, in the language of Aristotelian philosophy, "pure act," meaning that the divine life is at no point or in any respect conditioned by any reality external to God but is eternally complete and fully realized in itself. In this sense, God's life is intrinsically one of rest, because God does not have to "do" anything in order to be God; God is, so to speak, always already God. And yet this "rest" is inherently dynamic, since it is a life of mutual love realized in the eternal giving and receiving of the divine life itself in begetting of the Son by and the proceeding of the Spirit.

By contrast, because we live in the movement from potency to act (or from possibility to actuality), activity is inherent to the existence of material creatures—which is to say that we do need to "do" something in order to be the creatures we are. To be sure, because our status as creatures (and, still more specifically, as children of God) is established unilaterally and irrevocably from God's side, the "in order to" here does not refer to a requirement we have to fulfill, but simply describes the character of created existence as one of becoming. That we are children of God is entirely and exclusively a function of divine election, but as worldly creatures our being as children of God is lived out in time, in a process marked by birth, growth, and maturity, in which the shape of our lives is subject to constant change and development that ends only with death.[37] Within this process rest is always only a relative inactivity, which serves as an enabling condition (and thus the necessary corollary) of work, most obviously in the diurnal cycle of sleeping and waking, but also in any number of other regular alternations (e.g., summer and winter, seed-time and harvest) that mark the rhythms of earthly existence. Such rest—while entirely good and proper—is temporary and secondary, and while it, too, is included in the biblical understanding of Sabbath (see again Deuteronomy 5), Sabbath points as well to a different kind of rest: the one that "still remains for the people of God," which is precisely "God's rest," in which "those who enter . . . rest from their labors *as God did from his*" (Heb.

---

36. The writer of Hebrews juxtaposes the eschatological Sabbath not with the cultic Sabbath and its variants, but rather with the "rest" sought by the Israelites during their wilderness wanderings, but the distinction between earthly anticipation and final fulfillment is the same: "For somewhere it speaks about the seventh day as follows: 'And God rested on the seventh day from all his works' [Gen. 2:2]. And again in this place it says, 'They shall not enter my rest' [Ps. 95:11]. . . . For if Joshua had given them rest, God would not speak later about another day" (Heb. 4:4–5).

37. Assuming a traditionally Thomist interpretation of the angelic hosts as nonmaterial creatures, their existence is not characterized by temporal extension; but it does entail the (nontemporal) "history" of their accepting or rejecting of grace. See Ian A. McFarland, "When Time Is of the Essence: Aquinas and the *Imago Dei*," *New Blackfriars* 82, no. 963 (May 2001): 215, with reference to Aquinas, *ST* 1.62–63.

7. The Transformation of the World

4:9–10). This is rest conceived as its own end rather than a means to further work. But what kind of rest is that?

If we take our bearings from the doctrine of creation, we are reminded once again that the difference between God's "work" of the first six days and the divine "rest" on the seventh is not between activity and inactivity, since, on the one hand, the world is no less dependent on the power of God for its existence on the seventh day than the first; and, on the other hand, the work of the six days requires no more effort on God's part than does the rest on the seventh. The difference has rather to do with God's *way* of relating to the world: first bringing into being and then sustaining in being. But from the perspective of the creature, the latter relation is that which enables creaturely becoming, the activity or movement that defines the history of every creature's existence in space and time.[38] In other words, God's ceasing from the six days' work of bringing creatures into being is the condition of the possibility of creatures bringing themselves into being by using their natural capacities (viz., the created powers proper to creatures as the particular kinds of creatures they are) to live out the particular forms of temporal existence God has given them.[39] Within this temporal frame of becoming, creaturely "rest" can only be relative, since the complete cessation of all movement is death. Such relative rest has (again) the practical benefit of enabling periods of more intensive activity, but in the biblical perspective reflected in the various Sabbath cycles, they also point toward a more comprehensive perfection (in the etymological sense of "completion") of creaturely activity, which the writer of Hebrews describes as "God's rest" (4:10). Such rest evidently requires a shift to a mode of existence in which the movement that characterizes creaturely life in time and space is finished. In this respect it presupposes a death died once and for all that nevertheless allows for a life lived to God on the far side of death (cf. Rom. 6:9–10). That is, analogously to the way in which God's rest on the seventh day does not entail inertness or inactivity, so the "sabbath rest [that] remains for the people of God" (Heb. 4:9) is not lifelessness but rather life upheld in its completeness—and thus "not . . . by bread alone, but by every word that comes from the mouth of God."

Maximus the Confessor described this form of life, which is no longer characterized by becoming and yet is not for that reason either frozen or inert, as "ever-moving rest."[40] In so doing, he draws on Gregory of Nyssa's idea of *epektasis*, according to which eternal life takes the form of an ever-deepening

---

38. The same idea is reflected in physicists' concept of the world line, understood as the trajectory of an entity in space-time, each point of which defines a particular spatial and temporal location, and the whole of which defines the history of the entity whose line it is.

39. These created powers—the natural capacities of creatures—are secondary causes and, as such, operate only because and so long as they are continually upheld and enabled by God as primary cause. Nevertheless, within the sphere of creation they have genuine causal efficacy, even as one can recognize the power of a character to produce some outcome in the world of a novel while conceding that this (secondary) causal efficacy is absolutely dependent on the (primary) causal power of the author. See the discussion in Ian A. McFarland, *From Nothing: A Theology of Creation* (Louisville, KY: Westminster John Knox, 2014), 142–52.

40. *Aeikinētos stasis.* See Maximus the Confessor, *Quaestiones ad Thalassium* 59 (CCSG 22:53) and 65 (CCSG 22:285); *Opuscula Theological et Polemica* 16 (PG 91:185A); cf. *Ambiguum* 67 (PG 91:1401A). Although Alexis Torrance has suggested that the phrase is better translated as "ever-*dynamic* rest" (Alexis Torrance, *Human Perfection in Byzantine Theology: Attaining the Fullness of Christ* [Oxford: Oxford University Press, 2020], 74), Maximus's understanding of glory as participation in the life of a

176   *The Hope of Glory*

immersion into the divine life.[41] This immersion has an inherently paradoxical character, because, on the one hand, the fact that glorified life is rooted in God means that movement has come to an end, because it has reached that fullness of being that is its ultimate and unsurpassable goal; yet, on the other hand, because God's being is infinite, the creature's capacity to enjoy it has no limit and so is ever-expanding. In short, in glory we ascend by standing still, so that the resting in God that is a cessation from labor (viz., the activity by which we come to be who we are in time) is an ever-increasing intensification of life (viz., the enjoyment of who we are as beloved of God in eternity).[42] The rest toward which we look is a resting in God's word, which unlike created realities does not pass away (Isa. 40:8; Matt. 24:35 and par.; cf. 1 Pet. 1:24–25), but neither is its eternity to be understood in terms of an unchanging content fixed like words on a page. Such a perspective fails to reckon with the fact that the word of God is *living* (Heb. 4:12) and, indeed, a *person* (John 1:1, 14) who sustains us by addressing us ever anew to call forth from us ever-new responses, so that the more we depend on God, the more intimately we come to know and love God. An ever-moving rest.

And yet nothing would be further from the truth than to view this rest as a private matter between the individual and God. Having been spoken into being by the divine Word (*Logos* in Greek), we are individually finite *logoi* who subsist in and under the infinite Logos, but the eternal Logos does not speak us into existence in isolation. We are, rather, part of a vast diversity of created beings bound together not as a single system, but as "an interaction of systems innumerable."[43] To say with Maximus that the significance of any created logos can be understood only in light of the eternal Logos who spoke it forth means that each can finally be understood only in relation to the totality of other *logoi* that provide the context within which it lives, moves, and has its being.[44] It

---

God who is "beyond all motion and rest" in *Ambiguum* 15 (PG 91:1221A) seems to me good reason to stress the oxymoronic character of the phrase.

41. Gregory, in turn, derived the term *epektasis* from Paul: "the soul rises ever higher and will always make its flight yet higher—by its desire of the heavenly things 'straining ahead [*epekteinomenos*] for what is still to come' [Phil. 3:13], as the Apostle says." Gregory of Nyssa, *The Life of Moses*, trans. Abraham J. Malherbe and Everett Ferguson (New York: Paulist Press, 1978), 113 (2.225). Cf. his *On the Soul and the Resurrection*: "in the Beautiful no limit is to be found so that love should have to cease with any limit of the Beautiful"; in Gregory of Nyssa, *Dogmatic Treatises, Etc.*, vol. 5 of *Nicene and Post-Nicene Fathers*, 2nd series, ed. Philip Schaff and Henry Wace (Boston: Hendrickson, 1995 [1893]), 450.

42. "In another Scriptural passage the progress is a standing still [*ho de dromos . . . stasis esti*], for it says, 'You must stand on the rock' [Exod. 33:21]. This is the most marvellous thing of all: how the same thing is both a standing still and a moving. For he who ascends certainly does not stand still, and he who stands still does not move upwards. But here the ascent takes place by means of the standing [*entautha de dia tou hestanai, to anabēnai ginetai*]. I mean by this that the firmer and more immoveable one remains in the Good, the more he progresses in the course of virtue. . . . It is like using the standing still as if it were a wing to fly upward through its stability in the good." Gregory of Nyssa, *Life of Moses*, 117–18 (2.243–44; cf. *PG* 44:405B–C). Cf. Hans Urs von Balthasar, *The Last Act*, vol. 5 of *Theo-Drama: Theological Dramatic Theory*, trans. Graham Harrison (San Francisco: Ignatius, 1998 [1983]), 131 (quoting Adrienne von Speyr, *Objektive Mystik*, 74–75): "'In the midst of our vision of God' there is 'a joyful movement toward him in which we are always arriving at our goal and yet are still moving forward.'"

43. Austin Farrer, *Love Almighty and Ills Unlimited: An Essay on Providence and Evil* (London: Collins, 1962), 51.

44. See Maximus, *Ambigua ad Iohannem* 7 (PG 91: 1081B–C; cf. 1077A–B; 1081A). Note that in this way the unity of the creation does not depend on its forming part of a single causal nexus. If (as in much of the tradition) angels are immaterial, each angelic life is causally independent of all other creatures; likewise, if the creation is (as some cosmologists believe) a multiverse, then our universe is one causally isolated world among many. Nevertheless, insofar as all creatures, whatever their inter-worldly

7. The Transformation of the World 177

follows that to be addressed and thereby sustained eternally by God's word in glory is to experience oneself as addressed alongside myriad other creatures. To live with God is therefore to live with other creatures, because God's love for us is not separable from the love that brought the whole of creation into being. To rest in God is therefore to rest together with the whole of creation.

This obviously differs profoundly from our situation now. In the present any rest we experience can only be relative, because our living depends on our continued activity, which, in turn, entails an ongoing process of give-and-take with other creatures, and these creatures at various times and in different respects may appear as threats no less than as gifts to our well-being. As our knowledge of God now is partial (1 Cor. 13:12), so, too, is our knowledge of other creatures: we cannot see them (any more than we can see ourselves) as they appear in God's sight, because the latter is precisely not one in which a creature's value is a function of its utility—its capacity to give rise to experiences of pleasure or pain—as is invariably the case for us who view them in the context of time and space. Only in glory is such a vision possible: only there can the "leopard . . . lie down with the kid," because only then will "the earth . . . be full of the knowledge of the LORD as the waters cover the sea" (Isa. 11:6, 9).[45]

And yet the celebration of Sabbath now serves as a reminder of this destiny in the face of day-to-day temptations to view the world as nothing more than a struggle for existence in which our interactions with other creatures, human and nonhuman alike, are decided by more or less generous calculations of costs and benefits. In this age, Sabbath rest can only be partial, but it can nevertheless serve as an occasion to recall the destiny of creatures as irreducible to utility, to recognize that no creature exists merely for the sake of another; for since God has no need of creaturely intermediaries to bring about the ends God desires, no creature's significance in God's sight can be exhausted by (however much it may include) its contribution to other creatures' flourishing.[46] To observe Sabbath is thus (among other things) to engage with the world and its creatures on terms other than their usefulness or lack thereof, but in prayerful (and, invariably, only fitfully successful) effort to discern their intrinsic value as creatures.

---

causal relations, are created through the Word (John 1:3), none can finally be understood apart from all others, as components of an unimaginably complex utterance in which the place of each is defined by its relation to the rest.

45. The worry that the vision of a glorified leopard or wolf or lion that does not eat prey animals amounts to a denial of their carnivorous nature reflects the same sort of misunderstanding of the resurrection seen in the Sadducees' question about future marriage arrangements (see Matt. 22:23–33 and pars.). Even as there is no marriage or giving in marriage in the resurrection, neither is there hunting, and for the same reason: that in the resurrection the lives of material creatures, having come to an end, are no longer sustained by the "bread" of creaturely interaction, but, like angels in heaven, are upheld by God's word alone.

46. Here I part company with Aquinas, who limits the creatures who will populate the eschatological new heavens and earth to those that contribute to human felicity (*Ex consummatione igitur hominis consummatio totius naturae corporalis quodammodo dependet*; Thomas Aquinas, *Compendium Theologiae* 148; https://www.corpusthomisticum.org/ott101.html). My position is effectively that on Thomas's grounds no creature can be excluded, since the ways in which other creatures contribute to our being—and thus to our well-being—do not permit the sorts of clean lines to be drawn between different sorts of creatures that Thomas presupposes (and in this context, it is interesting to note that in the posthumously compiled Supplement to the *Summa Theologiae* 3.91.5, the argument is made that if plants and animals are to have a place in the renewed creation, either all or none of them must be included). For an insightful discussion of these matters in relation to Thomas in particular, see Paul J. Griffiths, *Decreation: The Last Things of All Creatures* (Waco, TX: Baylor University Press, 2014), 274–96.

178   *The Hope of Glory*

It is in this context that Jesus' declaration that "The sabbath was made for humankind, and not humankind for the sabbath" (Mark 2:27) should be understood. The point is certainly not that the Sabbath is something humans are free to exploit for their own benefit; that would simply erase the Sabbath altogether as in any way distinct from the other days of the week. But it is to challenge the temptation to view the (relative) inactivity of earthly rest as an end in itself, without reference to the eschatological rest to which it points. For because in this age rest can only be partial and relative, the choice posed by the Sabbath is not between activity and inactivity, but rather between different forms of activity. Jesus is thus the Lord of the Sabbath (Mark 2:28 and pars.), not in the sense that he ignores it (as his critics charged in, e.g., Matt. 12:2 and pars.; Luke 13:14; John 5:16; 9:16), but in that he discloses that its point is less to refrain from activity than to make one's activity an occasion for bearing witness to God's desire for the well-being of creatures (see, e.g., Luke 13:16).[47]

Because Jesus' behavior on the Sabbath follows the logic of jubilee laid out in his inaugural sermon in the Nazareth synagogue, his witness to the promise of entering into God's rest is not best understood as indifference to earthly rest but rather as promoting such rest, understood not as inactivity in the abstract, but rather as life (with its necessary alteration of relative activity and inactivity) freed from the extremes of affliction and want that mar creaturely existence in this age. For insofar as the life that is to be brought to glory is just this earthly life, faithful witness to the hope of glory means regarding and engaging other creatures as beings destined for glory, and thus working to counter all those circumstances of their present existence that are inconsistent with it. Such work is not, of course, undertaken in the belief that it will itself achieve or even hasten our coming into glory, which cannot be earned by human effort but only received as a gift of God on the far side of life in space and time. Still, although the hope of glory is not a hope for the future of this world (i.e., the sort of hope for a utopian transformation of the conditions of earthly existence that breeds either titanism or despair), it is nevertheless a hope *for* this world (specifically, its eternal vindication before God) that is inseparable from treating every creature as the intended object of divine vindication. Concretely, this means bearing witness to the promise of Sabbath: a rest that is not the cessation of activity, but a fullness of life no longer fractured or diminished by powers that run counter to its flourishing. Rest—but a rest that is living, active, and thus "ever-moving."

---

47. In light of the indifference to traditional Sabbath observance in the New Testament (with the rather oblique exceptions of Matt. 24:20 and Luke 23:56), N. T. Wright has argued along these same lines that "the Lord's Day might be thought of . . . not in terms of things not to be done but rather of undertaking specific things that it is good and appropriate to do, not of refusal to do certain types of work so much as of determination to do certain other types—acts of healing, of mercy, of creativity, of justice, of beauty, of love." N. T. Wright, *Scripture and the Authority of God: How to Read the Bible Today* (San Francisco: HarperOne, 2011), 168–69.

Conclusion
A Theology of Glory

The foregoing chapters have quite explicitly sketched out a theology of glory. This would seem to be problematic for a Lutheran like myself, given Martin Luther's strident rejection of theologies of glory in favor of what he called a theology of the cross. One way to address that problem would be to point out that Luther was referring to method, not content. That is, he was not rejecting the propriety of talking *about* eschatological glory, but rather to doing theology as though one already had access to an eschatological point of view by "look[ing] upon the invisible things of God as though they were clearly perceptible in those things that have actually happened."[1] Instead, Luther argued, the true theologian confesses that in this life we know of God only what God has given us to see in the person of Jesus and so "comprehends the visible and manifest things of God seen through suffering and the cross."[2] Luther's point was not to deny the reality of the "invisible things" of God (e.g., the glorious attributes associated with God's "eternal power and divine nature," to which Paul refers in Rom. 1:20), but rather to stress precisely their *invisibility*, which, he argued, means that they are not accessible during this life, when we know "only in part" (1 Cor. 13:12). Under these conditions our knowledge of divine attributes must be derived exclusively from what we learn from the visible, earthly, and inglorious humanity of Jesus, which God has established as the instrument and reference point for all teaching about divine things.[3]

It would, however, be too facile to dismiss Luther's concerns about theologies *of* glory as irrelevant to the attempt to talk *about* glory that is intrinsic to Christian eschatology. For to the extent that a theology about glory looks to the promise of heaven above rather than earth below, it can all too easily distract the theologian from the flesh-and-blood realities of life in this world, attention to which would seem to be demanded by the Christian prayer that God's will should be done "on earth as it is in heaven" (Matt. 6:10). Admittedly, the fact that the earthly realization of God's will is a matter of prayer reflects the conviction that its fulfillment (like the immediately preceding petition for the coming of the kingdom, with which it is arguably in apposition) is the work of God rather than human beings. After all, the glory of the kingdom is an object

---

1. Martin Luther, *Heidelberg Disputation*, §19, in *Career of the Reformer I*, vol. 31 of *Luther's Works* [hereafter *LW*], American ed., ed. Harold J. Grimm (Philadelphia: Fortress, 1957), 40.

2. Luther, *Heidelberg Disputation*, §20, in *LW* 31, 40.

3. "[W]hoever wishes to deliberate or speculate soundly about God should disregard absolutely everything except the humanity of Christ." Martin Luther, Letter to Spalatin (February 12, 1519) in *D. Martin Luthers Werke: Kritische Gesammtausgabe*,121 vols. (Weimar: Hermann Böhlau 1883–2009), Part 4, Briefe/Briefwechsel, 1:226.

180 *The Hope of Glory*

of hope, and "hope that is seen"—that is, the fulfillment of which is the predictable outcome of intra-worldly processes of cause and effect—"is not hope" (Rom. 8:24). And yet if the fact that "we hope for what we do not see" demands that "we wait for it with patience" (Rom. 8:25), this can hardly be taken to justify indifference to the shape of life here and now; for Paul identifies "the hope of glory" with "Christ among you" (Col. 1:27), and he makes this point in the context of discussing his own role as a "minister" (*diakonos*) of the church, which includes "completing what is lacking in Christ's afflictions" on its behalf (Col. 1:24–25). Such a perspective would seem to imply that a faithful theology *about* glory will properly take the form of what Luther describes as a theology *of* the cross: taking its measure from the commitment to creaturely well-being in the present that Jesus not only instantiates in his ministry, but also explicitly cites as confirmation of his own messianic status (Matt. 11:4–6 and par.).

In line with these concerns, I have attempted in the preceding pages to challenge a purely contrastive view of the relationship between life now and the life to come. Thus, while I have described the two states in terms of the distinction between the present reality of life sustained by "bread" (viz., resources derived from other creatures) and the future hope of life upheld solely by God's word, I have also argued that one of the implications of the gospel is that in its message of forgiveness we already experience something of what it will mean to live by God's word alone. For to be forgiven is to receive the news that one's identity is not defined by "works" (whether conceived in terms of what we have done or what has been done to us), but exclusively by God's graciously unilateral decision to claim us as God's children apart from any merit or demerit on our part (see John 1:12; 1 Pet. 1:23). Although this experience does not free us from the need to continue to cultivate the myriad relationships with other creatures that together constitute the "bread" needed to sustain our earthly lives, it does change our understanding of these relationships: in light of the gospel, it becomes clear that the point of sustaining one's life is no longer to protect against the threat of death, for the assurance of the power and finality of God's love means that death, though still an enemy (1 Cor. 15:26), can no longer be victorious (1 Cor. 15:54–57; cf. Rom. 8:38–39); instead, the gospel frees us to use our lives in service of the well-being of others, resisting those forces that seek to thwart God's will for life (Deut. 30:19; Ezek. 18:23, 32; John 3:16).[4]

The Challenge of the Cross

At this point, however, another, rather different problem emerges. For Jesus explicitly links his having come "that they may have life, and have it abundantly" with his status as a servant: the "good shepherd" who "lays down his life for

---

4. A Christian "cannot ever in this life be idle and without works toward his neighbors, for he will necessarily speak, deal with, and exchange views with men. . . . Man, however, needs none of these things for his righteousness and salvation. Therefore he should be guided in all his works by this thought and contemplate this one thing alone, that he may serve and benefit others in all that he does, considering nothing except the need and advantage of his neighbor." Martin Luther, *The Freedom of a Christian*, in *LW* 31, 364–65.

Conclusion 181

the sheep" (John 10:10–11; cf. Luke 22:27). Moreover, he goes on to make it clear that he sees this willingness to lay down one's life as incumbent upon all those who would be his disciples: "If any wish to come after me, let them deny themselves and take up their cross and follow me. For those who want to save their life will lose it, and those who lose their life for my sake will find it" (Matt. 16:24–25 and pars.; cf. Matt. 20:26–28 and par.). As already noted, Paul sees his own role as a minister of Christ in just these terms: characterized by rejoicing in those sufferings through which he somehow carries on and completes the saving significance of Christ's afflictions (cf. Gal. 6:17). Here a theology of the cross takes on a potentially sinister aspect, since for Paul the "hope of sharing the glory of God" (Rom. 5:2) seemingly entails not simply confronting the flesh-and-blood realities of suffering, but actively embracing them: "we also boast in our sufferings, knowing that suffering produces endurance, and endurance produces character, and character produces hope" (Rom. 5:3–4, NRSV). From this perspective, hope seems less a motivation for resisting suffering than grounds for seeking it out, leading to the risk that the hope of future glory comes to be understood as a call to masochism in the present.[5]

Feminist and womanist theologians have made an especially trenchant case that cross-centered theologies should be rejected on the grounds that their practical effect has been to augment rather than relieve human suffering—especially as experienced by women.[6] Of unparalleled importance here is the work of Delores Williams, with her uncompromising insistence, "There is nothing divine in the blood of the cross."[7] Importantly, not all theologians who identify as womanist or feminist share Williams's views.[8] Yet her position remains profoundly compelling because it is rooted in precisely the same conviction that drove Luther to insist on a theology of the cross in the first place: namely, that Jesus should be the source and measure of all Christian talk about God. In so doing, however, Williams insists that to place Jesus at the center of theological reflection means to attend to what he himself *did*—the concrete shape of his ministry in Galilee, Samaria, and Judea—rather than to what was *done to him* in his arrest and execution.[9] There is much to commend in this position, for if Jesus is indeed the Word made flesh, then his own deliberate activities—healing the sick and lame, giving sight to the blind, preaching good news to the poor (Matt. 11:4–5 and par.)—are arguably a much better index of the content of the divine will than the activities of those who opposed him, whose captivity to sin was precisely the occasion for his coming into the world in the first place (see Matt. 1:21).

---

5. See the discussion on p. 40 above.

6. See especially Delores S. Williams, *Sisters in the Wilderness: The Challenge of Womanist God-Talk* (Maryknoll, NY: Orbis, 1993); and Rita Nakashima Brock and Rebecca Ann Parker, *Proverbs of Ashes: Violence, Redemptive Suffering, and the Search for What Saves Us* (Boston: Beacon, 2002).

7. Williams, *Sisters in the Wilderness*, 148.

8. For attempts to articulate a womanist and a feminist theology of the cross, respectively, see JoAnne Marie Terrell, *Power in the Blood?: The Cross in the African American Experience* (Maryknoll, NY: Orbis, 1998); and Deanna A. Thompson, *Crossing the Divide: Luther, Feminism, and the Cross* (Minneapolis: Fortress, 2004). For a range of reflections by North American theologians (both women and men) on the place of the cross in Christian theology, see *Cross Examinations: Readings on the Meaning of the Cross Today*, ed. Marit Trelstad (Minneapolis: Fortress, 2006).

9. Williams, *Sisters in the Wilderness*, 165-67.

182   *The Hope of Glory*

There are, however, two problems with this position: one exegetical and the other pastoral. Exegetically, it is simply impossible to square the wholesale rejection of the cross in the economy of salvation with the consistent witness of the New Testament on its central place in God's reconciling activity (e.g., John 12:32–33; 1 Cor. 1:17–18; Gal. 6:14; Eph. 2:16; Col. 1:20; Heb. 12:2; 1 Pet. 2:24). And while it is certainly true that the actions of Jesus' enemies against him cannot be understood to reveal God's will in the same way that Jesus does through his ministry, the fact that Jesus himself declares that he came "to give his life a ransom for many" (Matt. 20:28 and par.), along with his followers' subsequent insistence that he was crucified "according to the definite plan and foreknowledge of God" (Acts 2:23; cf. Isa. 53:2–10; Matt. 8:17; John 11:48–52) cannot be ignored when assessing the theological significance of the crucifixion. Pastorally, rejecting the cross leads to a rejection of Christian hope as well: the language of victory and vindication associated with Jesus' resurrection is set aside along with the cross as dangerously triumphalist, with the result that eschatological hope is replaced by a purely this-worldly horizon of survival in the face of the continuing onslaught of sin.[10] And when death finally comes, it does not lead to encounter with a transcendent Creator, but only a return to the earthly matrix of created forces out of which new, but equally temporary life may emerge.[11]

Feminist and womanist rejections of a theology of the cross can thus be seen as a specifically Christian form of the refusal of hope described in chapter 2: morally compelling in their refusal of the false consolations of much traditional Christian teaching, and yet finally inconsistent with the way in which the New Testament affirms the cross as the definitive sign of a hope that does not disappoint. And yet however strong the biblical evidence linking the cross with glory may be, the obstacles to combining them into a coherent account of eschatological hope are considerable. Two dangers in particular stand out. The first reflects precisely the concerns of feminist and womanist critics of cross-centered theologies: the risk of focusing so strongly on the cross as the cause of glory that cruciform suffering becomes the point of the Christian life now, with hope deferred to an indefinitely distant and otherworldly future. The second risk is the converse: that of allowing the promise of glory to eclipse the continuing relevance of the cross as a reminder of the cost of discipleship by reducing the cross to "a harmless non-offensive ornament . . . that doesn't force us to confront the power of Christ's message and mission."[12] The first

---

10. Williams, *Sisters in the Wilderness*, 158–61.

11. See, e.g., Rosemary Radford Ruether, *Sexism and God-Talk: Toward a Feminist Theology* (Boston: Beacon, 1984), 257–58.

12. James H. Cone, *The Cross and the Lynching Tree* (Maryknoll, NY: Orbis, 2011), xiv–xv. In this context, one might compare the theologies of the cross on display in the hymns "The Old Rugged Cross" and "Were You There (When They Crucified My Lord)?" Although the lyrics of the former hymn describe the cross as "the emblem of suffering and shame," nothing in the text suggests that there is any real shame associated with it. Quite the contrary, it is described more in terms of a quaint family heirloom, like grandmother's old gingham dress. Inert and entirely under the possessor's control, it is a fetish to which one longs to "cling," and which is sufficiently valuable to allow the possessor to "exchange it some day for a crown." It is an emblem of glory: the sign of a God whose measure has been taken, and with whom one has the easy relations as of a shopkeeper whose merchandise is both attractive and inexpensive. By contrast, in "Were You There?" the cross is as far from being a personal trophy as could possibly be imagined: one does not cling to it like a prized heirloom, but rather recoils from it in trembling horror.

Conclusion   183

error, in which suffering earns a future reward amounts to just the sort of quest to achieve glory through our own efforts that Luther opposed as "works righteousness"; the second is a manifestation of the "cheap grace" that results when Luther's emphasis on the saving power of the cross apart from works becomes an excuse for disregarding Jesus' demand to engage the flesh-and-blood realities of life here and now.[13]

Faithful confession of the gospel rejects both these alternatives. It is false to Jesus' proclamation that the kingdom is now at hand (Mark 1:15; Matt. 12:28 and par.; Luke 17:21) to view suffering (and thus earthly life as a whole) as present means to a purely future end; and it is false to Jesus' proclamation that our vindication is yet to come to use the promise of glory to downplay the place of suffering in the work of faithful witness to the gospel.[14] In this way, the hope of glory can neither be separated from nor identified with the cross.[15] At the same time, simply to talk about the cross is no more a guarantee of good theology than the cry of "Lord, Lord" is a mark of faithful discipleship (Matt. 7:21–23). As James Cone has observed, "The cross can heal and hurt; it can be empowering and liberating but also enslaving and oppressive. There is no one way in which the cross can be interpreted."[16] He himself seeks to provide a healing understanding of the cross for contemporary North Americans by juxtaposing it with the lynching tree—the preeminent mark of racial terrorism in the United States. The lynching tree provides Cone the means to address the two dangers identified above: on the one hand, the "cross needs the lynching tree to remind Americans of the reality of suffering—to keep the cross from becoming a symbol of abstract, sentimental piety"; and on the other, "the lynching tree also needs the cross, without which it becomes simply an

---

13. For the classic diagnosis of "cheap grace" from a Lutheran perspective, see Dietrich Bonhoeffer, *Discipleship*, vol. 4 of *Dietrich Bonhoeffer Works*, trans. Barbara Green and Reinhard Krauss (Minneapolis: Fortress, 2003).

14. Von Balthasar provides a forceful reminder that the glory of eternity does not entail a forgetfulness of the cross: "We must not . . . forget that the eschatological Jerusalem has no other temple but God *and the Lamb*, that it is not illuminated by sun or moon, but by the glory of *God*, 'and its lamp was *the Lamb*' (Rev. 21:22f.). Moreover, the whole city is entrusted, not to God, but to the Lamb, and it 'comes down in the splendour of God's glory' (21:9f.) only as the Bride of the Lamb. . . . The glory of God is nowhere, not for a single instant, separated from the Lamb." And the Lamb appears "standing as if it had been slaughtered" (Rev. 5:6). Hans Urs von Balthasar, *Seeing the Form*, vol. 1 of *The Glory of the Lord: A Theological Aesthetics*, trans. Erasmo Leiva-Merikakis (San Francisco: Ignatius, 1989), 438.

15. My approach to the relation between the cross and glory is thus very different from that proposed by Christopher Southgate in his *Theology in a Suffering World: Glory and Longing* (Cambridge: Cambridge University Press, 2018). Although conceding that glory can be used in Scripture in ways that point toward the divine transcendence, his primary strategy is to treat glory semiotically, as a sign of divinity, which comes in three forms: *gloria mundi* (glory in the natural world), *gloria crucis* (glory in suffering), and *gloria in excelsis* (eschatological glory). While I appreciate Southgate's desire to challenge the equation of glory with worldly estimations of beauty, it seems to me that the refusal to separate talk of glory from the cross is very different from treating suffering as itself glorious; here it seems to me that the critiques of feminist and womanist thinkers retain their full force. And while there is a glory of this world (Luke 4:6; Rev. 21:24) that is not just a manifestation of human sin, there seems to me an important difference between any *gloria mundi* and the glory of God to which the world and its creatures may bear witness (Ps. 19:1; Isa. 6:3). The idea that divine glory is hidden in the world and needs to be discerned through careful exegesis of quotidian reality seems to me to miss the point of biblical accounts of the experience of glory as immediate and overwhelming, rather than something that needs to be uncovered through hermeneutical ingenuity (see, e.g., Exod. 24:15–18; 40:34–35; 1 Kgs. 8:10–11; 2 Chr. 7:1–4; Ezek. 1:26–28; Luke 2:9; Acts 7:54–56; cf. Isa. 40:5; Matt. 24:30 and pars.).

16. Cone, *The Cross and the Lynching Tree*, xix.

184   *The Hope of Glory*

abomination. It is the cross that points in the direction of hope, the confidence that there is a dimension to life beyond the reach of the oppressor."[17]

Cone here identifies the knife-edge on which a true theology of the cross is poised: the cross must be preached in a way that keeps the reality of this-worldly, flesh-and-blood suffering firmly in focus; and it must also be preached in a way "that points in the direction of hope." But (and here the critique of feminists and womanists comes again to the fore), how can the cross point to hope without leading to a theology that enjoins passive submission to earthly suffering and a correspondingly otherworldly account of glory? Cone himself appeals to his own experience: he affirms the cross's saving significance, "because I have seen with my own eyes how that symbol empowered black people to stand up and become agents of change for their freedom."[18] Of course, preaching the cross—as Cone himself acknowledges—has also produced very different effects, ranging from a sentimentality that is indifferent to questions of human agency to a glorification of suffering that annihilates it. And yet it has been the claim of Christians from Paul through Luther to Cone himself that reading our own stories of suffering alongside, in, and through the story of the cross somehow promotes life. How is this possible?

Answering this question requires first of all careful exegesis of the place of the cross in Jesus' story. On the one hand, it is the end of his life, as reflected in John's record of Jesus' final words from the cross: "It is finished" (John 19:30).[19] It is not, however, properly viewed as his life's goal or aim. For although the Gospels are emphatic that Jesus believed that his earthly ministry would terminate with his death on the cross (Matt. 16:21; 17:22–23; 20:17–19 and pars.), and that he came in order to "lay down [his] life" (John 10:15) in just this way (John 3:14; 12:32), to stop there is to misconstrue completely the place of Jesus' death in the economy of salvation, which he himself clarifies as follows: *"For this reason* the Father loves me, because I lay down my life *in order to take it up again"* (John 10:17). Laying down his life is not an end in itself, but only a means toward the true point of Jesus' coming: that he should "take it up again"—and thereby be in a position to raise up others "on the last day" (John 6:40, 44, 54; cf. 5:25–29). God does not love death, but life (Ezek. 18:32; cf. Prov. 8:36); and the Father's love for Jesus is correspondingly rooted in Jesus' commitment to the triumph of life, in which the reclamation of his own life becomes the means for his giving life to others (cf. Heb. 7:25).

The cross thus points to hope just to the extent that it is the *end* of Jesus' life, but not the *purpose* of his life: Jesus did not come to die, but to live; but life can only triumph once death has been left behind. It is in this context that it is important to emphasize one final time that resurrection is not a resuscitation, neither a return to earthly life nor its extension on another plane. To be

---

17. Cone, *The Cross and the Lynching Tree*, 161–62; cf. 158: "Salvation through the cross is a mystery and can only be apprehended through faith, repentance, and humility"; still the cross is "an 'opening to the transcendent' for the poor who have nowhere else to turn—the transcendence of the spirit that no one can take away, no matter what they do."

18. Cone, *The Cross and the Lynching Tree*, 145.

19. When speaking of the cross as the end of Jesus' story, "the cross" should be taken as synecdoche for the credal trio, "crucified, died, and was buried." That is, to speak of the cross is to refer to the end of Jesus' human lifespan, as that which causes his death, which is, in turn, confirmed by his burial.

Conclusion 185

raised from the dead is to be freed from the threat of death ("death no longer has dominion over him," Rom. 6:9), and that happens not through evading death, but by having died "once for all," so as to live again on different terms—"to God" (Rom. 6:10). For Jesus to be resurrected is not for him to leave his earthly life, as lived from Bethlehem to Golgotha, behind; on the contrary, the life "revealed in the flesh" that Jesus lays down is the very same life that is "vindicated in Spirit" (1 Tim. 3:16).

In developing a theology of the cross consistent with the hope of glory, it is therefore crucial to distinguish death as a necessary prelude to risen life from the very different claim that undergoing death is a meritorious act that earns eternal life. If Jesus lays down his life "in order to take it up again," the laying down is simply a logical precondition of the taking up (since only one who has died can be raised from the dead), not a moral one. Similarly, the claim that Jesus, "having been made perfect [*teleōtheis*] . . . became the source of eternal salvation for all who obey him" (Heb. 5:9) simply affirms that Jesus saves by virtue of his complete (another possible translation of *teleōtheis*) assumption of the whole of human life from birth to death.[20] Even Philippians 2, which seems at first glance to affirm a cause-and-effect relationship between Jesus' suffering and death on the one hand and his resurrection on the other ("*Therefore* God exalted him even more highly and gave him the name that is above every other name," 2:9) cannot really bear such an interpretation. For if Jesus is the Word who was with God in the beginning ("in the form of God," according to Phil. 2:6), then the "name that is above every other name" (i.e., the divine name YHWH) cannot be viewed as something he acquired only afterward and as a reward for his earthly ministry, since it is his by nature, intrinsically and inalienably. It follows that Jesus' resurrection and exaltation, too, are not a reward for his suffering, but rather the confirmation of his status as the eternal Word.

A theology of the cross is therefore not one that sees the cross as a place of vicarious punishment or redemptive suffering that would make it in any sense the goal or aim of Jesus' life. Life, not death, is not the point of the incarnation (John 10:10). But neither does it allow the cross to be rejected as soteriologically irrelevant—as nothing more than the monstrous manifestation of sin's resistance to the advent of the kingdom rather than (as the New Testament clearly and consistently teaches) an integral part of Jesus' mission. A theology of the cross is rather one that sees the cross as the end of Jesus' life, and thus as a suffering that is significant *precisely in that it marks the termination of the reality and the possibility of suffering*. When the cross is understood in this way, Jesus' injunction that his followers must bear the cross is thus not that they should seek out suffering as a positive good, but rather that they should understand two things: that suffering is intrinsic to life lived in "the present evil age" (Gal. 1:4), and that it has a definite end. To confess Christ crucified and risen is therefore to acknowledge the pervasive and inescapable reality of suffering, but also to recognize that suffering does not endure. In this way, the cross at once stands for the apotheosis of suffering—since on the cross suffering afflicts life to such

---

20. "Since, therefore, the children share flesh and blood, he himself likewise shared the same things, so that through death he might destroy the one who has the power of death, that is, the devil, and free those who all their lives were held in slavery by the fear of death" (Heb. 2:14–15).

186   *The Hope of Glory*

an extent as to destroy it—but also suffering's limit, since with death suffering has an end, after which the powers and principalities can do no more.

The Hope of Glory

Of course, were the cross nothing more than the end of suffering, it would simply show the triumph of the forces opposed to life and thereby vanquish hope rather than sustain it. The hope of glory—of new, risen, and imperishable life lived to God—is that the end of suffering is not the end of life and, more specifically, that it is just the life that has undergone suffering that is vindicated in glory.[21] The promise is not of more life in the sense of life's infinite extension on a new plane. Even if such a life somehow excluded the possibility of further suffering, it would betray the Christian hope because it would ultimately mean that the significance of earthly life would finally diminish to zero, like an object in the rearview mirror gradually shrinking to the vanishing point. For Christian hope is a hope for *this* life. It is not, to be sure, a utopian hope that we will, with sufficient good will and ingenuity, acquire the capacity either to render life within time and space free of the calculus of cost and benefit associated with our need to acquire "bread" or to overcome the destructive power of sin and death. That sort of triumphalism, whether pursued on Christian or non-Christian grounds, only redoubles the destructive power of the very evils it seeks to overcome. Creation has its own glory (1 Pet. 1:24; Rev. 21:26; cf. Matt. 4:8) and may witness to God's glory (Ps. 119:1), but created glory is nevertheless quite distinct from the glory of God (Isa. 42:8; 48:11; John 12:43). The realization of the hope of glory therefore awaits the coming of "new heavens and a new earth, where righteousness is at home" (2 Pet. 3:13), and where the pain of this life is not forgotten, but somehow, in a way we simply cannot now imagine, redeemed, such that the whole of one's life, in spite of the ambiguity of its present form as both sinning and beset by sin, may be glorified.

Yet to affirm the inherently otherworldly fulfillment of glorification in this way is not to subscribe to a simple deferral of Christian hope in the mode of an otherworldly fantasy. Granted that in the present life "we see only a reflection, as in a mirror," and so "know only in part" (1 Cor. 13:12), nevertheless, even "seeing the glory of the Lord as though reflected in a mirror," we are already now "being transformed . . . from one degree of glory to another" (2 Cor. 3:18). Although we continue to live by bread, we experience with the gospel the first fruits of what it means to "live to God" (Rom. 6:10) as those who are sustained by God's word alone, living by the promise that our lives are neither validated by what we have done or invalidated by what we have failed to do, but have their worth established beyond our every capacity or incapacity by the God who calls us as "children . . . and joint heirs with Christ" (Rom. 8:17), for "those

21. This distinction between life and suffering distinguishes Christian understanding of resurrection from accounts of reincarnation in which life is identical with suffering (as explicitly stated in the First Noble Truth of Buddhism), and from the corresponding equation of the end of suffering with the end of life (as in Buddhism's Third Noble Truth—although it is important to recognize that this does not imply that nonexistence is the goal of Buddhism, since in Buddhism any talk of a goal reflects the presence of *taṇhā*, or desire, whereas enlightenment entails the cessation of all desire—including the desire for nonexistence).

Conclusion 187

whom he called he also justified; and those whom he justified he also glorified" (Rom. 8:30).

A properly Christian hope of glory is therefore inseparable from a theology of the cross because it takes death seriously as the end of life and the "last enemy" (1 Cor. 15:26). That is, it recognizes that death (including the more or less extended and intense experiences of suffering that precede it) not only marks life's boundary but is inimical to life—for how can that which cuts life off be anything other than its enemy? With death, life is over; our tales, however significant or insignificant they may appear, come to an end. And yet in taking death seriously, the Christian hope also takes earthly life seriously. For according to this hope the life we live now and that ends in death is no mere prelude to some new, far longer and more interesting story, in comparison with which the goodness of life in this world is at best merely instrumental, an ephemeral means to a more substantial end. To proclaim the glory of the crucified and risen Lord and the resurrection of the dead is rather to insist that it is precisely *this* life, as lived in time and space between birth and death, that is the object of divine interest. The hope to which we look is thus one in which our earthly lives, having been lived in flesh (and, as such, sustained by the "bread" of relations with other creatures), should be vindicated in the Spirit by the power of that same word by which the heavens and all things were made (Ps. 33:6; John 1:3).

This way of conceiving the end of human life has implications for how life is to be lived now. For it means that the lives that will in glory be sustained supernaturally (i.e., directly by God's word rather than, as is currently the case, through the mediation of created causes) are none other than the lives we are living now. We live in the assurance that "we are God's children now" (1 John 3:2) and so a "new creation" (2 Cor. 5:17), so that in looking to the shape of life in glory, our attention is properly directed not to some distant, otherworldly horizon, but to the circumstances of our living in the present. And if the life to which we look forward in heaven is just the vindication of this earthly life, then we cannot do otherwise than seek to anticipate that life now, recognizing that the life to come is not a further series of episodes following on this life, but precisely the disclosure of the eternal significance of what transpires in this world: "just as you did it to one of the least of these . . . you did it to me" (Matt. 25:40).

Such action is not motivated by the illusion that we will thereby realize the kingdom in history, for the "kingdom of God is not coming with things that can be observed" (Luke 17:20). Rather, it is undertaken in the recognition that we who have "died to sin can no longer go on living in it" (Rom. 6:2): those who have been called to glory will naturally seek to live lives consistent with the life to come, because they understand their actions now as the raw materials of their lives in glory. Such attempts will always be imperfect, constrained by the finitude of material resources, threatened by the prospect of death, and marred by the power of sin, which even in the lives of the saints is ever-present, often unrecognized, and never fully understood. Even the noblest efforts to live in the light of glory will need to be redeemed, because even the most faithful saint can never be more than a justified sinner.

But it is precisely this promise of redemption that makes the gospel empowering. For redemption is the assurance that the cross and the whole trail of suffering for which it stands both is and is not the final word. It is the final

188 *The Hope of Glory*

word in that it marks an end to life, the final attack that is the goal but also the limit of all other assaults by the principalities and powers against God's creation.[22] Yet it is not the final word, because God raises up the dead who, having truly died, can no longer be threatened by death. And here we see how it is that the symbol of the cross can (to cite Cone's words once more) empower people "to stand up and become agents of change for their freedom." It is precisely because the cross, though the instrument of life's destruction, poses a limit to the powers of destruction—a limit that is definitively overcome by the promise and power of the resurrection—that the cross, in spite of the intentions of the Roman Empire, is able to give rise to hope. "Death has been swallowed up in victory . . . through our Lord Jesus Christ. Therefore," Paul can write, "be steadfast, immovable, always excelling in the work of the Lord, because you know that in the Lord your labor is not in vain" (1 Cor. 15:54, 57–58).

Why is the labor of the faithful not in vain? Because it will bring in the kingdom? No. Because it will defeat sin, death, and the devil? No. Because it will earn the laborer an imperishable crown? No. Our labor is not valuable because it is meritorious, or because it is effective: our sin renders merit impossible, and the constraints of our finitude render questions of effectiveness ultimately moot. The reason our labor is not in vain is that for all its shortcomings, it stands under the promise of redemption, the promise that while sin and death will have their say, they will not have the final say. Theirs is not the last word. The last word is God's, the Word that was in the beginning. And it is a word of life.

Such is the hope of glory.

---

22. The following exchange from the film *The Maltese Falcon* gets it right:
  Kasper Gutman: "Well, sir, there are other means of persuasion besides killing and threatening to kill."
  Sam Spade: "Yes, that's . . . that's true. But, they're none of them any good unless the threat of death is behind them."

Bibliography

Adams, Marilyn McCord. *Christ and Horrors: The Coherence of Christology*. Cambridge: Cambridge University Press, 2006.

———. *Horrendous Evils and the Goodness of God*. Ithaca, NY: Cornell University Press, 1999.

Adorno, Theodor W. *Minima Moralia*. Translated by E. F. N. Jephcott. London: Verso, 1978.

Agamben, Giorgio. *The Kingdom and the Glory: For a Theological Genealogy of Economy and Government*. Translated by Lorenzo Chiesa. Stanford, CA: Stanford University Press, 2011 (2007).

Ahlstrom, Sydney E. *A Religious History of the American People*. New Haven, CT: Yale University Press, 1972.

Alighieri, Dante. *A Translation of the Latin Works of Dante Alighieri*. Westport, CT: Greenwood Press, 1969 (1904).

Anatolios, Khaled. *Deification through the Cross: An Eastern Christian Theology of Salvation*. Grand Rapids: William B. Eerdmans, 2021.

Augustine. *The City of God against the Pagans*. Edited and translated by R. W. Dyson. Cambridge: Cambridge University Press, 1998.

———. *Confessions*. Translated by Henry Chadwick. Oxford: Oxford University Press, 1991.

———. *On Genesis*. Edited by John E. Rotelle, OSA. Translated by Edmund Hill, OP. Hyde Park, NY: New City Press, 2002.

———. *The Writings against the Manicheans and against the Donatists*. Vol. 4 of *Nicene and Post-Nicene Fathers*. Edited by Philip Schaff. 1st series. Grand Rapids: William B. Eerdmans, 1984 (1887).

Balthasar, Hans Urs von. *Dare We Hope "That All Men Be Saved"? with a Short Discourse on Hell*. Translated by Dr. David Kipp and Rev. Lothar Krauth. San Francisco: Ignatius, 1988.

———. *The Last Act*. Vol. 5 of *Theo-Drama: Theological Dramatic Theory*. Translated by Graham Harrison. San Francisco: Ignatius, 1998 (1983).

———. *Seeing the Form*. Vol. 1 of *The Glory of the Lord: A Theological Aesthetics*. Translated by Erasmo Leiva-Merikakis. San Francisco: Ignatius, 1982 (1961).

———. *A Short Primer for Unsettled Laymen*. Translated by Michael Waldstein. San Francisco: Ignatius, 1985.

———. *Theology: The New Covenant*. Vol. 7 of *The Glory of the Lord: A Theological Aesthetics*. Translated by Brian McNeil. Edinburgh: T&T Clark, 1989 (1969).

———. *Theology: The Old Covenant*. Vol. 6 of *The Glory of the Lord: A Theological Aesthetics*. Translated by Brian McNeil and Erasmo Leiva-Merikakis. Edinburgh: T & T Clark, 1991 (1967)

Barth, Karl. *Church Dogmatics*. 13 vols. Edited by G. W. Bromiley and T. F. Torrance. Edinburgh: T&T Clark, 1956–1974.

190   *Bibliography*

———. *Dogmatics in Outline*. Translated by G. T. Thompson. New York: Harper & Row, 1959.

———. *The Resurrection of the Dead*. Translated by H. J. Stenning. Eugene, OR: Wipf and Stock, 2003 (1933).

———. *The Word of God and the Word of Man*. Translated by Douglas Horton. N.p.: Pilgrim Press, 1928.

Bava Metzia. In The William Davidson Talmud. https://www.sefaria.org/Bava_Metzia.59b.1?lang=bi&with=all&lang2=bi.

Bayer, Oswald. *Martin Luther's Theology: A Contemporary Interpretation*. Translated by Thomas H. Trapp. Grand Rapids: William B. Eerdmans, 2008 (3rd German ed., 2007).

Beckwith, Christopher I. *Greek Buddha: Pyrrho's Encounter with Early Buddhism in Central Asia*. Princeton, NJ: Princeton University Press, 2015.

Berneri, Marie Louise. *Journey through Utopia*. New York: Schocken Books, 1950.

Bloch, Ernst. *The Principle of Hope*. 3 vols. Translated by Neville Plaice, Stephen Plaice, and Paul Knight. Oxford: Basil Blackwell, 1986 (1954–1959).

Blomberg, Craig, and Sung Wook Chung, eds. *A Case for Historic Premillennialism: An Alternative to "Left Behind" Eschatology*. Grand Rapids: Baker Academic, 2009.

Blumenthal, David R. *Facing the Abusing God: A Theology of Protest*. Louisville, KY: Westminster/John Knox, 1993.

Bonhoeffer, Dietrich. *Creation and Fall: A Theological Analysis of Genesis 1–3 / Temptation*. New York: Macmillan, 1959.

———. *Discipleship*. Vol. 4 of *Dietrich Bonhoeffer Works*. Edited by Geffrey B. Kelly and John D. Godsey. Translated by Barbara Green and Reinhard Krauss. Minneapolis: Fortress Press, 2003.

———. *Ethics*. Vol. 6 of *Dietrich Bonhoeffer Works*. Edited by Clifford J. Green. Translated by Reinhard Kraus, Charles C. West, and Douglas W. Stott. Minneapolis: Fortress Press, 2005.

Braaten, Carl E. *The Future of God*. New York: Harper & Row, 1969.

Brock, Rita Nakashima, and Rebecca Ann Parker. *Proverbs of Ashes: Violence, Redemptive Suffering, and the Search for What Saves Us*. Boston: Beacon, 2002.

Bulgakov, Sergius. *The Sophiology of Death: Essays on Eschatology: Personal, Political, Universal*. Translated by Robert J. De La Noval. Eugene, OR: Cascade, 2021.

Burrell, David B., Carlo Cogliati, Janet M. Soskice, and William R. Stoeger, eds. *Creation and the God of Abraham*. Cambridge: Cambridge University Press, 2010.

Calvin, John. *Institutes of the Christian Religion*. Edited by John T. McNeil. Translated by Ford Lewis Battles. Philadelphia: Westminster Press, 1960.

Camus, Albert. *The Myth of Sisyphus*. Translated by Justin O'Brien. New York: Vintage, 1961.

———. *The Rebel: An Essay on Man in Revolt*. Translated by Anthony Bower. New York: Vintage, 1991 (1956).

Caputo, John D. *Against Ethics: Contributions to a Poetics of Obligation with Constant Reference to Deconstruction*. Bloomington: Indiana University Press, 1993.

Catechism of the Catholic Church. 2nd ed. Vatican City: Libreria Editrice Vaticana, 1997.

Cavanaugh, William. *Torture and Eucharist: Theology, Politics, and the Body of Christ*. Malden, MA: Blackwell, 1998.

Chung, Sung Wook, and David Mathewson. *Models of Premillennialism*. Eugene, OR: Cascade, 2018.

Cobb, John B., Jr., and David Ray Griffin. *Process Theology: A Basic Introduction*. Philadelphia: Westminster, 1976.

Cohn, Norman. *The Pursuit of the Millennium. Revolutionary Messianism in Medieval and Reformation Europe and Its Bearing on Modern Totalitarian Movements*. 2nd ed. New York: Harper & Row, 1961.

Bibliography 191

Compendium of Creeds, Definitions, and Declarations on Matters of Faith and Morals. 43rd ed. Edited by Heinrich Denzinger, Peter Hünermann, et al. San Francisco: Ignatius Press, 2012.

Cone, James H. *Black Theology and Black Power.* New York: Seabury, 1969.

———. *The Cross and the Lynching Tree.* Maryknoll, NY: Orbis, 2011.

———. *God of the Oppressed.* New York: Seabury, 1975.

———. *Martin & Malcolm & America: A Dream or a Nightmare?* Maryknoll, NY: Orbis, 1991.

———. *The Spirituals and the Blues.* New York: Seabury, 1972.

Copeland, Rebecca L. *Created Being: Expanding Creedal Christology.* Waco, TX: Baylor University Press, 2020.

Corsini, Eugenio. *Apocalisse di Gesù Cristo secondo Giovanni.* Turin: Società Editrice Internazionale, 2002.

Cross Examination: Readings on the Meaning of the Cross Today. Edited by Marit Trelstad. Minneapolis: Fortress Press, 2006.

Cullmann, Oscar. *The Immortality of the Soul or the Resurrection of the Dead: The Witness of the New Testament.* London: Epworth, 1964.

Dalferth, Ingolf U. *Creatures of Possibility: The Theological Basis of Human Freedom.* Grand Rapids: Baker Academic, 2016 (2011).

———. *Crucified and Resurrected: Restructuring the Grammar of Christology.* Translated by Jo Bennett. Grand Rapids: Baker Academic, 2015 (1994).

Davis, Ellen F. *Scripture, Culture, and Agriculture: An Agrarian Reading of the Bible.* Cambridge: Cambridge University Press, 2009.

Davis, Stephen T., ed. *Encountering Evil: Live Options in Theodicy.* New ed. Louisville, KY: Westminster John Knox, 2001.

Deane-Drummond, Celia. "The Technologization of Life." In *Technofutures, Nature and the Sacred: Transdisciplinary Perspectives,* 139–57. Edited by Celia Deane-Drummond, Sigurd Bergman, and Bronislaw Szerszynski. Farnham, UK: Ashgate, 2015.

Derrida, Jacques. "Différance." In *Margins of Philosophy,* 1–28. Translated by Alan Bass. Chicago: University of Chicago Press, 1982.

———, and Jean-Luc Marion. "On the Gift: A Discussion between Jacques Derrida and Jean-Luc Marion." In *God, the Gift, and Postmodernism,* 54–78. Edited by John D. Caputo and Michael Scanlon. Bloomington: Indiana University Press, 1999.

Engels, Friedrich. "Socialism: Utopian and Scientific." In *The Marx-Engels Reader,* 683–717. 2nd ed. Edited by Robert C. Tucker. New York: W. W. Norton, 1978.

Erasmus, Desiderius, and Martin Luther. *Luther and Erasmus: Free Will and Salvation.* Edited by E. Gordon Rupp and Philip S. Watson. Philadelphia: Westminster, 1969.

Farrer, Austin. *Love Almighty and Ills Unlimited: An Essay on Providence and Evil.* London: Collins, 1962.

Fitzmyer, Joseph A. *The Gospel according to Luke I–IX: A New Translation with Introduction and Commentary.* New York: Doubleday, 1981.

Florensky, Pavel. *The Pillar and Ground of the Truth: An Essay in Orthodox Theodicy in Twelve Letters.* Translated by Boris Jakim. Princeton, NJ: Princeton University Press, 2004.

Forde, Gerhard O. *The Captivation of the Will: Luther vs. Erasmus on Freedom and Bondage.* Edited by Stephen Paulson. Grand Rapids: William B. Eerdmans, 2005.

Frank, David A. "Arguing with God, Talmudic Discourse, and the Jewish Countermodel: Implications for the Study of Argumentation." *Argument and Advocacy* 41 (Fall 2004): 71–86.

Frei, Hans W. *The Identity of Jesus Christ: The Hermeneutical Bases of Dogmatic Theology.* Eugene, OR: Wipf and Stock, 1997 (1975).

Goodacre, Marc. *The Case against Q: Studies in Markan Priority and the Synoptic Problem.* Harrisburg, PA: Continuum, 2002.

Gray, John. *Straw Dogs: Thoughts on Humans and Other Animals.* New ed. London: Granta, 2003.

Gregory of Nyssa. "An Address on Religious Instruction." In *Christology of the Later Fathers,* 268–325. Edited by Edward R. Hardy. Philadelphia: Westminster Press, 1954.

————. *Gregory of Nyssa: Dogmatic Treatises, Etc.* Vol. 5 of *Nicene and Post-Nicene Fathers.* Edited by Philip Schaff and Henry Wace. 2nd series. Boston: Hendrickson, 1995 (1893).

————. *The Life of Moses.* Translated by Abraham J. Malherbe and Everett Ferguson. New York: Paulist Press, 1979.

Gregory the Great. *Forty Gospel Homilies.* Translated by David Hurst. Collegeville, MN: Cistercian Press, 1990.

Griffiths, Paul J. *Decreation: The Last Things of All Creation.* Waco, TX: Baylor University Press, 2014.

Gutiérrez, Gustavo. *A Theology of Liberation: History, Politics, and Salvation.* Edited and translated by Sister Caridad Inda and John Eagleson. Maryknoll, NY: Orbis, 1973.

Halpern, Paul, and Paul Wesson. *Brave New Universe: Illuminating the Darkest Secrets of the Cosmos.* Washington, DC: Joseph Henry Press, 2006.

Hart, David Bentley. "The Devil's March: *Creatio ex nihilo,* the Problem of Evil, and a Few Dostoyevskian Meditations." In *Creation ex nihilo: Origins, Development, Contemporary Challenges,* 297–318. Edited by Gary A. Anderson and Markus Bockmuehl. Notre Dame, IN: University of Notre Dame Press, 2018.

————. *The New Testament: A Translation.* New Haven, CT: Yale University Press, 2017.

————. *That All Shall Be Saved: Heaven, Hell, and Universal Salvation.* New Haven, CT: Yale University Press, 2019.

Hefner, Philip. *Technology and Human Becoming.* Minneapolis: Fortress Press, 2003.

Hegel, G. W. F. *Phenomenology of Spirit.* Translated by A. V. Miller. Oxford: Oxford University Press, 1977 (1807).

————. *Reason in History: A General Introduction to the Philosophy of History.* Translated by Robert S. Hartman. New York: The Library of Liberal Arts, 1953 (1840).

Hjelde, Sigurd. *Das Eschaton und die Eschata: Eine Studie über Sprachgebrauch und Sprachverwirrung in protestantischer Theologie von der Orthodoxie bis zu Gegenwart.* Munich: Christian Kaiser, 1987.

Hodge, Charles. *Systematic Theology.* Grand Rapids: William B. Eerdmans, 1940 (1872).

"Humanist Manifesto II." American Humanist Association. https://americanhumanist.org/what-is-humanism/manifesto2/.

Hyams, Edward. *The Millennium Postponed: Socialism from Thomas More to Mao Tsetung.* London: Secker & Warburg, 1974.

Impey, Chris. *How It Ends: From You to the Universe.* New York: W. W. Norton & Company, 2010.

Intergovernmental Panel on Climate Change. *Climate Change 2022: Impacts, Adaptation and Vulnerability.* February 28, 2022. https://www.ipcc.ch/report/ar6/wg2/.

Irenaeus of Lyon. *Against Heresies.* In *The Apostolic Fathers with Justin Martyr and Irenaeus.* Vol. 1 of *Ante-Nicene Fathers.* American ed. Edited by Alexander Roberts and James Donaldson. Grand Rapids: William B. Eerdmans, 1985 (1885).

James, William. "The Will to Believe." In *The Will to Believe and Other Essays in Popular Philosophy,* 13–33. Cambridge, MA: Harvard University Press, 1979 (1897).

Bibliography

Jameson, Frederic. *Archaeologies of the Future: The Desire Called Utopia and Other Science Fictions*. London: Verso, 2005.

———. *The Political Unconscious*. Ithaca, NY: Cornell University Press, 1981.

Jeanrond, Werner G. *Reasons to Hope*. London: T&T Clark, 2020.

Jerome. *De Viris Illustribus*. https://www.newadvent.org/fathers/2708.htm.

John Paul II, Pope. *Centesimus annus*. 1991. https://www.vatican.va/content/john-paul-ii/en/encyclicals/documents/hf_jp-ii_enc_01051991_centesimus-annus.html.

———. "General Audience, Wednesday, 25 June 1997." June 25, 1997. https://www.vatican.va/content/john-paul-ii/en/audiences/1997/documents/hf_jp-ii_aud_25061997.html.

Jones, Robert P. *White Too Long: The Legacy of White Supremacy in American Christianity*. New York: Simon & Schuster, 2020.

Julian of Norwich. *The Showings of Julian of Norwich*. Edited by Denise N. Baker. New York: W. W. Norton, 2005.

Justin Martyr. *Dialogue with Trypho*. In *The Apostolic Fathers with Justin Martyr and Irenaeus*. Vol. 1 of *Ante-Nicene Fathers*. American ed. Edited by Alexander Roberts and James Donaldson. Grand Rapids: William B. Eerdmans, 1985 (1885).

Kaneda, Toshiko, and Carl Haub. "How Many People Have Ever Lived on Earth." Population Reference Bureau, updated November 15, 2022. https://www.prb.org/articles/how-many-people-have-ever-lived-on-earth/.

Keller, Catherine. *Apocalypse Now and Then: A Feminist Guide to the End of the World*. Minneapolis: Fortress Press, 2005 (1996).

Kelsey, David H. *Human Anguish and God's Power*. Cambridge: Cambridge University Press, 2020.

———. *Imagining Redemption*. Louisville, KY: Westminster John Knox, 2005.

Kierkegaard, Søren. *Training in Christianity and the Edifying Discourse Which "Accompanied" It*. Translated by Walter Lowrie. Princeton, NJ: Princeton University Press, 1944.

Kilby, Karen. "Julian of Norwich, Hans Urs von Balthasar, and the Status of Suffering in Christian Theology." *New Blackfriars* 99, no. 1081 (May 2018): 298–311.

Kolb, Robert. *Bound Choice, Election, and Wittenberg Theological Method: From Martin Luther to the Formula of Concord*. Grand Rapids: William B. Eerdmans, 2005.

Kolb, Robert, and Timothy J. Wengert, eds. *The Book of Concord: The Confessions of the Evangelical Lutheran Church*. Minneapolis: Fortress Press, 2000.

Kurzweil, Ray. *The Singularity Is Near: When Humans Transcend Biology*. London: Duckworth, 2016.

Lactantius. *The Divine Institutes*. In *Fathers of the Third and Fourth Centuries*. Vol. 7 of *Ante-Nicene Fathers*. American ed. Edited by Alexander Roberts and James Donaldson. Grand Rapids: William B. Eerdmans, 1975 (1886).

Lindsey, Hal, with C. C. Carlson. *The Late Great Planet Earth*. Grand Rapids: Zondervan, 1970.

Lloyd, Vincent. *Religion of the Field Negro: On Black Secularism and Black Theology*. New York: Fordham University Press, 2018.

Löwith, Karl. *Meaning in History: The Theological Implications of the Philosophy of History*. Chicago: University of Chicago Press, 1957.

Luther, Martin. *D. Martin Luthers Werke: Kritische Gesammtausgabe*. Edited by J. K. F. Knaake et al. 67 vols. Weimar: H. Böhlau, 1883–1997.

———. *Luther's Works*. American ed. Edited by Harold J. Grimm. 55 vols. Philadelphia: Fortress Press / St. Louis: Concordia Publishing House, 1957–1986.

Lynch, William F. *Images of Hope: Imagination as Healer of the Hopeless*. Notre Dame, IN: University of Notre Dame Press, 1965.

Lyotard, Jean-François. *The Postmodern Condition: A Report on Knowledge*. Translated by Geoff Bennington and Brian Massumi. Minneapolis: University of Minnesota Press, 1984.

Martin, Adrienne. *How We Hope: A Moral Psychology*. Princeton, NJ: Princeton University Press, 2013.

Maximus the Confessor. *Ambigua*. In *Sancti Maximi Confessoris Opera Omnia*. Vol. 91 of *Patrologiae cursus completus: Series graeca*. Edited by J.-P. Migne. Cols. 1031–1418. Paris, 1865.

———. *On Difficulties in the Church Fathers: The Ambigua*. 2 vols. Edited and translated by Nicholas Constas. Cambridge, MA: Harvard University Press, 2014.

———. *On Difficulties in Sacred Scripture: The Responses to Thalassios*. Translated by Maximos Constas. Washington, DC: Catholic University of America Press, 2018.

———. *On the Cosmic Mystery of Jesus Christ: Selected Writings from St. Maximus the Confessor*. Translated by Paul M. Blowers and Robert Wilken. Crestwood, NY: St. Vladimir's Seminary Press, 2003.

———. *Opuscula Theological et Polemica*. In *Sancti Maximi Confessoris Opera Omnia*. Vol. 91 of *Patrologiae cursus completus: Series graeca*. Edited by J.-P. Migne. Cols. 9–286. Paris, 1865.

———. *Quaestiones ad Thalassium*. In *Sancti Maximi Confessoris Opera Omnia*. Vol. 90 of *Patrologiae cursus completus: Series graeca*. Edited by J.-P. Migne. Cols. 244–785. Paris, 1865.

———. *Selected Writings*. Translated by G. C. Berthold. New York: Paulist Press, 1985.

McFarland, Ian A. *In Adam's Fall: A Meditation on the Christian Doctrine of Original Sin*. Malden, MA: Wiley-Blackwell, 2010.

———. *From Nothing: A Theology of Creation*. Louisville: Westminster John Knox, 2014.

———. "Present in Love: Rethinking Barth on the Divine Perfections." *Modern Theology* 33, no. 2 (April 2017): 243–58.

———. "The Problem with Evil." *Theology Today* 74, no. 4 (January 2018): 321–39.

———. "When Time Is of the Essence: Aquinas and the *Imago Dei*." *New Blackfriars* 82, no. 963 (May 2001): 208–23.

———. *The Word Made Flesh: A Theology of the Incarnation*. Louisville, KY: Westminster John Knox, 2019.

Mellert, Robert B. *What Is Process Theology?* New York: Paulist Press, 1975.

Meyendorff, John. *A Study of Gregory Palamas*. Translated by George Lawrence. Crestwood, NY: St. Vladimir's Seminary Press, 1964.

Milbank, John. *Beyond Secular Order: The Representation of Being and the Representation of the People*. Malden, MA: Wiley Blackwell, 2014.

———, and Adrian Pabst. *The Politics of Virtue: Post-liberalism and the Human Future*. London: Rowman and Littlefield, 2016.

Moloney, Francis J., SDB. *The Apocalypse of John: A Commentary*. Grand Rapids: Baker Academic, 2020.

Moltmann, Jürgen. *Theology of Hope: On the Ground and the Implications of a Christian Eschatology*. Translated by James W. Leitch. London: SCM, 1967 (1965).

Moravec, Hans. *Robot: Mere Machine to Transcendent Mind*. Oxford: Oxford University Press, 1999.

Morrison, Toni. *Beloved*. New York: Alfred A. Knopf, 1998.

———. *The Source of Self-Regard: Selected Essays, Speeches, and Meditations*. New York: Alfred A. Knopf, 2019.

Morse, Christopher L. *The Difference Heaven Makes: Rehearsing the Gospel as News*. London: T&T Clark International, 2010.

Bibliography 195

Mott, John R. *The Evangelization of the World in This Generation.* New York: Student Volunteer Movement for Foreign Missions, 1905.

Mühling, Markus. *T&T Clark Handbook of Christian Eschatology.* Translated by Jennifer Adams-Maßmann and David Andrew Gilland. London: Bloomsbury T&T Clark, 2015 (2007).

Nellas, Panayiotis. *Deification in Christ: The Nature of the Human Person.* Translated by Norman Russell. Crestwood, NY: St. Vladimir's Seminary Press, 1997.

Newbigin, Lesslie. *The Gospel in a Pluralist Society.* London: SPCK, 1989.

Newheiser, David. *Hope in a Secular Age: Deconstruction, Negative Theology, and the Future of Faith.* Cambridge: Cambridge University Press, 2019.

Newman, John Henry. *An Essay in Aid of a Grammar of Assent.* Notre Dame, IN: University of Notre Dame Press, 1979 (1870).

Nicholas of Cusa. *Nicholas of Cusa on God as Not-Other: A Translation and Appraisal of "De li non aliud."* Translated by Jasper Hopkins. 3rd ed. Minneapolis: Arthur J. Banning Press, 1987.

"Nobody Knows Who I Am." negrospirituals.com. https://www.negrospirituals .com/songs/nobody_knows_who_i_am.htm.

Origen of Alexandria. *Spirit and Fire: A Thematic Anthology of His Writings.* Edited by Hans Urs von Balthasar. Translated by Robert J. Daly, SJ. Washington, DC: Catholic University of America Press, 1984 (1938).

Paine, Thomas. *The Age of Reason: Being an Investigation of True and of Fabulous Theology.* Cambridge: Cambridge University Press, 2013 (1794).

Pannenberg, Wolfhart. *Systematic Theology.* 3 vols. Translated by Geoffrey W. Bromiley. Grand Rapids: William B. Eerdmans, 1991–1998 (1988–1993).

Papias. *Fragments of Papias.* In *The Apostolic Fathers, with Justin Martyr and Irenaeus.* Vol. 1 of *Ante-Nicene Fathers.* American ed. Edited by Alexander Roberts and James Donaldson. Grand Rapids: William B. Eerdmans, 1985 (1885).

Parker, Theodore. *Ten Sermons of Religion.* Boston: Crosby, Nichols, and Company, 1853.

Pieper, Josef. *Faith, Hope, Love.* Translated by Mary Francis McCarthy, SND. San Francisco: Ignatius, 1997 (1986).

Pinn, Anthony B. *Why Lord? Suffering and Evil in Black Theology.* New York: Continuum, 1999.

Plato. *Gorgias and Timaeus.* Translated by Benjamin Jowett. Mineola, NY: Dover, 2003 (1892).

Rahner, Karl. *Jesus, Man, and the Church.* Vol. 17 of *Theological Investigations.* Translated by Margaret Kohl. New York: Crossroad, 1981.

———. *Theology, Anthropology, Christology.* Vol. 13 of *Theological Investigations.* Translated by David Bourke. New York: Seabury, 1975.

Ratzinger, Joseph. *Eschatology: Death and Eternal Life.* 2nd ed. Translated by Michael Waldstein. Washington, DC: Catholic University of America Press, 1988 (1977).

Raup, David, and Steven M. Stanley. *Principles of Paleontology.* 2nd ed. New York: W. H. Freeman, 1978.

Rauschenbusch, Walter. *Christianity and the Social Crisis.* New York: Macmillan, 1907.

"Regolamento della Consulta Medica della Congregazione delle Cause dei Santi, 23.09.2016." September 23, 2016. https://press.vatican.va/content/salastampa/ it/bollettino/pubblico/2016/09/23/0666/01504.html.

Richardson, Cyril C., ed. and trans. *Early Christian Fathers.* New York: Macmillan, 1970.

Rogers, Eugene F. *Sexuality and the Christian Body: Their Way into the Triune God.* Oxford: Blackwell, 1999.

Bibliography

Roth, John K. "A Theodicy of Protest." In *Encountering Evil: Live Options in Theodicy*, 1–37. New ed. Edited by Stephen T. Davis. Louisville, KY: Westminster John Knox, 2001.

Rubenstein, Richard. *After Auschwitz: History, Theology, and Contemporary Judaism.* 2nd ed. Baltimore: Johns Hopkins University Press, 1992 (1966).

Ruether, Rosemary Radford. *Sexism and God-Talk: Toward a Feminist Theology.* Boston: Beacon, 1984.

Scheeben, Matthias Joseph. *Nature and Grace.* Translated by Cyril Vollert, SJ. New York: Herder, 1954.

Schleiermacher, Friedrich. *On Religion: Speeches to Its Cultured Despisers.* Edited and translated by Richard Crouter. Cambridge: Cambridge University Press, 1996.

Schmid, Heinrich. *Doctrinal Theology of the Evangelical Lutheran Church.* 3rd ed. Translated by Charles A. Hay and Henry E. Jacobs. Minneapolis: Augsburg, 1961 (1899).

"Secular Humanist Declaration." Council for Democratic and Secular Humanism. https://secularhumanism.org/a-secular-humanist-declaration/.

Segundo, Juan Luis. *A Theology for Artisans of a New Humanity.* 5 vols. Translated by John Drury. Maryknoll, NY: Orbis, 1973–1980.

Sender, Ron, Shai Fuchs, and Ron Milo. "Revised Estimates for the Number of Human and Bacteria Cells in the Body." *PLoS Biology* 14, no. 8 (August 2016): https://journals.plos.org/plosbiology/article/file?id=10.1371%2Fjournal .pbio.1002533&type=printable.

Seneca. *Seneca Ad Lucilium Epistolae Morales.* 3 vols. Translated by Richard M. Gummere. London: William Heinemann, 1917.

Sonderegger, Katherine. *The Doctrine of God.* Vol. 1 of *Systematic Theology.* Minneapolis: Fortress Press, 2015.

Southgate, Christopher. *Theology in a Suffering World: Glory and Longing.* Cambridge: Cambridge University Press, 2018.

Suchocki, Marjorie Hewitt. *The End of Evil: Process Eschatology in Historical Context.* Albany: State University of New York Press, 1988.

Tanner, Kathryn. *Christ the Key.* Cambridge: Cambridge University Press, 2010.

———. *Christianity and the New Spirit of Capitalism.* New Haven, CT: Yale University Press, 2019.

———. *Economy of Grace.* Minneapolis: Fortress Press, 2005.

———. *Jesus, Humanity and the Trinity.* Edinburgh: T & T Clark, 2001.

Taylor, Mark C. *Erring: A Postmodern A/theology.* Chicago: University of Chicago Press, 1984.

Teilhard de Chardin, Pierre. *The Future of Man.* Translated by Norman Denny. New York: HarperCollins 1964 (1959).

Terrell, JoAnne Marie. *Power in the Blood?: The Cross in the African American Experience.* Maryknoll, NY: Orbis, 1998.

Tertullian. *Against Marcion.* In *Latin Christianity: Its Founder Tertullian.* Vol. 3 of *Ante-Nicene Fathers.* Edited by Alan Menzies. Grand Rapids: William B. Eerdmans, n.d.

Thiel, John E. *Icons of Hope: The "Last Things" in Catholic Imagination.* Notre Dame, IN: University of Notre Dame Press, 2013.

Thomas Aquinas. *Compendium Theologiae.* https://www.corpusthomisticum.org/ ott101.html.

———. *Of God and His Creatures: An Annotated Translation (with Some Abridgement) of* the Summa Contra Gentiles *of St. Thomas Aquinas.* Translated by Joseph Rickaby, SJ. London: Burns and Oates, 1905.

———. *Summa Theologiae.* 60 vols. Blackfriars ed. London: Eyre & Spottiswood, 1964–1981.

Bibliography 197

Thompson, Deanna A. *Crossing the Divide: Luther, Feminism, and the Cross*. Minneapolis: Fortress Press, 2004.

Tipler, Frank J. *The Physics of Immortality: Modern Cosmology, God, and the Resurrection of the Dead*. New York: Doubleday, 1994.

Torrance, Alexis. *Human Perfection in Byzantine Theology: Attaining the Fullness of Christ*. Oxford: Oxford University Press, 2020.

Tran, Jonathan. *The Vietnam War and Theologies of Memory: Time and Eternity in the Far Country*. Oxford: Wiley-Blackwell, 2010.

Transhumanism and Transcendence: Christian Hope in an Age of Technological Enhancement. Edited by Ronald Cole-Turner. Washington, DC: Georgetown University Press, 2011.

Turner, Denys. *Julian of Norwich, Theologian*. New Haven, CT: Yale University Press, 2011.

Volf, Miroslav. *The End of Memory: Remembering Rightly in a Violent World*. Grand Rapids: William B. Eerdmans, 2006.

Ward, Peter D., and Donald Brownlee. *The Life and Death of Planet Earth: How the New Science of Astrobiology Charts the Ultimate Fate of Our World*. New York: Times Books, 2003.

———. *Rare Earth: Why Complex Life Is Unusual in the Universe*. New York: Copernicus Books, 2000.

Warfield, Benjamin Breckenridge. "The Millennium and the Apocalypse." In *Biblical Doctrines*, 643–64. Oxford: Oxford University Press, 1929.

Warren, Calvin L. *Ontological Terror: Blackness, Nihilism, and Emancipation*. Durham, NC: Duke University Press, 2018.

Watson, Francis. *Gospel Writing: A Canonical Perspective*. Grand Rapids: William B. Eerdmans, 2013.

Watson, Philip S. *Let God Be God: An Interpretation of the Theology of Martin Luther*. Philadelphia: Fortress Press, 1947.

Webster, John. *Word and Church: Essays in Christian Dogmatics*. Edinburgh: T&T Clark, 2001.

Weinberg, Steven. "Steven Weinberg on the Relationship between Scientific Inquiry and Everyday Living." Interview by Bill Moyers. *A World of Ideas*. September 23, 1988. https://billmoyers.com/content/steven-weinberg-scientific-inquiry/.

Westermann, Claus. *God's Angels Need No Wings*. Translated by D. L. Scheidt. Philadelphia: Fortress Press, 1979.

White, Thomas Joseph, OP. *The Incarnate Lord: A Thomistic Study in Christology*. Washington, DC: Catholic University of America Press, 2015.

Widdicombe, Peter. "The Wounds and the Ascended Body: The Marks of Crucifixion in the Glorified Christ from Justin Martyr to John Calvin." *Laval théologique et philosophique* 59, no. 1 (February 2003): 137–54.

Wiesel, Elie. *A Jew Today*. Translated by Marion Wiesel. New York: Random House, 1978.

———. *The Oath*. Translated by Marion Wiesel. New York: Random House, 1973.

Williams, Dolores. *Sisters in the Wilderness: The Challenge of Womanist God-Talk*. Maryknoll, NY: Orbis, 1993.

Winner, Lauren. *The Dangers of Christian Practice: On Wayward Gifts, Characteristic Damage, and Sin*. New Haven, CT: Yale University Press, 2018.

Wright, N. T. *New Heavens, New Earth: The Biblical Picture of the Christian Hope*. London: Grove, 1999.

———. *The Resurrection of the Son of God*. London: SPCK, 2003.

———. *Scripture and the Authority of God: How to Read the Bible Today*. San Francisco: HarperOne, 2011.

Scripture Index

OLD TESTAMENT

Genesis
1:2	148n34
1:3	172
1:6–9	148n34
1:9	172
1:21	148n34
1:31	6, 47, 89, 131–32, 165
2	167n22, 172n35
2:1–2	172
2:1–3	166
2:2	172n35, 174n36
2:3	172
2:7	142–44
2:16–17	118, 137
3	167n22
3:1–7	89n1
3:14–19	160
3:19	136, 139, 144
3:21	138n8, 143n19
3:22	117–18
4:7	89n1
5:24	137
6:1–3	117
6:3	118, 137
6:6–7	55n54
7:11	126
9:22	166
12:1–3	64, 128
12:3	65, 67, 69
15:1	84
17:1–8	128
18:17–33	53
18:27	139
28:12	127n33
28:14	69
50:20	153

Exodus
3:1–12	128
3:15	114
5:6–9	77
5:15–18	77
5:22–23	77
6:1–8	77
6:9	77
16:18	68
20:8–11	173
20:10	68
22:21–27	67
24:15–18	183n15
33:21	176n42
40:34–35	183n15

Leviticus
25:2–5	68
25:2–6	173
25:8	173
25:13	173
25:23	173
25:42	173
26:6	67

Numbers
15:27–30	73
16:33	141
23:19	55n54

Deuteronomy
5	174
5:14	68
5:15	173
8:3	14, 65, 122
10:18	67
21:23	72
25:4	68
30:19	180

Judges
13:1–20	128

1 Samuel
2:6	138n6
15:29	55n54

1 Kings
8:10–11	183n15
8:27	130n45
8:30–43	128
22:19	126, 127n33
22:19–20	127
22:21	127n33

Nehemiah
9:6	148
9:28	128

Job
3:9	19
4:18	127n33
7:9	138, 141
10:9	139
13:15	57n58
17:13–16	138n6
26:6	131n46, 138n6
26:8–12	148n34
34:15	139

Psalms
6:5	118, 131, 138, 141, 145
19:1	183n15
33:6	187
49:13–14	138n6
51:3–5	123
57:3	128
80:14	128
89:9	148n34
90:3	139
90:10	117
95:11	174n36
103:14	139
103:19	126
103:20	127n33
104:24–26	148n34
115:17	144
119:1	186
130:3	8, 123
130:3–4	8
139:8	131n46, 138n6
139:15–16	140
147:14	68
148:2	127n33

199

Scripture Index

Proverbs
8:36	184
15:11	138n6
22:10	172n35

Ecclesiastes
3:2	118
3:20	139
9:5	118
9:10	131, 138, 141
12:7	139, 143

Isaiah
1:17	67
6:1–3	127
6:2	127n33
6:3	183n15
7:14	68
11:6	177
11:6–9	67
11:9	129, 177
13:6–9	122–23
25:6	149
32:17	67
38:18	131, 138, 141, 145
38:18–19	118
40:5	183n15
40:8	176
40:28	172
42:8	186
45:15	47
48:11	186
50:4	9
53:2–10	182
53:4–6	52, 72n27
58:1–11	40
60:15	173
61:2	173
61:7	173
63:15	128
65:17	20, 126, 131
65:20	118
65:25	67, 148
66:1	126
66:22	20, 126, 131

Jeremiah
1:5	140
10:10	148
20:7–8	53
20:14–18	53
22:3	67
22:13–17	40
29:7	16, 166
32:21–23	52
46:10	123

Ezekiel
1:26–28	183n15
10:1	127n33
18:23	180
18:32	180, 184
33:11	90
34:25	67
37:1–14	162n9

Daniel
5:21	126
6:26	148
7:2–7	68
7:13	123
7:13–14	118
9:24–27	22n7
12:2	117n11, 129
12:2–3	138

Hosea
7:4	172n35

Amos
3:2	52
5:10–15	40
5:15	89
5:18–20	123
7:1–6	55n54
9:2	131n46, 138n6

Zechariah
8:12	67
8:17	89

Malachi
3:10	126

NEW TESTAMENT

Matthew
1:1	69
1:2–16	69
1:21	69, 72, 181
1:22	64
1:22–23	69
1:23	68, 135
2:14–18	69
2:15	64
2:17	64
2:23	64, 69
3:2	72
3:13–15	71
3:15	64
4:1–11	69
4:4	14, 65, 122
4:8	186
4:10	79n44

4:13–16	69
4:17	27, 72, 75, 77, 115, 155
4:18–20	78
4:21–22	78
5:1–2	40n4
5:3	74
5:10	40
5:17	64, 68
5:17–18	69
5:20	69
5:21–22	73
5:22	130n44
5:27–28	73
5:29–30	130n44
5:34	126
5:39–42	40n4
5:46–47	40n4
6:10	179
6:31–33	156n51
7:21–23	183
8:2–3	37n49, 75
8:5–10	37n49
8:5–13	73
8:11	119, 149
8:14–15	37n49, 74
8:16–17	72n27
8:17	182
8:28–33	81n47
9:2–7	37n49, 74
9:9	73, 78
9:10–11	72
9:13	70n20, 72
9:20–22	37n49, 75
9:22	80n46
9:23–25	37n49
9:27	69
9:27–30	37n49
9:34	69
9:35	37n49
10:1	79
10:1–6	69
10:2	78
10:3	78n42
10:5–8	79
10:8	165
10:28	139n11
10:32–33	79
10:42	74n34
11:2–5	75
11:4–5	165n17, 181
11:4–6	180
11:5	15, 74
11:12	27
11:19	72
11:29	139n11
12:1–4	69

Scripture Index

12:2 — 178
12:9–13 — 74
12:22–28 — 69
12:28 — 10n23, 161, 183
12:32 — 73n29
12:34 — 79n44
12:34–42 — 70
12:39 — 161
13:34–35 — 69
13:40–42 — 123
13:49–50 — 123, 129
14:7 — 68n15
14:26–31 — 79
15:1–6 — 73n28
15:1–14 — 69
15:7 — 79n44
15:15 — 79
15:22 — 69
15:22–28 — 37n49
15:24 — 69, 70n20, 77n39, 79
16:5–12 — 79
16:17–19 — 79
16:18 — 78, 80
16:18–19 — 131
16:21 — 184
16:23 — 79
16:24–25 — 181
17:1 — 78
17:4 — 79
17:22–23 — 184
17:24–27 — 81
18:6–7 — 74n34
18:10–14 — 74n34
18:14 — 131
18:17 — 73
18:20 — ixn4
18:21–22 — 74n30, 79
19:14 — 75n36
19:26 — 9n20
19:28 — 126n28
20:17–19 — 184
20:26–28 — 181
20:28 — 71–72, 182
20:29–34 — 37n49
20:30–31 — 69
21:1–5 — 69
21:6–11 — 70
21:9 — 69
21:12–13 — 69
21:32 — 75
21:45–46 — 69
22:1–10 — 119
22:1–14 — 149
22:15–33 — 69
22:18 — 79n44
22:23–33 — 138, 177n45

22:30 — 148n33, 159
23:1–36 — 69
23:13 — 79n44
23:15 — 69n17, 79n44
23:23 — 73n28, 79n44
23:25 — 79n44
23:27 — 79n44
23:29 — 79n44
23:33 — 79n44
24:1–30 — 163n12
24:3 — 116n6
24:14 — 27, 170n30
24:20 — 178n47
24:21 — 22n7
24:27 — 116n6
24:29–31 — 166
24:30 — 123, 183n15
24:35 — 176
24:36–39 — 171n33
24:37 — 116n6
24:39 — 116n6
24:42 — 171n33
25 — 123, 155
25:31–32 — 121
25:31–33 — 123
25:31–46 — 75, 91
25:34 — 123
25:34–40 — 165
25:37–38 — 123
25:40 — 74, 155, 187
25:41–43 — 123
25:41–46 — 129
25:44 — 123
25:45 — 74n34
25:46 — 130n42, 149
26:14–16 — 70n21
26:15–23 — 70
26:24 — 69
26:28 — 106
26:29 — 119
26:33–34 — 80
26:36–46 — 79
26:56 — 70n21, 79
26:57–66 — 69
26:64 — 115, 118
26:64–65 — 72
26:69–75 — 70n21, 79
27:37 — 72
27:46 — 54
27:52 — 117n11
27:52–53 — 141n15
28:17 — 146n27
28:19–20 — 27

Mark
1:4 — 72
1:15 — 27, 72, 183

1:16–18 — 78
2:1–11 — 69
2:5–7 — 72
2:14 — 78n42
2:17 — 72
2:27–28 — 178
3:14–15 — 79
3:18 — 78n42
3:19–22 — 70
4:27 — 77
5:1–20 — 81–82
6:3 — 10, 84
6:51–52 — 79
9:47–48 — 129
10:15 — 75n36
10:46–52 — 74
12:28–34 — 70n21
12:41–44 — 74
13:10 — 27
14:49 — 64
15:43 — 70n21
16:15 — 27
16:17–20 — 162
16:19 — 13

Luke
1:19 — 128n36
1:21–24 — 69
1:26–38 — 128
1:30–32 — 64
1:33 — 69
2:9 — 183n15
2:11 — 69
3:12–13 — 81
3:13 — 75n35
3:23–34 — 69
4:6 — 183n15
4:16–21 — 174
4:16–30 — 70
4:18 — 15, 165, 165n17
4:21 — 64
4:23–24 — 84
5:1–11 — 78n41
5:27–28 — 78n42
6:15 — 78n42
6:20 — 74
6:24 — 74
6:34 — 19n1
7:22 — 37n49
7:29 — 75n36
7:36–50 — 72
7:48–49 — 72
7:50 — 80n46
8:1–3 — 74
10:1–9 — 79
10:18 — 124
12:56 — 79n44

Scripture Index

Luke (*continued*)

Reference	Pages
13:10–13	74
13:11–16	40
13:14	178
13:15	79n44
13:16	178
13:23–28	123
14:13	165
14:14	142
17:20	27, 171, 187
17:20–21	154
17:21	ixn4, 85n50, 115–16, 155, 183
18:1–7	54
18:27	19n1
18:42	80n46
19:1–10	74, 80–81
19:10	72
20:36	7, 144
20:37–38	142
20:38	148
21:19	139n11
21:28	119, 123
22:27	24, 181
22:31–32	79–80
22:37	69
23:2	72
23:43	141
23:56	178n47
24:1–51	114n4
24:15–16	146n27
24:25–27	64
24:27	106
24:30–31	12
24:36–40	33
24:40	145
24:44	69
24:44–47	64
24:45–48	27
24:47	8

John

Reference	Pages
1:1	64, 68, 89, 106, 176
1:2	114
1:3	14, 62, 83, 118, 177n44, 187
1:12	142, 180
1:13	169
1:14	68, 115, 176
1:31	69
1:35–42	78n41
1:46	10
2:11	161
2:13–17	69
3:1	70n21
3:8	142
3:14	184
3:16	180
3:17	91, 156
3:18	124n23
3:34	10n23
4:22	69
4:48	161n5
4:54	161
5:2–9	37n49
5:14	72
5:16	178
5:19–23	114
5:22	91, 121n17
5:22–27	123
5:25–26	21n3
5:25–29	184
5:27	91, 121n17
5:29	123
5:46	64
6:2	161
6:14–15	70
6:24–66	70
6:26	120n15
6:39	156
6:40	142, 149, 156, 184
6:44	156, 184
6:54	142, 149, 156, 184
6:67–69	79
6:70–71	79n44
6:71	70n21
7:32–34	69
7:50–51	70n21
8:2–10	74
8:4	73
8:11	72
8:12–18	69
8:15–16	123
8:39–47	70
8:42	64
8:44	79n44
8:57	10
9:1–7	37n49
9:1–8	74
9:16	178
9:39	123
10:10	40, 149, 165n17, 185
10:10–11	181
10:15	25n19, 184
10:17	184
10:25	161
10:31–33	72
10:37–38	165n17
11:1–44	6
11:11–14	117n11
11:24–26	156
11:45–50	69
11:48–52	72, 182
12:27	139n11
12:31	124
12:32	76, 184
12:32–33	182
12:37–38	69
12:42	70n21
12:43	186
12:45	93
12:47	91, 123
13:1	134
13:35	165
14:9	93
14:11	165n17
14:12	10n23
15:15	66
16:11	72, 124
16:21–22	34n45
16:33	72, 84
17:1–5	143
17:3	149
17:5	119
17:22	154
18:36	128
19:12–16	72
19:30	114, 184
19:31–36	69
19:33–34	153n47
19:39	70n21
20:17	143
20:19	12
20:24–27	145
20:26	12
20:26–27	33
20:27	153n47
20:30	161
21:4	12, 146n27
21:9–13	12
21:14–15	146n27
21:15–19	80
21:18–19	84

Acts

Reference	Pages
1:3–9	114n4
1:11	117n9, 118, 134
1:15–22	79
2:14–40	79
2:23	182
2:24	12
2:25–26	19
2:36	113, 119
2:43	161
3:1–8	37n49
3:1–10	79
3:13	64
3:21	126n28, 129n41
3:26	69
4:12	25, 89
4:22	161
5:14–16	79

Scripture Index

5:31	8, 106
6:7	70n21
7:54–56	183n15
7:56	116n8
9:15	77n39
9:32–41	37n49, 79
10	80
10:36	119
10:38	165
10:42	91, 121
10:43	8
13:22–23	64
13:38	8
14:8–10	37n49
15:1–11	80
16:10	19n1
17	62n3
17:24	128
17:28	118
17:31	121
22:21	77n39
24:26	19n1
26:18	8
28:8	37n49

Romans

1:1	164
1:4	69, 114
1:17–18	48n29
1:19–20	48n29
1:20	179
1:23	48n29
2:5–10	90
2:8–9	129
2:15–16	135n1
3:5–6	90
3:21	64
3:23	8, 155
4:4–5	142
4:5	125, 152
4:13–16	80
4:17	145
5:2	1, 2, 181
5:2–3	33
5:3–4	33, 181
5:5	19, 39
5:6	125
5:12	137
5:17	137
5:18	129
5:20	125
6:2	124, 187
6:4	119, 140
6:6	139–40
6:9	7, 114, 144, 159, 185
6:9–10	175
6:10	9, 114, 144, 185–86

6:11	9, 21n3
6:13	140
6:22–23	149
7:21–24	124
7:24	140–41
7:25	125
7:26	125n25
8	34n45, 140n12
8:1	125
8:3	72
8:15–17	143
8:17	186
8:18	33, 36, 48n29, 150
8:19	161
8:19–21	160
8:21	126n28, 135, 147, 149
8:23	156, 159
8:23–24	19
8:24	x, 2, 19, 31, 50, 180
8:24–25	76, 159
8:25	180
8:28	66, 127n33
8:29	140
8:30	154, 187
8:31	2
8:38	51
8:38–39	180
8:39	14, 140
9:4–5	69n18
9:5	69
10:9	119
10:17	4n11
11:1	69n18
11:16–18	70
11:25	27
11:32	106, 129
12:4	66
12:9	89
12:12	19
14:10	121
15:18–19	161
15:26	165

1 Corinthians

1:1	164
1:9	66
1:17–18	182
1:26–29	33
2:8	116
2:9	109
3:13–15	141n14
3:15	125, 131, 152
4:5	129
4:10–13	33
5:5	74n30
5:9–11	74n30

5:11	73
7:17	66
7:31	156, 159
9:10	2
10:23	78n40
11	125
11:1	77n39
11:20–21	120
11:24	120
11:26	119
11:27–32	120
12:3	119
12:12	66
12:14–20	77
12:27–30	77
12:29–31	68
13:12	118–19, 142, 149, 177, 179, 186
14:12	78n40
15:3	72
15:3–4	69
15:10	66, 164
15:19	150
15:20	6, 161
15:20–21	143n18
15:22–23	145
15:23	116n6
15:23–24	161
15:26	117–18, 145, 180, 187
15:36	154
15:36–40	145
15:42	146
15:42–43	154
15:42–44	129, 159
15:44	12, 139, 144
15:46	141, 144
15:47	143
15:50	136, 143–44, 159
15:50–53	x
15:51	116, 137, 170n30
15:52	145
15:53	145
15:54	188
15:54–57	180
15:55	159
15:57–58	188
16:22	115

2 Corinthians

1:20	65, 68
3:2	2
3:12	39
3:18	186
4:10	140
4:16–17	x
4:17	16n33, 85, 150, 154

Scripture Index

2 Corinthians (*continued*)
5	139
5:1–3	136
5:6	141
5:7	x, 19
5:8	141
5:10	121, 135n1
5:14	140
5:14–15	21n3
5:14–17	9
5:16	9n20, 114
5:17	136, 145, 165, 187
5:19	9, 90
5:21	71–72
6:16	136
11:23–27	xi
12:1–4	126n26
12:2	126
12:7–9	54
13:4	9, 114

Galatians
1:4	72, 183
1:15	164
1:18	79
2:1–14	164
2:2	69n18
2:7–8	77n39, 79
2:7–9	69n18
2:9	79
2:10	165
2:11–14	79
2:20	125, 140, 164
3:13	72
3:16	65
4:4	69
4:4–5	64
4:4–7	143
4:25–26	126n27
5:14	165
5:22–23	165
5:25	155
6:2	77
6:14	182
6:17	181

Ephesians
1:20	13
2:10	156
2:12	39
2:16	182
4:12	78n40
5:2	72
5:13–14	159
6:12	165

Philippians
1:12–14	164

1:23	117n11, 138n7, 141, 149
1:29	52
2:6	185
2:7	113
2:9	114, 185
2:9–11	119
2:10–11	116
2:12	159
3:4–6	69n18
3:9	33
3:11	129
3:12	156
3:13	32, 176n41
3:19	129

Colossians
1:14	8, 106
1:15–17	64
1:16	127n33
1:19	65, 85, 89, 170
1:20	182
1:24	33, 52
1:24–25	180
1:27	ix, 2, 6, 13, 180
2:9	7, 65, 85, 89, 106, 170
2:12	140
2:14–15	72
3:3	125, 140
3:6	106

1 Thessalonians
1:10	22n9, 106
2:1–8	170n30
2:19	116n6
3:13	116n6
4	117n11
4:13	39
4:13–17	129
4:15	116n6, 117, 121, 141, 169
4:16–17	118
4:17	22
5:9	22n9
5:10	141
5:11	78n40
5:23	116n6, 139n11

2 Thessalonians
1:6–9	123
1:8	116n6
1:9	129
2:1	117
2:9	161
2:11–12	90
2:13	161

1 Timothy
1:1	68, 113
1:15	7
2:3–4	91, 106
2:4	129
2:6	72
3:16	185
4:10	2, 129, 129n41

2 Timothy
2:4	131
2:13	72
2:18	142
4:1	91
4:8	138n7, 149

Titus
1:2	149
2:11	106, 129
2:13	2, 20
2:13–14	113

Hebrews
1:1	64
1:2	64
1:3	64
2:4	161
2:7	135
2:9	6, 135
2:14–15	185n
2:17	10, 143
3:14	66n11
4:4–5	174n36
4:8	174n36
4:9	175
4:9–10	174–75
4:12	176
4:15	7, 71
5:9	185n20
6:4–6	73n29
6:11	2
6:19	139n11
7:25	184
7:27	115
9:12	115
9:26	115
9:27	137, 159
9:28	124
10:10	115
10:12	72
10:26–27	124
10:37	115
11:3	62n3
12:1	141
12:2	182
12:5–6	52
12:7–11	131

Scripture Index

13:8	119	3:10	126n28	20:4–6	20, 127, 165
13:14	16, 156, 166	3:12	126n28	20:7–15	22
		3:12–13	127n31, 186	20:8	165
James		3:13	20, 126, 131	20:10	129, 131
1:17	67			20:11–12	121
1:18	161	**1 John**		20:14	118, 129–30
1:21	139n11	1:1	64	20:14–15	123
1:27	165	1:2	115	21	128
2:1	116	1:18	8	21:1	20, 126, 131,
2:1–7	165	2:2	72		148n34
5:7–8	117n6	2:28	116n6	21:2	126n27
		3:2	118, 159, 161, 187	21:2–3	126
1 Peter		3:18–19	170n30	21:3	135
1:1	166	4:8	131, 148	21:4	34, 159
1:9	139n11	4:16	131, 148	21:6–8	129
1:10	64	5:16	73n29	21:8	96n20, 129
1:23	142, 180			21:14	166
1:24	186	**2 John**		21:21	148
1:24–25	176	9–11	73	21:22	183n14
2:11	166			21:22–23	127
2:22	71	**Revelation**		21:23	148, 163
2:23	40	1:7	118–19	21:24	183n15
2:24	182	2:10	149	21:26	150, 186
2:24–25	72n27	2:16	27n24	22:2	148
3:15	xi, 19, 59	3:11	149	22:3	150
3:15–16	109	3:20	77	22:5	148, 163
3:22	13	4:2–8	127	22:7	115
4:16	40	5:6	183n14		
4:17	115, 123	5:11	148	**APOCYRPHA**	
5:4	135, 149	5:11–12	127		
5:10	154n49	6:10	34, 54		
		7:9	148	**Sirach**	
2 Peter		7:14	22n7	34:1	19
1:4	64, 143	10:7	64		
1:17–18	128	13:10	22n9	**RABBINIC LITERATURE**	
2:4	129n40	13:11–13	161		
2:6	129n40	14:9–11	106	*Bava Metzia*	
2:9	129n40	14:19–20	161	59b	53n46
2:12	129n40	16:14	161		
3:4	116n6	18:13	139n11	**APOSTOLIC FATHERS**	
3:6–13	126n28	19:11–21	22		
3:7	129n40	19:20	131, 161	*1 Clement*	
3:8	137n4	20	24	Prologue	79n43
3:9	129	20:1–6	22		

Name and Subject Index

Adams, Marilyn McCord, 151n40
Adorno, Theodore, 42n9
advent, 24, 26, 26n21, 32n41, 77, 114, 116–
19, 122, 161, 171, 185. *See also* Jesus
Christ, second coming; Parousia
afterlife, 156
Agamben, Giorgio, 6n17
Ahlstrom, Sydney E., 28n26
Ambrose of Milan, 131n37
amillennialism, 26n22
annihilationism, 129
Anatolios, Khaled, 143n17
angels, 13, 71, 94n12, 127–28, 127n33,
128n36, 129n40, 134n56, 135n2,
137n3, 144n21, 148, 148n33, 159, 162,
162n9, 174n37, 176n44, 177n45
Anselm of Canterbury, 122n53
apokatastasis, 129, 129n41, 133. *See also*
universalism
ascension, 13, 79, 84, 114–17, 114n4, 116n7,
117n9, 160
ataraxia, 41, 41n5, 43
Augustine of Hippo, 20, 20–21n3, 33n44,
118n13, 143n19, 144n21, 146n27, 153,
161–62n6, 164, 164n15, 166n22

Balthasar, Hans Urs von, 3, 3n5, 4–5,
4nn10, 11; 4–5n12, 5nn13, 15; 130n43,
131n47, 147n28, 149n35, 176n42,
183n14
baptism, 7, 9, 9n21, 21n3, 50n33, 119,
140–41, 140n13, 163
Barth, Karl, ixn1, 23, 24n13, 25, 69n19,
106–7n62, 107, 107n63, 114nn3, 4;
118n12, 124n24, 134n56, 138n7,
150n37, 160n1, 171n34
Bayer, Oswald, 104n61
beatific vision, 142n16
Benedictus Deus, 117n11, 121, 125, 141n14
Berneri, Marie Louise, 30n35
Bloch, Ernst, 2–3n4, 32n41, 58n64
Blomberg, Craig, 34n46
Blumenthal, David, 53, 53n43, 55
body, 9, 11n25, 12n28, 16, 29, 33n44, 41,
77n38, 121–22, 124–25, 137, 138n8,

139–43, 139n11, 142n16, 144nn21, 22;
145–47; 146nn26, 27; 147n29, 153–54,
153nn47, 48; 159–60
soulish, 139, 139n9, 141, 144
spiritual, 12–13, 139, 139n9, 141, 143n19,
144, 159
See also Jesus Christ
Bonhoeffer, Dietrich, 101n48, 138n8,
183n13
Braaten, Carl E., 31n39
Brock, Rita Nakashima, 181n6
Buddhism, 41, 41n6, 56n57, 186n21
Bulgakov, Sergius, 165–66n20
Bultmann, Rudolf, 5n13

Calvin, John, 117–18n11, 142n15, 163n13
Camus, Albert, 30n35, 45, 46nn25, 26;
56n57, 57, 57nn60, 61; 59
Caputo, John, 42nn10, 12; 43nn15, 16;
45n24
Cavanaugh, William, 74n30
Chalcedon, Council of, 9, 139
chaos theory, 31n40, 44n19
Christology, Chalcedonian, 12, 64, 161n4,
10, 10n24
Chung, Sung Wook, 21n6
church. *See* Jesus Christ: body
Constantinople, Second Council of, 12
Cone, James H., x–xii, xn7, 24–25n17,
28n28, 73n29, 113n1, 128n37, 182n12,
183–84, 184n17, 188
Copeland, Rebecca L., 161n4
Corsini, Eugenio, 21n4
creation
from chaos, 51, 54n50
from nothing, ix, 46–47, 49–51, 51nn35,
37; 61, 89, 126n30, 174
goodness, 133n52, 151n40, 165
grace of, 63–64, 66, 83
new, 5, 9, 67, 136, 145, 163, 169, 171–72,
187
transfiguration, 5n13, 165–66n20
creatures, 6n17, 8, 14–15, 20, 23, 31, 47,
51–52, 54n50, 61–65, 61nn2, 4; 63n5,
71, 74, 83, 85, 89–90, 95, 115, 117–18,

206

Name and Subject Index

121, 126–28, 127n30, 128n36, 131–32, 133n52, 134, 134n56, 136, 137n3, 142–44, 143n19, 151, 162n9, 163, 163n12, 172, 174–75, 177–78, 177nn45, 46; 183n15
contingency, 61n3
as finite, 137, 137n3, 143, 144n21, 148n32, 168–69, 171, 176
flourishing, 70, 103, 163, 165, 177
relationships among, 13, 146–49, 152–53, 159, 161, 164, 169, 177, 180, 187
cross, 36, 54, 64, 72n27, 84n48, 85, 91, 93, 115, 115n5, 134, 153n47, 171, 179–88, 182n12, 183nn14, 15; 184nn17, 18
theology of, xi, 15, 179–82, 181n8, 182n12, 184–85, 187
Cullmann, Oscar, 145n25

Dalferth, Ingolf U., 115n5, 145n24
damnation, 25n19, 90, 100n44, 102–6, 132–34, 133n53, 134n56, 150
Dante Alighieri, 57, 58n62, 142n16, 151n39
Davis, Ellen F., 35n47
day of the Lord, 26n23, 121–23, 126n28. *See also* Last Judgment
Deane-Drummond, Celia, 28n29
death, x, 2, 6–7, 9, 11–12, 12n28, 14n32, 20, 34–36, 42, 55, 56n57, 90, 101n48, 103–4, 103n54, 106, 114n3, 115–18, 117–18n11, 118nn12, 13; 119n22, 122nn19, 20; 124, 124n23, 125, 129–31, 133n53, 134–35, 137–41, 138nn6, 8; 140n12, 141nn14, 15; 143–45, 144n23, 145n24, 146nn26, 27; 147n28, 149; 152n45, 156, 150–60, 169, 171, 174–75, 180, 182, 184–86, 185n20, 187–88. *See also* Jesus Christ
Derrida, Jacques, 42n11, 43n16
despair, xn7, 3n4, 39, 39nn1, 2; 43, 54–55, 55n55, 58, 99n38, 101, 104n60, 134, 178
Deus absconditus, 106n62, 107n63. *See* God: hiddenness
devil, 20–21n3, 79n44, 94n13, 131, 134n56, 161, 185n20, 188
Dionysius the Areopagite, 127n33
dispensationalism. *See* premillennialism

Engels, Friedrich, 28–29n30
epektasis, 150, 175, 176n41
Epicureanism, 41n5, 43, 56n57
Erasmus, Desiderius, 99–100, 99n38, 100n42
eschatology, ix, ixn1, 1, 3, 3nn5, 6; 5, 4–5n12, 20, 24, 26, 28n29, 31, 31n39, 91–93, 108, 113n1, 115–16, 122, 134–35, 135n1, 147, 156, 159, 179
Eucharist, 119–21, 125, 163–64, 164n16

evil, ix, 26n23, 40nn3, 4; 41, 46, 49, 51n35, 52n38, 54n50, 57nn58, 60; 85, 89–93, 89n1, 96–97n24, 99–100, 100n44, 103–8, 103n57, 107n62, 115, 121, 124, 127, 132–34, 138n8132nn48, 49; 133nn52, 55; 151–53, 151n40, 153n47, 165, 185–86
problem of, 51, 92, 103n57, 107n62, 132, 132n49

faith, ixn4, 1, 4–5, 4n11, 5n13, 19, 22n9, 24, 24–25n17, 25n18, 26n23, 33, 36, 46, 53n41, 54, 58–59, 62n3, 64n7, 66, 73n28, 80n46, 100, 100n43, 104n61, 106n62, 108, 113, 115, 119, 134n56, 147, 162–63, 162n11, 164n16, 184n17
fall, 64n7, 97, 97n27, 143, 160n2, 166n22
Farrer, Austin, 176n43
Fitzmyer, Joseph, 74nn31, 33
Florensky, Pavel, 131n47
Forde, Gerhard O., 92n6, 110n41
forgiveness, 8–9, 13–15, 50n33, 67, 72, 73n29, 75, 85, 95, 95n18, 99, 101–3, 105–6, 123, 132–34, 133nn53, 54; 151n38, 162, 169, 180,
Frank, David A., 53n46
Frei, Hans W., 76

glory, x–xi, 1–6, 8, 13–16, 13n30, 16n33, 33, 35–36, 36n48, 40, 51, 65, 67, 83–85, 103n57, 104, 107, 118n13, 129–30, 132, 135–36, 139, 141–42, 144–45, 146n27, 147–56, 148n32, 151nn38, 40; 159–61, 163, 166, 171–72, 175n40, 176–84, 182n12, 183nn14, 15; 186–87
of God, 1, 4n12, 5n14, 6n17, 8, 26–27n23, 48n29, 64, 108, 116, 129, 130, 133, 145n24, 154n49, 155, 163, 163n13, 181, 183nn14, 15; 186
hope of, ix–x, 2–3, 5–6, 13, 16, 135, 160, 178, 180, 183, 185–88
of Jesus, 5n13, 9, 12n29, 20, 24, 24n16, 91, 107, 109, 113–16, 119–21, 123, 134–35, 169
theology of, 5, 15, 179
God
as Creator, 10, 31, 46, 46n27, 47–48, 53n41, 61–62n3, 62–63, 62n4, 64n6, 70, 91, 101, 121, 130, 137, 161–62n6, 182
goodness, 52, 53n43, 55–57, 67, 73n29, 89, 94–95, 95nn16, 18; 98n30, 108, 132n49
hiddenness, 48–49, 52, 61, 66, 99, 104n61, 105, 126–27n30
invisibility, 48n29, 61–62, 61nn1, 2; 64, 70, 179, 182
knowledge of, 71, 106, 106n62, 177

208 *Name and Subject Index*

God (*continued*)
and limit experiences, 61–62n3
as Not Other, 62n4
nature, 48n29, 61–62n3, 63–64, 150, 179
omnipotence, 50–52, 51n35, 52n38, 90, 100, 132n49
protest against, 52–58, 53n41, 54nn48, 51; 55nn52, 54; 56n57, 57n58, 61, 132n49
as pure act, 174
sovereignty, 24n15, 31, 33n43, 34, 40, 49, 56, 56n57, 99, 131n46
as transcendent, 40n3, 61n3, 63, 64n6, 130n45, 182, 183n15, 184n17
as Trinity, 93, 143, 146
will, 4, 7–8, 40, 40n3, 46–51, 65–66, 89–92, 102–3, 106, 106–7n62, 115, 126, 126–27n30, 127n31, 131, 135, 148n33, 153, 163, 179–82
wrath, 22n9, 48n29, 94–96, 94n13, 95nn16, 18; 98–99, 99n34, 100n43, 101–7, 106n62, 123, 133
Goodacre, Marc, 74n32
gospel, xn7, 1, 7–9, 14–15, 25n18, 26–27, 63, 65n9, 73n29, 77n39, 82, 85n50, 92, 99, 102–4, 106, 115–16, 123, 125, 125n25, 133, 133nn52, 54; 135nn1, 2; 138n7, 140, 154–56, 161–62, 164, 169, 180, 183, 186–87
grace, 6n16, 14, 14nn31, 32; 20, 32n41, 33, 65n9, 66, 66n13, 71, 74, 94n11, 95n16, 99n38, 100–101, 101n47, 103n57, 104n60, 105, 107, 120, 122, 124n23, 125, 137n3, 138nn7, 8; 140, 142, 151, 151n38, 154n49, 163–64, 170, 172, 174n37, 183, 183n13. *See also* creation; redemption
Gregory I ("the Great"), Pope, 124, 134
Gregory of Nyssa, 65–66n10, 113n2, 127n33, 138n8, 143n20, 146n27, 150, 150n36, 175, 176nn41,42
Gregory Palamas, 140n13
Griffiths, Paul, ixn1, 30n34, 31n38, 135n2, 177n46
Gutiérrez, Gustavo, 75n34

Hart, David Bentley, 23n11, 96n20, 130n42, 132, 133nn52, 55; 151n40
heaven, 5–7, 5n14, 13, 15, 26, 30n35, 34, 54, 67, 69, 85, 89, 101n45, 103n54, 113–19, 116n8, 118n13, 121, 123, 125–29, 126–27nn29, 32, 33; 128nn34, 35, 36, 37; 129nn40, 41; 130–31, 130n45, 135–37, 137nn3, 4, 142n16, 145–46, 148, 148n33, 149n35, 151nn38, 40; 159, 160, 171, 171n33, 173m, 176n41, 179, 187
invisibility, 5n14, 115, 126–27, 126n26

new, 2, 15, 20, 26–27n3, 113, 125–27, 126n28, 127n31, 128, 136, 148–49, 163, 166, 170–71, 177n46, 186 (*see also* Jerusalem)
Hefner, Philip, 29n33
Hegel, G. W. F., 32n42, 33n44
hell, 95, 95n17, 98, 100n42, 103n54, 115, 129–31, 129nn38, 40; 130n44, 131n47, 133–35, 133n54, 139n11
Hjelde, Sigurd, ixn1
Hodge, Charles, 26, 27n24, 25; 126n28
Holocaust, the, x, 52–54, 52n38, 53nn41, 47; 54n50, 57
Holy Spirit, the, 13, 27n25, 73n29, 100, 104n61, 114, 143–44, 144n23
hope, ix–xii, xn7, 1–7, 2n3, 2–3n4, 4n12, 9, 13–16, 19–20, 19n1, 23–27, 24nn13, 17; 28n28, 30n35, 31–37, 32n41, 36n48, 39–44, 39nn1, 2; 41n7, 43n17, 46, 49–51, 54–59, 55–56n55, 57n60, 58n64, 61, 63, 65n10, 67–68, 68n16, 70–71, 73–74, 76–78, 81, 83–85, 84n48, 91, 107–9, 113, 115, 117–19, 122–28, 124n24, 131n47, 134–35, 134n56, 137–38, 138nn7, 8; 143n20, 147, 149–50, 150n37, 151n38, 155, 157, 159–60, 162–63, 165n20, 166–67, 169–70, 178, 180–88
false, 15, 19–20, 32, 34–37, 39, 44, 54, 56, 67, 84, 109
refusal of, 15, 39–40, 43, 49, 57n60, 58, 61, 182
theology of, 3–5. *See also* glory, hope of
hypostasis, 10–13, 10nn23, 24; 11n25, 12n28, 64, 139, 139n11, 140n13, 146
hypostatic union, 14n32

incarnation, ix, 8, 10–11, 11n26, 63, 64n6, 76, 83, 89, 102, 105, 116n7, 126–27n30, 138, 160, 160n2, 161n4, 185, 186n21
intermediate state, 117–18n11, 122n19, 141
Irenaeus of Lyon, 21n4, 22n8, 23n12, 139n9
Israel, 4nn8, 12; 8, 52–54, 65, 67–73, 68n16, 69nn18, 19; 70n20, 71n25, 74n33, 75–78, 77n39, 80, 82–83, 166, 173

James, William, 45
Jameson, Frederic, xn5, 29n30, 43n14, 43n16
Jeanrond, Werner G., 58n64
Jerome, 21n4
Jerusalem
earthly, 126n27, 141–42n15
heavenly, 126n27, 128–30, 150, 163, 183n14
new, 126, 148
Jesus Christ
as *autobasileia*, 68, 135, 174

Name and Subject Index

body, 50n33, 64, 66–68, 66n11, 77–78,
93n8, 113, 120, 125, 126n28, 135n2,
143n18, 145, 155, 163–64
death, 7–8, 12–13, 16, 24, 72, 84, 113–14,
127, 153n47, 164n15, 170, 184, 184n19
as Emmanuel, 68
Jewishness, 69–70, 69n17, 70n21, 72
as judge, 20, 90, 109, 113, 120–25,
124n24, 135n1, 138n7, 149, 170
as Logos, 176
as Messiah, 65, 67–69, 75, 162n11
natures, ix, 9–13, 10n23, 11nn25, 27, 64,
160, 160n2, 185
resurrection, ix, 1, 4nn8, 10; 5n15, 6, 8,
9, 12–13, 15, 68, 76, 84, 113–16, 114n4,
115n5, 116n7, 117n9, 161, 164nn15, 16;
170–71, 182, 185, 188
as Savior, 20, 64n7, 69, 71, 89, 116, 169
seated at God's right hand, 13, 20, 113–
14, 116, 116n8, 160 (see also ascension)
second coming, 20–22, 20n3, 24, 24n16,
27n25, 117, 119, 124, 166, 169 (see also
advent; Parousia)
Second Person of the Trinity, 10–11, 121
sinlessness, 71–72, 71n26
Son of God, 73n29, 114, 162n11
Son of Man, 5n15, 73n29, 116n8, 118–19,
121, 121n17, 123, 171n33
temptation of, 30n36
transfiguration, 5n15
wounds, 13, 145–46, 153nn47, 48
See also Word
John Paul II, Pope, 75n34, 118n13
Jones, Robert P., 28n27
jubilee, 173, 178
Julian of Norwich, 91–99, 91n4, 93n8,
94nn10, 11, 12, 13; 95nn16, 17, 18;
96n20, 23, 24; 97nn25, 27; 98nn30, 31,
32, 33; 99n34, 101–8, 106n62
justification, 155, 156n50
Justin Martyr, 21n4, 79n43

Kant, Immanuel, 47n29
Keller, Catherine, 24n13, 30n35
Kelsey, David H., 63n5, 152n45
Kierkegaard, Søren, 91
Kilby, Karen, 96–97n24, 99n36
King, Martin Luther, Jr., 28n28, 166n21
kingdom of God, 1, 3, 16, 20, 23–28, 26n21,
31, 33n44, 34, 68, 68n16, 74–79,
75n36, 81, 83, 85n50, 109, 115, 119,
123, 125–26, 128, 135–36, 143–44, 146,
148–49, 154–57, 156n51, 161, 162n11,
163–65, 163n12, 165n17, 165–66n20,
171, 173–74, 179, 183, 185, 187–88
kingdom of heaven. See kingdom of God
Kolb, Robert, 99n37
Kurzweil, Ray, 29n32

Lactantius, 21n4
Last Judgment, 15, 21–22, 118, 121–22,
122nn19, 20; 124–25, 124n23, 166
Lateran Council, Fourth, 108n65
Left Behind, 2, 2n2, 21
life, eternal, 159
Lindsey, Hal, 24n16, 25nn18, 19, 20; 34n46
Lloyd, Vincent, 2–3n4
logoi, 176
Luther, Martin, xi, 4n10, 65, 65n9, 77,
77n38, 91–92, 92n5, 97n24, 99–108,
100nn41, 42, 43, 44; 101nn45, 46, 47,
48; 102nn49, 50; 103n54, 57; 104nn58,
59, 60, 61; 106n62, 107n63, 153n48,
179–81, 179n3, 180n4, 183–84
Lynch, William, 19n1
Lyotard, Jean-François, 41n8

Martin, Adrienne, 2n3
Marxism, 28–29, 29n31, 34, 44, 57–58n61
Mary of Nazareth, 7, 8n19, 64, 77n39,
93n8, 113, 118n13
Mathewson, David, 21n6
Maximus the Confessor, 14n31, 47n29,
148n32, 160, 160n2, 175–76,
175–76n40
McFarland, Ian A., ixnn2, 3; 40n3; 49n32;
64nn6, 7; 115n5, 116n7; 137n3;
156n50; 167n22; 174n37; 175n39
Mellert, Robert B., 148n32
metanarrative, 41, 41n8, 43
Milbank, John, 31n37
millenarianism. See premillennialism.
millennium, 20–21, 21n5, 23–24, 26, 26n22,
30, 124, 165–66
miracles, 10n23, 24, 48, 126–27n30, 161–64,
161–62n6, 162nn10, 11; 164n16
Moloney, Francis J., SDB, 21n4
Moltmann, Jürgen, xnn6, 7; 3–5, 4n8, 5n13,
58n64
Moravec, Hans, 29n32
Morrison, Toni, 152
Morse, Christopher L. 126n29, 128n34
Mott, John R., 27n24
Mühling, Marcus, 1n1, 126n27
multiverse, 61n2, 127n32, 176n44

narrative, 12, 22, 42–43, 43n14, 57, 57n58,
59, 76, 80, 117n9, 141n15, 152–53, 171
naturalism, 40, 43, 46, 46n25, 50, 52, 56–57
nature, 4, 13–14, 29, 30n35, 32n41, 40,
46n27, 66, 71, 83, 101–2, 103n57,
113n2, 138n8, 139, 139nn9, 11;
140n13, 143–44, 145n25, 148, 160,
161–62n6, 162, 177n45. See also God;
Jesus Christ
Nellas, Panayiotis, 143n19
Newbigin, Lesslie, 85n50

210 *Name and Subject Index*

Newheiser, David, 43n15
Newman, John Henry Cardinal, 67n14
Nicene Creed, 5n14, 20, 114, 116, 126
Nicholas of Cusa, 62n4
Niebuhr, Reinhold, 31n38

open theism, 51n35
Origen of Alexandria, 21n5, 68

Paine, Thomas, 71
Pannenberg, Wolfhart, xn7, 116n7, 147n30
Papias of Hierapolis, 21n4, 80n45
Parker, Rebecca Ann, 181n6
Parker, Theodore, 166n21
Parousia, 1, 22n8, 27n24, 116–17, 116n6,
    117n9, 121, 141, 147n28, 170, 170nn30,
    31. *See also* advent; Jesus Christ:
    second coming
Paul the Apostle, ixxi, ixn4, 2, 6, 9, 12–13,
    16n33, 19, 22, 32–33, 34n45, 39–40,
    48n29, 51–52, 54, 62n3, 66, 66n11,
    69n18, 72, 73n30, 77n39, 79, 101n47,
    114, 116–18, 117n11, 120–21, 120n15,
    121n16, 124–25, 125n25, 126n27, 129,
    135n1, 136–37, 139–41, 139n9, 143–45,
    147, 149–50, 152, 154–56, 160, 164–65,
    169, 170n30, 176n41, 179–81, 184, 188
person. *See* hypostasis
Pieper, Josef, 32n41, 39nn1, 2
Pinn, Anthony B., 43n17
Plato, 46–47, 46n27, 144n22
premillennialism, 21–27, 21n6, 22nn7, 8;
    25nn15, 16; 25n19, 28n27, 31, 34–35,
    34n46, 124, 165
postmillennialism, 26–29, 26n22, 28nn27,
    28
postmodernism, 41–43, 41n8, 43n17
primary cause, 47, 50, 61–62, 175n39. *See
    also* God: as Creator
process theology, 51–52, 54n50
purgatory, 141n14
Pyrrho of Elis, 41n6

Rahner, Karl, 137n5, 141n14, 147n28
rapture, 22, 22n8, 24–25, 25n19, 26n21, 35
Ratzinger, Joseph, 6n16, 30n36, 122n20,
    143n18, 147n28, 163n12
Rauschenbusch, Walter, 26n23
redemption, ix, ixn1, 15–16, 19, 33, 33n43,
    35, 36n48, 40, 52, 54, 63n5, 66, 70–72,
    83, 98, 98n32, 108, 119, 124, 134n56,
    135n2, 140n13, 151n38, 152, 152n45,
    154, 159–60, 163–64, 170, 170n31, 173,
    187–88
  grace of, 63–64, 64n7, 66, 83, 170
rememory, 152–53

resurrection, x, 6–7, 7n18, 9, 9n21, 12n28,
    13, 15, 20–21, 20n2, 21n3, 85, 113,
    117–18n11, 118n12, 129, 138, 138n8,
    139n9, 141–42, 141–42n15, 142n16,
    143n18, 144–50, 145n25, 147n28,
    150n37, 153–56, 159, 169, 170n31,
    171, 177n45, 184, 186n21, 187. *See also*
    Jesus Christ
revelation, xi, 4, 7, 36, 62n3, 64n7, 65, 71,
    90–96, 103n57, 106–7, 106–7n62,
    115–16, 118–19, 126n26, 144, 152, 155,
    170
Rogers, Eugene F., 69n19, 134n56
Roth, John K., 54nn49, 51; 55nn52, 53, 55
Rubenstein, Richard, 46n26, 51n37, 52–53,
    52n38, 53n47, 56n56, 57, 57n61, 59
Ruether, Rosemary Radford, 182n11

Sabbath, 68, 171–75, 174n36, 177–78
sacrament, 13, 48, 50n33, 101n45, 119–20,
    163–64, 164nn15, 16
salvation, ix, 7, 21n6, 22n9, 25, 25n20,
    64n7, 69, 73n29, 78, 80–81, 80n46,
    89, 91, 98–103, 100n44, 122, 129n41,
    130n42, 131, 135n1, 142, 143n17, 160,
    160n2, 180n4, 182, 184–85, 184n17
sanctification, 155–56, 156n50, 161
Scheeben, Matthias Joseph, 144n23
Schleiermacher, Friedrich, 161n6
Schmid, Heinrich, 126n28, 129n39
Schweitzer, Albert, 3
Scotus, John Duns, 127n33
secondary cause, 47–50, 61–63, 65, 148n33,
    162, 165, 172, 175n39
Segundo, Juan Luis, SJ, 29n31
Seneca, 41n7
sin. *See* evil; forgiveness
social gospel, 1, 26–27, 27–28n26
Sonderegger, Katherine, 49n31, 61n1
Son of God. *See* Jesus Christ
soul, 12, 12n28, 20, 21n3, 34, 46, 53–54,
    64, 93, 94n11, 95n18, 96, 98n32, 102,
    106n62, 117n11, 121, 137, 139–41,
    139nn9, 11; 142n16, 144, 144n22, 160,
    176n41
Southgate, Christopher, 183n15
Spirit. *See* Holy Spirit, the
Strong, Josiah, 27–28n26
suffering, forgetfulness of, xi, 15, 20, 32,
    34, 37, 54, 151n38, 183

Tanner, Kathryn, 14n32, 31n37, 66n12,
    144n23
Taylor, Mark C., 42, 42n9
Teilhard de Chardin, Pierre, xn7, 29n33
Terrell, JoAnne Marie, 152n45, 181n8

Name and Subject Index

Tertullian, 21n4, 22n8
theodicy. *See* evil: problem of
Thiel, John E., 122n20, 151n38
Thomas Aquinas, 13–14n30, 47–48n29, 61n3, 71nn23, 24; 84n48, 127n33, 137n3, 142n16, 143n18, 161, 162nn7, 8, 9; 164n16; 174n37; 177n46
Thompson, Deanna A., 181n8
Tipler, Frank J., 29n32
Torrance, Alexis, 175n40
Tran, Jonathan, 152–53
transcendence. *See* God
transhumanism, 29, 29n33, 44, 57–58n61, 168n28
tribulation, 22, 22nn7, 8, 9; 26n21
Trinity. *See* God
Turner, Denys, 92n6

universalism, 95, 108, 129, 133, 133n52. *See also apokatastasis*
utopia, xn5, 28–29n30, 30–31, 30n35, 32n41, 43n16, 57–58n61, 178, 186

Victorinus of Pettau, 21n4
vocation, 66–70, 66n13, 74–75n34, 77–79, 77n39, 81–84, 154–56, 156n50, 164
Volf, Miroslav, 151n39, 152n42

Warfield, B. B., 23nn10, 11; 26, 26–27n23
Warren, Calvin L., 43n17
Watson, Francis, 74n32
Watson, Philip S., 99n37
Webster, John, 113n1
Weinberg, Steven, 44–45, 46n25, 59
Weiss, Johannes, 3
Westermann, Claus, 128n36
White, Thomas Joseph, OP, 84n48
Widdicombe, Peter, 153n48
Wiesel, Elie, 53nn41, 44, 45; 54n48, 55n55
Williams, Dolores, xi–xii, 181
Williams, Rowan, 132n50
Winner, Lauren, 9n21
Wright, N. T., 3n6, 139n10, 178n47
wounds, 33n44, 36, 153. *See also* Jesus Christ

www.ingramcontent.com/pod-product-compliance
Lightning Source LLC
LaVergne TN
LVHW010101300525
812408LV00012B/90